STOCK WATERING

STOCK WATERING

THE JUDICIAL VALUATION OF PROPERTY FOR STOCK-ISSUE PURPOSES

BY

DAVID L. DODD

INSTRUCTOR IN FINANCE, COLUMBIA UNIVERSITY

NEW YORK

COLUMBIA UNIVERSITY PRESS

1930

Published November, 1930

PRINTED IN THE UNITED STATES OF AMERICA
BY THE PLIMPTON PRESS · NORWOOD · MASS.

PREFACE

What is meant by " value "? Philosophers are not alone in being intrigued and plagued by this question. Economic theorists have long discussed the problem from the viewpoint of their peculiar interests in human conduct. Practical business economists have had to face it in fields such as those of taxation, of accounting, of corporation finance, and of real-estate operations. And, more and more, the courts have had to wrestle with it in the many fields of law where property must be " valued " in order to determine the rights of plaintiff and defendant.

Because economists and courts are dealing alike with the same type of values, economic values expressed in terms of money, it would seem highly appropriate for students of economics to join forces with students of law in the study of this common field of interest. With such an object in mind, a small group of faculty members and graduates of the Columbia University Schools of Law and Business has been studying the principles of valuation applied by the courts, as revealed by the American case law and by a limited portion of the foreign case law. Throughout this study, attention has been focussed on the extent to which the concept of the term, " value of the property," is affected by the peculiar purpose for which the valuation is being made. No one who is even casually familiar with the decisions, let us say, on public utility valuation for rate-making purposes as contrasted with valuation for tax purposes can doubt that both the standard of value and its methods of measurement may differ greatly as between different fields of law. But the precise nature and the extent of the differences still remain obscure. To clear up some of the more important distinctions is the primary object of the pending research.

Prior to the publication of a general volume on the entire subject of judicial valuation, the various members of this research group have been publishing special articles or monographs on valuation for particular legal purposes. Articles have already been published on valuation: (*a*) as a measure of recovery for insurance losses; (*b*) as a means of determining the cash payment claimed by a dissenting minority in a corporate consolidation; (*c*) as a test of solvency in bankruptcy cases; (*d*) as a measure of the " upset price " in a corporate reorganization; (*e*) as a basis for tax appraisals; (*f*) as a standard of public utility rate control; and (*g*) as a test of " impairment of capital" by a corporation through the payment of dividends.

The present study, by Mr. David L. Dodd of the Columbia University School of Business, considers a very different type of valuation from any of those that have been treated heretofore. The subject is the valuation of property to determine whether stock has been issued for an inadequate consideration — in short, the subject of stock watering. Stock, according to the statutes of most of our states, must be issued for cash, property or services equivalent to its full par value. But what is a full equivalent in property or in services? The answer depends on a valuation of that property or of those services.

Within the last few years, the new device of shares without par value has made such headway that it promises, before long, to supersede almost completely the old par-value stock. Mindful of this fact, a good many recent writers in the field of corporation finance have already tolled the death knell of the anti-stock-watering laws and have seen the end of all the vexatious legal problems of valuation that go with these laws. Their optimism has little foundation. Without a doubt, the non-par stock laws have changed and will still further change the law of shareholders' liabilities. But they can never, of themselves, make a dead issue of the problems of valuation with which stock watering has heretofore been associated. The removal of par value, to be sure, takes away the necessity of an equivalence between the assets on the one hand and the face value of the stock on the other hand. But it leaves with us a problem of a reasonable valuation of the assets on the corporate balance sheet. Creditors and stockholders may no longer be deceived by a fictitious *par* value; but they may still be deceived by a fictitious *asset* value. And the law will therefore continue to face the necessity of protecting investors who are thus deceived. For this reason, I think, Mr. Dodd's study will constitute, not merely the first thoroughgoing study of valuation under a law that is becoming obsolete, but also a guide to the statute makers and the judges who will have occasion to develop the modern law of non-par stock, so that it will not remain, as it tends to be at present, a device for depriving innocent investors of all protection against the wiles of unscrupulous promoters.

JAMES C. BONBRIGHT

COLUMBIA UNIVERSITY
May 15, 1930

CONTENTS

CHAPTER I

INTRODUCTION: THE PROBLEM AND THE LAW OF STOCK WATERING

Scope of Study

It is the object of this treatise to discuss the principles and methods of judicial valuation in connection with the issuance of corporate stock for property and services, and to raise some questions concerning the efficacy of the system of control implicit in our anti-stock-watering statutes. A study of the valuation by courts of non-cash considerations for which stock has been issued is justified by the obscurity of the concept of " value " to which the courts have appeared to adhere in cases which have arisen under our anti-stock-watering laws. As indicated in the preface, this investigation is a part of a larger study of the whole field of valuation the object of which is to determine whether and to what extent the basis of valuation is affected by the purpose for which the property is being valued.

In an article discussing the liability of shareholders on watered stock,[1] Professor Bonbright made the following twofold division of the problem: first, the question of evidence that the stock has in fact been " watered " judged by accepted legal standards; second, the question whether shareholders are liable, and if so to whom they are liable where existence of watered stock has been admitted by the defendant shareholders or proved by the plaintiff creditors.

For the purposes of his article, Mr. Bonbright discussed only the latter question, leaving for a later study the far more difficult problems suggested by the first question. These latter problems form the subject of the present treatise. They bring up the whole question as to the valuation of property and service which have been accepted by a corporation in exchange for its stock. By way of introduction, however, to the subject of valuation, it will be necessary in this chapter to discuss briefly the practice of stock watering, and to summarize the American law relating to shareholders' liability on

[1] Bonbright, James C., *Shareholders' Defenses against Liability to Creditors on Watered Stock* (1925), 25 Col. L. Rev. 408.

watered stock. A concluding chapter discusses the effectiveness of the anti-stock-watering laws in curbing the evils of overcapitalization and raises questions as to possible alternative ways of solving the problem.

It should be observed that this study is restricted to the problem of judicial valuation under the laws controlling *private* business corporations of all types. A study of the special problems involved in the control of public utility capitalization is not contemplated here. To be sure, the two problems are closely related. But the question of the regulation of public utility securities is so closely integrated with questions of public policy concerning adequacy of service, continuous operation, and rate control as to place the problem in a class by itself. It is generally conceded that the special nature of public utility enterprises justifies more rigid requirements with regard to their capitalization than would be desirable in the case of a private venture.[2]

It should be further noted that our concern is with watered stock having a *par value* and not with that more insidious form of stock watering involved in the issuance of non-par stock for property followed by an overvaluation on the corporation's books and financial statements. Under many of our state statutes which provide for the issuance of non-par shares, stock may be issued for an agreed consideration, consisting of services or property other than cash, without the necessity of the parties coming to any agreement concerning its value. Thus the promoter-shareholder is presumably relieved from all liability to creditors which might be based on an overvaluation of the consideration for which the stock is issued.[3] This very possibility of avoiding liability on overissued stock largely explains the recent popularity with promoters of shares without par value. Whether, and to what extent, the removal of a nominal par value from the face of share certificates is a real or fancied remedy

[2] Bonbright, James C., Railroad Capitalization (N. Y., 1920), c. V; Locklin, David P., Regulation of Security Issues by the Interstate Commerce Commission (Urbana, Ill., 1927); Baldwin, Donald C., Capital Control in New York (Phila., 1920); Heilman, Ralph E., *The Development by Commissions of the Principles of Public Utility Capitalization* (1915), 23 J. Pol. Econ. 888.

[3] Berle, Adolf A., Jr., *Problems of Non-par Stock* (1925), 25 Col. L. Rev. 43, reprinted in Berle, Adolf A., Jr., Studies in the Law of Corporation Finance (Chicago, 1928), c. IV; Bonbright, James C., *The Dangers of Shares without Par Value* (1924), 24 Col. L. Rev. 449.

for the evils of watered stock is a subject which we have reserved for later treatment.

We may note at this point, however, that an overissue of stock ordinarily goes hand in hand with an overstatement on the balance sheet of the value of the corporate assets received for the stock.[4] The one lends a semblance of support to the other, and the combination is more insidiously deceptive than excessive nominal valuation of stock certificates alone. Shares without par value break down this doubly deceptive combination by eliminating from the stock certificate any representation concerning the value of the consideration for which the shares were issued. They make no attempt to curb balance-sheet deception.

Nature and Methods of Stock Watering

In order to see in its functional aspects the problem of valuation which arises when corporate stock is issued for a consideration other than cash, it is necessary to point out some aspects of the practice of stock watering and the evils which are supposedly associated with it. Stock watering may be defined as the issuance of nominally full-paid stock in an amount exceeding the value of the assets against which the stock has been issued.[5] Aside from an issuance of stock

[4] Bonbright, *op. cit., supra* (note 3) at p. 455. This has not always been the case with stock watering in other countries. In England, for instance, Parliament sanctioned a splitting-up of shares by various railway companies which resulted in great increases in par values. The stipulation was made, however, that the water should be frankly shown on the books by offsetting special accounts on the debit side of the balance sheet, instead of being concealed by a write-up of asset values. Bonbright, *op. cit. supra* (note 2) at pp. 60–61. By the 1929 amendment of the British Companies Act, sect. 47, stock may be sold for cash at less than par, but the amount of the discount must be shown in the prospectus and in all subsequent balance sheets until written off.

[5] Various definitions of the phrase "watered stock" have been given by judges and by writers on finance. According to some, stock is watered when its par value exceeds the *value* of the corporate earning power; according to others, stock is watered when its nominal value exceeds the "fair value" of the shareholders' equity in corporate assets; according to still others, the watering is measured by the excess of the par values over the *actual investment* of the shareholders in the enterprise, irrespective of the present values which the property represented may now have attained. Choice of one definition or another generally depends on the particular writer's view as to sound financial practice, as there is a tendency to regard "stock watering" as a term of opprobrium to be applied to any capitalization which is deemed excessive.

A still further variation in the use of the phrase is to be noted on the part

for no consideration whatever, there are three prevalent methods by which an excessive or " fictitious " issue may be made.

The first method, being the most obvious, is probably the least prevalent of these devices. It consists in issuing certificates of " fully paid " stock for an amount of cash which is less than the par value of the stock.[6] The ease of detecting the discrepancy between the net value accretion in the assets of the corporation and the increase in nominal capitalization when this device is employed accounts for the rarity of its use.

The second method consists in the payment of stock dividends the value equivalent of which has not been added to the corporate assets. The use of this method of watering stock is less easily detected than the first, as it involves the difficult question of proper asset valuation, a cloak behind which an unscrupulous management may hide with considerable success. It is probably less deceptive than the third method, to be mentioned subsequently, largely because it is not adapted for use in connection with corporate promotion in its early stages and because the motive for doing it is strongest in the public utility field where its use is likely to be restricted by the regulations of the Interstate Commerce Commission and the public utility commissions of the several states. Prior to the era of security

---

of those writers who say that stock is watered if new stock is sold by a going concern at a price which is less than the current market price of the outstanding shares, even though the new issue is sold *pro rata* to old stockholders at a price equal to or above par value. The idea is that the new stock issue, even though it is balanced by a corresponding increase in assets, dilutes (i.e., " waters ") the value of the old shares. Writers who hold to this definition generally regard any stock dividend as a case of stock watering, even though it is issued in order to capitalize a genuine surplus from previously reinvested earnings.

In the main, the courts have held to the definition of watered stock as any stock issued in excess of the value of the consideration for which it has been exchanged, although there has been some tendency, at least among legal commentators, to refer only to an issue which exceeds the amount of consideration, *as valued in good faith* by the directors. See 5 Fletcher, Cyclopedia of Corporations (Chicago, 1918), sect. 3517, pp. 5837–38; 1 Cook, Corporations (8th. ed., N. Y., 1923), sects. 28–29, pp. 149–50. This identifies " watered stock " with the question whether the issue would be deemed invalid at law, and involves an unfortunate confusion between a financial fact and a legal rule. But the term has no definite legal standing, as it seldom appears in statutes or in statements of the common law. The terms, " fictitious issue " or " stock issued for inadequate consideration," are more common.

[6] See 5 Fletcher, *op. cit.*, sect. 3591, p. 5927 for cases.

regulation by these bodies, this device was often used by railroads and other public service corporations as a means of concealing the true rate of return on the capital actually invested, but commission control of security issues has largely put a stop to the practice or else subjected it to such a degree of publicity in accounts as to prevent it from being dangerously deceptive.[7] Furthermore, stock dividends are paid by going concerns whose credit is already dependent for the most part upon their established earning capacity rather than upon their nominal assets. In the case of a newly formed corporation the situation is likely to be different, since the book values of the assets have a greater influence on the investor and creditor in the absence of any record of earnings. When a corporation pays a stock dividend it has usually reached a point where its earning power is directly measurable by past records. Consequently, investors in the shares of the corporation as well as its creditors are less likely to be deceived by the nominal capitalization, although a large stock dividend may prevent the public from becoming aware of an abnormally high rate of earnings of the invested capital.

The third method of watering stock consists in issuing "fully paid" stock — usually at the time of promotion though it may be done subsequently — for property or services taken at an overvaluation. This method is by far the most prevalent and is probably the most harmful to the public. It has characterized a large part of all promotions,[8] and the devices for its execution have been so care-

[7] Recently, however, a number of large public-utility holding companies, whose securities are not subject to commission control, have resorted to the use of recurrent stock dividends, wholly or partly in lieu of cash dividends. The North American Company is an outstanding example. There has been much criticism of the practice on the ground that it unstabilizes the income (in cash equivalent) of the stockholder and that it creates the appearance of an income from dividends larger than the total earnings realized by the corporation. See DIVIDENDS PUT TO WORK, a pamphlet published by the North American Company, New York, for a statement of the criticism and an attempted answer.

[8] This was particularly true of our period of industrial combination or "trust" formation, from 1897 to 1903, inclusive. See U. S. INDUSTRIAL COMMISSION, REPORTS (1900–1902), Vols. I, II, XIII, and XIX, Index *s. v.* "Capitalization"; U. S. BUREAU OF CORPORATIONS, REPORT OF THE COMMISSIONER OF CORPORATIONS ON THE STEEL INDUSTRY (1911–1913), Pt. I, p. 14 *et seq.;* DEWING, ARTHUR S., CORPORATE PROMOTIONS AND REORGANIZATIONS (Cambridge, Mass., 1914); MEAD, EDWARD S., TRUST FINANCE (New York, 1903); Colton, Henry E., *Par Value versus No Par Value Stock,* 7 A. B. As. J. (1921), 671; United States v. United States Steel Corporation, 223 Fed. 55, 167 (D. C., D. N. J., 1915).

fully provided for in our statutory and court-made law as to make it a very effective medium for the overissue of securities. It is well adapted to conceal the fictitious character of the stock issued and throws upon the party who may complain of it the exceedingly difficult problem of proving an overvaluation of the consideration.

Motives for Stock Watering

A study of the origins of stock watering would take us afield from our major purpose, but one aspect of its genesis should be dwelt upon briefly at this point, since one of the purposes of this study is to suggest measures for reform looking to the abolition of stock watering or to the reduction of its evil consequences to a minimum. We refer to the reasons why stock watering is resorted to by promoters.

The essential features of a typical corporate promotion consist of: (1) the discovery by the promoter of an opportunity to make money, either through the direct purchase of valuable property, or through the purchase of an option on such property; (2) the capitalization of that opportunity at a figure which exceeds the cost of it to the promoter, through the direct or indirect issuance of corporate shares in exchange for it; and (3) the direct or indirect sale of these shares to the public by the promoter at a total price which exceeds the cost of the enterprise to him as he has assembled it. The difference represents the promoter's profit.

This profit, provided it is not excessive or obtained through deceit, may be looked upon as a legitimate payment for the performance of an indispensable economic service. An intermediary who, to use Mead's phrase,[9] devotes his efforts to bringing about a "coincidence of investment funds with investment opportunities" is rendering a service for which he is entitled to payment. The pro-

---

The prevalence of stock watering in railroad finance is discussed by Ripley, Wm. Z., Railroads, Finance and Organization (New York, 1915) and by Cleveland and Powell, Railroad Finance (New York, 1912).

[9] Mead, *op. cit.*, p. 62. *Cf.* Mead, Edward S., Corporation Finance (New York, 1928), Vol. I, c. II. In Allenhurst Park Estates v. Smith, 101 N. J. Eq. 581, 597, 138 Atl. 709, 716 (1927), the court remarked: "But that the promoter has his place in society and his usefulness in the world of business is beyond question. He is usually a man of vision, and his vision is not always dispelled by the sunlight of experience. Without him much of the material success and industrial progress of this country would not have been attained and scientific advancement would perhaps have been retarded."

moter must normally possess a peculiar degree of foresight with regard to the economic needs of society and an exceptional capacity for organization in order to assemble business propositions which will justify their existence by serving a social need.

This does not mean, however, that promoters' profits are always legitimate from the point of view of human welfare or that the promotion process should not be subject to some degree of social control. Our complaint is with the method by which he makes this profit and not with the fact that a profit is made.

The motive and methods of the promoter in seeking to make his profit do not differ in essentials from those of many merchants who deal in tangible commodities. The merchant's object is to "buy cheap and sell dear," the difference remaining in his hands, after all expenses are paid, being his profit. So it is with the promoter.

The merchant tags his wares "Price $1, Reduced from $2" and thus moves the goods from his shelves at a profit. "Reduced from $2" may be a pure fiction, but the merchant has discovered from experience that this is a useful device in persuading customers to believe that his wares are worth at least $1 per unit to them.

The same psychology which is a factor in the success of this merchandising device is operative in the sale of corporate shares and credit instruments. The promoter would like to be able to say to the investor and creditor — and through the device of stock watering does say, in effect, with regard to his shares of stock — "Price $50, Reduced from $100." That the merchandising device in the latter case takes the form of a statement of "Par value $100, Price $50" does not essentially alter the resultant influence on the buyer of a definite amount of corporate credit in the form of a loan or on the buyer of a fractional interest in the earnings and assets of a given corporation.[10]

[10] *Cf.* Mead, *op. cit. supra* (note 8) at p. 343, where he says: "Each share of stock bears the inscription 'par $100,' and in the mind of the speculative buyer the par value and the real value are identified. When the stocks are offered to him at $30 or $40 per share for the common, or at $60 or $70 for the preferred, with the assurance that the expected earnings of the company warrant its capitalization, the speculator is likely to consider the difference between the par value and the asking price as the measure of the bargain presented."

See also the testimony of General McNulta before the U. S. Industrial Commission with reference to the organization of the Distilling and Cattle Feeding Company (the Whiskey Trust). He said: "I think that they [those who entered the combination] thought that they were ahead for a while. In the first

In so far as the implied or expressed statements as to the value or worth of the thing offered for sale in each case are false, the analogy is perfect. In each case the publicity device mentioned assists the vendor in maintaining a desired margin in the selling price over and above his costs. By tagging his wares (shares of stock) with nominal values in excess of the worth of the assets which they represent, the promoter is able to retain a profit at the expense of those who rely upon the nominal amount of its capitalization in their dealings with the corporation.[11]

In the case of private companies, as distinguished from public utilities, this reliance takes two major forms. Either the prospective purchaser of the shares of watered stock who contemplates buying some of them from the promoter or his transferees is deceived by the nominal value of the shares and pays more for them than he would otherwise do, or else the creditor who lends money to the corporation is deluded by the nominal amount of the corporation's capital assets represented to have been contributed by the shareholders when the stock was originally issued and lends in larger amounts or at a lower rate of interest than he otherwise would do.[12]

The answer, then, to the question why the promoter desires to water his stock is that by this device he hopes to increase the dif-

---

place, they thought no distillery could compete for the trade, big or little; it was theirs; they owned it; and in the next place they got a lot of certificates, the value of which was probably two or three times the value of the distilleries which they represented, but it said dollars on them and they felt rich and carried them along." U. S. INDUSTRIAL COMMISSION, REPORTS (1900–1902), Vol. I, p. 236.

[11] It should be added, as another phase of stock watering as a stock-jobbing device, that low-priced shares have a much wider appeal to the public than have high-priced shares, and hence the promoter is able to get a higher price for them in the aggregate than he could get for a smaller number of shares representing the same interest in the enterprise but with no " water " in its capitalization. Not only is the high-priced share inaccessible to the owner of a small pocket-book, but the low-priced share appears to offer a better opportunity of a speculative rise in price. *Cf.* MEAD, *op. cit. supra* (note 8) at p. 309 *et seq.*

[12] The deceptive qualities of an inflated par value are probably not very effective once the shares become seasoned and are traded in on an organized market. Stocks listed on organized exchanges, or otherwise dealt in with considerable frequency, are bought and sold almost entirely on the basis of their present or potential equities in earnings without regard to their nominal values. The harm done to the invester, and for the most part to the creditor, occurs before earning power becomes established.

ference between the price he must pay for the properties and the price for which he can sell the securities representing the properties. He knows that, under American traditions of financing, people generally won't pay a price above par for stock in a new industrial corporation.[13] He therefore resorts to dilution as a means by which he can sell the stock at or below par and still make a profit. In doing this he is seeking a pecuniary reward for his services in conceiving and assembling the enterprise. But it is difficult to get people to buy promotion stock at a price which, quite frankly, includes a large payment to promoters for their services. While a proper payment for these services is just as much a true cost of the business as are the tangible assets, investors are not likely to see it that way. It follows that the promoters are under an impulse to make the par values *exceed* the cost to them of the assembled property by an amount at least equal to the price which they hope to get for their services. The temptation, however, is to go still farther and to stretch out the capitalization so that the promoter can sell the stock to investors *below par* and still realize enough to cover purchase costs plus promoter's profits. The bargain-counter instincts of investors mentioned above are thus exploited to the promoter's gain.

Just how far the promoter will attempt to stretch the stock issue depends largely upon his opinion concerning the credulity of the investors, together with the extent of his fear that if he goes too far he may be caught in a shareholders' liability suit even despite the very liberal interpretations by the courts as to what constitutes legal overvaluation. A promoter, even if he had nothing to fear from the law, would hardly capitalize a railway at ten times its construction cost, for the discrepancy would be too glaring to deceive anyone. But he might well capitalize the railway at twice the cost.

The second and less important reason for watering stock, from

[13] The situation in the case of bank stocks is different. They are ordinarily sold at a premium. Two reasons for this difference between industrial-share flotation and bank-stock flotation may be mentioned. In the first place, bank stocks are sold for cash. The investor knows that other purchasers of the stock are paying a cash price equal to his own payment and no question concerning the monetary value of the consideration is involved to cast doubt upon the financial integrity of the enterprise. In the second place, the investor in bank shares not only enjoys the benefit of careful governmental regulation, but, on the whole, the financial record of banks under this regulation has proven to be an enviable one from the standpoint of the shareholder.

the promoter's standpoint, is to create in the minds of creditors a more favorable impression than the corporation deserves in view of the economic value of its possessions. Security is the most essential aspect of credit extension. By watering stock the promoter gives to his corporation the appearance of having received a larger fund of wealth from its shareholders than it has actually received, with the result that the " equity " behind the creditors' claims seems larger than it really is. This may give to the corporation a more favorable borrowing capacity than it deserves.

In addition to the above reasons for stock watering, it is probable that certain motives which are not economic in character tend in the same direction. Pride and a certain unreasoned preconception in favor of large business units undoubtedly play a rôle in encouraging stock watering. To have promoted and to be connected with a " million-dollar corporation " may be an outward sign of successful achievement to which promoters aspire. Stock watering affords an easy route to that end.

From the point of view of corporation finance there are many more reasons for stock watering, not all of which are operative at the time of original incorporation. First, and perhaps the most important of these reasons, is the desirability of launching the enterprise with as little bonded debt as possible. By watering the common stock and giving substantial common-stock bonuses with original issues of bonds or preferred stock, the fixed charges may be kept down at the expense of stockholders' equities per share.[14] A corporation financed in this manner is in a sounder condition from the point of view of financial stability than it would be if it were bonded as heavily at the start as it would have to be in the absence of the use of bonus stock. Hence the latter is frequently a calculated element in the promoter's financial plan and stock watering is the result.[15]

A similar practice of giving stock bonuses with bonds may be resorted to at a time subsequent to the original financing in order to raise funds needed for expansion at a lower cost in terms of fixed charges than could otherwise be accomplished. It is not an uncommon practice for the company to obtain " fully-paid " stock for this

[14] Lyon, H., Corporation Finance (Boston, 1916), Pt. I, c. 3.

[15] A similar reason for watering stock exists at the time of a corporate reorganization, watered stock again being used as a means of accomplishing a reduction in fixed charges.

purpose by issuing it for overvalued property and having it donated back to the corporate treasury by friendly vendors.

A further reason for stock watering has been a desire on the part of those interested in a corporation which is facing failure to stave off the event of failure and liquidation. Such a concern either cannot issue and sell its bonds at all or else it can do so only by giving substantial stock bonuses with the bonds so that the investor may receive a speculative opportunity to offset the great risk incident to making a loan to such an enterprise. Under these circumstances corporations have been known to exchange stock, which had not theretofore been issued, for a consideration materially below its par value. In some instances stock has been given as a bonus with bonds. In others it has been sold for cash or other considerations at a price much below its face value. Stock issued under these circumstances is less apt to deceive those who have financial dealings with the corporation than an original issue. The reason for this has been suggested above. Going concerns tend to acquire credit status and general financial reputation in terms of their earning capacity, a reputation which is largely independent of the nominal value of their assets. In so far, however, as nominal capitalization is a factor in determining the financial standing of going concerns, the evils of watered stock are developed by this type of financial life-saving.[16]

Very similar in effect is the sale of stock below par by a going concern which is not threatened with failure but whose stock is currently quoted at a discount from par. Here the object is corporate development rather than financial resuscitation. The stock cannot be sold at par because the outstanding shares are available at a discount. The only effectual alternative to selling the stock below par may entail excessive indebtedness for the enterprise and unwholesomely burdensome fixed charges. Under these circumstances the

[16] For a discussion of the extent to which the courts will sanction the issuance of stock below par in order to save a company from insolvency under the rule of Handley v. Stutz, 139 U. S. 417, 11 Sup. Ct. 530 (1891), see BONBRIGHT, *op. cit. supra* (note 1) at p. 429. Sect. 16 of the recently enacted General Corporation Act of Ohio provides for the issue of par-value shares at a price less than par under special circumstances. The law contains provisions for the protection of the public when this is done. See General Code of Ohio, sect. 8623, subsection 16, as amended by Laws of 1929, p. 414 *et seq*. The committee which drafted the law had the rule of Handley v. Stutz, *supra*, in mind. See REPORT OF COMMITTEE RESPECTING REVISION OF OHIO CORPORATION LAW (Dec. 28, 1926), at p. 68.

wisest thing to do from the standpoint of existing interests is to market more stock at the best price which it will bring. The device of " treasury stock " is easily adapted to this situation and has been so used.[17]

Stock watering has also been used as a means whereby persons temporarily in control of a corporation perpetuate that control by issuing stock to friendly interests for overvalued property or services. This practice is comparatively rare, but some of the cases in the law books indicate that it has occasionally been resorted to.[18]

An additional reason sometimes advanced to explain the occurrence of watered stock is the desire to conceal from the public and from competitors the fact that excessive or exceptional profits are being made. It is sometimes urged that because a corporation is able to earn at a very high rate per cent on its capital stock, and hence to pay large dividends, competition is encouraged and sales resistance is met in the markets in which the corporation sells its product. Buyers of the product may complain if prices are raised, or are kept constant in a declining market, on the ground that large earnings per share or large dividends of the manufacturing corporation indicate that it enjoys an excessive margin of profit. To prevent this sales resistance by a concealment of the true rate of earnings, stock watering in the form of excessive stock dividends or prosperity reorganizations is sometimes resorted to. Although this argument has some degree of plausibility, the writer is inclined to assign to it a minor rôle in the genesis of stock watering.[19] It may be the primary

[17] See Chapter VIII, pp. 252–62, *infra*.

[18] Bowen v. Imperial Theatres, Inc., 13 Del. Ch. 120, 115 Atl. 918 (1922); Wildes v. Rural Homestead Co., 53 N. J. Eq. 425, 32 Atl. 676 (1895), *rev'd* on other grounds, 54 N. J. Eq. 668, 35 Atl. 896 (1896).

[19] A closely related reason for stock watering is the alleged tendency of public service corporations to dilute their capitalizations in order more effectively to argue before public service commissions and the Interstate Commerce Commission for the retention of existing rates at a given time, or for higher rates, on the ground that those in use do not yield more than a " fair return " on the " fair value " of the property used and useful to the public, or that existing rates do not yield even a fair return. See BONBRIGHT, *op. cit. supra* (note 1), c. I; LYON, *op. cit. supra* (note 14), pp. 85–86; MEAD, *op. cit. supra* (note 9), c. 20.

The notion that private corporations water their stock in order to charge higher prices for their products has been successfully refuted many times. See BONBRIGHT, *loc. cit.*; MEAD, *op. cit. supra* (note 8) c. 16; MEAD, *op. cit. supra* (note 9) at p. 225.

Some writers have suggested that excessive capitalization, so far from

reason for stock dividends, but in most cases the latter are not a means of watering stock as we have defined it for purposes of this study.

During the World War a special reason for stock watering existed. We refer to the Federal Excess Profits Tax which permitted corporations an exemption of eight per cent on their "invested capital" before the progressive tax rates commenced to apply. Although the tax law did not define "invested capital" in terms of the nominal capitalization of corporations, market values and physical appraisals were so difficult to obtain that a corporation tended to benefit in the amount of tax that it would have to pay by virtue of the presumption of larger investment implicit in the stated capitalization. Large nominal capitalizations fortified the argument of corporations for large deductions. Hence there was during this period a tendency to capitalize surpluses at excessive figures through stock dividends as well as to create such surpluses for stock dividend purposes by writing up the values of fixed assets on balance sheets.

An additional reason for stock watering is sometimes found in statutory attempts to control the capitalization of corporations. Ripley illustrates this in an article on railroad valuation.[20] A statute of the state of Washington relating to railroad capitalization limited the amount of bonds to be issued to an amount not in excess of twice the amount of stock and forbade the issuance of stock in excess of the value of the property received for it. Consequently, when a corporation which Ripley mentions wished to raise money on a bond issue it maintained the required ratio of stock to bonds by inflating the property valuations and issuing stock against the increase.

Finally, as chronicled by historians of our great industrial-combination movement in the late nineties and the years following, and as related by some of the promoters themselves, stock watering was an essential element in the method by which many owners of plants and security underwriters were induced to participate in the

---

staving off competition, may actually encourage it. If a company which is known to be overcapitalized shows an ability to earn dividends on its stock it may be presumed that a conservatively capitalized concern can earn at a still higher rate on its stock. Hence there is a temptation to go in and compete. See Mead, *op. cit. supra* (note 9) at pp. 224, 227–30; Erickson, H., Regulation of Public Utilities (Madison, Wisc., 1911), p. 50.

[20] Ripley, Wm. Z., *The Investor's Interest in Railroad Valuation,* 23 J. Pol. Econ. (Jan. 1915), 34–48.

organization of combinations on such terms as would still allow the promoter to make a profit.[21] It has been repeatedly testified, by those prominently connected with the promotional aspects of our industrial-combination movement, that without stock watering many of the combinations could not have been formed. Watered stock was the mystic solvent of difficulties which the promoter everywhere found useful and which from his standpoint was entirely legitimate in view of the anticipated enhancement of earning power which was contemplated as the essential *raison d'être* of each particular combination.

Alleged Evils of Stock Watering

Before turning to a consideration of the position of American law with respect to stock watering, it may be well to note briefly the evils supposed to be associated with the excessive issuance of stock, for the question may fairly be raised as to what interest the public has in the value of the consideration which a corporation receives for its shares.[22] But prior to a discussion of the evils of watered stock, it will be well to consider the purpose of a stated or par value for corporate shares.

Par value of a share of stock is significant solely as an accounting or publicity device. It is intended to be an advertisement of the value of the shareholders' contributions to the corporate treasury at the time the stock was originally disposed of by the corporation. The theory of legislatures in enacting statutes requiring full payment of corporate stock and imposing a liability to creditors upon holders of part-paid stock, as well as the theory of the courts in upholding a liability even in the absence of a statute, has been that the capital stock of a corporation is the basis of its credit. The

[21] Mead, *op. cit. supra* (note 8), c. 6, 17, 18, especially pp. 352–55; U. S. Industrial Commission, Reports (1900–1902), Vols. I and XIII, testimony of H. O. Havemeyer, C. R. Flint, Wm. H. Moore (especially at pp. 960, 961, 963), *et al.; ibid,* Vol. XIX, pp. 405–16, 616 *et seq.* See also Robinson, Maurice H., *The Distribution of Securities in the Formation of the United States Steel Corporation* (June, 1915), 30 Pol. Sci. Q. 277, describing the methods used by Wm. H. and J. H. Moore, who promoted many industrial combinations.

[22] For statements concerning the public's interest in the full payment of shares see Report of Committee Respecting Revision of Ohio Corporation Law, *supra* (note 16) at p. 77; U. S. Industrial Commission, Reports, Vol. XIX, *loc. cit. supra* (note 21); Hale, Wm. B., *A Field for Corporate Law Revision: Shareholders' Liability to Creditors* (1917), 12 Ill. L. Rev. 6, at p. 11.

general theory is perhaps best illustrated by a few quotations from the opinions of courts. Thus, the Court of Errors and Appeals of New Jersey has said:

The legislative purpose in exacting a statement of the amount of the capital stock, and of the names and residences of the subscribers, and of the amount subscribed by each, with the publicity of a published record of the certificate, was to provide a means of assuring the payment of debts contracted by the corporation. The legislature contemplated that subscriptions to the stock should be the capital with which corporations organized under the act should engage in business, on the credit of which the corporators were empowered to contract debts in the corporate name without any liability for such debts beyond the amount of their subscriptions to the stock. The capital stock subscribed is a substitute for the personal liability of partners in ordinary copartnerships and creditors are entitled to a *bona fide* exercise of the compulsory powers of the corporation to compel subscribers to pay in their subscriptions. Any arrangement between the agents of the corporation and subscribers for its stock that their subscriptions shall be merely colorable, or less onerous than they purport to be on the face of the subscription, is void as a fraud upon creditors.[23]

Judge Mitchell for the Supreme Court of Minnesota wrote an opinion as follows:

The capital of a corporation is the basis of its credit. It is a substitute for the individual liability of those who own its stock. People deal with and give their credit on the face of it. They have a right to assume that it has paid in capital to the amount it represents itself as having.[24]

And again, by the same court:

When a corporation represents that it has a paid-up capital of a given amount, it represents to the business world that at the time it issued the stock it received money or property to the full par value of the stock. The issuing of the stock of a corporation as paid up when it was not so in fact is a public and a private wrong — a cheat and a fraud — which enables the corporation to obtain credit and property by false pretenses.[25]

The Supreme Court of California said as follows:

But where a person accepts the ownership of stock which purports to be fully paid, a very different situation is presented. It cannot be said of him

[23] Wetherbee v. Baker, 35 N. J. Eq. 501, 511 (1882).

[24] Hospes v. Northwestern Manuf'g & Car Co., 48 Minn. 174, 197, 50 N. W. 1117, 1121 (1892).

[25] Wallace v. Carpenter Electric Heating etc., Co., 70 Minn. 321, 329–30, 73 N. W. 189, 191 (1897).

for a moment that he accepts the stock and enters upon the relation of stockholder to the corporation upon any understanding that his stock is liable for further calls on capital account, or that he, as an incident of his ownership and consequent relationship, assumes any such obligation. On the contrary, it is evident that he accepts the ownership of the stock and enters upon the relationship of stockholder with just the contrary understanding. What, then, is the principle upon which the holder of watered stock is, under any circumstances, held obligated to supply substance instead of water, to make good what it is pretended the corporation received but did not? The answer to this question is not in doubt. The stockholder is held upon the principle that one giving credit to a corporation is entitled to rely upon its ostensible capitalization as the basis for the credit given, and that when the corporation issues watered stock and thereby assumes an ostensible capitalization in excess of its real assets, the transaction necessarily involves the misleading of subsequent creditors, and, whether done with that purpose actually in mind or not, is at least a constructive fraud upon such creditors. In other words, the essence of the right of the creditors to brush aside the issuance of the stock as fully paid and to show that it was not such and to compel the payment of the balance upon it, is that its issuance as fully paid was as to him a fraud.[26]

The Supreme Court of Missouri:

No argument is needed to show that a requirement that the stock of a corporation shall be paid in money, or in labor or property at its money value, inures to the benefit of persons who may become creditors of the corporation, in that it requires the capital stock to be the representative of substantial values and insure the existence of a fund which must be within reach for the satisfaction of debts if the affairs of the corporation are managed as contemplated by law.[27]

The Supreme Court of the United States:

The capital stock of an incorporated company is a fund set apart for the payment of its debts. It is a substitute for the personal liability which subsists in private copartnerships. . . . It is publicly pledged to those who deal with the corporation, for their security. Unpaid stock is as much a part of this pledge, and as much a part of the assets of the company, as the cash which has been paid upon it. Creditors have the same right to look to it as to anything else, and the same right to insist upon its payment as upon the payment of any other debt due to the company.[28]

[26] Rhode v. Dock-Hop Co., 184 Cal. 367, 376–77, 194 Pac. 11, 15 (1920).
[27] Van Cleve v. Berkey, 143 Mo. 109, 129, 44 S. W. 743, 748 (1898).
[28] Sanger v. Upton, 91 U. S. 56, 60–61, 23 L. Ed. 220, 222 (1875).

The Court of Appeals of New York:

A deliberate and advised overvaluation of property thus purchased and paid for [in stock] is a fraud upon the law, and a violation of the conditions upon which the exemption of stockholders from liability under the provisions of the original statute is made to depend. It is a direct violation of the policy as well as of the terms of the law which demands payment, either in money or property at its value, of all of the capital stock of the company, as a condition of immunity of the stockholders from liability for debts of the corporation. The payment of an amount for property in excess of its value deprives creditors and the public of the security contemplated by the statute, and thus a fraud is perpetrated as well upon the law as upon creditors.[29]

And finally, the Chancery Court of Delaware has said as follows:

The fundamental principle is that shares of stock in a corporation are a substitute for the personal liability of partners, and the liability to pay for stock taken up to the par value thereof is a fund for the benefit of creditors of the company, and whoever takes shares of stock of a Delaware corporation assumes that liability for the benefit of creditors in case of insolvency of the company.[30]

The evils attributed to watered stock result from the misleading impression as to the size of the corporate capital which is given by the overcapitalization. The injury is of two kinds: first, the harm done to investors, whether they be general creditors, bondholders or stockholders, through the commitment of funds which they would not have contributed but for the deceptive capitalization of the corporation; and second, the harm done to consumers of the products or users of the services of corporations through the charging of excessive prices or through the poor character of the service rendered. A third objection to stock watering is really another phase of the second one. It is that unwarranted and excessive promotions are encouraged by the device of stock watering, resulting in a wasting of the capital resources of the country, and in the economic derangements incident to the failure of ill-conceived enterprises.[31]

[29] Douglass v. Ireland, 73 N. Y. 100, 104 (1878).

[30] Cooney Company v. Arlington Hotel Company, 11 Del. Ch. 286, 305, 101 Atl. 879, 887 (1917).

[31] Mead, writing in 1903, considered the chief evil of excessive capitalization to be a relative scarcity of *investment* securities. He regarded the low rate of return then obtainable on investment securities as a real social hardship and attributed the fact of this low return to the prevalence of speculative promo-

Let us examine the merits of each of these alleged evils, selecting the harm done to creditors for first consideration. It is customary for the apologists of stock watering to maintain that it is nonsense to suppose that creditors are in any way deceived by the capitalization of corporations. The protagonists of this particular form of misbranding admit that stock watering is a form of misrepresentation but say that it is unimportant for the reason that no one is misled by it, or at least that no creditor is misled by it.[32]

It is doubtless true that in most cases where a going concern is involved, short-term credit is extended to the enterprise largely upon the basis of its earning capacity and on the status of its liquid

---

tion. The demand for investment securities greatly exceeded the supply. The consequences, he said, were that men were kept at work long after they had reached the time for retirement, insurance premiums were excessively high, and interest rates paid by savings banks were exceedingly low — all of this because the speculative promoter capitalized the expected profits of industry into forms in which the investor could not purchase an interest. *Op. cit. supra* (note 8) c. 19. *Cf.*, on the other hand, Dos Passos, John R., Commercial Trusts (New York, 1901), pp. 50–60, where stock watering is vigorously defended on the ground that its use was essential to industrial and commercial development.

[32] Harno, Albert J, and Rice, Raymond F., *Non-par Value Stock* (1922), 56 Amer. L. Rev. 321, 323, 341; Ballantine, Henry W., *Stockholders' Liability in Minnesota* (1923), 7 Minn. L. Rev. 79, 90; Morawetz, Victor, A Treatise on the Law of Private Corporations (Boston, 1886), Vol. 2, sect. 830, pp. 801–802; Machen, Arthur W., Jr., A Treatise on the Modern Law of Corporations (Boston, 1908), Vol. I, c. 13, sect. 786. See also Report of Committee Respecting Revision of Ohio Corporation Law, *supra* (note 16), at p. 76; letter of A. W. Machen, draftsman of the seventh tentative draft of a Uniform Incorporation Act, which is printed at p. 144 of the Handbook of the National Conference of Commissioners on Uniform State Laws (St. Louis, 1920). It says, in part: "The old theory that the capital stock of a corporation is a trust fund for the payment of its debts, and that the State must see to it that this trust fund at least starts out by being intact is found in practice to be unfounded. Corporations do not in fact get credit on any such theory; and money-lenders have proved themselves to be much too hard-headed to act on any such legal fiction. Corporations get credit either on the actual value of their assets, or on the integrity and standing of their officers and managers, and not at all on the nominal value of stock. If anybody needs protection against watered stock it is not creditors but credulous investors in the company's securities."

Occasionally one encounters denials by courts that creditors rely upon the nominal capitalization of corporations. See Kunz v. National Valve Co., 29 Oh. C. C. 519, 531, 9 Oh. C. C. (n.s.) 593, 606–07 (1907); Richardson v. Mining Co., 23 Utah 366, 381–82, 65 Pac. 74, 78 (1901); Rubino v. Pressed Steel Car Co., 53 Atl. 1050, 1053 (N. J. Ch., 1903).

assets and current liabilities. Some limitation should be made even here, however, in view of the fact that works on credit analysis and the commercial credit-rating agencies appear to make use of certain ratios involving a consideration of the amount of the capitalization in their attempts to arrive at quantitative measures of credit risk.[33] But the harm done to creditors by watered stock is most likely to be effected in the early stages of the corporate history of the concern involved, before it has acquired a credit rating at the hands of the agencies and before it does its short-term borrowing on the basis of a current position. At the outset its loan credit tends to be based more largely upon the value of its fixed assets than upon the value of the particular kind of assets known to creditors as "liquid" or "current." Fixed assets are difficult for the short-term creditor to evaluate and hence he is likely to be deceived by the nominal amount of stock which was issued for them.

As to the bondholder, he is more likely to be deceived by false capitalization than is the short-term creditor. The ratio of the shareholders' equity to the bondholders' equity in the assets of a corporation may not be a very important basis for credit rating in the case where the enterprise is a well established one with some record of earnings.[34] But in the case of a new enterprise earning capacity is wholly prospective in the majority of cases [35] and asset

[33] See, for example, WALL, ALEXANDER, AND R. W. DUNNING, RATIO ANALYSIS OF FINANCIAL STATEMENTS (N. Y., 1928); THE FINANCIAL AUDIT AS VIEWED BY BANKERS (Publications of the Robert Morris Associates, 1922), p. 38. The leading credit-rating agencies profess to assign more favorable ratings to concerns having conservative capitalizations than to those having speculative capitalizations. A company which has a large shareholders' equity as compared with its funded debt is regarded as a better risk than one with a speculative capitalization in which the ratio of capital stock to funded debt is relatively small. If the capital stock is inflated through stock watering, however, it is obvious that the presumptions in favor of the conservative capitalization are not well founded. Where possible, the analyst avoids this pitfall by using the *market value* of the shareholders' equity in computing the ratio.

In the following cases investors and creditors claimed that they were deceived by reports of commercial agencies which were based upon false statements concerning the payment that had been made for capital stock: National Bank of Merrill v. Illinois & Wisconsin Lumber Co., 101 Wisc. 247, 77 N. W. 185 (1898); Davis v. Louisville Trust Co., 181 Fed. 10 (C. C. A., 6th. Cir. 1910).

[34] See BADGER, RALPH E., VALUATION OF INDUSTRIAL SECURITIES (N. Y. 1925); LYON, H., *op. cit. supra* (note 14), c. 2.

[35] Incorporation of going concerns and consolidation of going concerns are obvious exceptions.

values are therefore much more significant to the lender than in the case of the going concern. Further, most of the assets of the new enterprise will be fixed assets for which stock was issued. The bond financing involved may be an effort to raise working capital. In the face of the notorious difficulty of valuing fixed property, the bond creditor is very likely to be deceived by the nominal amount of stock outstanding, since he will tend to rely upon it in calculating the value of the stockholders' equity which furnishes him with a presumptive margin of safety in the form of an asset value back of his bond supposedly in excess of the face amount of the bond.[36]

The danger that stock watering may deceive creditors, while by no means negligible, is probably far less serious than is the danger of deception to innocent shareholders. There are two reasons for this. The first is the fact that the business of credit extension is a far more highly organized and sophisticated process than is the investment of funds in the shares of unseasoned business ventures. The trade creditor is likely to be a business man whose business requires him to study the problem of credit extension under varying circumstances. He is equipped by personal experience or the aid of a trained credit manager to deal with the risks involved on a much more intelligent basis when lending to a new corporation than is the buyer of low-grade stocks. The bank creditor is a trained specialist

[36] If it should be urged that the bond buyer is protected by the elaborate investigation of the enterprise which is generally made by the bankers who underwrite the bond issue, the answer is twofold: first, that even bankers have been known to be deceived by false capitalizations, since the valuation problem is as difficult for them as it is for others in some cases; and second, that not all bond issues are underwritten. For examples see Babbitt v. Read, 215 Fed. 395 (D. C., S. D. N. Y., 1914), *aff'd*, 236 Fed. 42 (C. C. A., 2d. Cir., 1916); Lloyd v. Preston, 146 U. S. 630, 36 Law Ed. 1111, 13 Sup. Ct. 131 (1892), *aff'g* Preston v. Cincinnati, C. & H. V. R. Co., 36 Fed. 54 (C. C., S. D. Ohio, W. D., 1888); Colonial Trust Co. v. McMillan, 188 Mo. 547, 87 S. W. 933 (1905); See v. Heppenheimer, 69 N. J. Eq. 36, 61 Atl. 843 (N. J. Ch., 1905); Gillett v. Chicago Title & Trust Co., 230 Ill. 373, 82 N. E. 891 (1907).

It is significant, however, that most suits by creditors against stockholders on watered stock are instituted by general creditors rather than by bond creditors. One reason for this is the fact that most of the suits recorded in the published reports of decisions are suits against shareholders of small industrial concerns which generally do not issue bonds. A further reason for the scarcity of bondholders' suits is the presence in most indentures of a waiver-clause by which the bondholder waives his right to sue stockholders on watered stock. For a discussion of the cases involving the clause see BONBRIGHT, *op. cit. supra* (note 1) at p. 423.

in the art of credit extension on a profitable basis and hence is not likely in the majority of cases to be greatly deceived by false nominal capitalizations. In cases where an issue of bonds by a new corporation is floated through the assistance of investment bankers the bond buyer is to a large extent, though not completely, protected by the investigation of the enterprise which the bankers will normally have made.

The second reason why the shareholder is more likely than the creditor to suffer financial loss due to stock watering is legal in origin. The present state of American law with regard to the rights of a stockholder is such that it is exceedingly difficult for him to procure compensation for the loss which he suffers because his stock was watered.[37] On the other hand, the creditor has a legal remedy which, though far from perfect in its operation, does afford some protection against the danger of personal loss due to stock watering.

We have considered, so far, the evils of stock watering from the standpoint of the investing public. It remains to discuss the possible effects of this practice on the public as consumers of commodities and services. Students of the subject have frequently expressed the opinion that the consumer may suffer from excessive corporate capitalization through the influence of the latter upon the prices charged for services or products and upon the character of the services rendered. The contention that stock watering results in increased charges and poor service has been urged particularly with reference to public utilities.[38] It has likewise been advanced with regard to industrial combinations or "trusts."[39] Careful and im-

[37] The almost complete failure of the law to protect injured stockholders has been frequently discussed. Berle, A. A., Jr., *Compensation of Bankers and Promoters through Stock Profits*, 42 HARV. L. REV. (1929), 748, 756–59; HALE, WM. B., *op. cit. supra* (note 22) at p. 8; BONBRIGHT, J. C., *op. cit. supra* (note 2) at pp. 451–52, *op. cit. supra* (note 1) at p. 410; BALLANTINE, HENRY W., PRIVATE CORPORATIONS (Chicago, 1927), p. 668, note 107; 1 COOK, ON CORPORATIONS (8th. ed., N. Y., 1923), sects. 39, 40, pp. 171–82; 5 FLETCHER, *op. cit. supra* (note 5) sects. 3519, 3587, at pp. 5842–43, 5915–16; 14 CORPUS JURIS, sects. 357, 613, 637, 696, at pp. 300–1, 452, 454–55, 477.

[38] Textbooks, governmental reports of investigations, and periodical literature abound with discussions of this subject. Extended references and quotations can be found in LOCKLIN, *op. cit. supra* (note 2), especially c. 1 and Appendix A, and in BONBRIGHT, *op. cit. supra* (note 2), c. 1 and 2 and Appendices A and B. The latter work discusses at length the effects of over-capitalization on railway rates and service.

[39] U. S. INDUSTRIAL COMMISSION REPORTS (1900–1902), Vol. 1, Pt. I, pp.

partial students of the practice of stock watering agree that it does have an undesirable effect upon rates and service.[40] Stock watering impairs corporate credit by encouraging the payment of excessive dividends on the one hand and by the disappointment of investors on the other. Impaired credit not only encourages undermaintenance, poor service, and high charges in the public utility field, but through its harmful effect on investors it hampers desirable development of resources in the industrial field.

A further significant injury done to consumers of the products and users of the services of industrial enterprises by the practice of stock watering is a loss or misapplication of the productive resources of the country which result from excessive capitalizations. Economic welfare depends in part on the nature and amount of the industrial output of the community. It is promoted by the wise expenditure of the annual savings of the public in the further production of consumable goods and services. The use of any privately acquisitive device such as stock watering which retards the flow of individual savings into industry, or diverts that flow to enterprises which fail because of the use of the device, is harmful to consumers because the results are reduced industrial output, the scrapping of capital goods, poor service, and the social costs of individual readjustments which are necessitated by the failure of enterprises. For purposes of discussion this subject may be divided into two parts: first, the effects of impaired confidence on the part of investors in corporate securities due to stock watering; and second, the harmful repercussions throughout the community of failures caused by stock watering. To the extent that financing through watered stock has impaired public confidence in the shares of new enterprises and caused a loss or destruction of values through forced liquidation of existing enterprises, the public suffers from retarded economic development and from the scrapping of capital goods.

248–49, Pt. II, p. 1080, Index *s.v.* " Prices," Vol. XIII, Digest, p. cxxix (Butler and Hopkins), Testimony pp. 497, 512, Vol. XIX, p. 618; COLLIER, WM. M., THE TRUSTS (New York, 1901), pp. 211, 215, 218; JENKS, JEREMIAH W., THE TRUST PROBLEM (New York, 1903), p. 105; REPORT AND PROCEEDINGS OF THE JOINT COMMITTEE OF THE SENATE AND ASSEMBLY APPOINTED TO INVESTIGATE TRUSTS (Albany, 1897), pp. 18–21; Dill, Jas. B., *Some Tendencies in Combinations Which May Become Dangerous,* PUBLICATIONS OF THE AMERICAN ECONOMIC ASSOCIATION, 3d Series, Vol. I (1900), p. 177.

[40] BONBRIGHT, *op. cit. supra,* note 2; LOCKLIN, *op. cit. supra,* note 2; RIPLEY, *op. cit. supra,* note 8.

The second phase of this subject relates to the series of readjustments which follow those corporate failures which probably would not have occurred had it not been for the presence of watered stock. In the railway field stock watering has been an important contributing factor in financial failures.[41] The immediate cause of many of them has been an excess of fixed charges over net revenues available to meet these charges, a disparity which can in many cases be traced in part at least to watered stock.[42] If the stock of these roads had stood for actual payment made to the corporate treasury, it is probable that failure would have been avoided. The reasons for this assertion are: first, the fact that actual payment for the stock reduces the sum which must in any individual instance be raised by the sale of bonds; and second, the existence of an actual stockholders' equity would in many cases have reduced the cost of capital loaned to the corporation. The result of actual full payment for the stock would have been lower fixed charges on two counts, and without any reduction in earning capacity to meet the smaller charges. But, in the main, the promotion of our railroads was not financed on the basis of actual payment for stock. In many instances practically the entire construction cost was defrayed from the sale of bonds and the stock was issued to construction companies and promoters for little or no consideration. Had the stockholders contributed real payment for their shares there would not have been the need for such heavy bond financing. The result would have been a lower ratio of debt to assets and a fair presumption is that failure due to excessive fixed charges might have been avoided in a number of instances.

The question may be raised, why the issuance of stock to promoters and construction companies for little or no consideration prevented the companies from floating still more stock among investors for cash. Why has it forced the companies to issue bonds instead? In the first place, there is serious doubt whether the promoters could have got a full cash payment for stock. In the second place, it may be assumed that the promoters wished to issue and sell

[41] Ripley, *op. cit. supra* (note 8), *passim*, especially c. 12 at p. 380 *et seq.*

[42] The failure of an enterprise can rarely be traced to any *single* cause, such as faulty financial structure, unwise expansion or mismanagement. In most instances a combination of adverse factors contributes to the result. On the other hand, one can say with considerable assurance that the absence of some one of the factors, such as excessive funded debt, would have prevented the failure.

as many bonds as possible, as they are more easily marketed in large amounts than stock. The presence of a large, apparent but unreal equity due to watered stock made it possible to float larger bond issues than otherwise — made it possible to issue bonds up to perhaps the full cost of the road. Finally, the presence of watered stock tended to prevent the shares of railway corporations, when once issued, from attaining a market value equal to par unless the companies became unexpectedly prosperous. Under these conditions, unless a sufficient amount of treasury stock had been reserved, it was impossible to finance extensions by new stock issues, since it was necessary to sell the latter for not less than par if the shares were to be fully paid and non-assessable. The result was that the railway corporations were forced to issue bonds to finance extensions.

A number of unfortunate consequences may result from the impairment of credit which is the logical sequence to this type of excessive bond financing superposed upon large issues of watered stock. In the first place, impaired credit sometimes leads to undermaintenance and poor service, both to the detriment of the community served. In the second place, the subsequent purchaser of the watered shares either suffers a decline in the market value of his holdings coupled with no return or only a negligible return upon his investment, or else the corporation resorts to the folly of paying unearned dividends on the stock. This latter practice is sometimes due to the fact that the excessive stock issue itself tends to create a quasi-fixed charge in the shape of an expectation of dividends that the earnings will not justify. Finally, the disparity between the actual fixed charges and net earnings, coupled with the payment of unearned dividends, may lead to failure of the enterprise. The latter may result in a reorganization which wipes out the common stockholders and may even result in the abandonment of mileage.[43] If mileage is abandoned, either as a part of a reorganization scheme or to postpone or avoid the necessity of a reorganization, economic paralysis develops in the territory previously served by the road and costly readjustments to the new situation must be made.

In the industrial field stock watering has also been the cause of

[43] Although railway mileage is rarely abandoned it does occur, and it is doubtless true that in last analysis a considerable proportion of discarded mileage has been due to overpromotion. It is reported that during the years 1923 to 1927, inclusive, the Interstate Commerce Commission authorized the abandonment of 3,052 miles of railroad engaged in interstate commerce. *United States Daily*, April 14, 1928.

an excessive ratio of fixed charges to income. The cause of many failures has been the absence of any real contribution by the shareholder to the corporate treasury. In contrast to the consequences of failure in the railway field, failure here is likely in many instances to lead to the abandonment of plants. The results, aside from the direct losses of investors, are unemployment of workmen, a falling off of retail trade in the immediate locality and a whole series of expensive readjustments growing out of the economic friction set up by the failure and abandonment of the enterprise which, but for the existence of watered stock in its financial structure, might never have occurred.

It has not been possible to subject the truth or falsity of the foregoing charges against stock watering to quantitative demonstration. That investors and creditors are sometimes deceived by false capitalizations is not open to question, but the number of those who are actually deceived and the extent of their pecuniary loss therefrom do not appear to be measurable. It is a demonstrable fact that there are numerous suits recorded in the law books in which creditors have alleged that they were deceived by watered stock as a part of their pleading in suits against stockholders for the recovery of an unpaid balance on shares of stock. In most of these actions they have not been required to demonstrate the truth of this assertion, the mere allegation being considered sufficient by the court for reasons suggested in the quotations above.[44] In the vast majority of cases

[44] BALLANTINE, *op. cit. supra* (note 32) at p. 90, *et seq.*; BONBRIGHT, *op. cit. supra* (note 1) at p. 421, his footnote (45); Hunt, Edwin S., *The Trust Fund Theory and Some Substitutes for It* (1902), 12 YALE L. J. 63, 78, *et seq.*; HALE, *op. cit. supra* (note 22) at p. 11. The rule is stated and the cases are collected in 6 FLETCHER, *op. cit. supra* (note 5), sect. 4095, p. 7034, his footnotes (15) and (16). The following statement by the Supreme Court of Minnesota indicates the position of most courts: " While the basis of the liability of the stockholders to the creditors for unpaid stock subscriptions is fraud, it is fraud in law, constructive fraud, rather than actual fraud; and it is not necessary for the creditors to prove affirmatively that they trusted the corporation in reliance upon the subscriptions. The presumption of reliance is raised when the creditor proves the issuance of the stock and that he subsequently trusted the corporation. It is true that this is not a conclusive presumption; it is one of fact and may be rebutted. The creditor must have relied upon the representation that the stock issued as fully paid was so in fact, or he was not misled or defrauded; but he is aided by the presumption or inference that he did rely upon the representation. . . . But it is not necessary for the creditor to plead or prove that he relied upon the representation, or the usual elements of actual fraud. And it is

the burden of proof of non-reliance on the part of the protesting creditor rests on the stockholder. Indeed, the writer cannot recall a single case in which the creditor has been required to *prove* that he actually relied upon the nominal capitalization except where the defending shareholder has adduced such evidence before the court as to cast serious doubt upon the fact of the creditor's reliance. The number of these court cases is probably almost worthless as evidence of the extent to which creditors are actually deceived by watered stock. Moreover, apparently only a tiny fraction of the worst cases of stock watering ever get into court.

Even less indicative of the extent of the deception are the cases in which subsequent innocent purchasers of shares of watered stock have protested in court against the original dilution, and the cases in which shareholders or corporations have sued for the recovery by the corporation of a secret profit made by the promoter through the overvaluation of the consideration for which his stock was issued. The position of the subsequent innocent purchaser of the shares is so hopeless that he rarely brings suit, while modern methods of forming corporations have been so cunningly devised by promoters that it is generally impossible to charge him with having made a *secret* profit which he has not disclosed to his fellow shareholders.[45] Suits of this nature are therefore comparatively rare when contrasted with the number of instances in which the promoter has probably made an illegitimate profit through excessive capitalization. And finally, the extent of the harm done to consumers due to the effect of stock watering on rates and the character of service

---

not fatal to his cause that as a matter of fact he had no personal knowledge of the amount of the professed capital stock, or of the shares held by any particular stockholder, or what was paid for them." Randall Printing Co. v. Sanitas Mineral Water Co., 120 Minn. 268, 274, 139 N. W. 606, 608 (1913).

See also the following: Smith v. Schmitt, 112 Or. 687, 710, 231 Pac. 176, 184 (1924); See v. Heppenheimer, 69 N. J. Eq. 36, 84, 61 Atl. 843, 862 (N. J. Ch. 1905); Vermont, etc., Co. v. Declez, etc., Co., 135 Cal. 579, 584, 67 Pac. 1057, 1059 (1902). But see Herron Co. v. Shaw, 165 Cal. 668, 671, 133 Pac. 488, 489 (1913).

A minority of courts ignore entirely the question of reliance by creditors upon the nominal capitalization. See BALLANTINE, *op. cit.*, at p. 88; BONBRIGHT, *op. cit.*, at p. 472.

[45] See Allenhurst Park Estates v. Smith, *supra*, note 9, and the cases therein cited. The leading cases are collected and discussed in BALLANTINE, *op. cit. supra* (note 37) at p. 168, *et seq.*

rendered by public utility enterprises as well as the extent of its harmful effect in causing needless failures and in slowing up industrial progress through impairing investment confidence are likewise immeasurable quantities. But while the extent of the harm done to various interests by stock watering cannot be quantitatively measured, the evidence is quite sufficient to show that the evil has been a serious one, and it is significant that even among writers with a distinctly *laissez-faire* outlook on business conduct there is far less disposition now than formerly to condone the practice or to belittle its dangers.[46]

Position of American Law with Respect to Stock Watering

Recognition of the undesirable effects of stock watering has led to the adoption in America of various devices for the social control of the practice. In the public utility field the capitalization of corporations is largely subject to the control or approval of public utility commissions or similar bodies. Where the consent of these commissions is necessary before corporate securities may be issued it is possible to prevent, or at least to restrict, stock watering through careful regulation of the value of the consideration for which stock is issued. And where commissions permit the issuance of stock at a price less than its par value, they are usually empowered to require the use of certain accounting methods which give publicity to the real nature of the transaction.

But the capitalization of purely private corporations is not subject to the same degree of public supervision. As a general rule these corporations may issue stock for almost any consideration which is deemed to be adequate by the directors. Almost the only check placed upon the practice is found in our statutory and judge-made law concerning the payment for capital stock and concerning the liability of stockholders to creditors on part-paid stock.[47] It is

[46] One of the most authoritative writers in the field of private finance, Mr. Hastings Lyon, who formerly defended the issuance of watered stock in his book on corporation finance, *op. cit. supra*, note 14, informs the writer that his present position, if he were to revise his discussion of the subject, would be far less tolerant.

[47] Further protection for the investor has been attempted through the enactment of laws regulating the sale of securities (the so-called Blue Sky Laws). The latest statutes of this type are collected in The Corporation Manual (31st. ed., New York, 1930), Pt. III, pp. 1727 to 2147. See also Reed, Robert R., and L. H. Washburn, Blue Sky Laws (New York, 1921); Elliott,

therefore pertinent to examine the position of American law with respect to the payment for capital stock before entering upon a discussion of the principles and methods of valuation which the courts have used in cases in which there was a dispute concerning the value of the consideration for which stock was issued.[48]

Not only at common law, but also by the statutes of practically all of the states, corporations are permitted to accept property and services, as well as cash, in payment for stock.[49] The rule permitting

---

JOHN M., THE ANNOTATED BLUE SKY LAWS OF THE UNITED STATES (Cincinnati, 1919); MILLS, CHAS. H., FRAUDULENT PRACTICES IN RESPECT TO SECURITIES AND COMMODITIES (Albany, 1925); 6 THOMPSON, ON CORPORATIONS (3d. ed., Indianapolis, 1927), sects. 4144–52; 7 FLETCHER, *op. cit. supra* (note 5), sect. 4421; 1 COOK, *op. cit. supra* (note 37), sects. 45c, 152; 2 *ibid.*, sect. 354; BALLANTINE, *op. cit. supra* (note 37) at p. 832 *et seq.;* annotations in 15 A. L. R. 262, 24 A. L. R. 523, 27 A. L. R. 1169, 30 A. L. R. 1331, 54 A. L. R. 498, 57 A. L. R. 1004. See also ASHBY, FORREST B., THE ECONOMIC EFFECT OF BLUE SKY LAWS (Phila., 1926). Other references are cited by BALLANTINE, *op. cit.*, at p. 833. And see REPORT OF THE COMMITTEE ON A UNIFORM SALE OF SECURITIES ACT, submitting a third tentative draft to the thirty-seventh annual meeting of the National Conference of Commissioners on Uniform State Laws, Buffalo, N. Y., Aug. 23–29, 1927.

These laws are mainly directed toward the regulation of the *sale* of securities rather than their issuance. But they are designed to protect the buyer of shares by preventing the public flotation of worthless shares.

In addition to the Blue Sky Laws referred to above, some further protection is provided for the investor by the law of "promoters' profits." See BALLANTINE, *loc. cit. supra* (note 45); EHRICH, MANFRED W., THE LAW OF PROMOTERS (Albany, 1916); ALGER, ARTHUR M., A TREATISE ON THE LAW IN RELATION TO PROMOTERS AND THE PROMOTION OF CORPORATIONS (Boston, 1897); 1 FLETCHER, *op. cit.*, sect. 135 *et seq.;* 1 THOMPSON, *op. cit.*, sect. 119 *et seq.* Though related to the problem attacked in this monograph, the whole subject of promoters' profits is so intricate and extensive that it deserves separate treatment. It has been purposely excluded from this inquiry.

[48] See in this connection, BONBRIGHT, *op. cit. supra*, note 1. The treatment of this subject which follows in the text has been advisedly abbreviated because of its exposition elsewhere. Liberal use has been made of Bonbright's treatment in this brief summary.

[49] The constitutional and statutory provisions are reviewed in 5 FLETCHER, *op. cit. supra* (note 5), sects. 3525–75. The best secondary source for the latest amendments is THE CORPORATION MANUAL, *supra*, note 47. Although the earlier constitutional clauses and statutes prohibited the issuance of stock for any consideration other than cash, it soon became apparent to legislators that industrial development would be retarded by such a stringent requirement. Consequently the laws were amended at a fairly early date to permit the issue of stock for considerations other than cash. Stevens, Robert S., *Stock Issues Under*

direct exchange of stock for property is a reasonable one since it makes it possible to avoid the roundabout and frequently expensive process of issuing stock for cash and then paying out the cash in the purchase of property.[50] This stock is usually issued under an agreement between the corporation and the subscriber that it shall be considered fully paid. Both at common law and under the statutes such an agreement is usually valid as between the parties, and the corporation is estopped to assert that the shareholders owe any further payment on their shares.[51]

---

the Uniform Business Corporation Act (1928), 13 CORN. L. Q. 399, 400–403. These amendments created the valuation problem which is discussed in this treatise. For an example of the shift in the terms of the statutes see STEVENS, *op. cit.*, in his footnotes (6) and (19). *Cf.* Schenck v. Andrews, 46 N. Y. 589 (1871); Boynton v. Hatch, 47 N. Y. 224 (1872); Schenck v. Andrews, 57 N. Y. 133 (1874); Boynton v. Andrews, 63 N. Y. 93 (1875).

[50] See the following for citation of cases in support of the rule that it is not necessary for a corporation to engage in the idle and roundabout ceremony of first disposing of its stock for cash and then expending the cash for property which it desires to purchase: 1 COOK, *op. cit. supra* (note 37), sect. 18, p. 130, footnote (2); 5 FLETCHER, *op. cit. supra* (note 5), sect. 3503, pp. 5805–8; CLARK, ON CORPORATIONS (3d. ed., St. Paul, 1916), p. 467; 14 CORPUS JURIS, sect. 594, footnote (62); 5 THOMPSON, *op. cit. supra* (note 47), sects. 3977, 3978, 3980 (*Cf.* sect. 3981); PALMER'S COMPANY LAW (London, 1929), p. 118.

Any deficiency in the value of the property turned over for stock is not cured by a preliminary exchange of checks between the vendor and the corporation. See American Tube & Iron Co. v. Hays, 165 Pa. St. 489, 30 Atl. 936 (1895); Rathbone v. Ayer, 121 App. Div. (N. Y.) 355, 105 N. Y. Sup. 1041 (1907), *rev'd.*, 196 N. Y. 503, 89 N. E. 1111 (1909).

The issue of stock for property in the formation of industrial consolidations has sometimes been preceded by a preliminary exchange of checks in order to give the appearance of an initial full payment for the stock. See U. S. INDUSTRIAL COMMISSION REPORTS (1900–1902), Vol. XIII, *Digest of Testimony*, pp. cix–cx, *Testimony*, pp. 93–94 (organization of the American Smelting & Refining Co.). The same type of transaction was used in financing the construction of the Union Pacific Railway. The construction company agreed to accept stock in part payment for work done. Since the law required the stock of the company to be paid for in cash at par, the Union Pacific gave its check to apply on construction account and the check was then given back to the Union Pacific in payment for stock. This fictitious "cash" transaction provided a formal compliance with the law and at the same time permitted the issuance of an excessive amount of stock for construction. See DAVIS, JOHN P., THE UNION PACIFIC RAILWAY (Chicago, 1894), p. 169.

[51] Exceptions are to be noted in a few jurisdictions where the courts interpret a subscription for stock at a price less than par as a twofold agreement (*a*) to issue stock, and (*b*) to accept less than par value in payment, and per-

Although the general common-law rule is that shareholders are not personally liable, even to creditors, for any unpaid balance on shares issued at a price less than par under an agreement between the corporation and the shareholders that they shall be considered fully paid, most courts recognize one exception in the form of a " fraud " liability to those creditors who may be presumed to have relied upon the fictitious capitalization.[52] Where property or services have been the medium of payment for corporate shares, the question of whether there was actionable fraud in the transaction generally resolves itself into a question of whether the property or services were valued in the manner contemplated by law.

Beginning at about the middle of the nineteenth century, more or less coincident with the development in this country of the use of the corporate device on a large scale, states began putting into their constitutions and statutes some provision as to the consideration for which stock might be issued, until at the present time practically every state has made such provision.[53] In many states the statutory or constitutional enactment forbade the issue of stock " except for money paid, labor done, or property actually received " and provided that " all fictitious increase of stock or indebtedness shall be void." [54] A provision of this sort occasionally creates a

---

mit the corporation to revoke its promise not to assess the stock but at the same time hold that the issuance of the stock was valid. See Bonbright, *op. cit. supra* (note 1), his footnote (6) at pp. 410–11.

[52] The courts of New York and of a few other states deny that there is any common-law liability on stock issued at a discount or for overvalued property. They insist that the shareholder's obligation rests solely upon his contract or upon the terms of a statute. See Bonbright, *op. cit. supra* (note 1) at pp. 411, 416.

Numerous judicial opinions and articles in legal periodicals as well as extended text treatments have been devoted to the grounds on which shareholders' liability to creditors is based. See: Bonbright, *op. cit.*, p. 409 *et seq.*; Ballantine, *op. cit. supra* (note 32); Ballantine, *op. cit. supra* (note 37) at pp. 669–80, 682; Hunt, *op. cit. supra*, note 44; Wickersham, G. W., *The Capital of a Corporation* (1909), 22 Harv. L. Rev. 319; *The Right of a Trustee to Recover Amount Unpaid on Capital Stock* (1924), 24 Col. L. Rev. 772. Perhaps the most notable judicial opinion on this question is found in Hospes v. Northwestern Manuf'g & Car Co., *supra*, note 24. *Cf.* the language of the Supreme Court of California in Rhode v. Dock-Hop Co., *supra*, note 26, quoted *supra*, pp. 14–15.

[53] Stevens, *op. cit. supra* (note 49) at p. 403. *Cf.* Fletcher, *loc. cit. supra*, note 49.

[54] See Fletcher, *loc. cit. supra*, note 49. The following are examples: Calif.

valuation problem in which the court is required by the pleading of the litigant parties to decide whether the property or services for which the stock was issued were so valued as to make it " fictitious " in whole or in part.[55]

Many states, however, have not been content with an enactment of the " money, labor and property " clause as noted above and have made various attempts at partial legislative definition of the *amount* of consideration which must be received in payment. Instead of relying upon the ambiguous term, " fictitious increase of stock," they declare that stock may be issued for property or services to the extent of the "value." thereof;[56] or the " money value " thereof;[57] or the " cash value " thereof;[58] or the " actual value " thereof, at the time of the issue.[59] Many of the statutes contain the further provision that in the absence of " fraud," or " actual fraud," in the transaction the judgment of the directors as to the value of the consideration other than cash shall be conclusive.[60]

Const. (1879), art. XII, sect. 11; Del. Const. (1897), art. IX, sect. 3; Mo. Const. (1875), art. XII, sect. 8; Ark. Const. (1874), art. XII, sect. 8; Calif. Civ. Code (as amended to 1923), sect. 359; Del. Rev. Code (1915), c. 65, par. 1928, p. 924; Mo. Rev. Stat. (1919), Vol. III, sect. 9740 (R. S. 1909, sect. 2981).

[55] The term " fictitious " is as vague as the term " value " and the courts have given no clear definition of either in stock-watering cases. See Coler v. Tacoma Railway & Power Co., 65 N. J. Eq. 347, 54 Atl. 413 (1903); Memphis, etc., Railroad Co. v. Dow, 120 U. S. 287, 7 Sup. Ct. 482 (1887); Peoria and Springfield Railroad Co. v. Thompson, 103 Ill. 187 (1882). *Cf.* BALLANTINE, *op. cit. supra* (note 37) at p. 663.

[56] For example, New York Stock Corporation Law, sect. 69 (L. 1923, c. 787, sect. 69); New Jersey General Corporation Act, sects. 48, 49 (P. L. 1896, p. 293, 2 Comp. Stat. N. J. [1911], p. 1630); 1 Cons. Stat. N. C. (1919), sect. 1158; Me. Rev. Stat. (1916), c. 51, sect. 54, p. 793.

[57] Alaska Comp. Laws (1913), sect. 811; Wisc. Stat. (1927), sect. 182.06; N. D. Comp. Laws Ann. (1913), sect. 4528 (R. C. 1905, sect. 4195); S. C. Civ. Code (1922), sect. 4303; N. H. Pub. Laws (1926), c. 225, sect. 11.

[58] Utah Comp. Laws (1917), sect. 862 (as amended by L. 1921, c. 22); Tenn. Ann. Code (Shannon, 1917), sects. 2076a14, 2126, 2303; N. D. Comp. Laws Ann. (1913), sect. 4528; Mo. Rev. Stat. (1919), sect. 10144.

[59] Md. Ann. Code (Bagby, 1924), sect. 41, par. 9, sect. 43, pars. 1, 2, 3(c), sect. 44, sect. 45; Gen. Corp. Act. Mich. (1921), sect. 53, Mich. Comp. Laws (1922), c. 175, sect. 9053 (53); Conn. Gen. Stat. (1918), sect. 3431; Dist. Col. Code (1901, as amended to June 7, 1924), sect. 613; Tex. Ann. Rev. Civ. Stat. (Vernon, 1925), art. 1308.

[60] Gen. Corp. Law of Del., art. I, sect. 14 (Del. Rev. Code [1915], d. 65, sect. 14, par. 1928, p. 924); N. Y. Stock Corp. Law, sect. 69 (L. 1923, c. 787, art. 7, sect. 69); Md. Ann. Code (1924), art. 23, sect. 49; Mich. Comp. Laws

Some states have gone still farther in their legislative attempts to prevent or control stock watering. A number of the statutes require a corporation which has issued shares of stock in payment for property to file with the secretary of state or other public official a sworn schedule describing in detail the consideration other than cash which the corporation has received for its stock, together with the valuation at which the same was received.[61] Occasionally the statutes contain penal clauses covering misstatements contained in such schedules.[62]

In addition to these clauses providing for the full payment of stock, most states have further provisions to the effect that shareholders shall be personally liable to creditors for any unpaid balance on their shares.[63] Although numerous defenses are available to share-

---

(1922), c. 175, sect. 9053 (53); Conn. Gen. Stat. (1918), sect. 3431; N. J. Gen. Corp. Act (1896), sect. 49 (P. L. 1896, p. 293, 2 Comp. Stat. [1911], p. 1630); N. C. Cons. Stat. (1919), sect. 1158; S. D. Rev. Code (1919), sect. 8775; Me. Rev. Stat. (1916), c. 51, sect. 54, p. 793; Ind. Acts 1929, c. 215, sect. 6(e), p. 732.

[61] Ill. Rev. Stat. Ann (Smith-Hurd, 1929), c. 32, sects. 4, 5, 28, 131, 145; Md. Ann. Code (Bagby, 1924), art. 23, sect. 43, pars. 3(c), 4, 5, sect. 44(b), (L. 1920, c. 545); Mich. Comp. Laws (Cahill's Ann. Sup., 1922), c. 175, sects. 9053(11), 9053(12), 9053(53); Mass. Gen. Laws (1921), c. 156, sects. 10, 16; Va. Const. (1902), sect. 167; Va. Ann. Code (1924), sect. 3788; Utah Comp. Laws (1917), sects. 862, 865; Vt. Gen. Laws (1917), sect. 4930; Mo. Rev. Stat. (1919), sects. 10144, 10145; Tex. Ann. Rev. Civ. Stat. (Vernon, 1925), art. 1308; Ohio Gen. Code, sect. 8623–(26), (Sect. 26 of Ohio Gen. Corp. Act, L. 1929, pp. 427–28); La. Bus. Corp. Act (Acts 1928, No. 250), sect. 18; R. I. Gen. Laws (1923), sect. 3495; Uniform Business Corporation Act, sect. 18.

This type of statute was probably copied from the British Companies (Consolidation) Act 1908, sect. 88 (now sect. 42 of the Companies Act of 1929). For discussions of these laws see: WICKERSHAM, *op. cit. supra* (note 52) at p. 336 *et seq.;* STEVENS, *op. cit. supra,* note 49; Uniform Business Corporation Act, annotations to sect. 18; REPORT OF COMMITTEE RESPECTING REVISION OF OHIO CORPORATION LAW (Dec. 28, 1926), at pp. 32, 77–78.

[62] Ill. Rev. Stat. Ann. (Smith-Hurd, 1929), sect. 150; Md. Ann. Code (Bagby, 1924), art. 23, sect. 49; Va. Ann. Code (1924), sect. 3788; Vt. Gen. Laws (1917), sect. 4930; La. Acts 1928, Act No. 250, sect. 18, par. iv; Mass. Gen. Laws (1921), c. 156, sect. 10(d); Uniform Business Corporation Act, sect. 18, par. ii.

[63] New York Stock Corporation Law, sect. 70 (L. 1923, c. 787, sect. 70); Gen. Corp. Act. N. J., sect. 21 (P. L. 1896, p. 284, 2 N. J. Comp. Stat., p. 1610, sect. 21); Ala. Civ. Code (1923), sect. 6992; Alaska Comp. Laws (1913), sect. 811; Conn. Gen. Stat. (1918), sect. 3435; N. C. Consol. Stat. (1919), sect. 1160; Ill. Rev. Stat. Ann. (Smith-Hurd, 1929), c. 32, sects. 51, 53; Del. Rev. Code (1915), c. 65, sect. 1934 (sect. 20 of Gen. Corp. Act); R. I. Gen. Laws (1923), sect. 3502; Ind. Acts 1929, c. 215, sect. 6(h), p. 773.

By way of illustration, the Delaware provision reads as follows: " When the

holders against this statutory liability, such as the fact that the particular shareholders who are being sued had no notice of the manner in which the stock was originally issued or that the creditors suing had such notice, it is none the less true that in a jurisdiction, such as New York, in which the courts refuse to recognize any liability of shareholders for the debts of the corporation at common law, this type of provision adds materially to the force of the " money, labor and property " clause in the origination of suits involving the valuation problem with which this treatise is concerned.[64] And although a majority of decisions appear to construe the clause as being merely declaratory of common law, a minority of courts have held to the contrary.[65]

These latter courts base the liability on statutory grounds rather than on the " trust fund," " holding out," or other conventional theories on which most courts are accustomed to rely in imposing liability at common law.[66] They hold, for example, that even creditors, on notice of the manner in which the stock was originally paid for, may recover an unpaid balance from shareholders because liability is a direct legal consequence of the statutory provision.[67] To this extent, at least, the legislation imposing a liability on shareholders has caused a departure from the common-law doctrine of fraud.

In addition to the foregoing legislation giving rise to valuation problems, some of the earlier statutes required the directors or trustees of corporations to file with the secretary of state, or other public official, periodic reports indicating the extent to which the capital stock of their corporation was fully paid up, and imposed upon them a joint and several liability to creditors who may have

---

whole capital stock of a corporation shall not have been paid in, and the assets shall be insufficient to satisfy the claims of its creditors, each stockholder shall be bound to pay on each share held by him the sum necessary to complete the amount of the par value of such share as fixed by the charter of the company or its certificate of incorporation, or such proportion of that sum as shall be required to satisfy the debts of the company. . . ."

[64] See BONBRIGHT, *op. cit. supra*, note 1.

[65] Many decisions on this point are collected in 7 A. L. R. 972. *Cf.* BONBRIGHT, *op. cit. supra* (note 1) at pp. 415–16, 421–22.

[66] BONBRIGHT, *op. cit.;* BALLANTINE, *op. cit. supra*, note 32. For other references see note 52, *supra*.

[67] See cases cited by BONBRIGHT, *op. cit. supra* (note 1), in his footnote (51) at p. 422.

relied upon the published statement, provided the report or certificate so filed should be proven to be false in any material representation.[68] In New York such a provision has given rise to numerous suits in which the principal allegation of the plaintiffs was that the report was materially false because the stock therein stated to have been fully paid up was in fact only nominally paid for, the consideration having been property taken at an overvaluation.[69]

The common-law doctrine together with the legislative provisions sketched above, form the basis for various types of suits which raise the issue of the value of property or services taken in exchange for stock. Both at common law and under the various statutes relating to stock watering the majority of suits attacking the valuation of property and services so exchanged are instituted by creditors of corporations, or by receivers, against the stockholders.[70] The

[68] N. Y. Laws 1848, c. 40, sect. 15; N. Y. Laws 1875, c. 611, sect. 21, which reads as follows: "If any certificate or report made, or public notice given, by the officers of any such corporation, shall be false in any material representation, all the officers who shall have signed the same shall be jointly and severally liable for all the debts of the corporation contracted while they are officers thereof." *Cf.* 7 N. Y. Ann. Cons. Laws (Birdseye, Cumming and Gilbert, 2d ed., 1918), p. 8717, sect. 35, L. 1909, c. 61, sect. 35, L. 1923, c. 787, sect. 61; N. J. Comp. Stat. (1911), p. 1633, sect. 52, N. J. P. L. (1896), p. 295.

See also, 6 FLETCHER, *op. cit. supra* (note 5), sect. 4156, discussing another type of statute which imposes a liability to creditors upon stockholders for a sum equal to the amount of stock held by each until the whole amount of the authorized capital stock shall have been paid in and a certificate filed to that effect.

[69] For example, Huntington v. Attrill, 42 Hun 459 (1886), *aff'd,* 118 N. Y. 365, 23 N. E. 544 (1890).

[70] A distinction is to be noted between stockholders' liability and promoters' liability. As has been noted in the text, stockholders are held liable to creditors either on common-law grounds of fraud, or under the statutes which impose such a liability. In addition to being subject to this liability as a stockholder the promoter may be held liable to the corporation for "secret profits" made out of the promotion. Much difficulty has been encountered by the courts in defining the status of promoters in relation to the corporate enterprises which they organize. See Isaacs, Nathan, *The Promoter: a Legislative Problem* (1926), 38 HARV. L. REV. 887.

But there is substantial agreement among the courts that the relationship of the promoter to the corporation is that of a fiduciary. In the absence of a statutory definition of the promoter's status, the courts have applied to his conduct the common-law rule that a fiduciary may not make a profit through his administration of the estate in his hands. On this theory they have erected a body of judicial precedent to the effect that promoters may not make "secret profits" from their promotive activities. Upon the promoter is imposed the

usual sequence of events is: first, a failure of the corporation; second, a partial liquidation of the obligations of the corporation through bankruptcy proceedings, equity receivership, foreclosure, or levy of execution; and third, a direct or representative suit at law or in equity by wholly or partially unsatisfied creditors of the corporation against the holders of allegedly unpaid stock.[71] The

duty of making full disclosure to an unbiassed board of directors, or to all of the existing shareholders, concerning the nature of his interest in the property which he proposes to sell to the corporation. See Allenhurst Park Estates v. Smith, *supra*, note 9, and references cited *supra*, note 47. But since the first board of directors is only nominally independent of the promoter, and since in most cases the original body of shareholders will consist entirely of the promoters and their nominees, this legal rule affords little protection to subsequent shareholders unless the latter can prove that "fraud" was practised by the promoter upon the directors, the corporation, or other shareholders. Arnold v. Searing, 73 N. J. Eq. 262, 67 Atl. 831 (1907), *aff'd*, 78 N. J. Eq. 146, 78 Atl. 762 (1910).

The law of promoters' liability for secret profits is intended, in part at least, to protect subsequent shareholders from an overvaluation of the consideration which is exchanged by the promoter for stock of the corporation. To the extent that this law is effective it is advantageous to creditors. On the other hand, the liability of stockholders to creditors is designed specifically for the protection of creditors, and although this liability is largely nullified by the difficulties of proving overvaluation and of obtaining judgment against shareholders even when overvaluation is proven, none the less it exercises some restraining influence upon excessive capitalization. Hence it tends to protect subsequent shareholders as well as creditors.

[71] Since a subscription for stock is a contract between the subscriber and the corporation, and since there is no direct contract relation between the subscriber and corporate creditors, the latter cannot bring an action at law against the former (in the absence of a statute which imposes a liability), to recover the unpaid balance on stock. Hence, shareholders' liability must usually be enforced by creditor's bill after the plaintiff has exhausted his remedies against the corporation, and after judgment has been obtained and execution thereon has been returned unsatisfied. The precise manner of bringing suit varies considerably among the different jurisdictions. For discussions of the remedies and procedure which the creditor may pursue see: BALLANTINE, *op. cit. supra* (note 37), sects. 200, 201, 216; *The Right of a Trustee to Recover Amount Unpaid on Capital Stock*, *supra*, note 52; *Right of Creditor of Insolvent Corporation to Sue Stockholder at Law upon Unpaid Subscription*, 7 A. L. R. 100; *Jurisdiction of Equity to Enforce Liability on Unpaid Subscription to Stock of a Corporation*, 46 L. R. A. (N.S.) 440; 14 CORPUS JURIS, sect. 1693 *et seq.*; 5 FLETCHER, *op. cit. supra* (note 5), sect. 3598; 6 *ibid.*, c. 56, subdivs. 12, 23, 24; 5 THOMPSON, *op. cit. supra* (note 47), sect. 3939, at p. 809; 7 *ibid.*, c. 150.

Whether or not shareholders' liability suits involve a jury trial depends upon the remedy which the plaintiff elects to pursue, upon statutory provisions,

cases of this nature which concern us are those in which the allegation of non-payment of shares is grounded in a contention that the property or services for which the stock was issued were overvalued in violation of common-law principles or statutory requirements. Occasionally, though more rarely, suits by creditors are directed against the trustees or directors for making a false report of the extent to which the capital stock was fully paid.[72]

Various other types of suits may be instituted by *stockholders* in which the principal issue is a question of the valuation of the consideration for which corporate stock was issued. The more significant forms of shareholders' suits are: (*a*) by minority shareholders to enjoin a contemplated stock issue on the ground that the par value of the stock to be issued exceeds the value of the consideration to be accepted;[73] (*b*) by shareholders to compel the cancellation of shares issued to others for an inadequate consideration;[74] (*c*) by share-

---

and upon other jurisdictional differences. For the most part the suits are brought in equity, and it is for this reason that one rarely encounters rulings by the court on the admissibility of evidence or instructions to juries concerning the measure of value which is to be applied in stock-watering cases. For exceptions see: Huntington v. Attrill, *supra,* note 69; The White Corbin Co. v. Jones, 155 N. Y. 475, 50 N. E. 289 (1898).

[72] For example, Huntington v. Attrill, *supra,* note 69. Another type of suit which is of comparatively rare occurrence involves disputes among creditors concerning their relative priorities. Manhattan Trust Co. v. Seattle Coal and Iron Co., 19 Wash. 493, 53 Pac. 951 (1898); *In re* L. M. Alleman Hardware Co., 181 Fed. 810 (C. C. A., 3d Cir., 1910), *rev'g* 172 Fed. 611 (D. C., M. D. Pa., 1909). *Cf. In re* Wyoming Valley Ice Co., 153 Fed. 787 (D. C., M. D. Pa., 1907).

[73] For example, Donald v. American Smelting & Refining Co., 61 N. J. Eq. 458, 48 Atl. 786 (1901), *rev'd,* 62 N. J. Eg. 729, 48 Atl. 771, 1116 (1901); Greer v. Amalgamated Copper Co., 61 N. J. Eq. 364, 49 Atl. 159 (1901); Coler v. Tacoma Ry. & Power Co., 64 N. J. Eq. 117, 53 Atl. 680 (1902), *rev'd,* 65 N. J. Eq. 347, 54 Atl. 413 (1903); Carver v. Southern Iron & Steel Co., 78 N. J. Eq. 81, 78 Atl. 240 (N. J. Ch., 1910); McMahon v. Pneumatic Transit Co., 85 N. J. Eq. 544, 96 Atl. 999 (1916); Gamble v. Queens County Water Co., 123 N. Y. 91, 25 N. E. 201 (1890), *rev'g* 52 Hun 166, 5 N. Y. S. 124 (1889); Rafferty v. Buffalo City Gas Co., 37 App. Div. (N. Y.) 618, 56 N. Y. S. 288 (1899).

[74] For example, Scully v. Automobile Finance Co., 12 Del. Ch. 174, 109 Atl. 49 (1920); Vineland Grape Juice Co. v. Chandler, 80 N. J. Eq. 437, 85 Atl. 213 (1912); Vogeler v. Punch, 205 Mo. 558, 103 S. W. 1001 (1907); Kunkle v. Soule, 68 Colo. 524, 190 Pac. 536 (1920); Soule v. Kunkle, 71 Colo. 221, 205 Pac. 529 (1922); American Macaroni Corp. v. Saumer, 174 N. Y. S. 183 (1919); Central Consumers' Wine & Liquor Co. v. Madden, 68 Atl. 777 (N. J. Ch., 1908); B. & C. Electrical Construction Co. v. Owen, 227 N. Y. 569, 126 N. E. 927 (1919) *aff'g* 176 App. Div. (N. Y.) 399, 163 N. Y. S. 31 (1917).

holders for a writ of mandamus to compel the corporate officers to recognize them as shareholders, the corporation resisting on the ground that the stock of the plaintiffs was issued for an inadequate or invalid consideration and is therefore void; [75] and (*d*) by shareholders to compel an accounting in voluntary liquidation of a corporation where shares were issued to others for an allegedly inadequate consideration.[76]

In addition to creditors' and stockholders' suits the problem of valuation is occasionally raised in *quo warranto* proceedings instituted to oust the corporation from its franchise to be a corporation on the ground that the stock was issued contrary to law.[77]

The foregoing list of suits or proceedings which raise the question of proper valuation of property exchanged for stock is not exhaustive, but it covers the principal types of actions which present the valuation problem to which this treatise is devoted. By far the largest number of suits have been by creditors to enforce a personal liability of shareholders, and consequently the major part of this study will be devoted to cases of this type. Many suits of the other types, however, have been read in the preparation of this monograph, and they will be referred to from time to time when their mention seems appropriate. Particular reference will be made to them whenever it appears that the nature of the action has given rise to principles of valuation which differ from those which prevail in creditors' suits.

The task of reading all American decisions relating to stock watering has proved to be a very formidable one. Accordingly, the writer has studied exhaustively the cases in certain important jurisdictions. This procedure was considered to be appropriate in view of the evident similarity of judicial attitude toward stock watering

[75] Bowen v. Imperial Theatres, Inc., *supra*, note 18. *Cf.* Fitzpatrick v. O'Neill, 43 Mont. 552, 118 Pac. 273 (1911); Arapahoe Cattle & Land Co. v. Stevens, 13 Colo. 534, 22 Pac. 823 (1889); Morgan v. Bon Bon Co., Inc., 222 N. Y. 22, 118 N. E. 205 (1917), *rev'g* 165 App. Div. (N. Y.) 89, 150 N. Y. S. 668 (1914); Edgerton v. Electric Improvement, &c., Co., 50 N. J. Eq. 354, 24 Atl. 540 (1892); Lothrop v. Goudeau, 142 La. 342, 76 So. 794 (1917).

[76] Cahall v. Lofland, 12 Del. Ch. 299, 114 Atl. 224 (1921), *aff'd*, 13 Del. Ch. 384, 118 Atl. 1 (1922).

[77] For example, State *ex rel.* Sanche v. Webb, 97 Ala. 111, 12 So. 377 (1892); State *ex rel.* White v. Citizens Light & Power Co., 172 Ala. 232, 55 So. 193 (1912); State *ex inf.* Attorney General v. Hogan, 163 Mo. 43, 63 S. W. 378 (1901).

in most jurisdictions. The reported decisions of the appellate courts in the following states were studied, and the writer believes that he has had the benefit of contact with *all* decisions of these courts which bear on the question here under review: New York, New Jersey, Delaware, and Missouri. In addition, the decisions of the appellate courts of Colorado, California, Illinois, and Washington have been studied with almost equal thoroughness. The leading cases decided by the federal courts and by the appellate courts of most other states have been studied and will be referred to from time to time in this discussion.

CHAPTER II

ITEMS THAT MAY NOT BE CAPITALIZED

Before considering the principles accepted by the courts in the valuation of property which is exchanged for stock, it is necessary first to note what types of property, or what other types of consideration, are valid for stock-issue purposes. Courts sometimes exclude certain considerations, not on the ground that they lack value, but on the ground that whatever may be their value, they do not constitute a valid consideration for the issue of stock.[1] It is not always possible, however, to conclude from the cases whether a finding that this or that item is not a " valid consideration " was intended to mean that no such item would be valid even if it admittedly had a considerable value, or whether the holding was merely intended to imply that, in the particular case at bar, the item was too plainly of little or no value to justify any waste of time in attempting to appraise it.

As has already been pointed out, the statutes of the various states stipulate certain items that may be accepted as a valid consideration for the issue of corporate stock. Three items are usually enumerated. In the language of the New York statute, " No corporation shall issue either shares of stock or bonds, except for money, labor done or property actually received. . . ." [2] Most considerations for which stock is issued clearly come under one of these three categories, but some of them raise doubts in the judges' minds as to whether they can reasonably be construed as either " property " or " labor done," as these terms are used in particular statutes. Thus an agreement to do labor in the future could certainly not qualify as " labor done." If admitted at all as a valid consideration, it would have to

[1] Lawyers will note the analogy here to the problem of " valid consideration " for contracts, where a distinction is drawn between considerations that may have " value in fact," but that have no " value in law," and other considerations that are said (by an absurd legal phraseology) to have " value in law " even though they may have no " value in fact." So far as the writer knows, however, there is no identity or even close similarity between what is valid for stock-issue purposes and what is valid or non-valid for contract purposes.

[2] N. Y. Stock Corp. Law (1923), sect. 69 (Laws 1923, c. 787).

be accepted as "property." But "property" is a term of many meanings, and courts have not always held that certain considerations are to be deemed "property" within the meaning of these particular statutes just because they would be accepted as property for other purposes. It is more than likely that here, as in other fields of law, the courts have often made their decisions as to whether a certain consideration is "property" depend on their opinion as to whether it should be deemed a valid basis for stock-issue purposes, rather than the reverse.[3]

Promoters' Services Rendered Prior to Incorporation

By far the most significant item which some courts have excluded from the valid considerations for stock issues is promoters' services

[3] It is possible that some courts tend to interpret the term "property" as it is used in the anti-stock-watering statutes, to signify *tangibles* only. They may infer this meaning from the fact that "money" and "property actually received" are frequently mentioned as alternative means of payment, or from the fact that some constitutions and statutes particularize with regard to the mode of payment. See, for example, art. ix, sect. 3 of the Constitution of Delaware, and sect. 14 of the General Corporation Act of Delaware (Rev. Code 1915, c. 65, sect. 14, par. 1928, p. 924), both of which enumerate money paid, labor done, or personal property, or real estate or leases thereof actually acquired, as appropriate means of payment for stock. See also, Mich. Comp. Laws (Cahill Ann. Sup., 1922), c. 175, sect. 9053 (53), which limits the property that may be taken in payment for stock to such as can be sold or transferred by the corporation or be subject to levy and sale on execution, or other process issuing from courts for the satisfaction of judgments or decrees against the corporation.

The following quotation from the opinion of Pitney, V. C., in a leading New Jersey case indicates a restriction of the term "property" to tangibles: ". . . So that, taking the aspect of the case most favorable to the defendants, the question which arises out of its ultimate analysis is, whether, under our statute above cited, it is competent and lawful to make up the valuation of the visible property to be purchased for stock issued, by adding to the actual market value, or cost of its reproduction, a sum of money ascertained by the capitalization of the annual profits expected to be realized from a favorable marketing of the product of the company by a suppression of competition. Or, as I believe I asked counsel in argument, can prospective profits, however promising, be considered as *property*, as that word is used in the statute above quoted?

"I repeat its language, 'the directors of any company incorporated under this act may purchase mines, manufactories or *other property* necessary for their business . . . and issue stock to the amount of the *value thereof* in payment therefor.'

"There the word 'property' must evidently be construed by its context

rendered prior to incorporation. In some jurisdictions, apparently, it is legitimate to capitalize these services, although it is dangerous to generalize on this point because of the fact that few cases have arisen in which the question was directly faced.[4] But some courts, notably those of New York, have construed the laws in their states as forbidding this practice.[5] They have held that promoters' services

---

which refers to something visible and tangible, and necessary for the business, and the amount of stock to be issued therefor is limited to the *value thereof*, that is, to the value of that *property*.

"If the question above put be the true one it seems to me that it answers itself and adversely to the contention of counsel of defendants." See v. Heppenheimer, 69 N. J. Eq. 36, 42–43, 61 Atl. 843, 846 (1905).

[4] The reason why the question has not often arisen is that promoters have generally refrained from issuing stock frankly and directly in exchange for their services. They have preferred to secure the same result by issuing an excessive amount of stock, ostensibly for specific assets of a more tangible nature. *Cf.* MASSLICH, *op. cit. infra*, c. IV, note 3. The reasons for adopting this more circuitous mode of payment will be discussed presently.

Holcombe v. Trenton White City Co., 80 N. J. Eq. 122, 82 Atl. 618 (1912), *aff'd*, 82 N. J. Eq. 364, 91 Atl. 1069 (1913), is the only creditors' suit found by the writer in which the court held that promoters' services rendered prior to incorporation could be capitalized. The validity of stock issued for promoters' services has been upheld more frequently in cases where the rights of creditors or of innocent purchasers of shares were not involved. See, for example, Fitzpatrick v. O'Neill, 43 Mont. 552, 118 Pac. 273 (1911); United German Silver Co. v. Bronson, 92 Conn. 266, 102 Atl. 647 (1917).

[5] Herbert v. Duryea, 34 App. Div. (N. Y.) 478, 54 N. Y. S. 311 (1898), *aff'd*, 164 N. Y. 596, 58 N. E. 1088 (1900); Lamphere v. Lang, 157 App. Div. (N. Y.) 306, 141 N. Y. S. 967 (1913), *rev'd* on other grounds, 213 N. Y. 585, 108 N. E. 82 (1915); Cooney Co. v. Arlington Hotel Co., 11 Del. Ch. 286, 101 Atl. 879 (1917), *mod.* and *aff'd*, 11 Del. Ch. 430, 106 Atl. 39 (1918). See also, *In re* Ballou, 215 Fed. 810 (D. C., E. D. Ky., 1914); American Macaroni Corp. v. Saumer, 174 N. Y. S. 183 (1919); Calivada Colonization Co. v. Hays, 119 Fed. 202 (C. C., W. D. Pa., 1902); Cahall v. Lofland, 12 Del. Ch. 299, 114 Atl. 224 (1921), on appeal, 13 Del. Ch. 384, 118 Atl. 1 (1922). *Cf.* Hayward v. Leeson, 176 Mass. 310, 57 N. E. 656 (1900); Allenhurst Park Estates v. Smith, 101 N. J. Eq. 581, 609–10, 138 Atl. 709, 721 (1927).

For discussions of the obligation of corporations to compensate promoters for services rendered in organizing them see: 17 A. L. R. 452, 481 *et seq.*; BALLANTINE, *op. cit. supra* (c. I, note 37), sect. 48, pp. 164–66; 4 COOK, *op. cit. supra* (c. I, note 5), sect. 707 at p. 2901 *et seq.*; 14 CORPUS JURIS, sect. 332, p. 282 *et seq.*; 1 THOMPSON, *op. cit. supra* (c. I, note 48), sects. 103–4; 1 FLETCHER, *op. cit. supra* (c. I, note 5), sect. 164; 5 *Ibid.*, sect. 3505; MACHEN, *op. cit. supra* (c. I, note 32), sects. 338–43, 361; EHRICH, *op. cit. supra* (c. I, note 47) at p. 151 *et seq.* Reference to these authorities will reveal that the courts are divided on the question whether a corporation can be compelled to reimburse promoters

do not fall into any of the three categories mentioned in the statutes — " money paid, labor done, or property actually received." " Labor done " might well seem to be a sufficiently broad concept to include promotion services, but the courts in New York and some other states have held to the contrary. Neither have these same courts seen fit to consider such services, when once rendered, as constituting a kind of intangible " property," distinct from the more solid assets, although we shall inquire at a later time whether they have not in effect permitted the same thing by assuming that the tangible assets may have become enhanced in value as a result of being assembled by the promoter.

The fact that other courts seem to have interpreted identical statutory clauses as permitting a direct capitalization of promotion services would seem to suggest that the split of authority may depend more largely on the judges' notions of good policy than on any literal interpretation of the legislative mandates. For there are indeed two sides to the question as to whether a capitalization of the services is proper. The affirmative side runs to the effect that a corporate enterprise is no less dependent on the services of a promoter than it is on the securing of an adequate building and equip-

---

for their necessary expenses and to pay them for their services in organizing corporations. There seems to be substantial agreement, however, that a corporation may generally render itself liable to compensate and reimburse for necessary and reasonable expenses and services by expressly promising to do so, or by any act from which an agreement to compensate or reimburse may be implied. This is particularly true if expenses were incurred or services were rendered with the understanding and expectation on the part of the promoters that reimbursement or compensation was to be provided by the corporation, or if the charter or statute authorizes such payment.

It is obvious that a certain amount of labor and initial outlay are absolutely necessary for the establishment of any corporation. The promoter not only performs this labor, but he also assumes the entire initial risk incident to the promotion. It seems only fair, therefore, that he should be reimbursed by the corporation for actual expenses incurred in the promotion, and that he should be compensated for his services and risk assumed so that the burden falls on all shareholders alike rather than on the promoter alone. There seems to be no reason, however, why the decision to pay the promoter a certain sum in this connection should not be made by unbiassed and independent parties, or, in the alternative, a full disclosure be made of the payment received by the promoter. Perhaps the denial by courts that stock may be used to compensate promoters for their services rests on the fact that directors are more likely to be excessively liberal or even reckless in disbursing stock than they would be when disbursing cash.

ment, and that payment for the one is just as necessary as is payment for the other. The negative view is that, granting both of these contentions, it does not follow that an allowance for the services should appear as an addition either to the book value of the fixed assets or to the par values of the outstanding capital stock. Just as the accountant frequently declines to sanction the valuation of many intangible assets at their true value, because he is well aware how speculative must be this value and how much temptation a director may be under to overstate it, so a court may plausibly decline to sanction the issuance of stock against promoters' services — with a concomitant write-up of the value of the assets on the balance sheet — simply because there is no objective basis for measuring the value of these services and because the promoter, without this objective basis as a guide, is almost sure to make the valuation excessive. To the argument that a promoter must be paid for his services, the reply may be made that he can and should secure his payment either by marketing at a premium the stock which he has received from the corporation in exchange for tangible assets which have cost him an amount equivalent to its par value, or by a direct payment to him for his services accompanied by a prompt and full disclosure of the amount of the payment in corporate accounts and other records which are made readily available to the public.[6]

It is important to note that, even in those states where the courts have declined to hold that promoters' services are a valid consideration for stock issues, no real exclusion of the services from capitalization has taken place. The only achievement has been to compel promoters to capitalize the services indirectly rather than directly. That is to say, the promoter, instead of issuing stock to himself in exchange for nothing but his services, has all or part of the stock issued to himself in exchange for physical assets to which he has title or on which he has secured an option. The value of these assets is estimated at far in excess of their actual cost to the promoter, who would justify this procedure on the ground that the

[6] The method of recoupment by the promoter through a sale of his stock at a premium has long been the practice in Germany. See c. IX *infra*, pp. 296–97. Under our present non-par stock laws it is relatively easy for the promoter to obtain compensation and a profit in the form of stock, since during the infancy of the corporation the promoter is in control and can have large quantities of stock issued to himself for only a nominal consideration.

property, when "assembled" and turned over to the corporation for the particular enterprise in question, is now worth far more than the separate parts were formerly worth. Thus, under the guise of a liberal valuation for purchased assets, he really makes an allowance for his own promotion services, and this practice, as we shall presently see, has not been effectively opposed by the courts. Unless the courts are willing to go the limit and drastically to disallow any valuation of property in excess of its cost to the promoters — a possibility which will be discussed in the concluding chapter of this study — it may be seriously doubted whether they would not be much wiser to sanction a direct capitalization of promotion services rather than to allow it in effect by a concealed overvaluation of the other assets. It was with this thought in mind that the recent Ohio General Corporation Act, perhaps the most carefully drafted of any corporation statute in the history of American law, expressly sanctions the payment by corporations of organization expenses and requires the balance sheet to carry a separate item to show these costs until they are written off.[7]

[7] Section 29 of the General Corporation Act of Ohio (approved March 8, 1927), Ohio Gen. Code, sect. 8623 (29), reads as follows: "A corporation may pay as cost of organization or reorganization the reasonable charges and expenses incident thereto and may also pay or allow reasonable compensation for the sale or underwriting, at the time of organization or thereafter, of its shares and securities or any part thereof, but all amounts so paid out or allowed or any balance thereof not previously charged off shall be stated on the books of the corporation and on every balance sheet prepared therefrom until the whole thereof has been written off." The draftsmen of this act stated that section 29 was derived from sect. 89 of the British Companies Act of 1908. They said in comment: "It is common practice to treat organization expenses and charges for financing as assets and to reduce the amount by an annual write-off. It is much better to expressly sanction this practice than to compel the concealment of such costs by exaggerated property accounts." REPORT OF COMMITTEE RESPECTING REVISION OF OHIO CORPORATION LAW (Dec. 28, 1926), at p. 81.

The language of section 29 does not clearly indicate whether this provision merely authorizes the corporation to pay the promoter's out-of-pocket expenses or the full value of his services. The comment of the draftsmen suggests that the former was all that was had in mind. Neither does the language of this section expressly authorize the issuance of *stock* in payment for promoters' services or other organization expenses. But section 22 provides that stock may be issued for "labor or services actually rendered to the corporations" and section 29 states that organization expenses may be paid by the corporation. The combined effect of the two provisions suggests that it would be legitimate to issue stock as compensation for such organization expenses as may be paid for under section 29. This hypothesis is strengthened by the fact that the ex-

Even, however, in those jurisdictions in which the courts have taken no positive position against the direct capitalization of promotion services, promoters have generally preferred to use the indirect method of overvaluing the tangible assets. It is not difficult to understand why they have chosen to attain their object by indirection. They well know that the value of their promotion schemes is a highly speculative and doubtful one, a claim for which is sure to be scrutinized by a court or a jury with far more skepticism than a claim for even a very liberal value on a given piece of real estate. They also know that this skepticism will be all the greater because of the fact that, if any litigation arises, it will most likely arise only after the enterprise has turned out to be a serious failure. And they are probably well aware that even modern concepts of property values have by no means outgrown the older close associations between property rights and tangible objects, with the result that a large tract of land, even if it were located on the desert of Sahara, would seem to the popular mind to have a greater claim to an " intrinsic value " than would a more intangible but no more useless plan of promotion.

Occasionally, however, the promoter has undertaken a direct capitalization of his services. In some cases he has had no other practical alternative because he has not found it convenient to secure either title or options to the tangible property as a basis on which he might issue the stock to himself. In other cases he has apparently been unaware of the legal dangers of so direct a method of stock watering and has been the victim of very poor advice on the part of counsel.[8]

---

pressed intention of the draftsmen, and the whole spirit of the law as enacted, envisaged full discretion on the part of directors with respect to the consideration which should be accepted for stock, except in case of a deliberate overvaluation on their part. Protection to creditors and other investors was intended to be provided by the publicity concerning the nature of the consideration accepted which is required by section 26, and by the similar provision in section 29 with respect to organization and underwriting expenses.

[8] For example, Cooney Co. v. Arlington Hotel Co., *supra,* note 5. One difficulty which the promoter encounters in collecting payment for his services lies in his peculiar legal relationship to the corporation prior to its formation. He cannot be an *agent* of the corporation because the principal is non-existent. This is perhaps the chief reason why courts refuse to allow the direct capitalization of his services as " labor done " for the corporation. There can be no doubt that they are " labor done " in the literal sense of the term, but as the law of promotion now stands, it is labor done by the promoter *for himself.* As a keen

Agreements to Render Future Services

Turning now to another type of consideration which the courts have refused to validate as payment for stock, we find that contracts or agreements to render services in the future [9] have received much the same treatment at the hands of the courts as have services of promoters rendered prior to incorporation. Those who have taken stock issued for future services have been held liable to corporate

---

student of promotion law put it in a recent article wherein he pleads for a statutory definition of the promoter's status and responsibilities: "It seems, then, that every attempt to fit the promoter into a common-law scheme has not only failed but has led to embarrassment and abuses. He tries to act as agent. The courts discover that he cannot. Call him an outsider, and you have not only a bald fiction but you make him free to deal at arms' length with the corporation and make secret profits. Call a halt by declaring him a fiduciary — a fiduciary with the burdens but none of the advantages of an ordinary fiduciary. You must modify the statement and retract it at every turn, and finally you find it leading to a recovery of secret profits that were assented to by everyone in interest, and that now can be recovered to enrich those who were never damaged. . . ." Isaacs, Nathan, *The Promoter: a Legislative Problem* (1926), 38 Harv. L. Rev. 887, 898–99.

Another and perhaps more important difficulty from the standpoint of the promoter himself is his desire to conceal from the investing public the fact that a large issue of stock has been made for promoter's services, an item which under the present laws governing the issue of par-value stock would create sales resistance by making investors and creditors suspicious of the value of the shares and, in view of judicial preference for physical property as the basis of value, would give creditors an excellent ground of complaint in case the enterprise should later get into financial difficulties.

[9] Some statutes expressly prohibit the issue of stock for services to be performed; *e.g.*, section 22 of the General Corporation Act of Ohio (Ohio Gen. Code, sect. 8623–22, Ohio Laws 1927, p. 18) reads as follows: "Promissory notes, drafts or obligations, of a subscriber or purchaser, shall not be accepted in payment for shares, nor shall shares be issued for future services." A similar provision is found in the laws of Maryland. See Md. Ann. Code (Bagby, 1924), art. 23, sect. 41, par. 6. *Cf.* subsection III, sect. 15 of the Uniform Business Corporation Act. This section provides that subscriptions for shares may be made payable "with necessary services actually rendered to the corporation." Section 16, subsection I, provides that "A certificate of stock shall not be issued until the shares represented thereby have been fully paid for."

See the following for discussion of the law and cases pertaining to the issue of stock for services: 5 Fletcher, *op. cit. supra* (note 5), sect. 3505; 1 Cook, *op. cit. supra* (note 5), c. II, sect. 18, pp. 131, 133; 5 Thompson, *op. cit. supra* (note 5), sect. 3966.

creditors for a sum equal to the par value of the stock,[10] and in some cases stock so issued has been held to be cancellable at the instance of the corporation or innocent shareholders.[11] In one case, where creditors' claims were not involved and where stockholders sued to compel directors of a dissolved corporation to account to a receiver for the benefit of innocent stockholders, the court held that, to the extent to which the directors had received regular dividends and liquidation dividends on shares of stock which were issued by and to themselves for services to be rendered, the defendant directors must account to the receiver.[12]

In some respects the accepted practices of accounting seem to support the position that a corporation may properly issue stock for services to be rendered. In listing the assets of an enterprise the accountant sees no valid reason for excluding payments that have

[10] Palmer v. Scheftel, 183 App. Div. (N. Y.) 77, 170 N. Y. S. 588 (1918); Palmer v. Scheftel, 194 App. Div. (N. Y.) 682, 186 N. Y. S. 84 (1921), *aff'd,* 236 N. Y. 511, 142 N. E. 263 (1923); Stevens v. Episcopal Church History Co., 140 App. Div. (N. Y.) 570, 125 N. Y. S. 573 (1910); Cooney v. Arlington Hotel Co., *supra,* note 5; Gillett v. Chicago Title & Trust Co., 230 Ill. 373, 82 N. E. 891 (1907); Hobgood v. Ehlen, 141 N. C. 344, 53 S. E. 857 (1906); Shipman v. Portland Const. Co., 64 Oreg. 1, 128 Pac. 989 (1913). *Contra:* Shannon v. Stevenson, 173 Pa. St. 419, 34 Atl. 218 (1896). See also: Shaw v. Ansaldi Co., Inc., 178 App. Div. (N. Y.) 589, 596–97, 165 N. Y. S. 872, 878 (1917); Davies v. Ball, 64 Wash. 292, 116 Pac. 833 (1911).

The force of Stevens v. Episcopal Church History Co., *supra,* is somewhat limited in this connection by the fact that the court probably decided the case primarily on the ground that the corporation received no real *contracts* for the rendition of future services. But, judging by the language of the court, it seems quite apparent that even if the court had found no defects in the alleged contracts it would still have decided that contracts for future services are not a valid consideration for the issuance of full-paid stock. The case is frequently cited by courts as a holding on this latter point.

[11] B. & C. Electrical Construction Co. v. Owen, 176 App. Div. (N. Y.) 399, 163 N. Y. S. 31 (1917), *aff'd,* 227 N. Y. 569, 126 N. E. 927 (1919); McCombs Producing & Refining Co. v. Ogle, 200 Ky. 208, 254 S. W. 425 (1923). *Cf.* Scully v. Automobile Finance Co., 11 Del. Ch. 355, 101 Atl. 908 (1917), on appeal, 12 Del. Ch. 174, 109 Atl. 49 (1920); Bowen v. Imperial Theatres, Inc., 13 Del. Ch. 120, 115 Atl. 918 (1922); Lothrop v. Goudeau, 142 La. 342, 76 So. 794 (1917). But see: Vineland Grape Juice Co. v. Chandler, 80 N. J. Eq. 437, 85 Atl. 213 (1912); Vogeler v. Punch, 205 Mo. 558, 103 S. W. 1001 (1907); Morgan v. Bon Bon Co., Inc., 165 App. Div. (N. Y.) 89, 150 N. Y. S. 668 (1914); *rev'd,* 222 N. Y. 22, 118 N. E. 205 (1917); Reed & Fibre Products Corporation v. Rosenthal, 153 Md. 501, 138 Atl. 665 (1927); Arapahoe Cattle & Land Co. v. Stevens, 13 Colo. 534, 22 Pac. 823 (1889).

[12] Cahall v. Lofland, *supra,* note 5.

been made in exchange for promises to render future services. Hence his inventory of assets will include such items as prepaid insurance, prepaid rent and prepaid interest. All of these items are valuable to a going concern, though their value may be wholly unrealized. The promoter regards in the same light his promise, or the promise of others, to render future services in promoting the welfare of the corporation. These services may consists in persuading prominent capitalists to take a financial interest in the enterprise, in inducing large potential users of the product to patronize the concern, in arranging favorable lines of credit with local bankers, or in other such services directed toward putting the enterprise on its feet as a going concern. As the promoter sees it, it is not only proper for the corporation to pay him in advance for these services but it is quite legitimate for the medium of payment to take the form of shares of stock. There are several reasons, however, for judicial denial that the latter may be done.

In the first place, a strict construction of the usual type of statute might hardly be thought to warrant the inclusion of future services. These statutes provide that stock may be issued for "money paid, labor done, or property actually received." Services to be rendered are clearly neither "money paid" nor "property actually received." The specific enumeration in the statutes and state constitutions of "labor done" as a valid consideration for stock issuance may be interpreted, by implication and without stretching the imagination, to exclude "labor to be done."

In the second place, courts know that corporate directors are more likely to be extravagant when making payments in stock than when their disbursements take the form of cash.[13]

In the third place, those items for which the corporation usually makes advance payment in cash, and which are listed as assets by the accountant, are either competitively sold in the market place and thus have a value to the enterprise which is fairly determinate, or else they are of such a nature that their value to the enterprise is direct and more or less obvious. On the other hand, the future services which the promoter attempts to capitalize are not usually

[13] *Cf.* Bailey v. Pittsburg & Connellsville Gas Coal & Coke Co., 69 Pa. St. 334, 342 (1871), where the court said: "When, by a proper subscription and payment of money, it has the possession of a capital in money, the interests of all the stockholders are motives to careful and prudent bargains, and will prevent the payment of their real cash for mere moonshine."

the subject of organized bargain and sale and are generally too intangible and indefinite in character to permit anything approaching accurate assessment of their value. This being the case, their use as a basis for stock issues is likely to lead to excessive watering of stock. Because of the indefinite nature of such promises their acceptance as payment for stock fails to conform to the basic legal and business assumption that the disposal of a corporation's capital stock will provide it with the means of conducting its business. Moreover, promises of this kind may not even be legally enforcible contracts. It may be doubted, for example, whether the promise of an individual to " promote the welfare " of a corporation is a sufficient consideration to create a legally binding contract. Both the indefinite character of the services to be rendered and the informal nature of the promises to render them have tended to cause courts to refuse to permit their capitalization.

Promissory Notes as Consideration for Stock

There is considerable similarity between the payment for stock in promises to render future services and payment with promissory notes. The principal difference between the two modes of payment is that the note is a promise to pay a definite sum of money and hence no problem of valuation is involved except for the factor of a discount for time and risk, whereas the promise to render future services involves both a question as to the value of those services, when rendered, and the problem of reducing that sum to a present value. These two methods of payment parallel each other so closely in their economic aspects that it is not surprising to find that the courts have taken much the same attitude toward both of them.

In neither situation do we find the factor of time discount discussed or decided. Perhaps the principal reason for this is the fact that a corporation normally has the power to extend the time for payment of stock subscriptions. Where the corporation has this power full and immediate payment of stock subscriptions is not a condition precedent to becoming a stockholder. Until full payment has been made, however, the subscriber is potentially responsible to creditors for the unpaid balance and may also be liable to the corporation for the benefit of other stockholders. Just as the mere agreement to render services in the future does not constitute " payment " for stock, so also the mere execution and delivery of an unsecured promissory note does not constitute satisfaction of a subscriber's liability to pay for his stock. This point is too obvious to require elaboration.

The courts do not agree, however, concerning the legal consequences of an issue of stock for promissory notes. The majority rule appears to be that where the statute or constitutional provision forbids the issuance of stock except for money paid, labor done, or property received, a note given in payment for stock is not a good consideration for the issuance of the stock for the reason that the note is neither " money paid " nor " property received."[14] Exception to this rule is sometimes made if the note is amply secured by collateral, particularly if the collateral is such that the corporation is authorized to invest its funds in it. On the other hand a minority of courts have held that even an unsecured promissory note is " property " and as such is a valid consideration for stock issuance.

The questions which most frequently arise in connection with promissory notes as a consideration for stock are: Can the corporation compel the maker of the note to pay it? Can the maker compel the corporation to cancel the note? Can an innocent transferee of the note enforce it? Can an innocent transferee of the stock issued for the note compel the corporation to recognize him as a stockholder? Can a receiver compel payment of the note for the benefit of creditors? Various answers have been given by the courts to these questions, but in general both the note and the stock are valid instruments in the hands of innocent parties. The note can be enforced by a receiver for the benefit of creditors or by transferees without

[14] Payment for stock with promissory notes has been the subject of extended treatment in legal texts. Our brief summary of the legal incidents of an issue of stock for promissory notes which follows in the text above has been derived from the following and from the cases there cited: 1 COOK, *op. cit. supra* (note 5, c. II), sect. 20, pp. 137–39; 14 CORPUS JURIS, sects. 590, 593, 599, 600, 818, 861, 862; 5 THOMPSON, *op. cit. supra* (note 5), sects. 3954, 3955; 5 FLETCHER, *op. cit. supra* (note 5), sects. 3512–14; annotations in 4 A. L. R. 1330, 35 L. R. A. (N.S.) 80, 52 *ibid.* 454. And see, with special reference to the aspect of the matter in which our particular interest lies, *Notes as Consideration for Issuance of Corporate Stock, etc.*, 58 A. L. R. 708, and a case note on *Taking Notes in Payment of Stock Subscriptions* (1928), 77 PENNA. L. REV. 285.

Some statutes prohibit the acceptance of promissory notes in payment for stock. See, *e.g.*, N. D. Comp. Laws (1913), sect. 4529 (R. C. 1905, sect. 4196); Ill. Rev. Stat. Ann. (Smith-Hurd, 1929), c. 32, sect. 28; Mass. Gen. Laws (1921), c. 156, sect. 16; Mo. Rev. Stat. (1919), sect. 10155; Ind. Acts 1929, c. 215, sect. 6(e), pp. 732–33; Uniform Business Corporation Act, sect. 16, subsection III.

notice. The validity of the note and of the stock, as between the corporation and the maker of the note, is open to greater question. Some courts hold that either the note or the stock or both are void as between the original parties or their transferees with notice. Other courts hold the reverse.

But despite the diversity among the courts concerning these several questions, the substance of the law with respect to promissory notes as consideration for stock is clear. Except in cases where the note is amply secured by the pledge of real or personal property the mere giving of a promissory note does not constitute *payment*.

Other Non-valid Considerations

Other items which courts have construed under varying circumstances as failing to constitute a valid consideration for "fully-paid" stock are: (*a*) the use of the name, prestige or influence of an individual;[15] (*b*) the performance of acts by directors which fall within their regular duties, even if these duties are only implied by the nature of the relationship between a corporation and its directors;[16] (*c*) the act of becoming a director of a corporation under an agreement by the latter to issue stock for that service;[17] (*d*) services of promoters or directors of a corporation in endorsing notes of the corporation as an incident to the financial conduct of its business;[18] (*e*) business plans of extremely problematical

[15] Randall Printing Co. v. Sanitas Mineral Water Co., 120 Minn. 268, 139 N. W. 606 (1913); Peninsular Savings Bank v. Black Flag Stove Polish Co., 105 Mich. 535, 63 N. W. 514 (1895); Central Consumers' Wine & Liquor Co. v. Madden, 68 Atl. 777 (N. J. Ch. 1908); Bowen v. Imperial Theatres, Inc., *supra*, note 11; Tooker v. National Sugar Refining Co., 80 N. J. Eq. 305, 84 Atl. 10 (1912); Webster v. Webster Refining Co. of Okmulgee, 36 Okla. 168, 128 Pac. 261 (1912); American Macaroni Corp. v. Saumer, 174 N. Y. S. 183, 184 (1919); York Park Building Assoc. v. Barnes, 39 Neb. 834, 58 N. W. 440 (1894). *Cf.* B. & C. Electrical Const. Co. v. Owen, *supra*, note 11. Other cases are collected in 5 Thompson, *op. cit. supra* (note 5), sect. 3965, and in 5 Fletcher, *op. cit. supra* (note 5), sect. 3506 *et seq.*

[16] For example, Cahall v. Lofland, *supra*, note 5; Palmer v. Scheftel, *supra*, note 10.

[17] Eyerman v. Krieckhaus, 7 Mo. App. 455 (1879); Central Consumers' Wine & Liquor Co. v. Madden, *supra*, note 15; Bowen v. Imperial Theatres, Inc., *supra*, note 11; Barnard v. Sweet, 74 Colo. 302, 221 Pac. 1093 (1923). *Cf.* Boulton Carbon Co. v. Mills, 78 Iowa 460, 43 N. W. 290 (1889).

[18] Cahall v. Lofland, *supra*, note 5; Schroeder v. Edwards, 267 Mo. 459, 184 S. W. 108 (1915).

value;[19] (*f*) unpatented formulas, trademarks, and inventions of such character as to raise a legitimate doubt in the minds of reasonable men as to whether their use as consideration for stock was not a mere device for circumventing the anti-stock-watering statutes;[20] and (*g*) services of directors or promoters in selling stock of a corporation, under certain circumstances.[21] This list is not exhaustive, but it is sufficiently long to bring into focus a tendency on the part of many courts to refuse to endorse the capitalization of intangibles whose value is so shadowy and difficult to estimate as to permit a substantial nullification of the object of the legislatures in enacting the statutes mentioned above, where it appears that innocent parties have been or are likely to be deceived by giving a freer rein to promoters.[22]

Although in a few instances the courts have held that stock issued for these items is valid against the corporation and as between parties on actual or constructive notice of the manner of its issuance,[23]

[19] Barnard v. Sweet, *supra,* note 17; Scully v. Automobile Finance Co., *supra,* note 11. *Cf.* the cases cited in note 20, *infra.*

[20] O'Bear-Nester Glass Co. v. Antiexplo Co., 101 Tex. 431, 108 S. W. 967, 109 S. W. 931 (1908); Gillett v. Chicago Title & Trust Co., *supra,* note 10; Webster v. Webster Refining Co. of Okmulgee, *supra,* note 15; State *ex rel.* Sanche v. Webb, 97 Ala. 111, 12 So. 377 (1892); Dean v. Baldwin, 99 Ill. App. 582 (1902); Van Cleve v. Berkey, 143 Mo. 109, 44 S. W. 743 (1898); Chisholm Bros. v. Forny, 65 Iowa 333, 21 N. W. 664 (1884). *Cf.* National Tube Works Co. v. Gilfillan, 124 N. Y. 302, 26 N. E. 538 (1891), *aff'g* 46 Hun 248 (1887); Whitehill v. Jacobs, 75 Wisc. 474, 44 N. W. 630 (1890); Kunkle v. Soule, 68 Colo. 524, 190 Pac. 536 (1920); Soule v. Kunkle, 71 Colo. 221, 205 Pac. 529 (1922). Other cases are cited in the following: 5 THOMPSON, *op. cit. supra* (note 5), sects. 3967, 3968; 14 CORPUS JURIS, sect. 596; 5 FLETCHER, *op. cit. supra* (note 5), sect. 3507.

[21] Stoecker v. Goodman, 183 Ky. 330, 209 S. W. 374 (1919); Vandeusen v. Ransom, 23 Oh. C. C. (N.S.) 194 (1912); Terrell v. Warten, 206 Ala. 90, 89 So. 297 (1921); Bivens v. Hull, 58 Colo. 338, 145 Pac. 649 (1914); Cahall v. Lofland, *supra,* note 5; Central Consumers' Wine & Liquor Co. v. Madden, *supra,* note 15; Kirkup v. Anaconda Amusement Co., 59 Mont. 469, 197 Pac. 1005, 17 A. L. R. 441 (1921). *Cf.* Davies v. Ball, 64 Wash. 292, 116 Pac. 833 (1911). But see: Standard Drilling Co. v. Slate, 205 Ky. 714, 266 S. W. 377 (1924); Denis v. Nu-Way Puncture Cure Co., 170 Wisc. 333, 175 N. W. 95 (1919); 5 FLETCHER, *op. cit. supra* (note 5), sect. 3524.

[22] Other types of consideration which are not valid for stock-issue purposes are discussed in the following: 5 THOMPSON, *op. cit. supra* (note 5), sects. 3954–71; 5 FLETCHER, *op. cit. supra* (note 5), sects. 3502–15; 14 CORPUS JURIS, sects. 593–96.

[23] For example, Whitehill v. Jacobs, *supra,* note 20; Vineland Grape Juice Co. v. Chandler, Arapahoe Cattle & Land Co. v. Stevens, Morgan v. Bon Bon Co., Inc., *supra,* note 11.

the general rule appears to be that, as between the holders of the stock and innocent parties, it is subject to numerous legal defects such as a liability of the holder to creditors of the corporation, the right of innocent shareholders to have the stock cancelled or declared by a court to be assessable for the benefit of the corporation, and the right of the corporation to refuse to recognize as a shareholder the holder of certificates so issued.

Most of the courts justify their decisions in these cases with statements to the effect that the items enumerated above do not constitute a valid consideration for the issuance of stock, or that their acceptance by corporations does not "constitute payment" for stock. Rarely do the courts say that they are wholly without value to the corporation accepting them, though it is apparent in some instances that this is the case. The reasons given for the rejection of these items are various. Some courts, like those of Texas, lay special emphasis upon the unsubstantial nature of these qualified property rights, and upon the fact that many of them are incapable of being subjected to the payment of debts of the corporation or sold by shareholders and the proceeds distributed by process of court.[24] On the other hand, other courts appear simply to be following what seems to them to be the letter of the statutes, as for instance, in holding that "services to be performed" are not "labor done" and that the disclosure of unpatented formulas, business plans and secrets are not "property actually received."[25] In still other instances, the courts evidently feel that the reality of the value, still more the

[24] O'Bear-Nester Glass Co. v. Antiexplo Co., *supra,* note 20. *Cf.* Webster v. Webster Refining Co. of Okmulgee, *supra,* note 15; General Bonding & Casualty Co. v. Moseley, 174 S. W. 1031 (Tex. Civ. App., 1915), *rev'd,* 110 Tex. 529, 222 S. W. 961 (1920); McCarthy v. Texas Loan & Guaranty Co., 142 S. W. 96 (Tex. Civ. App., 1911–1912).

Michigan has apparently attempted to avoid the difficulty in such situations by requiring that "only such property shall be taken in payment for capital stock as the purposes of the corporation shall require, and only such property as can be sold and transferred by the corporation, and as shall be subject to levy and sale on execution, or other process issued out of any court of competent jurisdiction for satisfaction of any judgment or decree against such corporation." Mich. Comp. Laws (Cahill, Ann. Sup. 1922), c. 175, sect. 9053(53). But the phrase "other process" is broad enough to include decrees and orders of chancery courts and, consequently, this provision does not prohibit taking patents, trade-marks, or the good will of a business, since they can be sold under recognized processes of equity courts. See Brown v. Weeks, 195 Mich. 27, 161 N. W. 945 (1917).

[25] See cases cited in notes 10, 11, 12, 15 and 20, *supra.*

proper assessment of it, is in such doubt as to make its inclusion a fertile excuse for stock watering. This is particularly the case where promoters cause the corporation to issue stock to themselves for services and the like without submitting the question of a reasonable value to the judgment of independent and intelligent directors.[26]

Significance of This Group of Cases

This group of cases clearly brings into view the functional or purposive nature of " valuation " as contrasted with " value " as the economist ordinarily uses the latter term. The modern economist's " value," or " market price," is an objective thing, the resultant of market forces. It is not encumbered with any particular mission or directive purpose in the affairs of men. True enough, it may be manipulated for a particular purpose and the level at which it is established by market forces, with or without manipulation, will necessarily influence the actions of men whose calculations must be based upon prevailing prices. In its normal aspects under free competition, however, it is an end of a process, a resultant of forces, rather than an instrument of reform or a force which is itself directed toward a particular end. On the other hand, the valuation of property or services for stock-issue purposes is more directly functional. When corporate shares were endowed with the characteristic of limited liability it was contemplated that the consideration paid

[26] For example, Cahall v. Lofland, *supra*, note 5; Gillett v. Chicago Title & Trust Co., *supra*, note 10. *Cf.* pp. 95–6, *infra*.

The danger of issuing " full-paid " stock for promotion services, secret formulas, trade-marks, patent rights, copyrights, good will or other intangibles, has received recognition in the proposed Uniform Sale of Securities Act (Blue Sky Law). See section 14 of the Third Tentative Draft of Uniform Sale of Securities Act, which was presented for consideration to the National Conference of Commissioners on Uniform State Laws, at its thirty-seventh annual meeting, Buffalo, N. Y., August 23–29, 1927. This section provides that the commission or commissioner who is charged with the administration of the act may require that securities issued in payment for various intangibles, such as those mentioned above, must be delivered to the commission or commissioner, or other satisfactory depository, to be held in escrow until all stockholders who have paid for their stock in cash have been paid certain minimum dividends. The commission or commissioner must be satisfied that the dividend or dividends were actually earned, and in case of dissolution or insolvency during the time such securities are held in escrow, the owners of them may not participate in the assets until after the owners of all other securities have been paid in full.

for them, as measured by their par values, should furnish a partial substitute for the unlimited liability of general partners and individual entrepreneurs for their respective debts. Thus it was supposed that the corporation would acquire a property substitute for the element of personal financial responsibility of the enterprisers on which creditors and investors had been accustomed to rely in the case of non-corporate business units. Such a substitute fulfills its function only to the extent that the consideration paid for the stock is a thing of substance in the value sense. Although it need not be something tangible in order to fulfill its purpose, it should have a value which is capable of some sort of objective measurement. Hence we find that in the above cases courts hold that for the purpose of paying for corporate stock the items mentioned are no consideration whatever.

In denying that they have any value for this purpose the courts do not assert that they have no economic or exchange value. They would doubtless admit, for example, that the purchase of the use of a man's name is a common practice and that the fact that a certain individual of reputation is connected with a given enterprise may be and often is of considerable value to that enterprise. They must recognize that in many instances enterprises have become a success due to the acquisition of a secret, though unpatented, process. Likewise, they are probably aware that the promoter fulfills a valuable economic service in conceiving and assembling new enterprises, a service without which the enterprises could not be formed. It must be evident to them that a promise to render future services, like promises to pay money, may have a present value when properly discounted for futurity and risk. But while all these intangible values may exist, they are too doubtful in quality and too uncertain in quantity to be fairly appraised by anyone, least of all by men whose self-interest dictates an almost unlimited optimism. Permission to capitalize them would open the way for flagrant abuses of the law.

There is a close parallel between the practice of courts in not allowing certain considerations, even if they have value, to enter into stock issues, and the accounting practice of not allowing certain assets, even if they have value, to appear on the books. An example of this practice is found in the treatment of the item of good-will, which, according to the accepted accounting convention, should not ordinarily be valued in accounts except when bought and then only at its cost price.[27] One reason for the similarity of treatment of these items is the fact that both balance sheets and other financial statements of corporations are publicity devices like the par value or stated value of shares. Owing to the danger of deception of persons who may rely upon the announced financial status of corporations, there is a tendency toward conservatism on the part of both judges and accountants who are called upon from time to time to certify the existence and worth of corporate assets. Both appear to be forcefully impressed with the danger inherent in giving publicity to the existence of values which are not demonstrably present except by mere statements of opinions unsupported by the presence of anything tangible to lend reality to the belief, or which, even if clearly existant, are likely to be regarded as ephemeral because of their intangible nature.

The accountants sometimes admit that their practice is not strictly logical, but justify it on the ground that, owing to the difficulty of assessing accurately the value of intangibles, it is better to err on the side of conservatism than to certify to a valuation which might easily turn out to be erroneous and therefore misleading. Courts are less frank and generally seek to avoid what appears to be an inconsistency by the discovery and elaboration of some esoteric legal reason for their decisions. But in each case a limitation is placed upon the circulation of misleading statements concerning the existence and value of assets.

[27] Hatfield, Henry R., Accounting (New York, 1927), c. 4, pp. 111–26; Kester, Roy B., Accounting, Theory and Practice (New York, 1922), Vol. I, p. 418, Vol. II, pp. 331–38; Montgomery, Robert H., Auditing Theory and Practice (4th ed. rev., New York, 1927), p. 230.

CHAPTER III

THE " GOOD FAITH " RULE VERSUS THE " TRUE VALUE " RULE IN STOCK-WATERING CASES

In the preceding chapter it was pointed out that the problem of determining whether stock has been watered involves not merely the question of finding the fair value of the consideration for which the stock was issued, but also the question as to whether the *type* of consideration was valid. This latter complication arises because of the fact that the courts sometimes refuse to consider certain items, such as promoters' services or agreements to perform future services, as constituting valid consideration even though they may conceivably be of great economic value to the corporation.

It remains to discuss in the present chapter a still further complication which arises from the generally accepted doctrine that, where stock is issued for property or services, the value placed upon this consideration by the corporate directors shall be accepted as final in the absence of " fraud." Under such a doctrine we have the problem of determining not merely whether the valuation was in fact excessive, but also whether it was " fraudulent," as that term is construed by the courts.

Unfortunately for purposes of analysis, the case decisions do not often make a clear-cut distinction between these two problems, (*a*) of finding whether the property was in fact overvalued, and (*b*) of finding whether it was " fraudulently " overvalued. This is true because the courts seldom discuss the question separately and almost never arrive at their conclusion, first by answering question one, and then by answering question two. The difficulty is made even greater because of the fact that there is no unanimity of opinion as to what is meant by a fraudulent overvaluation, some courts tending to construe " fraud " in a strict sense as denoting a wilful effort to deceive the plaintiffs, and other courts construing the term much more broadly as equivalent to any unreasonable overvaluation of the property.

As far as it is possible to do so, we shall discuss in the present chapter the significance of the majority rule that the valuation made by directors is final if it was made in good faith, and shall contrast this with the minority rule that the true value of the property rather than the opinion of the directors shall determine whether stock has been issued for a valid consideration. By disposing of the problem of good faith, the present chapter will prepare the way for an analysis of the central problem of this treatise which is that of discovering the standard or basis of valuation accepted by the courts in stock-watering cases. For reasons already suggested, however, it is impossible to dissociate completely the question of the good faith of the directors from the question of the standard of valuation itself. Even in the succeeding chapters, therefore, it will be necessary to recur to the question of good faith as affecting the decisions of the courts in the particular cases which are selected for analysis.

The "Good Faith" and the "True Value" Rules

The degree of finality of the directors' judgment as to the value of considerations for stock is the basis of the classification of courts into two groups: those which accept the so-called "good faith" rule, and those which accept the "true value" rule. According to the latter the question is simply, was the property in fact overvalued? According to the former the question is twofold: (*a*) was it in fact overvalued? and (*b*) if so, was the overvaluation made in bad faith? For clarity of discussion it seems desirable to consider the distinction between the two rules under two heads: first, what are the apparent differences between the two rules as revealed by the *opinions* of courts? and second, do the actual *decisions*, as contrasted with the *opinions*, support the conclusion that the difference between the two rules is anything more than a verbal one?

In a large majority of states judicial opinions express the view that a creditor who sues a shareholder for an unpaid balance on the ground that the stock was issued for overvalued property must prove more than the mere *fact* of overvaluation. He must also prove that the overvaluation was "fraudulent"—that is, that it was not made in "good faith" by the directors.[1] Such is the com-

[1] It should be noted that shareholders' liability rests upon the good faith of the *directors* and not upon the good faith of the defendant stockholders themselves. There is nothing in the statutes or in the common law which makes the opinions of the *shareholders* as to the value of property of any importance in determining whether or not there has been an issue of stock for overvalued property.

At first thought it may seem unjust to hold shareholders liable for fraudumon law in the absence of a statute prescribing the terms under which stock may be issued, but the common-law rule has been reinforced by statutory provisions in many states.[2] After stating that stock may be issued for " money paid, labor done, or property actually received, to the extent of the value thereof in payment therefor " these statutes state that when stock is issued for property, the judgment of the directors as to the value of such property shall be " conclusive in the absence of fraud." [3] But the term, " fraud," like the term, " value," has numerous meanings and the consequence is that judicial opinions fall into several groups depending upon the meaning of " fraud " which is accepted by the various courts.

a) *Various meanings of " good faith."* — Confining our attention to judicial utterances alone, the distinction between the " good faith " and " true value " rules is more than twofold, for the " good faith " courts may be divided into several classes. At one extreme are those courts that state that they require proof of fraudulent overvaluation in the strictest sense of the word " fraud." That is, there must be deliberate overvaluation with the intent to deceive creditors as to the real nature of the property and thus to get them to extend credit when they might not do so if they knew the real truth.[4] These courts seem to feel that creditors are seldom actually

---

lent or unreasonable action on the part of the directors, but the result is not as unfair as it may seem to be, on its face. For in practically every promotion there is an almost complete identity between the will of the directors and the will of the original recipients of stock issued for property. In normal cases the directors who authorize the original issue of stock for property are either the promoters who have title to or options on the property and who receive the stock in exchange therefor, or they are mere dummies acting on behalf of the promoters. The cogency of this point is apparent when it is observed that, with few exceptions, courts hold that innocent transferees of stock issued for overvalued property are not liable to creditors for an unpaid balance on stock. See Bonbright, *op. cit. supra* (c. I, note 1) at p. 417 *et seq.* See also, with reference to the strangeness of the rule which holds shareholders responsible for bad faith on the part of the directors: Rhode v. Dock-Hop Co., 184 Cal. 367, 194 Pac. 11 (1920); Andrews v. Panama Oil Co., 50 Cal. App. 764, 195 Pac. 963 (1920); Schenck v. Andrews, 57 N. Y. 133, 143 (1874); Ballantine, *op. cit. supra* (c. I, note 32) at p. 89 *et seq.; Ballantine, op. cit. supra* (c. I, note 37) at p. 677 *et seq.;* Report of Committee Respecting Revision of Ohio Corporation Law, *supra* (c. I, note 16) at pp. 75–76.

[2] See Bonbright, *op. cit.;* Ballantine, Henry W., Private Corporations (Chicago, 1927), sect. 207 *et seq.* See also the discussion *supra,* pp. 27–34.

[3] Statutes of this type are cited *supra,* c. I, note 60.

[4] Taylor v. Walker, 117 Fed. 737, 739 (C. C., N. D. Ill., N. D., 1902), *aff'd,*

deceived by false capitalizations and hence, unless it can be shown not only that creditors were actually deceived, but also that the directors intended to deceive them, they see no reason for imposing a liability upon shareholders. They cling tenaciously to a reference to morality by making " fraud " in its generic sense the ground on which they will decide cases of this sort. Unless the attitude of these courts is less definite than the mode of its expression connotes, it would seem that recovery by a creditor in these jurisdictions would be almost hopeless for the obvious reason that the defendants are not apt to admit that the property was deliberately overvalued by their directors with intent to deceive creditors. In the absence of this admission the plaintiff would have great difficulty in applying an objective standard for the measurement of the directors' *motives.*

Second, there are those courts which use " fraud " frankly in a " constructive " sense, as denoting deliberate overvaluation. They will not require proof or even evidence that the property was overvalued in order to mislead creditors. Proof of such a motive will impeach the transaction but this proof will not be required. For example, the directors might have deliberately overvalued the property with no thought of any creditors, in order to facilitate their stock-jobbing efforts or to induce some potential competitor to come into a new combination. Yet the stockholders would still be liable to creditors. The majority of "good faith" courts fall within this class. Most of them appear to be willing to give judgment for the plaintiff if he can show the fact that the property was overvalued and that this was done deliberately by the directors.[6]

127 Fed. 108 (C. C. A., 7th Cir., 1903); Hobgood v. Ehlen, 141 N. C. 344, 346–47, 53 S. E. 857, 858–59 (1906); Clayton v. Ore Knob Co., 109 N. C. 385, 389–90, 14 S. E. 36, 38 (1891); Penfield v. Dawson Town & Gas Co., 57 Neb. 231, 239–40, 77 N. W. 672, 675 (1898); Kroenert v. Johnston, 19 Wash. 96, 52 Pac. 605 (1898); National Bank of Merrill v. Illinois & Wisconsin Lumber Co., 101 Wisc. 247, 251–54, 257, 77 N. W. 185, 188, 189 (1898); Carp v. Chipley, 73 Mo. App. 22, 33 (1898); Streator Car Seat Co. v. Rankin, 45 Ill. App. 226, 229 (1892). For other cases see: 5 THOMPSON, *op. cit. supra* (c. I, note 47), sect. 3992; CLARK, ON CORPORATIONS (3d ed., St. Paul, 1916), p. 470.

[6] ". . . The fraud is consummated by the issue of stock as full-paid stock, under the act of 1853, which has not been fully paid for in value by the property for which it is issued, *and it does not depend upon any fraudulent intent other than that which is evidenced by the act of knowingly issuing stock for property to an amount in excess of its value.* All that is necessary to establish the legal fraud and take the stock issued out of the immunity assured to

Of course, it should be far easier to prove that property was deliberately or knowingly overvalued than that it was so valued with an *intent* to deceive the plaintiff.

The third, and last, class of "good faith" courts is represented by the courts of New Jersey. These courts, while subscribing in name to the "good faith" rule, as indeed the statute requires,[6] nevertheless set such high standards of "good faith" that creditors really seem to have a fair chance of prosecuting their claims to successful judgment. They adhere to the principle that "fraud," as that term is used in the statute, may exist even where the directors genuinely believed that the property was worth the value placed upon it. They carry the meaning of constructive fraud one step farther than the courts in the preceding class by indicating that a merely imprudent, or unreasonable overvaluation, even if not deliberately made, establishes a liability. In the language of a much quoted opinion:

When such differences are brought before judicial tribunals, the judgment of those who are by law entrusted with the power of issuing stock "to the amount of the value of the property," and on whom, therefore, is placed the first duty of valuing the property, must be accorded considerable

stock honestly issued in pursuance of the act of 1853 is to prove two facts: 1st. That the stock issued exceeded in amount the value of the property in exchange for which it was issued; and, 2d. That the trustees deliberately, and with knowledge of the real value of the property overvalued it, and paid in stock for it an amount which they knew was in excess of its actual value. The value may be determined in any action in which the question arises upon such evidence as may be given, having respect to the circumstances and the nature of the property, and the *scienter* and guilty action of the trustees may be proved either directly or inferred from circumstances." Douglass v. Ireland, 73 N. Y. 100, 104 (1878). (Our italics.) See also the authorities cited *infra*, notes 17–20, inclusive.

[6] 2 Comp. Stat. N. J. (1911), p. 1630 (sect. 49 of the Gen. Corp. Act., P. L. 1896, p. 293), as follows: "Any corporation formed under this act may purchase mines, manufactories or other property necessary for its business, or the stock of any company or companies owning, mining, manufacturing or producing materials, or other property necessary for its business, and issue stock to the amount of the value thereof in payment therefor, and the stock so issued shall be full-paid stock and not liable to any further call, neither shall the holder thereof be liable for any further payment under any of the provisions of this act; and in the absence of actual fraud in the transaction, the judgment of the directors as to the value of the property purchased shall be conclusive . . ." This section has since been repealed and other provisions have been substituted therefor. New Jersey Laws 1917, c. 195, pp. 566–68.

weight. But it cannot be deemed conclusive when duly subjected to judicial scrutiny. Nor is it necessary that conscious overvaluation or any other fraudulent conduct on the part of these primary valuers should be shown to justify judicial interposition. Their honest judgment, if reached without due examination into the elements of value, or if based in part upon an estimate of matters which really are not property, or if plainly warped by self-interest, may lead to a violation of this statutory rule as surely as would corrupt motive.

The cases in this state to which we are referred [citing cases] in support of the proposition that the honest judgment of the managers of a corporation, with respect to matters *intra vires*, cannot be disturbed at the instance of stockholders; all relate to transactions for which the legislature has set up no other criterion than the discretion of those managers. But the original issue of corporate stock is a special function, in the exercise of which the legislature has fixed the standard to be observed, and it is the duty of the courts, so far as their jurisdiction extends, to see that this standard is not violated, either intentionally or unintentionally.[7]

Such a broadening of the term, "fraud," shifts the emphasis from the purely moral ground of wilful misstatement with intent to deceive to that of the prudence, honesty, business sagacity and disinterestedness of the directors.[8] If actually adhered to, this

[7] Donald v. American Smelting & Refining Co., 62 N. J. Eq. 729, 731–32, 48 Atl. 771, 772–73 (1901). Although this case did not involve the rights of creditors, the opinion as quoted in the text was approved and adopted by the New Jersey courts in subsequent suits in which the plaintiffs were creditors rather than stockholders. See v. Heppenheimer, 69 N. J. Eq. 36, 61 Atl. 843 (1905); Holcombe v. Trenton White City Co., 80 N. J. Eq. 122, 82 Atl. 618 (1912), *aff'd,* 82 N. J. Eq. 364, 91 Atl. 1069 (1913). For discussions of the American Smelting & Refining Co. case and of the New Jersey rule in general, see: Wickersham, Geo. W., *The Capital of a Corporation* (1909), 22 Harv. L. Rev. 319; Wallstein, Leonard M., *The Issue of Corporate Stock for Property Purchased — a New Phase* (1906), 15 Yale L. J. 111.

The Supreme Court of California has recently adopted the New Jersey attitude toward payment for stock in property. Hasson v. Koeberle, 180 Cal. 359, 365–67, 181 Pac. 387, 389–90 (1919). A number of other courts have subscribed to similar views. See cases cited in notes 29–34 *infra.*

[8] Compare the following definition of the term "actual fraud" by a New Jersey court: "The expression, 'actual fraud,' as used in the cases last mentioned, must be interpreted to mean and include any device by which the stock of a corporation passes to a stockholder without payment in full, either in cash or by property purchased, 'to the amount of the value thereof,' and that an intentional overvaluation of property, upon the understanding that a portion of the stock issued should be returned for distribution among the directors voting for the purchase without payment by them, is such a device, and falls

identification of good faith with reasonable and unbiased judgment should result in a real advantage to those who object to directors' valuations.

b) *Meaning of "true value" rule.* — At the opposite extreme from that which insists on proof of malicious as well as deliberate overvaluation are those jurisdictions in which the courts uphold the so-called "true value" standard of liability and reject completely the defense of good faith, or even of reasonable judgment of the directors. These courts have assumed the break completely with the general American precedent. This is notably the position in Missouri. The same rule, somewhat modified at times, has occasionally been supported by judicial utterances in other jurisdictions,[9] but nowhere else has the doctrine been stated so uncompromisingly as in Missouri. The nature of the rule is best indicated by a quotation from a leading case:

> Upon a review of all the cases decided by the appellate courts of this State since the adoption of the Constitution of 1875, the ruling in all of which will be found to be in harmony, it is impossible to escape the conviction that in this State, whatever may be the case in some of the other States, the American Trust Doctrine, as suggested by Mr. Justice Harlan, has indeed been "reinforced" by its Constitution and Statutes; and that the proposition that the stock of a corporation must be paid for "in meal or in malt," in money or in money's value, is not a mere figure of speech, but really has the significance of its terms. It may be paid for in property, but in such case the property must be the fair equivalent in value to the par value of the stock issued therefor; that it is the duty of the stockholders to see that it possesses such value; that when a corporation is sent forth into the commercial world, accredited by them as possessed of a capital in money, or its equivalent, in property, equal to the par value of its capital stock, every person dealing with it, unless otherwise advised, has a right to extend credit to it on the faith of the fact that its capital stock has been so paid and that the money or its equivalent in property will be forthcoming to respond to his legitimate demands. In short, that it is the duty of the stockholder, and not of the creditor, to see that it is paid; hence, the inquiry in a case between a creditor and a stockholder when property has been paid in for the capital stock of the corporation, is not whether the

---

within the definition of 'actual fraud' as intended by the court of errors and appeals." Easton National Bank v. American Brick & Tile Co., 69 N. J. Eq. 326, 329, 60 Atl. 54, 55–56 (1905). *Cf.* Douglass v. Ireland, *supra,* note 5; WALLSTEIN, *op. cit. supra,* note 7.

[9] See cases cited *infra,* notes 42–58.

stockholder believed or had reason to believe that the property was equal in value to the par value of the capital stock; but whether, in point of fact, it was such equivalent.[10]

On the face of it this rule appears to shift the center of the inquiry from the opinions of the directors or incorporators as to the value of the consideration accepted for stock in lieu of a cash payment, to the question of fact, "What was the property worth?" Whether, in actual practice, this shift of emphasis makes any material difference in the results reached is a subject which will be discussed presently. Ostensibly, however, the "true value rule" would seem far more favorable to complaining creditors than the "good faith rule," for, not only would it eliminate the creditors' most difficult problem of proving that the directors' valuation was *deliberately* excessive, but it would also destroy the probative force of the directors' optimistic expectations concerning the eventual worth of the property.

If there be any injustice in this rule of law it is toward the stockholders who may have to suffer from the honest mistakes of their directors. As one "good faith" court puts it:

It cannot be properly claimed, in giving construction to the power conferred on them [the trustees or directors] by the amendatory act [Ch. 333, N. Y. Laws, 1853] that the property purchased, and every part thereof, should be *indispensable* for the prosecution of the business of the company, or that the sum allowed therefor should be its *precise, actual,* intrinsic value

[10] Van Cleve v. Berkey, 143 Mo. 109, 135–36, 44 S. W. 743, 750 (1897). Although the court was here concerned with an issue of stock by a corporation organized under the laws of Illinois, it later applied the same rule to corporations organized under the laws of Missouri. Berry v. Rood, 168 Mo. 316, 67 S. W. 644 (1902). See also Babbitt v. Read, 215 Fed. 395 (D. C., S. D. N. Y., 1914), *aff'd,* 236 Fed. 42 (C. C. A., 2d Cir., 1916). In Meyer v. Ruby Trust Mining & Milling Co., 192 Mo. 162, 189, 90 S. W. 821, 827 (1905), the court rephrased the rule as follows: "The rule in this State, therefore, is that unpaid subscriptions on capital stock of a corporation, constitute a trust fund for the benefit of creditors, and that whilst incorporators may turn over property instead of cash in payment of stock, that property must be fully equal to the value placed upon it, and its value is determined by the fact and not by the opinions of the persons turning it over, even though they may have honestly believed it to be worth the amount certified. . . ."

The rule still appears to be the law in Missouri. Hodde v. Hahn, 283 Mo. 320, 331, 222 S. W. 799, 802 (1920); Hastings v. Scott, 248 S. W. 973 (Mo. App., 1923).

(and that to be determined by the verdict of a jury), for the exemption of a stockholder from the liability which the original act imposed, in case the whole capital was not actually paid in cash. Such a construction would defeat the evident object of the law, which clearly was to encourage the formation of companies, by the appropriation of manufactories, mines and other property, proper for their business, and at a fair valuation, instead of money, as the capital therefor. No person could be expected to become a stockholder, and pay his money or appropriate his property, and he, nevertheless, be held liable to a contribution in favor of creditors, to the extent of the stock issued for such property, if a jury should, subsequently, and at an indefinite and unlimited period thereafter, find that the trustees had, under a mistake, but in an honest exercise of their judgment, concluded, erroneously, either that the property was in fact, as disclosed by subsequent events, *not absolutely indispensable*, or *actually worth* the *full* sum allowed for it. . . .

The construction given to the act by the court below, in its effect, imposes a *penalty* on the *stockholder* in a company for a mistake and erroneous judgment of its trustees in the faithful and honest discharge of their duties. . . .[11]

The judge who wrote the above opinion, and a number of other judges and writers on corporation law and finance, have urged that the enforcement of the "true value" rule is impracticable on the ground that such a severe interpretation of the law will unduly restrict industrial development and thus put a check upon the rapid growth of corporate enterprises.[12] It is difficult to deny such a contention if the "true value" rule is followed literally by the courts, for it is apparent that a damper would be placed upon the enthusiasm of promoters if the stock which they put out is to be subject to an uncertain and perpetual liability in favor of the resourceful creditor of the corporation who may subsequently be able to bring to light such facts as would persuade a jury that the directors, although honest, were guilty of a mistake in valuing the property.

[11] Schenck v. Andrews, 57 N. Y. 133, 142–43 (1874).

[12] Clayton v. Ore Knob Co., 109 N. C. 385, 395, 14 S. E. 36, 40 (1891); Richardson v. Treasure Hill Mining Co., 23 Utah 366, 380, 65 Pac. 74, 77 (1901); Schenck v. Andrews, *supra* (note 11) at pp. 143, 147; Van Cott v. Van Brunt, 82 N. Y. 535, 540 (1880); Kroenert v. Johnston, 19 Wash. 96, 105, 52 Pac. 605, 608 (1898); WALLSTEIN, *op. cit. supra* (note 7) at p. 115. *Cf.* MEAD, *op. cit. supra* (c. I, note 8) at pp. 352–55.

Actual Significance of the Assumed Differences between the "Good Faith" Rules and the "True Value" Rule

All of the above refers simply to opinions rather than to actual decisions; to what the judges say rather than to what they do. It is now necessary to inquire whether the differences between the several verbal rules are real or only nominal. In actual practice are the courts in the "true value" jurisdictions like Missouri more likely to find a defendant shareholder liable than are the courts in the more typical "good faith" jurisdictions? Are the judicial utterances by the various types of "good faith" courts to be taken literally, or do all such courts react alike to a given set of circumstances surrounding stock issues?

In order to get light upon these questions the writer has examined an extensive sample of cases with a view to determining whether these distinctions mean what they purport to mean, or indeed, whether they mean anything at all.

a) The supposed rule requiring proof of intent to deceive.—As has been noted, a minority of courts have said that the valuation certified by the directors will not be impeached unless the plaintiffs allege and prove that the directors deliberately overvalued the consideration accepted for stock and that they did so with an actual intent to deceive.[13] It has been noted further that this question

[13] In addition to the cases cited in note 4, *supra*, see the following: Troup v. Horbach, 53 Neb. 795, 74 N. W. 326 (1898); Coffin v. Ransdell, 110 Ind. 417, 11 N. E. 20 (1886); Young v. Erie Iron Co., 65 Mich. 111, 31 N. W. 814 (1887); Graves v. Brooks, 117 Mich. 424, 75 N. W. 932 (1898); Jones v. Whitworth, 94 Tenn. 602, 30 S. W. 736 (1895); Farrell v. Davis, 85 Or. 213, 222, 161 Pac. 94, 703 (1917); Andrews v. Panama Oil Co., 50 Cal. App. 764, 767, 195 Pac. 963, 964 (1920); Southwestern Portland Cement Co. v. Latta & Happer, 193 S. W. 1115, 1125 (Tex. Civ. App., 1917).

Other cases in which the opinions lay special emphasis upon the necessity of alleging and proving "actual fraud," but without clearly defining the latter in terms of intent to deceive, and which are cited by legal authorities as standing for the "intent" rule, are as follows: Bank of Fort Madison v. Alden, 129 U. S. 372, 9 Sup. Ct. 332 (1889); Coit v. Gold Amalgamating Co., 119 U. S. 343, 7 Sup. Ct. 231 (1886); Whitehill v. Jacobs, 75 Wisc. 474, 44 N. W. 630 (1890); American Tube & Iron Co. v. Baden Gas Co. and Hays, 165 Pa. St. 489, 30 Atl. 936 (1895); Bruner v. Brown, 139 Ind. 600, 38 N. E. 318 (1894); Whitlock v. Alexander, 160 N. C. 465, 76 S. E. 538 (1912); Kelly v. Fletcher, 94 Tenn. 1, 28 S. W. 1099 (1894). See also: 5 Thompson, *loc. cit. supra*, note 4; 42 L. R. A. 602, note.

of intent for which the shareholders are held responsible is avowedly a question of the state of mind of the directors. The courts which subscribe to this doctrine seem to be influenced by the common-law rule and by the phraseology of statutes which stress the presence of " fraud," or " actual fraud," as the basis for the imposition of a liability upon shareholders for the benefit of creditors. Judged by their language, " fraud " connotes an actual intent to deceive.

However, an examination of the actual decisions in these cases, and of the evidence upon which they were made to rest, reveals a discrepancy between the expressed rule, if literally interpreted, and the practice under it. The nominal standard of " actual fraud " or " intent to deceive " becomes *constructive fraud* in practice. The sole effect which the rule appears to have upon the litigant parties relates merely to the *form* which the pleadings must take. Failure on the part of the plaintiff to allege in his bill that the directors overstated the value of the consideration accepted for stock in order to deceive creditors may cause a demurrer to the bill to be sustained. If such is the case no question of valuation comes before the court. But if the bill is properly drawn there is no ground in the decisions of these courts for the conclusion that the standard of valuation is affected by the nominal requirement that intent to deceive must be alleged and proven. As has been noted above, this verbal requirement appears to be liberal to shareholders and on its face would seem to be an effective barrier to the imposition of a liability. But in practically all of the cases cited the courts have either found an overvaluation upon the same varieties of evidence which lead other courts to a like conclusion, or else they have been no more liberal in giving judgment for the defendant than these other courts would have been in the face of identical evidence.

The reason is not far to seek. The actual state of the directors' minds and the character of their motives are matters on which courts rarely have the benefit of direct testimony. Any conclusions which they may reach on that head must of necessity be inferred from circumstantial evidence. In practice the evidence upon which these cases have been decided has related more particularly to the question whether men of reasonable prudence and honesty would have valued the property at the price put upon it by the directors than to the motives of the particular directors. Hence " fraud " in these cases is really constructive fraud, an inference concerning the directors' motives deduced from evidence which in other jurisdictions would be relied upon to support a finding that the directors deliberately or imprudently overvalued the property, or that it was in fact overvalued regardless of the directors' state of mind.[14]

b) *The deliberate-overvaluation rule.* — The majority of "good faith" courts do not insist that an "actual intent to deceive" be proven as a condition precedent to the enforcement of the legal consequences of watering stock.[15] But, although most of them say

[14] The phrase "actual fraud" which is found in a number of statutes would seem to justify a requirement that positive rather than constructive dishonesty should be proven if the word "actual" was used as distinguished from "constructive." But, with one exception, the writer has not encountered a single decision in which this adjective was held to add significance to the mere word "fraud." The exception is Hobgood v. Ehlen, *supra,* note 4, wherein the court took some pains to distinguish "actual" from "constructive" fraud and insisted that the Delaware statute under which the corporation was chartered imposed a penalty upon the former. This pronouncement of the North Carolina court is weakened by the fact that the distinction has not been made by the Delaware courts themselves, and by the further fact that the distinction was not necessary to the decision since the property was obviously and grossly overvalued. See *contra,* McCombs Producing & Refining Co. v. Ogle, 200 Ky. 208, 254 S. W. 425 (1923), in which the court said that the "actual fraud" referred to in the Delaware statute could be inferred from circumstances.

The New Jersey courts, under a statute making the judgment of the directors conclusive "in the absence of *actual* fraud in the transaction," go to great lengths in broadening the meaning of the term "fraud." See the cases cited in footnotes 7 and 8, *supra.* And see our discussion of the "reasonable judgment rule" *infra,* pp. 72–78. *Cf.* the language of the New York court quoted in footnote 5, *supra.*

[15] Douglass v. Ireland, *loc. cit. supra,* note 5; National Tube Works Co. v. Gilfillan, 124 N. Y. 302, 306–7, 26 N. E. 538, 539 (1891); Northwestern Mut. Life Ins. Co. v. Cotton Exchange Real Estate Co., 46 Fed. 22, 24–25 (C. C., E. D. Mo., E. D., 1891), 70 Fed. 155 (C. C., E. D. Mo., E. D., 1895); Kelly v. Clark, 21 Mont. 291, 318, 326, 328, 53 Pac. 959, 963, 966, 967 (1898); Barnard v. Sweet, 74 Colo. 302, 307, 221 Pac. 1093, 1095 (1923); Coleman v. Howe, 154 Ill. 458, 469, 470–71, 39 N. E. 725, 727, 728 (1895); Cohen v. Toy Gun Mfg. Co., 172 Ill. App. 330, 348 (1912); Hastings Malting Co. v. Iron Range Brewing Co., 65 Minn. 28, 32–34, 67 N. W. 652, 653–54 (1896); Babbitt v. Read, *supra,* note 10; Clinton Mining & Mineral Co. v. Jamison, 256 Fed. 577, 580 (C. C. A., 3d Cir., 1919); Berry v. Rood, 168 Mo. 316, 328, 67 N. W. 644, 647 (1902); Meyer v. Ruby Trust Mining & Milling Co., 192 Mo. 162, 188–89, 90 S. W. 821, 827 (1905); Elyton Land Co. v. Birmingham Warehouse & Elevator Co., 92 Ala. 407, 425, 9 So. 129, 135 (1890); Gates v. Tippecanoe Stone Co., 57 Oh. St. 60, 78, 48 N. E. 285, 287 (1893); Donald v. American Smelting & Refining Co., 62 N. J. Eq. 729, 731–32, 48 Atl. 771, 772 (1901); Anthony & Scovill Co. v. Metropolitan Art Co., 190 Mass. 35, 39, 76 N. E. 289, 290 (1906).

that a mere overvaluation in fact is not conclusive evidence of overvaluation of the kind necessary to impeach the transaction,[16] they maintain with substantial unanimity that a deliberate overvaluation is *ipso facto* "fraudulent" or made in "bad faith."

Some courts, notably those of New York, have said explicitly that "bad faith" consists in deliberately (i.e., with knowledge) overvaluing the consideration accepted for stock.[17] They have also stated that a proper valuation is the sum which the directors honestly believed the consideration to have been worth.[18] More-

---

The cases cited, *infra,* notes 17–22, inclusive, for the rule that *deliberate* overvaluation is sufficient to charge shareholders with a liability are to a like effect. See also the discussion and cases cited in the following: 14 CORPUS JURIS, sect. 1489; BALLANTINE, *op. cit. supra* (note 2), pp. 659–61; 5 THOMPSON, *op. cit. supra* (note 4), sects. 3393–96; CLARK, *op. cit. supra* (note 4), pp. 470–71; 5 FLETCHER, *op. cit. supra* (c. I, note 5), sects. 3576, 3578.

[16] See McClure v. Paducah Iron Co., 90 Mo. App. 567, 576 (1901), for a statement of the rule and citation of a number of cases. See also the authorities cited in note 20, *infra.*

[17] For example, Douglass v. Ireland, 73 N. Y. 100, 104–5 (1878); Lake Superior Iron Co. v. Drexel, 90 N. Y. 87, 92–93 (1882); Rathbone v. Ayer, 121 App. Div. (N. Y.) 355, 363, 105 N. Y. S. 1041, 1046 (1907), *rev'd* on dissent of Kellogg, J., 196 N. Y. 503, 89 N. E. 1111 (1909); Bottlers Seal Co. v. Rainey, 243 N. Y. 333, 344, 153 N. E. 437, 441 (1926); McClure v. Paducah Iron Co., 90 Mo. App. 567, 584–85, 588 (1901); Hastings Malting Co. v. Iron Range Brewing Co., *loc. cit. supra,* note 15; The Boulton Carbon Co. v. Mills, 78 Iowa 460, 43 N. W. 290 (1889); Gilkie & Anson Co. v. Dawson Town & Gas Co., 46 Neb. 333, 348–50, 64 N. W. 978, 982–83 (1895); Kaye v. Metz, 186 Cal. 42, 50–52, 198 Pac. 1047, 1050–51 (1921); Tooker v. National Sugar Refining Co. of N. J., 80 N. J. Eq. 305, 314–17, 84 Atl. 10, 15–16 (1912); Coler v. Tacoma Railway & Power Co., 64 N. J. Eq. 117, 130–31, 53 Atl. 680, 685 (1902), *rev'd* 65 N. J. Eq. 347, 350, 54 Atl. 413, 414 (1903); Lea v. Iron Belt Mercantile Co., 119 Ala. 271, 276–77, 24 So. 28, 29 (1898), 147 Ala. 421, 425, 42 So. 415, 416 (1906); Sprague v. National Bank of America, 172 Ill. 149, 50 N. E. 19 (1898); Coleman v. Howe, 154 Ill. 458, 469, 39 N. E. 725, 727 (1895); Turner v. Bailey, 12 Wash. 634, 643, 42 Pac. 115, 118 (1895); Kelly v. Clark, 21 Mont. 291, 318, 53 Pac. 959, 963 (1898); Scully v. Automobile Finance Co., 12 Del. Ch. 174, 181, 109 Atl. 49, 52 (1920); Allen v. Grant, 122 Ga. 552, 557, 50 S. E. 494, 496 (1905); Young v. Erie Iron Co., 65 Mich. 111, 122, 31 N. W. 814, 820 (1887); Enright v. Heckscher, 240 Fed. 863, 869 *et seq.,* (C. C. A., 2d Cir., 1917); Lester v. Bemis Lumber Co., 71 Ark. 379, 386, 74 S. W. 518, 521 (1903); Medler v. Albuquerque Hotel & Opera House Co., 6 N. M. 331, 345, 28 Pac. 551, 555 (1892). *Cf.* The First National Bank of Chanute v. Northup, 82 Kan. 638, 109 Pac. 672 (1910); Chittenden v. Thannhauser, 47 Fed. 410 (C. C., S. D. N. Y., 1891).

[18] See the cases cited *supra,* note 17, and the following: Richardson v. Treasure Hill Mining Co., 23 Utah 366, 381, 65 Pac. 74, 77–78 (1901); Whitehill

over, it will be observed that in many of these cases the courts have adhered to the rule that a gross and obvious overvaluation of a consideration whose value is well known or easily ascertained is strong evidence of "bad faith" or "fraud," and that the presumption of fraud thus raised is in some cases conclusive unless rebutted in a manner satisfactory to explain away the apparent bad faith.[19] On the other hand, these courts are among the ones which strenuously maintain that a mere mistake or error in judgment on the part of the directors concerning the value of the consideration accepted for stock is not sufficient to charge shareholders with a liability for unpaid stock,[20] or that a margin must be allowed to cover differences of opinion concerning the value where the latter is not obvious.[21]

---

v. Jacobs, 75 Wisc. 474, 480–81, 44 N. W. 630, 631 (1890); Coit v. North Carolina Gold Amalgamating Co., 119 U. S. 343, 345, 30 L. Ed. 420, 421, 7 Sup. Ct. 231, 232–33 (1886); Northwestern Mutual Life Ins. Co. v. Cotton Exchange Real Estate Co., 70 Fed. 155, 157 (C. C., E. D. Mo., E. D., 1895); Arapahoe Cattle & Land Co. v. Stevens, 13 Colo. 534, 541, 22 Pac. 823, 825 (1889); Dailey v. Foster, 17 N. M. 654, 658–59, 134 Pac. 206, 207–8 (1913); Schenck v. Andrews, 57 N. Y. 133 (1874); Boynton v. Andrews, 63 N. Y. 93, 95 (1875); Hasson v. Koeberle, 180 Cal. 359, 366, 181 Pac. 387, 389 (1919); Elyton Land Co. v. Birmingham Warehouse & Elevator Co., *loc. cit. supra*, note 15; Macbeth v. Banfield, 45 Or. 553, 569, 78 Pac. 693, 698 (1904); State Trust Co. v. Turner, 111 Iowa 664, 671–72, 82 N. W. 1029, 1031–32 (1900); Alpha Portland Cement Co. v. Schratweiser, 221 Fed. 258 (C. C. A., 2d Cir., 1915), *aff'g* 215 Fed. 982 (D. C., E. D. N. Y., 1914); Grant v. East & West Railroad Co. of Ala., 54 Fed. 569, 576–77 (C. C. A., 5th Cir., 1893). For other cases see: 42 L. R. A. 593n; 14 Corpus Juris, 962, sect. 1489.

19 The leading cases are collected in the following: 5 Thompson, *op. cit. supra* (note 4), sect. 3994; 5 Fletcher, *op. cit. supra* (note 15), sect. 3578, especially footnotes (38), (49–52); 14 Corpus Juris, sect. 1489, especially footnote (89); Clark, *loc. cit. supra*, note 15; Ballantine, *op. cit. supra* (note 2) at p. 659; 42 L. R. A. 608n.

20 The leading cases are collected in the following: 5 Thompson, *op. cit.*, sect. 3993; 5 Fletcher, *op. cit.*, sect. 3576, especially his footnote (99); 14 Corpus Juris, sect. 1489, especially his footnote (84); Clark, *op. cit.*, 469; Ballantine, *op. cit.*, 660.

21 For example, Elyton Land Co. v. Birmingham Warehouse & Elevator Co., *loc. cit. supra*, note 15; McBride v. Farrington, 131 Fed. 797, 803–4 (C. C., W. D. N. Y., 1904); Clinton Mining & Mineral Co. v. Jamison, 256 Fed. 577, 582 (C. C. A., 3d Cir., 1919); Hobgood v. Ehlen, 141 N. C. 344, 354–55, 53 S. E. 857, 861 (1906); Goodman v. White, 174 N. C. 399, 401, 93 S. E. 906, 908 (1917); Barnard v. Sweet, 74 Colo. 302, 307, 221 Pac. 1093, 1095 (1923); Gamble v. Queens County Water Co., 123 N. Y. 91, 25 N. E. 201 (1890), *rev'g* 52 Hun 166, 5 N. Y. S. 124 (1889); Medler v. Albuquerque Hotel & Opera House Co.,

The practical effect of these and similar rules is that the directors' valuation is upheld unless it appears that the latter knew or *ought to have known* that their valuation was excessive. In effect, the courts quite frankly recognize that the directors are forced to guess at the value of much of the property which is accepted in payment for stock and refuse to impeach their estimate unless evidence is presented showing either (*a*) that they knew their valuation was excessive, or (*b*) that no reasonable business man contemplating the purchase of the property *could* have valued it at the figure placed on it by the directors. In brief, " fraud " in these cases means " constructive fraud." Whether or not in any given case this sort of fraud was present will be a question of fact to be determined by the jury or other fact-finding body, unless the overvaluation is either admitted or is so obvious as to leave no question of fact to be decided.[22]

After examining the nature of the evidence considered in this majority group of " good faith " cases and observing the actual decisions which the courts have reached in them, we are driven to the conclusion that the directors' valuation will not be impeached if the evidence shows that they had no positive ground for believing that their estimate was wrong. The absence of the requirement that an actual intent to deceive must be shown has no measurable effect upon the decisions. Both here and under the " intent " rule, discussed above, " constructive fraud " is the operative basis upon which any

---

6 N. M. 331, 345–46, 28 Pac. 551, 555 (1892). See also: 42 L. R. A. 600n, 602n; BALLANTINE, *op. cit.*, 660; Warren, Edward H., *The Progress of the Law: Corporations* (1921), 34 HARV. L. REV. 282, 286. But see: Boynton v. Andrews, 63 N. Y. 93, 95–6 (1875); Rathbone v. Ayer, 121 App. Div. (N. Y.) 355, 365, 105 N. Y. S. 1041, 1048 (1907), *rev'd* on dissent of Kellogg, J., 196 N. Y. 503, 89 N. E. 1111 (1909); Huntington v. Attrill, 118 N. Y. 365, 382, 23 N. E. 544, 548 (1890); See v. Heppenheimer, 69 N. J. Eq. 36, 61 Atl. 843 (1905).

It has been held in Illinois that unless there has been an exercise of independent judgment in the determination of the value of property, no margin is to be allowed to cover errors or differences of opinion. De Shelter v. American Spring Water Supply Co., 182 Ill. App. 403 (1913). But see Garden City Sand Co. v. American Refuse Crematory Co., 205 Ill. 42, 46, 68 N. E. 724, 725 (1903).

[22] Lake Superior Iron Co. v. Drexel, 90 N. Y. 87 (1882); Whitlock v. Alexander, 160 N. C. 465, 76 S. E. 538 (1912); Huntington v. Attrill, *supra*, note 21; Hobgood v. Ehlen, *supra*, note 4. See cases cited in 5 THOMPSON, *op. cit. supra* (note 20), sects. 3994, 4009; 5 FLETCHER, *op. cit. supra* (note 20), sect. 3578.

impeachment of the directors' valuation is made to rest. We find no persuasive evidence that a legal conclusion of overvaluation would be reached under one rule and not under the other. The pleadings of the parties may be required to differ under the two rules, but there is no evidence that the proofs on the question of overvaluation may not be identical.

c) The "reasonable judgment" rule. — Other courts, notably those of New Jersey, have insisted upon some standard of conduct other than mere negative honesty on the part of directors in determining the value of non-cash considerations for purposes of stock payment. The first definite expression of this attitude by the courts of New Jersey is found in the language of Dixon, J., quoted *supra* at page 61. The sense of the statement quoted is that creditors or others who object to the valuation certified by the directors may go behind even the honest opinion of the latter and question the sufficiency of the consideration in terms of the sum of money which an unbiassed or disinterested person would pay for the property after making an intelligent, or at any rate a businesslike, investigation of the factors affecting its value for the purposes contemplated.

As has been noted above [23] this language was used in a case in which the rights of creditors were not involved and in which the nature of the action did not require the plaintiff to make out a complete case on the issue of overvaluation. However, the language quoted has been carried forward by the courts of New Jersey and not only cited with approval but adopted in cases involving the issue of overvaluation and the rights of creditors with respect thereto. In *See v. Heppenheimer*,[24] after quoting the language of the Donald case with approval, the court stated its interpretation of the purport of the statute as follows:

> The intention of the legislature . . . manifestly was, that the capital stock of all corporations should *at the start* represent the same value whether paid for in property or money. That result can only be obtained by supposing that the property is to be appraised at its actual cash value, precisely as if a board of directors with the whole capital stock actually paid in cash is dealing at actual "arm's-length" as real purchasers with the owner of the property proposed to be purchased as a real vendor without any interest in the directors to overvalue the property or other interests inconsistent with the real interest of the stockholders as such.
>
> . . . .

[23] Footnote 7, *supra*.

[24] *Supra*, note 21.

After all, it seems to me that the true test, under this statute, as applied to the case here in hand, is this: if the company actually had to its credit in the bank the sum of $5,000,000 would it have been willing to have paid that price in cash for the property in question for the uses and purposes to which it proposed to devote it; would the property be worth that sum in cash to the company?

Any less severe test will, it seems to me, fail to satisfy the letter and spirit of the two sections of the act before recited, which seem to me clearly to require that the shares of capital stock of any company organized under the act in force when this company was organized should be of equal value whether paid for in cash or property purchased.[25]

In *Holcombe v. Trenton White City Co.*[26] we find this rule reaffirmed with special emphasis upon the necessity that the directors act not only honestly, but disinterestedly, and with intelligent recognition of the business facts bearing upon the question of value which were available to them.

Turning now to other jurisdictions, one notes many expressions of the courts which approach the sense of the language used by the New Jersey courts. In *Hasson v. Koeberle* [27] we find the court defining its position as follows:

" the rule is that where the corporation and stockholders have agreed upon a given valuation for the property transferred, such valuation is binding and conclusive unless it is fraudulent in purpose or effect. But if the parties have put upon the property a valuation in excess of what they knew or believed to be its true value, this is a constructive fraud upon the creditors and the stock will be deemed paid only to the extent of the actual value of the property received in exchange for it. . . ." [Citing cases.]

We are also of the opinion upon a review of the cases that, however morally righteous was the belief of the corporators, if it was reached without intelligent examination into the elements of value, or by including items not really " property," or by the influence of self-interest, the issue would be as much a violation of the statutory and constitutional provisions as though it had been dictated by corrupt motives. [Citing cases.] It may be remarked

[25] 69 N. J. Eq. 36, 55–56, 61 Atl. 843, 851 (1905). As noted, *infra* (c. VI, p. 159), the New Jersey statute was amended by Chapter 15 of Laws of 1913 (N. J. Pub. Laws 1913, p. 28) to conform to the language of this opinon. *Cf.* Dailey v. Foster, *supra*, note 18, where the language of the opinion in the *See* case is quoted as expressive of the proper standard. See also Grafton County Electric Light & Power Co. v. State, 78 N. H. 330, 332, 100 Atl. 668, 669 (1917).

[26] 80 N. J. Eq. 122, 159–61, 82 Atl. 618, 634 (1912), *aff'd*, 82 N. J. Eq. 364, 91 Atl. 1069 (1913).

[27] 180 Cal. 359, 363, 365–66, 181 Pac. 387, 388, 389 (1919).

at this point that in determining whether or not the corporators did in fact honestly and intelligently believe the Ord Mountain claims to be worth one million dollars the circumstances attending and following the transfer should be taken into consideration. Immediately following the transfer, shares of the par value of one dollar each and of the total par value of five hundred thousand dollars were returned to the corporation. A short time thereafter several thousand of these shares were sold to the respondents at five cents a share. These circumstances cast grave suspicion, to say the least, upon the existence of any honest and intelligent belief that the Ord Mountain claims were worth one million dollars.

And at a later point in its discussion the court said:

It was the duty of the court [below] to determine this value [present cash value] by ascertaining as nearly as possible what a reasonably prudent investor who contemplated spending his own money would have been willing to pay for the Ord Mountain claims under the circumstances under which the corporators acted on the date of the transfer.[28]

The Illinois courts purport to enforce the same standard of an intelligent and unbiased estimate of the reasonable cash value of the consideration accepted in payment for stock. This is evidenced by repeated reiteration by the courts of that state that "fair cash value" is the only proper basis of corporate capitalization; that in estimating this value the directors must act disinterestedly, that is, their judgment must be independent of self-interest; and that no presumption in favor of the propriety of the directors' estimate will be indulged by the courts unless there was a "valid contract of bargain and sale," that is, unless the parties who represented the corporation and the vendor dealt at arm's length. Thus, in *Gillett v. Chicago Title & Trust Co.*,[29] where mere figureheads of the promoters accepted (in their capacity as directors of the corporation) rights to an unwritten play and prospective patents on scene-shifting devices in payment of a subscription of $1,999,600 of "fully-paid" stock, the court said:

The law required the directors, in collecting that subscription, to obtain from MacKaye "money or money's worth" to the full amount of the subscription. [Citing cases.] "Money or money's worth" means cash or its equivalent. If the directors saw fit to accept property in lieu of cash they

[28] 180 Cal. 359, 366–67, 181 Pac. 387, 390 (1919). See also Rhode v. Dock-Hop Co., 184 Cal. 367, 370, 194 Pac. 11, 12 (1920).

[29] 230 Ill. 373, 82 N. E. 891 (1907).

could only take it at its fair cash market value. If it had no ascertainable market value, then the only price at which the directors could purchase it was such price as could be realized by selling it to others for cash.[30]

And subsequently the court said:

It will no doubt be agreed that the rights transferred to the corporation by the contract were without market value. It was then the duty of the directors, before accepting the rights transferred by this contract in payment of this large subscription, to ascertain whether those rights had value, and if so, what the value was. The natural and reasonable method to be pursued in determining that question would have been to have applied to men not interested in the promotion of MacKaye's scheme, who were of wide experience in the production of great spectacular plays, for their views in reference to the worth of the rights MacKaye proposed to transfer. No such investigation was made. No other steps were taken to ascertain the value of the rights MacKaye proposed to transfer, such as would have been taken by directors seeking to deal honestly and fairly with the assets of the corporation. *It was the duty of these directors to ascertain the value of those rights precisely as they would have done had they intended to invest money in such rights themselves,* and that they did not do. It is no doubt true that if the directors, in the fair, honest and intelligent exercise of their judgment, make a mistake and accept property at a price greater than its real value, such can not be regarded as a fraudulent overvaluation of the property; but that rule only applies where the transaction constitutes a valid contract of bargain and sale, made in good faith on the part of the directors and in the intelligent exercise of fair and honest judgment on their part. There was no such transaction here. The transfer to the corporation was a mere sham. It was, in fact, a sale by MacKaye to MacKaye, and was, in law, a fraud.[31]

To like effect is the following from the opinion in *Cohen v. Toy Gun Manufacturing Co.*: [32]

The law requires that the directors of a corporation obtain money or money's worth to the full amount of a stock subscription. If they see

[30] 230 Ill. at p. 408, 82 N. E. at p. 904. For similar statements see: Cohen v. Toy Gun Manufacturing Co., 172 Ill. App. 330, 347 (1912); De Shelter v. American Spring Water Supply Co., 182 Ill. App. 403, 412 (1913); Dee Co. v. Proviso Coal Co., 290 Ill. 252, 258, 125 N. E. 24, 26 (1919); Thayer v. El Pomo Mining Co., 40 Ill. App. 344, 347 (1890); Sprague v. National Bank of America, 172 Ill. 149, 50 N. E. 19 (1898), modifying 66 Ill. App. 320 (1896).

[31] 230 Ill. at pp. 410–11, 82 N. E. at pp. 904–5. Our italics.

[32] *Loc. cit. supra,* note 30.

fit to accept property in lieu of cash, they can only take it at its fair cash market value, or if it has no ascertainable market value, only at such a price as might be realized by selling the property to others for cash. They should ascertain the value of such property precisely in the same manner as they would do if they were about to invest their own money therein. The rule, that a mistake by directors in accepting property at too high a valuation in payment of a stock subscription cannot be regarded as a fraudulent overvaluation, applies only where the transaction constitutes a valid contract of bargain and sale, made in good faith by the directors, and in the intelligent exercise of fair and honest judgment on their part, and does not apply to a sham transaction. [Citing cases.]

Similarly, in *Garden City Sand Co. v. American Refuse Crematory Co.*[33] the court said:

Where a corporation desires property for corporate uses and the owner of the property desires to purchase stock, an exchange is equivalent to paying money for the property and the vendor paying it back for shares of stock. In such a case the corporation may agree with the stockholder as to the value of the property to be taken in payment for the stock, but the transaction must constitute a valid contract of bargain and sale made in good faith, in the exercise of fair and honest judgment.

Other instances of similar language are cited in the footnote.[34] In many of these additional examples the language is not quite so specific as that found in the quotations which have been given. But in all of the cases cited there is evidence that the courts regard an unbiassed estimate by the average prudent business man of the "fair," or "reasonable," cash value of the consideration as an appropriate basis of corporate capitalization.

[33] 205 Ill. 42, 48, 68 N. E. 724, 726 (1903).

[34] Whitlock v. Alexander, 160 N. C. 465, 473, 76 S. E. 538, 541 (1912); Tuttle v. Rohrer, 23 Wyo. 305, 316, 149 Pac. 857, 859 (1915); Kelly v. Clark, 21 Mont. 291, 334, 53 Pac. 959, 969 (1898); State Trust Co. v. Turner, 111 Iowa 664, 671–72, 82 N. W. 1029, 1031 (1900); Hastings Malting Co. v. Iron Range Brewing Co., 65 Minn. 28, 34, 67 N. W. 652, 654 (1896); Jones v. Whitworth, 94 Tenn. 602, 606–7, 30 S. W. 736, 737 (1895); Elyton Land Co. v. Birmingham Warehouse & Elevator Co., *loc. cit. supra,* note 15; Grant v. East & West Railroad Co. of Ala., 54 Fed. 569, 576–77 (C. C. A., 5th Cir., 1893); Boynton v. Andrews, 63 N. Y. 93, 94–95 (1875); Babbitt v. Read, 215 Fed. 395, 416 (D. C., S. D. N. Y., 1914), *aff'd,* 236 Fed. 42 (C. C. A., 2d Cir., 1916); Union Pacific R. Co. v. Blair, 48 Utah 38, 44–45, 156 Pac. 948, 950 (1916); Barnard v. Sweet, 74 Colo. 302, 307–8, 221 Pac. 1093, 1095 (1923); Shickle v. Watts, 94 Mo. 410, 417, 7 S. W. 274, 276 (1887); Lamprecht v. Swiss Oil Corporation, 32 Fed. (2d) 646, 651–52 (C. C. A., 6th Cir., 1929).

On close examination of the judicial decisions as distinguished from the opinions we find that under none of the several verbal rules discussed above is the directors' judgment conclusive, and that under each of them " constructive fraud " is the ground on which the directors' valuation is impeached. Although in the group of cases here under discussion the courts say that the directors' judgment must not only be honest to be upheld, but must be prudently, disinterestedly and intelligently exercised, we have been unable to detect any measurable effect of this language upon the decisions. That is, these courts are not noticeably either more or less severe in their anti-stock-watering decisions than those courts which subscribe to a less rigid nominal standard.

The reason for the apparent uniformity of result despite the obvious diversity of opinion is twofold. On the one hand, the language which forms the basis for separating the " reasonable cash value " courts from the ordinary run of " good faith " courts is found in cases wherein the overvaluation was so apparent as to result in judicial condemnation regardless of any nominal grounds upon which the decisions might have been based. On the other hand, despite the dissimilarities in modes of expression which courts have used in justifying their decisions in stock-watering cases, all courts appear in practice to uphold the directors' valuation where it is not plainly wrong, or to impeach it where the evidence indicates that, even after allowing the directors the benefit of all reasonable doubt, the valuation was not such as would have been made by reasonably prudent and intelligent business men investing their own funds rather than those of the corporation. The fact that it is possible to point to isolated cases in which the courts were noticeably more severe in their decisions than in others does not necessarily mean that the basis of valuation entertained by the former is different from that of the latter. It may simply mean that the standard of measurement is such that reasonable men may well differ as to the outcome of any particular application of it.[35] To illustrate, if a motor-vehicle law defines " reckless driving " as travelling at a rate in excess of forty miles per hour, the test is measurable and can be applied directly to any given alleged violation of the law, but if the

[35] For example, Gilkie & Anson Co. v. Dawson Town & Gas Co., *supra*, note 17; *contra*, Penfield v. Dawson Town & Gas Co., 57 Neb. 231, 77 N. W. 672 (1898). Douglass v. Ireland, *supra*, note 17; *contra*, Brockway v. Ireland, 61 How. Pr. 372 (1880).

law defines reckless driving as travelling at a " dangerous rate of speed " a factor of judgment is introduced into the criterion of law observance.

Neither the courts nor the legislatures have developed any crystallized rule or test of overvaluation for stock-issue purposes analogous to the " forty miles per hour " test of reckless driving. After a considered examination of both the opinions and decisions of many courts in stock-watering cases we have reached the conclusion that the diversity of decisions in these cases is due to the absence of such a well-defined test rather than in any supposed diversity of principle which may be erected upon the verbal differences which one can unearth from the opinions.

d) Cases decided under the " true value " rule. — The attitude of the leading " true value " court is sufficiently indicated by the language quoted on page 63 *supra*. Language of similar import is to be found in a number of opinions by the courts of Missouri, the home of the " true value " rule.[36] The contrast between the " good

[36] The development of the " true value " rule in Missouri may be traced in the following cases: Shickle v. Watts, *supra*, note 34; Farmers Bank of Frankfort v. Gallaher, 43 Mo. App. 482 (1890); Leucke v. Tredway, 45 Mo. App. 507 (1891); Shepard v. Drake, 61 Mo. App. 134 (1895); Wolfolk v. January, 131 Mo. 620, 33 S. W. 432 (1895) (" good faith " dictum); Carp. v. Chipley, 73 Mo. App. 22 (1898) (" good faith " dictum); Van Cleve v. Berkey, 143 Mo. 109, 44 S. W. 743 (1898); Berry v. Rood, 168 Mo. 316, 67 S. W. 644 (1902); Shields v. Hobart, 172 Mo. 491, 72 S. W. 699 (1903); Rumsey Manufacturing Co. v. Kaime, 173 Mo. 551, 73 S. W. 470 (1903); Meyer v. Ruby Trust Mining & Milling Co., 192 Mo. 162, 90 S. W. 821 (1905); Anheuser-Busch Brewing Association v. Park Novelty Co., 120 Mo. App. 513, 97 S. W. 209 (1906); Rogers v. Stag Mining Co., 185 Mo. App. 659, 171 S. W. 676 (1915); Babbitt v. Read, *supra*, note 10; Hodde v. Hahn, 283 Mo. 320, 222 S. W. 799 (1920); Hastings v. Scott, 248 S. W. 973 (Mo. App., 1923).

Examination of the above cases will disclose that wherever the " true value " rule has been emphasized by the court the facts of the case have been such as to justify the decision even under the " good faith " rule. In practically all of these cases the overvaluation was obvious, and it is this fact which weakens the contention that the " true value " rule is peculiarly stringent. Judged by their decisions the Missouri courts do not appear to be any more friendly to the creditor who sues on watered stock than are some other courts which do not subscribe to the " true value " doctrine. We have not been able to discover any close case in the Missouri decisions wherein a judicial conclusion that there was an overvaluation was reached which, on the basis of the same facts, might not well have been reached by " good faith " courts.

On the question of valuation the Missouri courts have been tending in the direction of recognizing that value is a matter of opinion about which reason-faith" rule and the "true value" rule is indicated by the following quotations: [37]

In the law of this subject, there are two rules governing the valid valuation of property against which stock of a corporation may be issued as full paid. Of one rule, Van Cleve v. Berkey, 143 Mo. 109, 44 S. W. 743,

able men may differ. In the latest decision cited (Hastings v. Scott) we find a frank recognition of this fact and an admission that some latitude must be allowed to cover differences of opinion. This is the rule elsewhere.

Although the vogue of the "true value" rule in Missouri is supposedly grounded in the language of its constitution and statutes (see Babbitt v. Read, *supra*), there is, on the basis of these enactments, no evident reason why the Missouri courts should deviate from the view which generally prevails in other American jurisdictions. The constitutional clause (Mo. Const. 1875, art. xii, sect. 8) is identical in its wording with the constitutions and statutes of other states. The section of the statutes which imposes a liability upon shareholders to the extent of the unpaid balance on stock is in no sense unique. See Mo. Rev. Stat. 1879, sects. 736, 745; Mo. Rev. Stat. 1889, sects. 2517, 2519; Mo. Rev. Stat. 1899, sects. 985, 987; Mo. Rev. Stat. 1909, sects. 3004, 3006; Mo. Rev. Stat. 1919, sects. 9764, 9766. Although Mo. Laws of 1911, pp. 148–49, amending Rev. Stat. 1909, sect. 399 (*Cf.* Mo. Rev. Stat. 1919, art. vii, sect. 10144), relating to the formation of manufacturing and business corporations, required the articles of incorporation to contain an itemized description of each parcel of property turned in as payment for capital stock and a statement of the actual cash value of each, the courts have said that this new provision did not abolish the "true value" rule, but was intended to reënforce it. Rogers v. Mining Co. and Hastings v. Scott, *supra*.

An examination of the Missouri legislation reveals that it contains no terms which explicitly impose a duty upon shareholders to see that their stock is in fact fully paid. It must be conceded that the "true value" rule in Missouri is a result of statutory construction by its courts, and it may plausibly be claimed that this interpretation was designed best to realize the intention of the legislators, but we can find no peculiar wording of the statutes to justify it, nor do we find, after an examination of the Missouri decisions, that in actual operation the Missouri interpretation has yielded unique results.

[37] See also Babbitt v. Read, *supra*, note 10; McClure v. Paducah Iron Co., *supra*, note 16; Richardson v. Treasure Hill Mining Co., *supra*, note 18; State Trust Co. v. Turner, *supra*, note 18; Tuttle v. Rohrer, *supra*, note 34; Whitlock v. Alexander, *supra*, note 34; Union Pacific R. Co. v. Blair, *supra*, note 34; Kelly v. Clark, *supra*, note 34; Taylor v. Cummings, 127 Fed. 108 (C. C. A., 7th Cir., 1903); Kroenert v. Johnston, *supra*, note 4; First National Bank of Chanute v. Northup, *supra*, note 17; Hastings v. Scott, *supra*, note 36; 14 Corpus Juris, sects. 1488–89; 5 Fletcher, *op. cit. supra* (note 20), sect. 3576; 5 Thompson, *op. cit. supra* (note 20), sects. 3991–92; Clark, *op. cit. supra* (note 15), at pp. 468–70; 10 Cyc. 473–77; 42 L. R. A. 602n; Ballantine, *op. cit. supra* (note 2), sect. 207; Wickersham, *op. cit. supra*, note 7; Wallstein, *op. cit. supra*, note 7; Bonbright, *op. cit. supra*, c. I, note 3; Hale, *op. cit.*

42 L.R.A. 592 (followed of necessity in Babbitt v. Read [D.C.] 215 Fed. 408, 236 Fed. 42 [C.C.A., 2d]), interpreting the Missouri Constitution, is the leading case. The rule requires that the value of the property must actually equal the amount of the stock regardless of any question of fraud, fraudulent intent, or the honest opinion of stockholders as to its worth. Under this rule, having its foundation largely if not entirely on interpretations of state laws, the only question for the jury is, Was the property worth the amount of the stock? This is known as the "true value" rule. In it, motive, intent and good faith are disregarded and the one thing to be shown is that the property conveyed for the stock was its equivalent in money and was worth in dollars the face of the shares. The other rule, of which Coit v. Gold Amalgamating Co., 119 U.S. 343 . . . is cited as the leading case, is known as the "good faith" rule, in which it is recognized that value is a matter about which men may honestly differ, and in which the further question of intention, good faith and fraud are submitted to the jury. Under this rule, to be sure, no device is tolerated to avoid an honest valuation, yet a margin is allowed for honest differences of opinion, and generally the transaction will be upheld even as against subsequent creditors if the valuation was honestly made, although it appear there was an error of judgment and that the valuation was in fact incorrect [citing authorities]. Of course, the transaction is always impeachable for fraud, and gross or intentional overvaluation is itself proof of fraud [citing authorities]. There is little if any distinction in the cases between actual fraud and fraudulent intent in overvaluation.[38]

. . . .

In those States which adopt the "true-value" rule, motive, intent, and good faith are disregarded. In order for a subscriber to relieve himself he must show that the property conveyed in satisfaction of the subscription was its equivalent in money, and was worth in dollars the face of the shares. In those States which adopt the "good-faith" rule it is recognized that value is a matter about which men may honestly differ. In them it is therefore held, that if the parties fairly and in good faith value the property conveyed in payment of the subscription, the courts will not go behind their assessment. But under either rule there must be payment, and if it is not made the subscriber remains liable as for an unpaid subscription.[39]

. . . .

---

supra, c. I, note 22; STEVENS, *op. cit. supra*, c. I, note 49; BALLANTINE, *op. cit. supra*, c. I, note 32; *The Right of a Trustee to Recover Amount Unpaid on Capital Stock* (1924), 24 COL. L. REV. 772; Thompson, Seymour D., *Payment for Shares in Property* (1902), 36 AM. L. REV. 840.

[38] Clinton Mining & Mineral Co. v. Jamison, 256 Fed. 577, 579–80 (C. C. A., 3d Cir., 1919).

[39] Allen v. Grant, 122 Ga. 552, 556–57, 50 S. E. 494, 496 (1905).

In some jurisdictions, where the value of the property taken in exchange is less than the par value of the stock, it appears to be the rule that creditors can enforce their claims against stockholders to the extent of the difference between the par value of the stock and the actual market value of the property, the value being taken as of the time of the exchange, and the absence of fraud being regarded as immaterial [citing cases]. In other states if the exchange is made in good faith, both parties believing that the property is really worth as much as the par value of the stock taken in exchange for it, the transaction is valid as against the creditors; but if there is fraud, or bad faith, or if the property is taken at a valuation known or believed by the parties to be in excess of its real market value, the creditors may impeach the transaction and obtain the benefit of the difference between the par value of the stock and the reasonable value of the property at the time of the exchange.[40]

. . . .

In jurisdictions where the good faith rule is recognized and the appraisement is honestly made, the property turned in is deemed to be payment for the stock to the extent of the price at which it is so turned in and accepted, and the stockholder is protected to the same extent as if the amount so paid had been paid in cash. See 10 Cyc. 475, 476 and cases there cited. In this State, however, the so-called "true value rule" has received the indorsement of the courts and must be held to be in force. By this rule nothing except money or money's worth is to be regarded as payment for shares of capital stock in corporations, regardless of whether the transaction was entered into in good faith or not. By this rule one who subscribes for and receives stock of a corporation must pay therefor the par value thereof, either in money or in money's worth, so that the real assets of the corporation at the outset at least shall square with its books. When either by fraud, accident or mistake, stock of a corporation, so subscribed for and delivered, has not been so paid for in money or money's worth, the holder thereof, wherever the true value rule is in force, is liable to the creditors of the corporation to the full extent of the difference between the par value of the stock and the money or money's worth paid or turned over to the corporation in payment therefor.[41]

After a careful examination of the Missouri cases we have come to the conclusion that the "true value" rule as adopted by the courts of that state has not resulted in any measurable effect upon the decisions with regard to the question of valuation of non-cash considerations given for stock. We have not found a single Missouri

[40] R. H. Herron Co. v. Shaw, 165 Cal. 668, 672–73, 133 Pac. 488, 490 (1913).

[41] De Shelter v. American Spring Water Supply Co., 182 Ill. App. 403, 411 (1913).

case in which overvaluation was found on the basis of facts which would not sustain a finding of overvaluation in a "good faith" state. It is true that in Missouri a demurrer to the plaintiff's bill will not be sustained for failure to allege fraud in the transaction whereby the stock was issued, and it is likewise true that "good faith" courts will sometimes sustain such a demurrer, but this is a mere matter of procedure or pleading which apparently does not affect the decision on the question of overvaluation if that question is raised by the pleadings. Moreover, even in "good faith" jurisdictions it is not necessary to allege fraud in terms if the allegations in the bill with respect to overvaluation are supported by proof which would sustain a charge of "fraud" as that term is variously interpreted by the several courts.

Although the text-writers referred to in footnote 37 *supra* have cited cases from several other jurisdictions in support of the "true value" rule, our examination of these and many other cases, with the possible exception of those decided by the Illinois courts, leads us to no other conclusion with regard to the operative effect of the rule than that stated above concerning the Missouri decisions.[42]

[42] The limited applicability of the rule in Iowa is admitted in State Trust Co. v. Turner, *supra,* note 34. The rule here seems to be that where the consideration is grossly and obviously overvalued no plea of fraud is necessary. See also Boulton Carbon Co. v. Mills, 78 Iowa 460, 43 N. W. 290 (1889). A similar rule has been upheld in Louisiana; Webre v. Christ, 130 La. 450, 58 So. 145 (1912).

Two Maine cases are frequently cited in support of the "true value" rule, but all that appears to have been decided in those cases is that the directors' judgment is not conclusive in all cases, particularly in the face of facts proving a gross and deliberate overvaluation. Libby v. Tobey, 82 Me. 397, 19 Atl. 904 (1890); Gillin v. Sawyer, 93 Me. 151, 44 Atl. 677 (1899).

Hastings Malting Co. v. Iron Range Brewing Co., *supra,* note 34, which is occasionally cited for the rule cannot properly be so classified. See Ballantine, Henry W., *Stockholders' Liability in Minnesota* (1923), 7 MINN. L. REV. 79, 92–93. The case stands for the rule that no presumption of good faith on the part of the directors will be indulged where the facts disclose a gross overvaluation of property whose value is ascertainable. As stated by the court: "Where the facts are undisputed, and the overvaluation is so great as to show that the stockholder ought to have known it if he had exercised ordinary business prudence, his actual belief or intention in the premises will not avail him; he will be presumed to have intended the reasonable and natural consequences of his act, which is to defraud creditors in case of the insolvency of the corporation." This language is the basis for including the case in footnote 34, *supra.*

Although in Kelly v. Clark, *supra,* note 34, the court quoted Van Cleve v.

Wherever we find language in the opinions which is suggestive of the "true value" rule we find a fact situation which, under pleadings raising the issue of overvaluation, would have resulted in the same decision in any jurisdiction regardless of the nominal rule to which the court might subscribe.

We have previously classified Illinois under the "reasonable judgment" rule and this, we believe, reflects a proper interpretation of the attitude of the Illinois courts. But the language of an inferior

---

Berkey, *supra*, note 36, with apparent approval, the opinion in the Kelly case clearly lays down the "good faith" rule despite the decision adverse to the shareholders.

The rule that stock must be paid in "money or in money's worth" expressed in Wetherbee v. Baker, 35 N. J. Eq. 501 (1882), is hardly sufficient ground for classifying this case under the "true value" rule in the face of the obvious overvaluation disclosed by the evidence.

In New York the question whether the "good faith" or the "true value" rule should prevail was raised to some extent in Boynton v. Hatch, 47 N. Y. 224 (1872), but in so far as the question was involved it was decided in favor of the "good faith" rule. See comments in Schenck v. Andrews, *supra*, note 18, and in Douglass v. Ireland, *supra*, note 5. The rule that no fraud need be alleged or proven where there has been a gross and obvious overvaluation was announced in Boynton v. Andrews, *supra*, note 18.

In Goodman v. White, *supra*, note 21, some of the language used by the court is suggestive of the "true value" rule, but other language in the opinion justifies the classification of this decision under the "reasonable judgment" rule. The evidence disclosed a gross and obvious overvaluation which was sufficient ground for the decision. *Cf.* Hobgood v. Ehlen, *supra*, note 21; Whitlock v. Alexander, *supra*, note 34.

Gates v. Tippecanoe Stone Co., *supra*, note 15, is frequently cited in support of the "true value" rule. The facts were such that any court would have held the shareholders liable to creditors. Moreover, the point decided in the case was that an actual intent to deceive creditors need not be shown in order to charge shareholders with a liability. This is pointed out in Kunz v. National Valve Co., 9 Oh. C. C. (N.S.) 593 (1907), where the "good faith" rule was followed. All suspicion of the applicability of the "true value" rule in Ohio has been eliminated by section 25 of the new General Corporation Act. (Ohio Gen. Code, sect. 8623–25; Ohio Laws 1927, pp. 19–20; Ohio Laws 1929, p. 427).

Neither Macbeth v. Banfield, *supra*, note 18, Richardson v. Treasure Hill Mining Co., *supra*, note 12, nor Union Pacific R. Co. v. Blair, *supra*, note 34, each of which has been cited in support of the "true value" rule, can properly be so regarded.

The courts of Washington have vacillated from a weakly expressed "true value" rule to a frank "good faith" attitude. Turner v. Bailey, *supra*, note 17; Adamant Manufacturing Co. of America v. Wallace, 16 Wash. 614, 48 Pac. 415 (1897); Kroenert v. Johnston, *supra*, note 4; Dunlap v. Rauch, 24 Wash.

Illinois court in a recent decision[43] declares the validity of the "true value" rule, and hence a brief review of the Illinois cases is in point here. A number of the early Illinois cases plainly stand for the "good faith" rule.[44] However, as early as 1890, the courts of that state began to emphasize the rule that shareholders of an insolvent corporation would be liable to creditors unless there had been given for the stock the "equivalent in money or in money's worth" and that the latter phrase meant "cash or its equivalent."[45] Some text-writers have used the presence of the "money-or-money's-worth" phrase in judicial opinions as the basis for classifying the courts which use it under the "true value" rule. But this phrase is frequently used by courts which accept the "good faith" rule.[46]

The opinion in *National Bank of America v. Pacific Ry. Co.*[47]

620, 64 Pac. 807 (1901); Lantz v. Moeller, 76 Wash. 429, 136 Pac. 687 (1913); Kennedy v. Norton, 91 Wash. 244, 157 Pac. 684 (1916); Hills v. Skagit Steel & Iron Works, 122 Wash. 22, 210 Pac. 17 (1922). Granting that the language in some of these opinions leans in the direction of the "true value" rule, there is no evidence that it caused the decisions to vary from the results which might well have been reached under the "good faith" rule. In the face of evidence of gross and obvious overvaluation the mere statement that money or money's worth must be paid for stock, or that the judgment of the directors is not conclusive, can hardly be called a declaration of allegiance to the Missouri principle.

For cases involving some analogy to the "true value" attitude see: Anthony & Scovill Co. v. Metropolitan Art Co., *supra*, note 15; Torbett v. Eaton, 49 Hun 209, 1 N. Y. S. 614 (1888), *aff'd*, 113 N. Y. 623, 20 N. E. 876 (1889).

[43] See the language quoted above p. 81 from De Shelter v. American Spring Water Supply Co., *supra*, note 41.

[44] Peck v. Coalfield Coal Co., 11 Ill. App. 88 (1882); Streator Reclining Car Seat Co. v. Rankin, 45 Ill. App. 226 (1892); Coleman v. Howe, *supra*, note 17; Farwell v. Great Western Telegraph Co., 161 Ill. 522, 44 N. E. 891 (1896). See also Taylor v. Cummings, *supra*, note 37; *In re* Beachy & Co., 170 Fed. 825 (D. C., E. D. Wisc., 1909).

[45] Thayer v. El Pomo Mining Co., *supra*, note 30; Coleman v. Howe, *supra*, note 17; Sprague v. National Bank of America, *supra*, note 30; Dean v. Baldwin, 99 Ill. App. 582 (1902); Garden City Sand Co. v. American Refuse Crematory Co., *supra*, note 33; Gillett v. Chicago Title & Trust Co., *supra*, note 31; Cohen v. Toy Gun Manufacturing Co., *supra*, note 30; De Shelter v. American Spring Water Supply Co., *supra*, note 30; Dee Co. v. Proviso Coal Co., *supra*, note 30; Linden Bros. v. Practical Electricity & Engineering Publishing Co., 309 Ill. 132, 140 N. E. 874 (1923).

[46] See cases and references cited in note 37, *supra*, and in c. VII, *infra*, footnote 48.

[47] 66 Ill. App. 320 (1896).

introduced the rule that the directors' valuation would not be upheld as against creditors unless it was such as would have been approved by a discreet and prudent business man. On appeal to the Supreme Court of Illinois in *Sprague v. National Bank of America*[48] the judgment below imposing a liability upon shareholders to creditors was affirmed, with a slight modification in the directions to the trial court with regard to the manner of determining the exact amount for which the defendants were liable. The defendants contended that they could not properly be charged with a liability for any alleged deficiency in value in the absence of proof of fraud. Despite this contention the court held them liable on the basis of the proven facts of the case. In so far as the "true value" rule does not require proof of fraud the decision in this case might be classed as conforming to the "true value" standard. But even the "good faith" courts hold that no proof of a direct fraud is necessary where the facts indicate "constructive" fraud in the sense of deliberate or obvious overvaluation. The facts of the case clearly indicated that the directors paid no attention whatever to the value of the consideration which they accepted for the stock issued, and that there was a very substantial discrepancy between the nominal value of the stock and any reasonable estimate of the value of the consideration accepted. Hence, a "good faith" court might reasonably be expected to have reached the same conclusion as that arrived at by this court. The court further elaborated the principles of law governing the legal consequences of such transactions by stating that the bargain made by the directors would not be upheld *unless it was made in good faith and in the exercise of judgment, fairly and honestly directed*. Moreover, the court said that no presumption in favor of the validity of the directors' valuation would be made unless the transaction effected was the result of *bargain and sale* between the parties. In this case no independent judgment was brought to bear upon the question of the value of the consideration accepted. The vendors were the vendees in effect, if not in fact. In substance the case stands for the rule that unless independent and honest judgment is exercised in the determination of the value of the consideration accepted for stock, that is, unless the corporation and the vendor of the property deal substantially at arm's length, the valuation determined by the directors will not be conclusive as against creditors. Moreover, if the transaction is effected without

[48] *Supra*, note 30.

the exercise of honest judgment it will not be necessary for creditors to allege and prove fraud in order to recover.[49]

In the next case, *Dean v. Baldwin*,[50] the rights of creditors were not involved, but the court did not recede from its rule that the directors' valuation must be a fair and honest estimate in order to be sustained. This was followed by *Garden City Sand Co. v. American Refuse Crematory Co.*,[51] wherein the court applied the reasonably-prudent-and-intelligent-conduct rule to transferees of stock in holding them liable to creditors. The language of the court at page 46 of the opinion suggests the applicability of the "good faith" rule with regard to the question of value, but at page 48 this is limited by a statement that although the corporation may agree with the stockholder as to the value of the property to be taken in payment for stock, the "transaction must constitute a valid contract of bargain and sale in good faith, in the exercise of fair and honest judgment." The court re-emphasized the fact that the question of value related solely to the time at which the stock was issued for property and not subsequently. The evidence disclosed a gross and obvious overvaluation of a patent-right by self-interested parties, a fact situation which even the most liberal of "good faith" courts would have condemned without the assistance of the limitation stated above concerning the necessity of arm's-length dealing and independent judgment.

We have already quoted at some length the opinion of the court in the next important case, *Gillett v. Chicago Title & Trust Co.*[52]

[49] We have found no basis in either the opinion or the decision of the court in this case for the contention of Mr. William B. Hale that the court relied upon the subsequent history of the enterprise in determining that the shareholders were liable to creditors. According to Hale "actual value of the property in the light of subsequent events was therefore the determining factor as to how fully the stock had been paid." It is true that the cause of the failure of the enterprise was such as could not have been foreseen by the organizers at the time the company was formed, and it is quite possible that in the absence of this cause the company might have proven to be a success. But we find no evidence that the court relied upon subsequent events in reaching its decision. On the contrary, there is clear language in the opinion of the Supreme Court of Illinois (its instructions to the trial court), basing the amount of the liability upon the difference between the par value of the stock issued and the net value of the consideration paid to the company *at the time it was so paid*. See Hale, Wm. B., *A Field for Corporate Law Revision: Stockholders' Liability to Creditors* (1917), 12 Ill. L. Rev. 6, 9.

[50] *Supra*, note 45. [51] *Supra*, note 45. [52] *Supra*, p. 74.

Here, too, there was a gross and obvious overvaluation of intangibles having a purely prospective value, and the valuation was made by self-interested parties and their nominees. The court elaborated the "money-or-money's-worth" phrase, and stated that the directors' estimate must relate to the "fair cash market value" of the consideration. It contributed to the stature of the "independent judgment" requirement by stating that the directors must ascertain the value of the consideration "precisely as they would have done had they intended to invest money in such rights themselves." The following language from the opinion is a clear expression of the attitude of the Illinois Supreme Court with regard to the "good faith" rule:

> It is no doubt true that if the directors, in the fair, honest and intelligent exercise of their judgment, make a mistake and accept property at a price greater than its real value, such can not be regarded as a fraudulent overvaluation of the property; but that rule only applies where the transaction constitutes a valid contract of bargain and sale, made in good faith on the part of the directors and in the intelligent exercise of fair and honest judgment on their part.

As we have previously indicated, this opinion brought the Illinois court substantially to the position of the courts of New Jersey. It is worthy of note, however, that the Illinois viewpoint was developed in cases involving such gross and obvious overvaluation that no such careful definition of position was essential to the decision reached if the decision is judged by the standards elsewhere applicable.

Cohen v. Toy Gun Manufacturing Co.[53] closely parallels the Gillett case in its facts and in the opinion. The necessity of an exercise of independent judgment and the limited applicability of the rule that a margin may be allowed to cover errors of judgment are here re-emphasized. In the face of evidence disclosing an obvious overvaluation the rule that fraud need not be charged in terms in the bill, if facts supporting such a charge are alleged, is repeated.

It is difficult to say whether the next case, *De Shelter v. American Spring Water Supply Co.*,[54] really represents a deviation from the Illinois precedent established by the cases reviewed above. The language of the court quoted *supra*, at page 81, clearly declares the validity of the "true value" rule. But the court's authority for the statement that this rule is the proper standard was the Gillett case,

[53] *Supra*, note 45.

[54] *Supra*, note 30.

supra, in which the "true value" rule was not mentioned in terms. The question of the applicability of the "good faith" rule was raised in the De Shelter case by the contention of the defendant shareholders that such overvaluation as had been found by the trial court was due to an error in honest business judgment on the part of the directors, and that in consequence the issue of stock should not be impeached except for fraud shown otherwise than by mere proof of the fact of overvaluation. The court's reply to this contention is found in the quotation above referred to. But the defendants contended, further, that where the value of the property turned in for stock is not definitely ascertainable, a reasonable latitude for differences of opinion should be allowed. The court characterized this as a mere restatement of the "good faith" rule and said that the merits of the contention were fully covered by the language of the supreme court in the Gillett case where it was said that if the consideration "had no ascertainable market value, then the only price at which the directors could purchase it was such price as could be realized by selling it to others for cash." This, the appellate court said, was a specific application of the "true value" rule to the identical state of facts that counsel for the defendants insisted gave rise to the "margin for error rule."

As we view the Gillett case, the decision therein was grounded on the evidence of gross and obvious overvaluation of apparently worthless intangibles by self-interested parties. The opinion did contain *dicta* to the effect that property whose value was not readily ascertainable could not be turned in for stock at a greater price than could be obtained by selling it to others for cash, but the application of that principle necessarily involves an estimate by the directors of the "fair cash value," and further *dicta* in the opinion clearly indicate that it is only in the absence of an exercise of independent judgment, fairly and honestly directed, and in the absence of arm's-length dealing, that the directors' opinion as to the value is totally ignored. If, then, the Gillett case stands for a "true value" rule, it differs from the variety of that rule which is followed by the Missouri courts, where the directors' judgment is supposedly ignored. Regarding the Gillett case in the light of its facts, we may say that in so far as the decision in that case stands for the principle that no margin shall be allowed to cover differences of opinion, the principle is tantamount to and in no wise differs from the rule universally applied that where there is a gross and obvious overvaluation of the consideration this fact alone is strong evidence of a legal overvaluation which the defendants must rebut by positive proof if they are to be allowed to escape liability.

Because of the confusing state of facts reported in the De Shelter case it is impossible to say whether or not the decision was an unusually severe one from the standpoint of stockholders. A and B purchased at a bankruptcy sale, for $11,000 cash, the tangible property, good will, contracts, and accounts of a bankrupt concern which had been engaged in the business of selling mineral water. The property purchased was appraised in the bankruptcy proceedings at $27,000. H and S were unsuccessful rival bidders, having offered $10,750 for the property and business connections of the enterprise. A and B then formed the defendant corporation and transferred the property purchased to it in full payment of $49,800 of stock. They ran the business for about two years, during which period they reinvested about $10,000 in the enterprise from earnings made from its operation. They then sold the business and property to H and S for $31,425.48.

The plaintiff had obtained a judgment for $20,000 against the corporation organized by A and B for personal injuries sustained while in its employment, and sought by his bill to recover from A and B on account of an alleged unpaid balance on the stock. Testimony concerning the value of the consideration received by the company for its stock ranged from $7,000 to $100,000. The case was referred to a master who rejected the price paid by A and B for the property at the bankruptcy sale as evidence of its value and who by a process of his own determined from all of the evidence that the value of the property when turned in by A and B in payment for the stock in question was $31,425.48, the identical price for which A and B had two years later sold the property to H and S after reinvesting some $10,000 of earnings from the business. The ostensible basis for this conclusion was the fact noted by the appellate court that the property was substantially the same at the time of the sale to H and S as it was at the time A and B bought it. The trial court approved the findings of the master and gave judgment for the plaintiff against A and B, each in the amount of one-half or the difference between the par value of the stock issued and $31,425.48.

On appeal the judgment was affirmed. The appellate court said that the findings of the master and of the trial court must be given due weight, and unless manifestly wrong should not be overthrown as contrary to the evidence. Admitting the difficulty of valuing the property in question, the court said that from its review of the evidence it could neither demonstrate the mathematical accuracy of the conclusions reached below nor say that they were manifestly wrong. Hence, it said that the case must be decided in the light of a valid conclusion reached below that the property was overvalued by $18,374.52. It then turned its attention to the defendants' contention that the transaction could not be set aside except for fraud. The outcome we have indicated above.

Although the valuation sustained by the court appears to have been largely arbitrary, and to have been based to a considerable extent upon events subsequent to the time when the stock was issued, nevertheless, the decision does not appear to have been unduly severe. The property had just been bought at a forced sale for approximately one-fifth of the face value of the stock which was issued for it soon thereafter, and no independent judgment was exercised in determining the amount of the stock. Moreover, the valuation fixed by the trial court was less arbitrary than it seems, in view of its finding that the property sold to the corporation was substantially the same as that which was sold two years later to the rival bidders at the bankruptcy sale. It seems to the writer that this latter disposal of the property involved the elements of bargain and sale upon which the Supreme Court of Illinois had insisted in the Gillett case and that the former sale of the property to the corporation did not. Hence the court was justified in assuming that the price paid at the latter sale was a fair index of the reasonably estimated cash price which the corporation might have paid for the property.

Without question the *opinion* in the De Shelter case supports the "true value" rule, though we do not agree that the court's citation of the Gillett case as authority for the rule was justifiable on logical grounds. More important is the fact that the decision in the case might well have been reached by a "good faith" court without the aid of the "true value" doctrine.

No subsequent decision by the Supreme Court of Illinois has been found which goes as far as the De Shelter case in accepting the "true value" rule. In *Dee Co. v. Proviso Coal Co.*[55] we find the court imposing a liability upon shareholders even though it found no reason to question the good faith or honesty of the defendants.

[55] *Supra*, note 30.

But in that case no independent judgment was exercised in determining the valuation; a large amount of stock was issued for non-existent good will; and prospective profits of a small coal-marketing enterprise, the amount of which resulted from very unusual circumstances, were capitalized at 10 per cent without any clear justification therefor. This case could hardly be cited for the "true value" rule unless the essence of that doctrine is contained in the principle that mere honesty on the part of the directors is not a bar to recovery by creditors. "Good faith" courts sometimes say that mere honesty on the part of the directors is a bar to recovery by creditors, but they also impeach transactions of the type involved here on the ground of constructive dishonesty, inferring the latter from evidence similar to that which was before the court in the Dee case. Similarly, in *Ryerson & Son v. Peden,*[56] the consideration was obviously overvalued; non-existent good will was capitalized; and the entire transaction whereby the stock was issued was effected by self-interested parties. Stressing the necessity of arm's-length dealing between the corporation and the vendors of property where stock is issued for the latter, the court said that payment in property is no payment except to the extent of the *true value* of the property. But the evidence so clearly indicated an overvaluation that the decision might well have been grounded in a more liberal rule, even if we assume that by the mere use of the term "true value" the court thereby indicated its preference for the "true value" rule.

Finally, in *Linden Brothers v. Practical Electricity & Engineering Publishing Co.,*[57] where a considerable amount of stock was issued for an unprofitable publishing business and its list of subscribers, and where no independent judgment had been employed in determining the amount of stock to be issued, the court summarized the law of Illinois concerning the payment for stock with non-cash considerations as follows:

> There is no uncertainty about the law or the justice of it and the duty of the courts to enforce it in accordance with its language and intent. The capital stock of a corporation is a trust fund for the security of those who deal with the corporation, and the stockholders are bound to make it good to creditors. The law requires stockholders to give money or money's worth to the full amount of their subscriptions, and money or money's worth

[56] 303 Ill. 171, 135 N. E. 423 (1922); 318 Ill. 105, 148 N. E. 845 (1925).

[57] *Supra,* note 45.

means cash or its equivalent. Payment for stock may be made in property, and when payment is so made the property must be reasonably worth the sum at which it is taken. If property has an ascertainable market value it can only be taken at its fair cash market value, and if it has no market value it can only be taken at such price as could be realized when selling it to others for cash. The transaction must be equivalent to paying money for the property, and must constitute a valid contract of bargain and sale made in good faith and in the exercise of judgment fairly and honestly exercised.[58]

Regarding the Illinois cases as a whole it seems that, although in recent years there has been some tendency on the part of the courts to phrase their opinions along the lines of the " true value " rule, there is little ground to believe that the decisions vary materially from the probable outcome of the cases if they had been tried under a standard which is nominally less severe from the standpoint of promoters and shareholders. The principal reason for this seems to be that in practically every one of the cases the evidence disclosed either a deliberate overvaluation or an obvious overvaluation which no reasonable man would deny. Indeed, it is a noteworthy fact that the most elaborate expositions of the " true value " rule are to be found in those cases in which it was mere dictum, since the facts were such as to lead even the most lenient of courts to condemn the directors' valuation.

Our examination of the cases in which the so-called " true value " rule has been asserted in one form or another has not indicated that the predilection of some courts for this mode of expressing the basis for their decisions has had any measurable effect upon the standard of valuation which the courts actually apply in stock-watering cases. The verbal simplicity with which the difference between the two rules is stated obscures the fact that the court or jury is compelled to estimate or guess at the value under either rule. In the practical application of the two rules the limits within which this guessing may occur are substantially identical.

Conclusions Concerning the Effects of the " Good Faith " and " True Value " Rules

The conclusion which we draw from our somewhat lengthy review of the several " good faith " rules as opposed to one another and to

[58] 309 Ill. 132, 136, 140 N. E. 874, 876 (1923).

the "true value" rule is that the distinctions are largely verbal. In the reported cases the application of either rule, aside from the purely procedural aspects of bringing a question of valuation before the court for trial, seems to lead to the same decision as could readily be reached under the other. The reason, in part, for this apparent uniformity of decision in the face of diversity of opinion, lies in the fact that the large majority of cases which are appealed to courts of record have involved such apparent overvaluation and such obvious attempts on the part of promoters to evade the laws, that even the most liberally inclined courts could not find an acceptable justification for upholding what was done. Practically all the language which justifies the classification of judicial opinions under the several rules is therefore *dictum.*

On the other hand, there is little or no ground for making a practical distinction between the operation of the several rules, because the question in any case before the fact-finding body resolves itself into a query as to what was a *reasonable* valuation of the property as made by directors in the exercise of ordinary business judgment based on the circumstances that were evident at the time. This is necessarily so because of the nature of the property capitalized. In most instances its value can only be estimated. If the directors have exercised ordinary business prudence, and have valued the property as though they were purchasing it for their own use, the judgment will ordinarily be in favor of the defendants regardless of the nominal rule to which the court happens to subscribe. If, on the other hand, they made no serious attempt to value the property; or if they ignored the plain and obvious business facts of the situation in making their valuation; or if they arranged to have the valuations made by irresponsible "dummies" who knew nothing about the property; or if, by their prior or subsequent action, they demonstrated within a reasonable degree of certainty that they knew or should have known that they were overvaluing the property, — the judgment will ordinarily go against them.

In effect, the standard of conduct for which all of the courts hold directors and shareholders responsible is that of ordinary business prudence. This is well illustrated by the attitude adopted by many courts toward a mere formalistic valuation of the consideration accepted for stock. We have already noted that our corporation statutes, which originally permitted the issuance of stock for cash only, were early amended to permit the direct issue of stock for property.[59] The object of this change in the law was not only to eliminate the useless step of first issuing the stock for cash, but to facilitate the formation of corporate enterprises in many cases where initial cash payment would have been impossible. As most of the courts have interpreted the statutes, however, this change was not intended to give promoters a free hand concerning the issue of stock for property. In effect the new statutory provisions permitted the issuance of stock for property or services to the " extent of the value thereof," and since other clauses of the statutes imposed a liability upon shareholders to creditors to the extent of the unpaid balance on their stock (or in an amount equal to the face value of their stock until it should be fully paid and a certificate to that effect made and recorded), a duty was imposed upon the directors to *deliberate* upon the question of the value of non-cash considerations for which they proposed to issue stock and to issue the latter only to the extent of the value of those considerations. The feasibility of the whole scheme from the standpoint of public policy was dependent upon the exercise of reasonable judgment concerning this matter by the directors, who were authorized to superintend the issuance of stock and to see to it that payment was made for it in accordance with the spirit of the statutes.

From the standpoint of the promoters the changed laws seemed to be a great boon, since those laws made the promoters or their nominees the judges of whether or not the stock was fully paid. The usual method of forming corporations then as now was ritualistic in nature. Either the promoters themselves, or dummies nominated by them, acted as original incorporators and directors and through a series of formalities arranged for the issuance of large quantities of stock to themselves in exchange for property without putting up any cash, or at best only a nominal amount of cash. It is not surprising, therefore, that the courts should have recognized the danger of " watered stock " resulting from this procedure nor that they should have set up some required norm of conduct as a check upon the promoter's optimism. This they have done in a number of jurisdictions by open criticism in stock-watering cases of any failure on the part of the directors to deliberate upon the value of the consideration for which they authorized stock to be issued, and by penalizing stockholders for the fact that the directors' valuation was not a reasonable one.

[59] *Supra*, c. I, footnotes 49, 50.

It is not to be inferred that a failure of the directors to place a valuation upon the consideration, or the fact that they did not act as unbiased, independent parties, of itself makes the stock liable to assessment by creditors. The effect of the presence of such procedure upon the judicial decisions appears to be that of casting upon the defendant shareholders the burden of proof to show that the directors' valuation was reasonable, whereas, in the absence of such procedure the benefit of any doubt as to the reasonable value of the consideration would normally be given to the shareholders.

In the large majority of cases that have been studied, a merely perfunctory valuation by the directors, or a total absence of any valuation on their part, or an excessive valuation by directors who were not really acting independently of the vendors, has lead to a holding that the stock is not full paid. This appears to be true whether the plaintiff be a creditor or a shareholder.[60]

[60] For judicial criticism of complete failure to appraise the consideration, and of the presence of self-interest or lack of independence on the part of the appraisers, see the following: Enright v. Heckscher, *supra*, note 17; *In re* Manufacturers' Box & Lumber Co., 251 Fed. 957 (D. C., D. N. J., 1918); Gardner Valve Manufacturing Co. v. Halyburton, 87 N. J. Eq. 689, 102 Atl. 893 (1917); Holcombe v. Trenton White City Co., *supra*, note 7; Ecuadorian Association, Ltd. v. Ecuador Co., 71 N. J. Eq. 757, 65 Atl. 1051 (1907); Wolcott v. Waldstein, 86 N. J. Eq. 63, 97 Atl. 951 (1916); Wetherbee v. Baker, *supra*, note 42; See v. Heppenheimer, *supra*, note 7; Easton National Bank v. American Brick & Tile Co., 69 N. J. Eq. 326, 60 Atl. 54 (1905), *aff'd* in part, 70 N. J. Eq. 722, 64 Atl. 1095 (1906), *rev'd* in part, 70 N. J. Eq. 732, 64 Atl. 917 (1906); Bryson v. Conlen, 144 Atl. 723 (N. J. Ch., 1929); Donald v. American Smelting & Refining Co., *supra*, note 7; Strickland v. National Salt Co., 72 N. J. Eq. 170, 64 Atl. 982 (1906), 77 N. J. Eq. 328, 76 Atl. 1048 (1910), *aff'd* on other grounds, 79 N. J. Eq. 182, 223, 81 Atl. 828, 832 (1911); Gillett v. Chicago Title & Trust Co., *supra*, note 29; Dee Co. v. Proviso Coal Co., *supra*, note 30; Cohen v. Toy Gun Manufacturing Co., *supra*, note 30; Garden City Sand Co. v. American Refuse Crematory Co., *supra*, note 33; Sprague v. National Bank of America, *supra*, note 30; Cooney Co. v. Arlington Hotel Co., *supra*, c. II, note 5; Scully v. Automobile Finance Co., *supra*, note 17; Bowen v. Imperial Theatres, Inc., *supra*, c. II, note 11; Cahall v. Lofland, *supra*, c. II, note 5; *In re* Pipe Line Oil Co., 289 Fed. 698 (C. C. A., 6th Cir., 1923); Thurston v. Duffy, 38 Hun 327 (1885), *contra*, Knowles v. Duffy, 40 Hun 485 (1886); Bole v. Murray, 233 Pa. 589, 82 Atl. 943 (1912); McBryan v. Universal Elevator Co., 130 Mich. 111, 89 N. W. 683 (1902); Atwell v. Schmitt, 111 Or. 96, 225 Pac. 325 (1924); Smith v. Schmitt, 112 Or. 687, 231 Pac. 176 (1924); McClure v. Paducah Iron Co., *supra*, note 17; Raleigh Investment Co. v. Bunker, 285 Mo. 440, 227 S. W. 121 (1920); Osgood & Moss v. King, 42 Iowa 478 (1876); Hobgood v. Ehlen, *supra*, note 4; Gates v. Tippecanoe Stone Co.,

The stress laid by the courts upon this failure to appraise the consideration in an intelligent and disinterested manner fortifies our contention that the basis of corporate capitalization which the courts have in mind in these stock-watering cases is essentially one of reasonable business conduct. No intelligent person who is in business for profit buys his business property without giving considerable attention to what it is worth. This is particularly true where the property is not regularly bought and sold and for which there is, in consequence, no market test of its value. It is entirely logical, therefore, and is consistent with a standard of reasonable judgment in making valuations for stock issue purpose, for the courts to permit the presence of self-interest, or the absence of any exercise of intelligent judgment on the part of the directors, to swing the balance against those who are called upon to defend the results of a purely formal procedure by the directors. A clear judicial expression to this effect is found in the following:

> The judgment of the directors of a corporation upon the value of property or stock to be taken and accepted by the corporation in exchange for its own stock in payment of a subscription contract, the exercise of which, when acted upon, is made conclusive by statute, refers to an honest attempt to determine the value of the property or stock by a board of directors representing the corporation alone, and jealous of its rights and interests, and anxious to secure for the corporation all that it is justly entitled to. Anything less than that is dishonest and fraudulent. The directors may be honestly mistaken. They may exercise a very poor judgment and make a very poor bargain, but this is wholly immaterial so long as they have no personal interests of their own to further and act fairly and honestly by the corporation they profess to represent. . . . But when it also appears, as it does here, that the parties transferring these options to the corporation at such a gross overvaluation were the very parties who pretended to accept the transfer on behalf of the corporation and that they alone were in control of the corporation and that the personal interest of each was subserved by the acceptance of the transfer in exchange for the stock, it conclusively establishes fraud. In the transaction involved here there was not such an exercise of judgment by the directors as to the value of the options as the statute intended should be exercised by a board of directors in the purchase of property or stock, and for that reason the pretended

supra, note 15; Elyton Land Co. v. Birmingham Warehouse & Elevator Co., *supra*, note 15.

See Wallstein, *op. cit. supra*, note 7, for a discussion of the exercise of *impartial judgment* on the part of the directors in the valuation of non-cash considerations which are accepted for stock.

exercise of judgment by the directors is not conclusive upon any creditor of the corporation.[61]

Broadly speaking, the shareholder seems to be at the greatest disadvantage in New Jersey and Illinois where the courts have insisted upon the presence of all the important elements which should be involved in the exercise of an unbiassed and intelligent judgment concerning the value of the consideration which is accepted for stock. In Missouri, on the other hand, we do not find that the severe nominal standard of " true value " has placed any unusual burden upon the shareholder. In fact, every finding of overvaluation by the Missouri courts which we have examined has been consistent with the results reached under the ordinary " good faith " rule that a deliberate or reckless overvaluation constitutes the offense against which the anti-stock-watering statutes were directed. These are distinctly impressionistic conclusions, however. Their validity can hardly be demonstrated because of the unique character of each case and because of the presence of obvious overvaluation in practically all of the cases have been decided in most jurisdictions.

[61] Atwell v. Schmitt, 111 Or. 96, 106–7, 225 Pac. 325, 328 (1924).

CHAPTER IV

THE STANDARD OF VALUATION AS DEFINED BY STATUTES AND COURTS

Peculiar Nature of the Valuation

Neither the tendency of courts to take into account the opinion of the directors concerning the value of property exchanged for corporate stock, nor their refusal to permit the capitalization of the considerations mentioned in Chapter II, indicates the *standard* and *methods* of valuation which the courts apply in stock-watering cases. These questions will now be considered.

It may be well to note first the peculiar type of property which is generally involved where creditors bring suit to hold stockholders liable on unpaid shares. Very rarely in litigation of this kind does the dispute arise with respect to property that has an active market or that is freely reproducible at a definitely set price. Property of this latter type is generally purchased by the corporation for cash which it receives from the proceeds of a sale of treasury stock below par.[1] The assets which are exchanged directly for stock, by an issuance of shares either to the promoters or to the owners of the property, generally include such items as: (*a*) a patent which may be deemed more or less essential to the manufacture of the article for which the company is incorporated; (*b*) a leasehold on the only practicable location for the enterprise in question; (*c*) mining claims; (*d*) options on or ownership in a group of manufacturing enterprises which it is proposed to consolidate. All of these cases raise the same difficulties in the valuation, namely, that on the one hand there is no objective test of value set by competing bids and offers in an active market, and that on the other hand no value can be set by reference to the cost of securing similar property. For there is always a real or an alleged element of uniqueness in the property in question which makes it impossible to measure its value to the corporation by reference to the cost of some other property which has a readily ascertainable market.[2]

[1] Pages 252–62, *infra*.

[2] The value of some property can be measured only in terms of its usefulness to a particular enterprise. Marshy waste land adjoining a stone quarry

It is not surprising that these peculiar difficulties of valuation arise almost invariably in stockholders' liability suits, for it is just such types of property which promoters take pains to select in order to evade the legal requirements that stock shall be issued at not less than par. Their very purpose in financing the enterprise by means of a direct issuance of stock for property has been to issue stock greatly in excess of the price for which the property could be bought by cash purchase, so that they may use the excess in part as a reward for their promoters' services and in part as a means of raising cash capital for the corporation through the sale below par of stock donated by the promoters to the company. It would be quite impossible for them to accomplish this purpose by an issue of stock to themselves for property which has an obvious and clearly ascertainable market value, since in this case the discrepancy between the par value of the stock and the market value of the property would clearly expose the stock watering. The promoters are, therefor, under the necessity of securing some property which they may plausibly claim to have a unique value from the point of view of the new corporation, with the result that they can identify the value of this property with whatever value they place upon the new enterprise as a going concern.[3]

---

may be of no value to the owner in any use to which he can put it and yet be extremely valuable to the quarry company as a dumping ground for shale and other dross of the industry. The value of this property to the enterprise cannot be determined without reference to its capacity to contribute to the success of the particular concern. Its serviceability to this concern is the only criterion for the measurement of its value to the concern because it lacks independent realizability, there being no market for identical properties which may serve as a basis for comparison and measurement of its value to the specific enterprise. Even if a price could be realized for it because it has an alternative use, there is no warrant for the assumption that this price would reflect its value to the stone-quarrying corporation.

Promoters almost invariably attempt to justify large issues of stock by a generalization of this idea of unique value. They regard it as being applicable to all types of property acquired by them for use in their promotion schemes. And, as will later appear, the courts have lent a friendly ear to this sort of reasoning by granting that " value to the corporation for its use " is an element which may properly be taken into account in determining the value of property for stock-issue purposes.

[3] For a frank admission by a lawyer that property with a readily ascertainable value does not meet the requirements of promotion, see Masslich, C. B., *Financing a New Corporate Enterprise* (1910), 5 Ill. L. Rev. 70, 72.

It follows that in nearly all stockholders' liability cases the courts can make little or no use of the two measures of value on which they place greatest reliance in other types of litigation, such as ordinary damage cases; namely, the market value of the property and the cost of reproducing substantially similar property.

In addition to the special difficulties of valuing property in stock-watering cases, emphasis should be given to one fundamental distinction between the effect of valuation for stock issuance and of valuation, let us say, for purposes of taxation, for compensation under the law of eminent domain, or for measurement of loss in damage cases. In all these cases the effect of the valuation upon the cash settlement is direct. For example, if the valuation for tax purpose is relatively high, the tax will be relatively high. The size of the tax-base has a direct pecuniary effect upon the expenses of the taxpayer and upon the revenue of the tax authority. Thus the tax-base is an exact, quantitative instrument for the measurement of the rights and obligations of the parties. On the other hand, the valuation of property for stock-issue purposes has no such direct effect, either upon the profits of the promoter or upon the losses of those who may be deceived by an overvaluation. The par value of stock issued for property does not *fix,* but only incidentally influences the price which the promoter can get for his stock — the influence being upon the feelings of the purchasers as to the value of the stock because of the amount of its par value. Moreover the loss to the creditor due to stock watering is frequently limited by the amount of his claim rather than by the amount of overvaluation. The creditor is damaged to the extent of his loss, which is frequently less than the amount of " water " in the stock. This lack of direct correspondence between the amount of overvaluation and the amount of the cash settlement may account, in part, for the loose standard of valuation which courts apply in stock-watering cases, for it frequently relieves courts of the necessity of finding any very exact value in order to decide disputes between creditors and shareholders.

Statutory Definitions of " Value "

We come now to the central problem of our study, namely, to the problem of the basis of valuation which courts apply to property and services in stock-watering cases. Watered stock, we say, refers to stock issued in excess of the value of the assets received in exchange therefor. But what do we mean by the " value of the assets " and how is this " value " to be determined?

There are two possible ways of discovering the standard of valuation which a court applies in any particular type of litigation. The first way is to read the formal definitions of value which the court accepts in its written opinions. The second way is to study the types of evidence which the court excludes or includes as bearing on a proper valuation. In most cases the first means of discovering the accepted standard of value, namely, the study of judicial definitions, leads to almost negative results, for the concepts of value which the court itself entertains are too vague to permit of a nice definition. As will be seen presently, this situation applies notably to the type of valuation which we are discussing.

In defining the word " value " for the purposes of deciding whether stock has been watered, courts frequently do nothing but repeat the qualifying adjectives that are used in the statutes and constitutions of the various states. These statutory definitions include such phrases as " reasonable value," " full value," " cash value," " fair valuation," " fair value," " actual value," " real value," " true money value," " real present cash value " and other similar expressions.[4] Terms such as these are merely question-begging phrases and really add nothing to the mere word " value." So far as can be discovered from an intensive study of the cases, the courts have made no real distinctions between these various statutory definitions of value, and it is doubtful whether any cases would have been decided differently if one rather than the other of the above definitions had been used by the jurisdiction in question.

The only statutory definitions that might possibly contain real color in their adjectives are those rare ones which use some variation of the concept of market value. Thus, both the statute and the constitution of Kentucky set " market price " as the standard, whereas the China Trade Act of 1922 uses " fair market value " as the test. Conceivably, either of these two definitions might lead a

[4] *Cf.* Chapter I, footnote 49. Section 15 of the Uniform Business Corporation Act provides for the issuance of stock for considerations other than cash, " the fair valuation of which, to the corporation, is not less than the aggregate par value of the shares subscribed for," and makes no attempt to define the term, " fair valuation." Section 17 declares that the valuations made by directors, incorporators or shareholders shall be conclusive. An attempt to protect the public against excessive valuations is made through the publicity provisions of section 18.

court to accept market value as distinct from value to the owner in deciding stock-watering cases. A review of the cases interpreting Kentucky law, however, does not lend support to this hypothesis.[5] Indeed, these cases show no indication whatever that the adjective " market " has in any way restricted the court's interpretation of the concept " value of the property." There is not the slightest indication, for example, that the Kentucky courts have taken the " value of the property " to mean the market value in the sense of the price for which that property might actually have been sold to some *outside* buyer.

Judicial Definitions of " Value "

Coming now to the judicial definitions of value as distinct from statutory definitions, we find the courts repeating the meaningless phrases which have become current in all types of judicial valuation, phrases such as " fair value," " cash value," " real value," " intrinsic value " and the like. Aside, however, from these vain attempts at formal definition, the courts have sometimes thrown a little light on the question of the standard of value by statements such as these: (*a*) that value *as distinct from* cost to the promoter or to the vendor of the property is the proper test as to whether or not there has been overcapitalization;[6] (*b*) that the value is to be taken at the time when the property was exchanged for the stock rather than at some prior or subsequent time;[7] (*c*) that value should be taken to mean

[5] Altenberg v. Grant, 85 Fed. 345 (C. C. A., 6th Cir., 1898); Mayfield Water & Light Co. v. Graves County Banking & Trust Co., 170 Ky. 56, 185 S. W. 485 (1916); Jones v. Bowman, 181 Ky. 722, 205 S. W. 923 (1918); Taylor v. Citizens' Oil Co., 182 Ky. 350, 206 S. W. 644 (1918); Detroit-Kentucky Coal Co. v. Brickett Coal & Coke Co., 251 Fed. 542 (C. C. A., 6th Cir., 1918); Stoecker v. Goodman, 183 Ky. 330, 209 S. W. 374 (1919); Lamprecht v. Swiss Oil Corporation, 32 Fed. (2d) 646 (C. C. A., 6th Cir., 1929). *Cf.* Peden Iron & Steel Co. v. Jenkins, 203 S. W. 180 (Tex. Civ. App., 1918).

[6] See pp. 111–33, *infra*.

[7] This is the expressed rule in most jurisdictions. Huntington v. Attrill, 118 N. Y. 365, 374, 381–82, 23 N. E. 544, 546, 548 (1890); Morgan v. Bon Bon Co., 222 N. Y. 22, 28, 118 N. E. 205, 206 (1917); White Corbin & Co. v. Jones, 86 Hun 57, 59, 34 N. Y. S. 203, 204 (1895), *rev'd* on other grounds, 155 N. Y. 475, 50 N. E. 289 (1898); R. H. Herron Co. v. Shaw, 165 Cal. 668, 674–75, 133 Pac. 488, 490–91 (1913); Clinton Mining & Mineral Co. v. Jamison, 256 Fed. 577, 583 (C. C. A., 3d Cir., 1919); Taylor v. Walker, 117 Fed. 737, 739 (C. C., N. D. Ill., N. D. 1902), *aff'd*, 127 Fed. 108 (C. C. A., 7th Cir., 1903); National Bank of America v. Pacific Railway Co., 66 Ill. App. 320, 330 (1896), *mod.* and

aff'd, 172 Ill. 149, 161, 169, 50 N. E. 19, 23, 26 (1898); De Shelter v. American Spring Water Supply Co., 182 Ill. App. 403, 411 (1913); State Trust Co. v. Turner, 111 Iowa 664, 671–72, 82 N. W. 1029, 1031–32 (1900); Hastings Malting Co. v. Iron Range Brewing Co., 65 Minn. 28, 34, 67 N. W. 652, 654 (1896); Holcombe v. Trenton White City Co., 80 N. J. Eq. 122, 151–53, 82 Atl. 618, 631 (1912), *aff'd,* 82 N. J. Eq. 364, 91 Atl. 1069 (1913); Farrell v. Davis, 85 Or. 213, 220, 161 Pac. 94, 96, 703 (1916, 1917); Finletter v. Acetylene Light, Heat & Power Co., 215 Pa. 86, 90, 64 Atl. 429, 430 (1906); Richardson v. Treasure Hill Mining Co., 23 Utah 366, 380, 65 Pac. 74, 77 (1901); Union Pacific R. Co. v. Blair, 48 Utah 38, 54–56, 156 Pac. 948, 954 (1916) (by McCarthy, J., on application for rehearing); State, *ex rel.* White v. Citizens Light & Power Co., 172 Ala. 232, 237, 55 So. 193, 195 (1912); Hasson v. Koeberle, 180 Cal. 359, 365–67, 181 Pac. 387, 389–90 (1919); Coit v. North Carolina Gold Amalgamating Co., 14 Fed. 12, 15 (C. C., E. D. Penna., 1882), *aff'd,* 119 U. S. 343, 30 L. Ed. 420, 7 Sup. Ct. 231 (1886); Northwestern Mutual Life Ins. Co. v. Cotton Exchange Real Estate Co., 46 Fed. 22, 24 (C. C., E. D. Mo., E. D., 1891); Northern Trust Co. v. Columbia Straw-Paper Co., 75 Fed. 936, 937 (C. C., N. D. Ill., 1896); *In re* Wyoming Valley Ice Co., 153 Fed. 787, 794 (D. C., N. D. Penna., 1907); *In re* L. M. Alleman Hardware Co., 181 Fed. 810, 813 (C. C. A., 3d Cir., 1910); Alpha Portland Cement Co. v. Schratweiser, 221 Fed. 258, 259 (C. C. A., 2d Cir., 1915), *aff'g,* 215 Fed. 982 (D. C., E. D. N. Y., 1914); Garden City Sand Co. v. American Refuse Crematory Co., 205 Ill. 42, 46, 68 N. E. 724, 725 (1903); John R. Proctor Land Co. v. Cooke, 103 Ky. 96, 104, 44 S. W. 391, 393 (1898); Young v. Erie Iron Co., 65 Mich. 111, 122–23, 31 N. W. 814, 820 (1887); Kelly v. Clark, 21 Mont. 291, 333–34, 53 Pac. 959, 969 (1898); Gilkie & Anson Co. v. Dawson Town & Gas Co., 46 Neb. 333, 358, 361, 64 N. W. 978, 1097, 1099–1100 (1895) (dissent of Commissioner Ragan); Penfield v. Dawson Town & Gas Co., 57 Neb. 231, 77 N. W. 672 (1898); McCarter v. Pitman, Glassboro & Clayton Gas Co., 74 N. J. Eq. 255, 261, 69 Atl. 211, 213 (1908); Gardner Valve Mfg. Co. v. Halyburton, 87 N. J. Eq. 689, 693–94, 102 Atl. 893, 894–95 (1917); Hills v. Skagit Steel & Iron Works, 122 Wash. 22, 26, 210 Pac. 17, 18–19 (1922). *Cf.* Rehfuss v. Moore, 134 Pa. 462, 474, 19 Atl. 756, 758 (1890).

But in a number of cases (including some of the above) it seems quite probable that the courts relied to some extent upon subsequent events in assessing the value, though the position of each court is not always made clear by its verbal statements. Lamprecht v. Swiss Oil Corporation, 32 Fed. (2d) 646, 649, 652 (C. C. A., 6th Cir., 1929); Hills v. Skagit Steel & Iron Works, *loc. cit. supra;* Scully, v. Automobile Finance Co., 12 Del. Ch. 174, 180, 109 Atl. 49, 51–52 (1920); Foster v. Belcher's Sugar Refining Co., 118 Mo. 238, 263, 24 S. W. 63, 70 (1893); Thurber v. Thompson, 21 Hun 472, 474–75 (1880); Garden City Sand Co. v. American Refuse Crematory Co., *loc. cit. supra;* De Shelter v. American Spring Water Supply Co., *supra;* Eggleston v. Pantages, 93 Wash. 221, 228, 160 Pac. 425, 428 (1916); Clinton Mining & Mineral Co. v. Jamison, *loc. cit. supra;* Kennedy v. Norton, 91 Wash. 244, 245, 157 Pac. 684 (1916); Huntington v. Attrill, 118 N. Y. 365, 380–81, 23 N. E. 544, 548 (1890); *In re* Wyoming Valley Ice Co., *loc. cit. supra;* Richardson v. Treasure Hill Mining Co., 23 Utah 366, 378–79, 65 Pac. 74, 77; Hasson v. Koeberle, *loc. cit. supra.* For reasons noted *supra,* c. III, footnote 49, we have not included Sprague v.

value *to the corporation* [8] or value for the corporate purposes rather than value in an outside market. But while these definitions point vaguely in a general direction, they do not lead to any precise standard. The notion of a highly individualized value of property for the particular use of the corporation, as contrasted with its value to anyone else, or to the general market, implies on its face a capitalization of prospective profits as the only general method of determining the value of business property for a specific use; but no hint is given in the simple statement of this basis of valuation as to how the prospective earnings are to be estimated or at what rate they should be capitalized.

Recognition by the courts that the "value of the property to the corporation" must be considered in shareholders' liability cases, implies that the mere fact that the promoter bought property for $1,000,000 and turned it over to his own corporation immediately afterward for $2,000,000 of stock will not be accepted as conclusive evidence that the stock is part-paid. For the promoter may have driven a shrewd bargain and may have bought property for half of its value to the corporation. Moreover, the price paid by the promoter is likely to represent more nearly the value of the property separate from the new organization, whereas the value of the property to the company includes a share in the enlarged value of the assembled new enterprise.

To illustrate this point let us take the case of a consolidation of a score of competing paper mills on which the promoter has options to purchase them for $5,000,000 in cash. Although as a usual rule the promoter is not financially able to make an outright purchase of this magnitude, it is conceivable that he might buy the plants for $5,000,000 cash and at once transfer them to a newly organized corporation for $10,000,000 of its stock. Yet, if a court should later

---

National Bank of America, 172 Ill. 149, 50 N. E. 19 (1898), in this latter group of cases. It must be admitted, however, that some of the later Illinois cases appear to support Hale's contention.

In addition to the above cases many of those cited in c. VIII, *infra*, suggest a reliance by the courts upon subsequent events. This is particularly true of the treasury-stock cases and those in which the subsequent conduct of the promoters in disposing of their stock has been accepted as evidence of deliberate overvaluation. See also 5 THOMPSON, *op. cit. supra* (c. I, note 47), sect. 3996; 5 FLETCHER, *op. cit. supra* (c. I, note 5), sect. 3576; 14 CORPUS JURIS, sect. 1489.

[8] See pp. 215–22 *infra*.

be required to investigate this transaction in a stockholders' liability suit, it would not necessarily hold that only half of the stock had been paid for or that every share of the stock was only fifty per cent paid-up; for the plants, brought together under a single ownership and management, might have a much greater value than the sum of their separate values — the increment being due to the expectation of less competition and of greater operating efficiency.[9] There may be, from the viewpoint of the corporation, a balance of legitimately recognizable value attaching to the enterprise as a totality over and above the sum of the values which are separately assignable to the several plants.

It is thus a prospectively estimated " value of the new enterprise as a going concern " that is the test of whether there has been an overissue of stock.[10] But how is one to determine this value? By

[9] See discussion, *infra*. pp. 205–14.

[10] It is here assumed that the promoter and his associates turn over to the corporation all, or substantially all, of the physical property of the enterprise in one lump. If this were not the case — if part of the stock were issued separately for the land, another part for one plant, another for a second plant, etc. — there would be difficulty in the way of valuing each parcel on the basis of the value of the enterprise as a going concern. Troublesome problems of imputation or allocation of the enhanced value resulting from the combination would be raised. This explains why official investigators of the trust movement in the State of New York reported that " both common and preferred stock were issued in bulk for the several properties acquired, studious care being exercised to conceal the details of payments for particular properties and to avoid the disclosure of the processes whereby values represented by stock issues were computed." Report of the Joint Committee of the Senate and Assembly Appointed to Investigate Trusts (Albany, 1897), Senate Document (N. Y.) No. 40, p. 19. This report indicated that occasionally the supposed enhancement in value due to combination of competitors was smuggled into the capitalization under excessive and often entirely fictitious allowances for " goodwill," " patents," " trade-marks," " brands " and the like.

In a number of cases courts have accepted the validity of an increment to the value of separate parts, due to their combination, as an item which may be capitalized. See cases *loc. cit. supra*, note 9. But the courts have not developed any theory of imputation by which combination value shall be allocated to the separate parts, for, as a rule, they are not required by the facts and pleadings of the cases to do so.

It would seem to be logical in cases such as that stated in the text, to value each separate item at its market price (which would be the cost to the promoter, unless he drove a genuine " bargain," or unless he made payment in securities issued to him for the properties), and to consider the excess value of the whole enterprise over the sum of these separate " values " as a " going concern value," or, more frankly, as a monopoly value in those instances where

the market price of the combined property viewed as a going concern? No, for there is no market for it except the market created by the corporation which is paying for the property in stock. Cash bids for whole corporate businesses as going concerns are rarely made. Still more rare are cash bids for whole enterprises *prior to* their organization. Is the value to be determined by the market value of the new stock? No, for the new stock will not be placed on the market until after it has been issued; and one cannot expect the promoter to know what the market price will be when it is issued.[11] Moreover, there is seldom a *bona fide* active market for a

a monopoly position is attained. This, however, is just what promoters do not like to do. As has been noted, *supra*, c. II, pp. 43–45 and note 4, p. 41, the desire of the promoter is to mix thoroughly the tangibles with the intangibles, rather than to place a large claim for "going value" or "promoter's services" alone and in plain view. Consequently, we find that the promoter generally turns over practically the entire aggregate of property to the corporation in a lump sum, with all the increments due to "intangibles" firmly interwoven. See Masslich, C. B., *Financing a New Corporate Enterprise* (1910), 5 ILL. L. REV. 70, 73–75.

But even when this cannot be done, and even when the promoter is compelled to have the different items of property turned over separately, his case is not so bad as it might seem. For if he turns over one particular plant at an inflated price in stock he will urge that the plant, through its strategic importance — that is, its power to hamper the new enterprise through competition if it is not bought — has a "value to the corporation" far in excess of its market value or of its cost to him. Indeed, this method is frequently used by promoters to assemble their projects so that the property that they control will be indispensable to the new enterprises which they promote. Thus it is that the promoter need not (as he frequently cannot) acquire the entire property which is essential to the consolidation in order fully to capitalize the value of his "idea."

[11] One exception to this statement may be noted. Sometimes the promoters and their banking associates agree, prior to incorporation of the enterprise, that the promoters shall donate back to the treasury of the company a certain proportion of the stock issued to them for the property and the bankers underwrite the public sale of this treasury stock at a fixed price. At other times there is not an underwriting agreement but an agreement that the company itself shall offer the treasury stock at a definite price. In both cases the promoter knows in advance the price at which the stock will be offered for sale in the market, and where there is an underwriting agreement he knows the price which the corporation will obtain for these shares. But the courts have been quite willing to admit the contention of the promoters that these are sacrifice prices agreed upon by the originators of the enterprise as the cheapest method of raising necessary working capital and that they bear no necessary relationship to the value of the property originally exchanged for a larger block

new issue. Such a market as there is will be " pegged " by the bankers who are interested in the flotation of the new securities. May the cost of the property to the promoters be accepted as the measure of the value of the property to the corporation? No, since the promoters may have procured the property at a genuine " bargain " and the cost to them may be far removed from the " value of the property to the corporation." [12] May the value of the property to the corporation be measured by the cost of reproducing the physical property? No, for in many instances the property is not reproducible in this sense. This is true in the case of patents, copyrights, secret formulas, mineral rights, land that is uniquely situated, and good will. Furthermore, it cannot be maintained that the cost of physical reproduction of a score of competing plants, which have been combined into a monopoly enterprise by the promoter, accurately measures the " value to the corporation " of the combined properties. Not only would this standard of valuation ignore time utility as an element in value, but it would ignore many other factors which go to make up a " going-concern value." May the " value of property to the corporation " be measured by capitalizing expected earnings? Logical considerations seem almost to require that this be the standard, since a corporate enterprise has a value largely because it may bring profits to its shareholders. Yet there are very few adjudicated cases in which this standard has been frankly accepted and several in which it has been held to be inappropriate. The fact situation in the large majority of cases fails to make the application of this standard a practicable means of solving the question of valuation before the court.

Although most courts in cases involving the issuance of stock for property have gone no further in defining a standard of value than to imply or say that the test is " value to the corporation," a few

---

of stock. The bearing of such transactions upon the value of the property and upon what the directors thought the value was is discussed in chapter VIII, *infra*.

Another exception is encountered where stock is issued for property by a going concern whose shares have a market value. See Donald v. American Smelting & Refining Co., 62 N. J. Eq. 729, 48 Atl. 771, 1116 (1901), *rev'g*, 61 N. J. Eq. 458, 48 Atl. 786 (1901); Enright v. Heckscher, 240 Fed. 863, (C. C. A., 2d Cir., 1917); Strickland v. National Salt Co., 72 N. J. Eq. 170, 64 Atl. 982 (1906); 77 N. J. Eq. 328, 76 Atl. 1048 (1910), *aff'd* on other grounds, 79 N. J. Eq. 182, 81 Atl. 828, 832 (1911); Lamprecht v. Swiss Oil Corporation, *supra*, note 7.

[12] See pp. 118–33, *infra*.

of them, notably the courts of New Jersey, have attempted to make the matter more explicit by stating that the par value of stock which is issued for property should not exceed the amount of *cash* that might reasonably and properly have been paid by a board of directors for the property in question, in case a cash sale rather than a direct exchange of stock had been involved. This position is derived from the view that a direct issuance of stock for property is designed simply to accomplish the same result that would be accomplished in a more circuitous way by the sale of stock for cash at par and by the application of the proceeds of this sale to the purchase of the property needed by the corporation. It rejects the popular assumption that a larger amount of stock may fairly be issued for property than would reasonably be paid in a cash sale — an assumption based on the view that promotion stock is normally worth less than par because of the risk involved in the venture — and it implies that creditors may make good their claim that stock has been watered if they can prove beyond reasonable doubt that intelligent and prudent directors, acting in the interest of the corporation rather than in the interest of the promoters alone, would not have been willing to pay out of the treasury a cash sum equal to the par value of the stock which has been issued for the property.

This adherence to a " reasonable cash standard " of valuation has been perhaps most clearly expressed by the New Jersey court in *See v. Heppenheimer* in the language quoted *supra*, page 72.

This statement has often been cited with approval not only by the New Jersey courts in subsequent cases but also by the courts of other states. Whether the doctrine is really taken seriously, or whether, on the other hand, the common American assumption that the stock of a new enterprise cannot normally be worth par has not caused the courts to depart in their actual decisions from this strict, cash-value rule, is a question which is reserved for discussion after a detailed study of the cases.

The Concept of Value as Revealed by the Evidence Which Courts Consider in Stock-watering Cases

It is a general situation in all types of judicial valuation, whether the purpose of the valuation be for taxation, for condemnation by power of eminent domain, for public utility rate-making, or for any other object, that the *real* principles of valuation which the courts accept can be discovered, if at all, only by a study of those considerations which the courts treat under the heading of " evidence " of the value. In all of these types of litigation, to be sure, the courts start out with an assumed standard or concept of value, such as " market value " or " value to the owner " or " real value." They then purport to take into account such factors as capitalized earning power, or reproduction cost, or actual cost, only in so far as these items are relevant " evidence " of the one thing which it is desired to find, namely, the *value* of the property. Invariably, however, their definition of " value of the property " is so very vague that it is almost meaningless except in so far as it is given content by the rules that are generally discussed under " evidence." The real meat of the substantive law, then, is to be found only in a study of what purports to be evidence of fact but what is really a mixture between the finding of fact and the setting of a legal standard.[13]

What has been said in the last paragraph applies to valuations for stock-issue no less than to valuations for other purposes. The professed or implied standard of " value to the corporation " is a vague and nebulous concept without definite content or meaning. Most courts have qualified the concept through their insistence that only a " deliberate " overvaluation will support a liability of shareholders to creditors, and some courts, notably those of New Jersey, have rephrased the concept in terms of the " reasonable cash price " which a board of directors would pay. But these verbally accepted standards are not always taken literally by the very courts that announce them; and even if they were to be taken seriously, their meaning would not be apparent without a close study of their application to the facts of the particular cases that have arisen.

For the reasons just stated, the four following chapters of this study will concern themselves with the types of evidence which may be presented by one side or the other as proving that property has or has not been overvalued in a case involving a charge of stock watering. Our primary interest will be not so much in discovering the detailed rules of evidence for their own sake, as in revealing the standard or concept of value which a court discloses through its acceptance or rejection of the evidence that is offered.[14]

[13] See Dickinson, John, Administrative Justice and the Supremacy of the Law in the United States (Cambridge, Mass., 1927), pp. 167–74, 307–32. See also the references cited *supra*, c. III, note 22.

[14] In some fields of jurisprudence certain types of evidence have, by a process of judicial fixation, become crystallized into rules of law which are de-

Chapter V discusses the use of some form of *cost* as evidence of the value of the property: (*a*) original cost; (*b*) estimated replacement cost; and (*c*) cost to the promoter or other vendor who sold the property to the corporation.

Chapter VI considers earning power, realized or prospective, as a basis of valuation. This chapter deals with certain questions raised by the use of capitalized earning power as a measure of going concern value.

Chapter VII discusses a group of cases which involve several special aspects of the earning-power basis of capitalization: the issue of stock against mere potential values; the capitalization of a supposed enhancement in value due to combination of separate properties; " value to the corporation," or going-concern value, as an instance of capitalizing earning power; and some implications of the " reasonable cash value " rule.

Chapter VIII closes the discussion of evidence with a miscellaneous group of types of evidence tending to show that the defendant stockholders, or the responsible directors, did not themselves regard the property in question as worth the par value of the stock that was issued against it.

---

terminative of cases in which the specific types of evidence appear. For example, there is the " Stop, Look and Listen " rule in negligence cases in the field of damages. It is so generally understood by reasonable men that ordinary prudence requires one who is approaching an unguarded grade crossing of a railroad to stop, look and listen before attempting to cross, that proof of his failure to do so conclusively shows him to have been negligent in the eyes of the law. It is a complete defense at law for the defendant to prove such failure. Proof of it has, by judicial precedent, become crystallized into the rule of law that *ipso facto* the plaintiff was guilty of negligence.

It would be helpful, in our search for the basis of capitalization in stock-watering cases, if we could discover similar rules of law. For example, it would help to clarify the concept of " value to the corporation " if we should find that in every case wherein the promoter capitalized his property at more than it cost him in cash, the court held that there was an overvaluation, or that in every case wherein the promoters turned back to the corporation a part of the stock issued to them for property the court found an overvaluation. So far as the writer knows, however, there are no such definite rules in stock-watering law. Every stock-watering case involves a number of variables, each of which is more or less pertinent to the question of overvaluation. It is not surprising, then, that the courts have not developed a pattern which will fit every case, or even any substantial group of cases. Stock-watering law is almost a " wilderness of single instances."

CHAPTER V

COST OF THE PROPERTY AS EVIDENCE OF ITS VALUE

The Relationship between Cost and Value

Economic theory makes a sharp distinction between the cost of a commodity and its value. Cost refers to the price that was necessary, or that would be necessary, to secure the commodity; value refers to the price for which the commodity can be sold (" market value ") or else to the price that represents its worth to its owner (" value to the owner ").

But while making a distinction between cost and value, economic theory also recognizes a relationship between the two — a relationship that under some conditions is remote and under other conditions becomes an identity.

Both the distinction and the relationship between the two concepts are recognized by the courts as well as by the economists. The cost of any given property, say the courts, is not to be taken as representing in itself the value of this property. But it may be and usually is considered by them as *evidence* of this value, and under certain conditions it will be taken as the exact *measure* of value.

Unfortunately, however, the courts, not being trained in economic analysis, do not always preserve the clear-cut distinction between cost and value that is generally observed by the economists. In certain types of valuation, particularly in public utility valuation for purposes of rate-making, they have confused the term " fair value of the property " with what the economist would insist was the *cost* of the property rather than its value.[1] In stock-watering cases, on the other hand, the courts have been fairly clear in distinguishing between value and cost and have been fairly ready to concede that the amount which was paid for the property by a promoter or other vendor need not represent its *value* to the purchasing corporation.

For the purposes of our case study it will be convenient to consider three classes of cost that may be offered as evidence of the

[1] Hale, Robert L., Valuation and Rate-Making (New York, 1918).

value of property: (*a*) original cost of the property; (*b*) replacement or reproduction cost; (*c*) cost to the promoter or other vendor who sells the property to the corporation.

The first two classes of cost may be dismissed with a few words, as they figure only rarely in stock-watering litigation. On the other hand, the cost to the promoter or other vendor is perhaps as significant as any other type of evidence in stock-watering cases, and it therefore requires extended treatment.

Original Cost of the Property as Evidence of Its Value

In most kinds of judicial valuation, such as that arising in damage cases, the original cost of constructing or purchasing the property is relevant evidence of its present value only when no more pertinent evidence is available, or when there is good reason to suppose that subsequent material changes in value have not taken place. Not infrequently, where the original purchase or construction of the property is recent, original cost may be accepted as a rough measure of current replacement cost, which in turn may be taken as evidence of present value.

In stock-watering cases, however, original cost has not even been offered in evidence except on very rare occasions.[2] Even in those cases in which it has appeared as a part of the evidence, we do not find that it is relied upon to a material extent, and in a number of the cases it has been assigned practically no weight as evidence of the value. The reason for this is apparent when we recall that in stock-watering cases the courts are frankly concerned with the value of the property *at the time it was taken in payment for stock*. For obvious reasons the original cost of the property will not be pertinent to the question of the value *at that time* unless the cost was incurred at approximately the same time. In those few instances where this has been the case the original cost is substantially identical with the cost of reproduction and has been treated as such by the courts.[3]

From the promoter's standpoint the principal objection to original

[2] McClure v. Paducah Iron Co., *supra*, c. III, note 16; Gamble v. Queens County Water Co., *supra*, c. I, note 73; Hastings Malting Co. v. Iron Range Brewing Co., *supra*, c. III, note 15; Berry v. Rood, *supra*, c. III, note 36; Union Pacific R. Co. v. Blair, *supra*, c. III, note 34; Northwestern Mutual Life Ins. Co. v. Cotton Exchange Real Estate Co., *supra*, c. III, note 15.

[3] For example, Gamble v. Queens County Water Co., *supra;* Northwestern Mut. Life Ins. Co. v. Cotton Exchange, etc., Co., *supra*.

cost as a measure of the value of property for purposes of corporate capitalization is that it provides no stimulus to promotion.[4] This accounts in part, perhaps, for the rejection of this test of value by the courts, but its deficiencies as a measure of present value doubtless contribute to that result to a still greater extent.

Replacement Cost as Evidence of Value

The dominant weight given in many types of valuation, such as valuation for public utility rate control or valuation for measurement of damage liability, to the estimated cost of replacing the property is in striking contrast with the scant attention that this kind of evidence receives in stock-watering cases. As suggested in the previous chapter, the reason for this lies chiefly in the nature of the property that is valued in typical suits involving shareholders' liability. As a rule, the property turned over by the promoter is not of a standardized nature with an easily ascertainable replacement cost. Instead, it includes property of a more or less unique nature, such as a patent, or a site of land particularly available for an amusement park, or a group of manufacturing enterprises each of which was necessary, or is alleged to have been necessary, for the effectiveness of a consolidation or merger. Moreover, the date to which the valuation applies is frequently so remote in the past as to exclude the possibility of estimating the replacement cost with accuracy.

Nevertheless, there have been a few cases where the court has apparently given some weight to the estimated cost of replacing all or part of the property in question, and the more important of these cases may now be mentioned.

In *See v. Heppenheimer*[5] the receiver of the Columbia Straw-Paper Company sought to collect an unpaid balance on stock. The stock had been issued for thirty-nine competing mills engaged in the manufacture of wrapping paper from straw. The total amount of stock issued to form the consolidation was based upon an estimate of future profits computed on the assumption that the enterprise would dominate the industry and that it would be in a position to charge monopoly prices for the product. The ultimate question for decision in the case was whether the stock was paid up in a manner

[4] *Cf.* U. S. Industrial Commission, Reports (1900–1902), Vol. XIX, pp. 408–12.

[5] 69 N. J. Eq. 36, 61 Atl. 843 (1905).

such as would relieve the shareholders from liability to creditors. Restating the issue, the court said that the question raised by the pleadings was whether it was legitimate and proper to base the valuation of property for stock-issue purposes upon a capitalization of anticipated profits. This question the court answered in the negative, but its decision imposing a liability upon shareholders for an unpaid balance on the stock rested upon the special circumstances of the case.[6]

Among the many factors contributing to the court's decision were the following: (*a*) the company was organized by "dummies" who knew nothing of the straw paper business; (*b*) the directors and shareholders who authorized the issuance of the stock for the mills were totally ignorant of the value of the properties and of the business risks incident to their operation; (*c*) there was no independent and unbiased appraisal of the properties such as was contemplated by the statute; (*d*) the only appraisal that was made was a self-interested one made on behalf of the promoters, and the basis of its computation was a capitalization of anticipated profits; (*e*) in computing these profits the promoters assumed that a monopoly would be attained. This assumption ignored the ease with which the plants could be reproduced and operated at a profit in an artificially maintained market; (*f*) large stock bonuses were given to the purchasers of bonds; and finally, (*g*) the plants were obtained on options the total amount of which was only about half of the amount of stock issued in order to take them up.

In the face of so many factors upon which the decision was grounded it is not possible to state precisely the rôle played by the fact that the properties involved were easily reproducible. It seems probable, however, that this was an important element in the decision reached. On its face it appears unreasonable to compute the value of a consolidation of competing plants by capitalizing anticipated profits, if, in the estimate of profits, the fact that the plants are easily reproduced is ignored. There is considerable language in the opinion to indicate that the court accepted the view just stated.[7] For this reason we regard the *See* case as one in which a significant rôle was played by the cost of reproduction as evidence

[6] *Cf.* Railway Review v. Groff Drill & Machine Tool Co., 84 N. J. Eq. 321, 91 Atl. 1021 (1914), *aff'd,* 84 N. J. Eq. 508, 96 Atl. 1103 (1915); Gamble v. Queens County Water Co., *supra,* note 2.

[7] 69 N. J. Eq. 36, 42–50, 64, 72, 61 Atl. 843, 846–49, 854, 857 (1905).

of value, even though no exact data concerning that cost appeared in the evidence.

Gamble v. Queens County Water Co.[8] was a suit by minority shareholders to enjoin an issue of $60,000 in bonds and $50,000 in capital stock for a completed waterworks constructed by one of the directors of the defendant company. The proposed issues had been approved by a large majority of the shareholders, but the minority shareholders (the plaintiffs here) contended that, inasmuch as the construction of the property had cost the vendor director only about $69,000, including interest on the investment during construction and an allowance of $8,000 for supervision, the proposal would contravene the section of the New York Stock Corporation Law which permitted the issue of stock for property only to the extent of the " value thereof."

Judgment below was for the plaintiff on the basis of the finding of the trial court that the net cost of the property was $61,000. On appeal to the New York Court of Appeals the judgment below was reversed and a new trial ordered to proceed in accord with the principles of law announced by the Court of Appeals. These principles required the taking into account not only of the costs of supervision and interest during construction, but also of a fair profit to the contractor, the increase in the market value of pipe over the actual cost of the pipe laid, the potential losses to the defendant company due to competition of the new waterworks if it were not bought, and, finally, the prospects of an enhanced value of the property in the future due to the growth of the community served. The court said that the question was whether $110,000 was a *reasonable price* for the company to pay in view of all the factors just mentioned.

The standard of valuation suggested by the rules laid down by the court is a combination of cost of reproduction as a lower limit and the capitalized value of prospective earnings as an upper limit. Cost of reproduction was definitely included by the ruling of the court that a reasonable valuation would cover a fair profit to the contractor as well as the enhancement in the value of the pipe represented by the difference between spot prices at the time the completed works were offered to the company and the actual cost of the pipe to the contractor. Perhaps if creditors' rights had been involved, the court would not have been so liberal in allowing the

[8] *Supra,* c. I, note 73. *Cf.* Union Pacific R. Co. v. Blair, *supra,* note 2.

inclusion of anticipated profits, but the fact remains that under the circumstances of the case the cost of reproducing the property played a significant role in determining the outcome of the suit. The judgment below, based upon an exclusion of certain elements in the cost of reproducing the property, was reversed largely because of that exclusion.[9]

In *McClure v. Paducah Iron Co.*[10] a creditor sued to collect from shareholders an alleged unpaid balance on stock issued for an idle furnace. The furnace belonged to a Missouri corporation which had bought it secondhand. It had dismantled it at its original location, transported it to Missouri and erected it there at a cost of $113,000. This corporation became indebted to its directors and in order to liquidate the debt it sold the furnace to a Kentucky corporation in full payment for $100,000 of the stock of the latter company. The stock was then distributed among the directors of the Missouri corporation (the individual defendants in this suit) in satisfaction of their claims, at the rate of $100 of stock for every $50 of debt due.

The Kentucky corporation dismantled the furnace and had it reërected on its property in Tennessee. The cost of dismantling, transportation, and modernized reërection in Tennessee was $40,000. The Kentucky corporation became insolvent and this suit ensued.

The evidence disclosed that the original cost of the furnace erected in Missouri was $113,000; that a large part of this cost covered transportation and erection expense; that even then it was only a secondhand furnace; that the sale of the furnace to the Kentucky corporation was, in part at least, an arrangement whereby the Missouri corporation could liquidate its debt to the defendants; that the defendants took their stock at the rate of twice the face amount of their debt; and that a new and modern furnace could have been erected in Tennessee for not over $100,000. The only opposing evidence was testimony by the defendants that the company would have paid $100,000 in cash for the furnace if it had had the cash.

The evidence mainly relied upon by the court in adjudging the defendants liable to the plaintiff creditor was the fact that a modern, new furnace could have been erected in Tennessee for $100,000, whereas the one acquired by the company for $100,000 of stock was an old one located a great distance from the point at which it was

[9] *Cf.* Shickle v. Watts, *supra*, c. III, note 34.

[10] 90 Mo. App. 567 (1901).

intended to be used, and the fact that the defendants took the stock so issued as though it were worth only fifty cents on the dollar.

As we see it, the court regarded the cost of erecting even better facilities as conclusive evidence that the old furnace was overvalued, and it regarded the manner in which the directors disposed of the stock as evidence that they were well aware that they were overvaluing the furnace. This is a reasonable interpretation of the decision, although not an inevitable one. It should be observed that the plaintiff's claims were relatively small and all that the court had to find to sustain its judgment was sufficient overvaluation to cover those claims. An additional element supporting the decision was the fact that the defendants controlled both the selling and the purchasing corporation.

Finally we may quote from the language of the court in *Grant v. East & West R. Co.*[11] where the propriety of capitalizing a railroad at a figure at least as great as its cost of reproduction, provided this sum is supported by earning power, is emphasized. The court said:

> There could be no fraud or badge of fraud in such a purchaser [at a forced sale] claiming the benefit of his bargain, and valuing his property, when repaired and extended, according to its capacity to make net earnings, and according to what it would cost to build and equip such a road, then and there, if it had never been built, and the right of way had yet to be acquired, and the road built from the stump. On this subject it can hardly be claimed that the testimony is conflicting.[12]

Judged by these cases, cost of reproduction may at times be pertinent evidence of the present value of property for purposes of stock issue, but no case has been found where cost of reproduction has been accepted as conclusive evidence of that value, nor have we found a case in which the sole evidence offered was this type of cost. In consequence it is impossible to attach a precise significance to cost of reproduction as evidence in stock-watering cases. It is clear, however, that there may be circumstances wherein it may be the decisive evidence. For example, it is doubtful whether a court would allow shareholders to escape a liability to creditors where the amount of stock issued for property exceeds its cost of reproduction, provided the time element is not important.[13] On the other hand,

[11] 54 Fed. 569 (C. C. A., 5th Cir., 1893).

[12] *Ibid.*, p. 576.

[13] See Atwell v. Schmitt, 111 Or. 96, 225 Pac. 325 (1924). But a court might uphold a valuation which exceeded the reproduction cost of the *tangible* property alone.

would a court ever impose a liability where it is shown that the cost of reproduction is in excess of the amount of stock issued for the property? Probably it would do so if the evidence showed that the company could not reasonably have paid as much as the reproduction cost for the property. For example, a factory equipped and adapted for the manufacture of bicycles might cost $1,000,000 to duplicate and yet a price of $500,000 for it might be unconscionably high if the machinery is to be junked and the structure used to house a woolen mill.

Cost to the Promoter as Evidence of Value

Although neither the original cost of constructing or purchasing the property, nor the estimated cost of replacement, has played a significant rôle in valuation to determine whether stock has been fully paid, the cost of the property to the promoter has played a highly important rôle. Even this type of cost, however, is rarely if ever accepted as sufficient evidence in the absence of other substantiating circumstances.

The cost to promoters of property acquired by them and later turned over to the corporation appears in various forms. In some instances the promoters purchase the property with their own cash or with cash supplied to them for the purpose by others.[14] In other instances they make a partial payment in cash and later fulfill a promise to deliver to the vendors of the property certain of the securities to be issued for the property.[15] These securities may be

[14] For example, Rathbone v. Ayer, *supra*, c. III, note 21; Lea v. Iron Belt Mercantile Co., *supra*, c. III, note 17; Northwestern Mut. Life Ins. Co. v. Cotton Exchange Real Estate Co., *supra*, c. III, note 15; Babbitt v. Read, *supra*, c. III, note 10; *In re* Phoenix Hardware Co., 249 Fed. 410 (C. C. A., 9th Cir., 1918); Libby v. Tobey, *supra*, c. III, note 42; De Shelter v. American Spring Water Supply Co., *supra*, c. III, note 30; Hastings Malting Co. v. Iron Range Brewing Co., *supra*, c. III, note 34; Berry v. Rood, *supra*, c. III, note 36; Rumsey Manufacturing Co. v. Kaime, *supra*, c. III, note 36; Flint v. Sebastian, 317 Mo. 1344, 300 S. W. 798 (1927); Hebberd v. Southwestern Land & Cattle Co., 55 N. J. Eq. 18, 36 Atl. 122 (1896); Gamble v. Queens County Water Co., *supra*, note 2; Atwell v. Schmitt, *supra*, note 13.

[15] Garden City Sand Co. v. American Refuse Crematory Co., *supra*, c. III, note 33; Elyton Land Co. v. Birmingham Warehouse & Elevator Co., *supra*, c. III, note 15; Wallace v. Carpenter Electric Heating Manufacturing Co., *supra*, c. I, note 25; Gilkie & Anson Co. v. Dawson Town & Gas Co., *supra*, c. III, note 17; Penfield v. Dawson Town & Gas Co., *supra*, c. III, note 35; Wolcott v. Waldstein, *supra*, c. III, note 60; Finletter v. Acetylene Light, Heat & Power Co., *supra*, c. IV, note 7.

either bonds or stock, or both. Sometimes the promoters effect a purchase by a small cash payment and an assumption of debt, which latter may or may not be assumed later by the corporation.[16] In other cases the promoters have acquired property without making any cash payment whatever. In such instances the vendor to them accepts payment solely in corporate securities and assumptions of liabilities by the corporation.[17] In still other cases, where stock is issued to the promoters for mere options to purchase property, the cost of them is nil except for their time and expense in securing the options.[18] Likewise, where the corporation reimburses the promoter in cash for all actual outlays incurred in acquiring the property and issues him stock in addition, the cost to the promoter is nil.[19]

Although economists generally accept the theory that commodities which are competitively produced and sold tend, " in the long run," to sell at prices equal to their respective costs of production, they also agree that at any given moment the cost of producing a commodity bears no necessary or definite relation to its value. The same absence of relationship exists at any given time between the cost to the present owner, who is not the original owner or producer, and value or price of the thing owned. The price at which one may be willing to sell a certain commodity may be affected by the price which one paid for it. But this mental attitude will not necessarily influence the terms of its sale nor will it necessarily determine the command which the thing owned may have over other commodities in direct exchange. At any given time people may pay too much or too little for property, and the significance of the quantitative terms will ordinarily change with the times.

The ultimate question to be decided in an action by a creditor to

[16] Huntington v. Attrill, *supra,* c. III, note 21; *Cf.,* Bottlers Seal Co. v. Rainey, *supra,* c. III, note 17.

[17] National Bank of Merrill v. Illinois & Wisconsin Lumber Co., 101 Wisc. 247, 77 N. W. 185 (1898); Scott v. Barton, 285 Mo. 427, 226 S. W. 958 (1920); Wetherbee v. Baker, *supra,* c. I, note 23; See v. Heppenheimer, *supra,* note 5 (with respect to those vendors who accepted payment in securities); Tooker v. National Sugar Refining Co., *supra,* c. II, note 15; Bailey v. Pittsburg & Connellsville Gas Coal & Coke Co., *supra,* c. II, note 13.

[18] Douglass v. Ireland, *supra,* c. III, note 5; Davies v. Ball, 64 Wash. 292, 116 Pac. 833 (1911); Atwell v. Schmitt, *supra,* note 13.

[19] *In re* Universal Rubber Products Co., 15 Fed. (2d) 62 (D. C., W. D. Penna., 1926); Enright v. Heckscher, *supra,* c. III, note 17; Clinton Mining & Mineral Co. v. Jamison, *supra,* c. III, note 15.

enforce a shareholder's liability on part-paid stock is whether and to what extent the plaintiff should recover. If the rule of law in this connection were that whenever property has been turned over to a corporation for an amount of stock in excess of the value of the former, a liability arises for the difference, then a mere finding of the fact of overvaluation would be conclusive of the ultimate question. But since, by judicial construction and by the terms of many of the statutes, the liability arises in most cases because of *fraud,* actual or constructive, the condition precedent to liability on the part of the stockholder must be something other than the mere fact of overvaluation. Excessive and unreasonable valuation [20] is the essential in the majority of cases. Hence, we should expect to find two types of evidence in every such case. The first would be designed to prove whether or not the value of the consideration was less than the par value of the stock issued therefor. The second would be intended to show whether or not any overvaluation, assuming it to have been made, was the result of an honest mistake in judgment, which might reasonably have been made by the average prudent business man acting in the light of conditions prevailing at the time the stock was issued.[21]

From a logical standpoint we cannot say that evidence concerning the cost of property to promoters should, of necessity, fall within the limits of either of the above types, since it does not follow that property is worth either more or less than it cost the promoter, or exactly what it cost him, and, *a fortiori*, it does not follow that the directors were actually or constructively aware of a discrepancy. In all ordinary cases this would be true, whether the promoter effected the purchase with cash or with the promise of only a part of the securities which he later arranged to have issued to himself for the thing purchased, for he may have acquired the property at a genuine bargain. Under certain hypothetical circumstances, however, the cost of property to the promoter might well be regarded as conclusive evidence that he overvalued the property when he

[20] *Cf.* Chapter III, *supra.*

[21] In most cases, however, the courts do not distinguish the two types of evidence, or rather the two questions on which the evidence is thought to bear. It is frequently impossible to determine whether the court is reviewing the proofs as evidence which is pertinent to the one or to the other. In actual effect the two questions are for the most part lumped together in the composite query, "was the valuation such as a prudent business man might have made *under the circumstances.*"

exchanged it for stock, and that he knew that he was doing so. This would be the case if the property consisted entirely of readily reproducible goods which the promoter bought at the regular market price and which he immediately turned over to a corporation at an advance in price. Property of this type does not often appear in stock-watering cases, however, because it does not suit the promoter's purpose.[22] As a rule, the kinds of property which one encounters in stock-watering cases possess some degree of uniqueness, and hence no logical inference concerning its present value can be deduced from the mere fact that the promoter paid a certain sum for property at some time in the past.[23]

Even in those cases where the net cost of property to the promoter is nil, we cannot draw any conclusive inference that the property is worthless at the time or later. A promoter may obtain options to buy property at a price of $100,000 without paying anything for the options. The identical property may be worth $200,000 to an enterprise which is capable of financing its exploitation. Under such circumstances no necessary inference of overvaluation follows from proof of the fact that the promoter delivered the optioned property to a newly organized corporation in exchange for $100,000 in first mortgage bonds and $100,000 in stock, of which latter he returned $50,000 to the corporate treasury to be sold for a working capital of $25,000. After delivering the mortgage bonds to the former owners by way of payment of the option price, the promoter has in hand $50,000 of stock which does not necessarily represent an overvaluation, if by " value " is meant the average prudent business man's estimate of the economic worth of the property to the corporation which acquired it in the manner indicated.

Although, for the reasons just suggested, the cost of property to the promoter is not conclusive proof of its value at the time when it

[22] *Cf.* pp. 98–99, *supra.*

[23] But see the following: Atwell v. Schmitt, *supra,* note 13; Enright v. Heckscher, *supra,* note 19; Flint v. Sebastian, *supra,* note 14. *Cf.* Babbitt v. Read, *supra,* note 14. In these cases it appeared that the promoters acquired property at relatively low prices and turned it over to the corporation immediately at a very considerable advance in price when identical property, or equally good property for the corporation's purpose, could then have been acquired at prices equal to or less than the prices paid by the promoters. In only one of these cases, however, did the court fix the value of the property at exactly its cost to the promoters. Flint v. Sebastian, *supra.* But a liability was imposed upon defendant shareholders in each case.

was exchanged for stock, it may nevertheless be admitted as *evidence* of that value, along with other evidence.

A study of the cases discloses that more or less probative significance is assigned to the cost of the promoter's interest, depending upon the circumstances of each particular case. For example, in *Atwell v. Schmitt* [24] where the promoters acquired, at a cash cost of not over $400, options to purchase about 3,000 acres of orchard land at about the prevailing market price for such land, other equally good land being obtainable at the same price, and immediately in their capacity as the sole directors of a corporation organized for the purpose of acquiring this land, authorized and issued to themselves $200,000 of stock for the options, the court held that the transaction was *conclusively fraudulent* and that nothing had been paid on the stock.[25] It said, in part:

> It is obvious that if these options, upon which nothing had been paid and which merely conferred the right to purchase the optioned lands for a price equal to, if not in excess of, their market value, and which had been procured at but slight expense and under circumstances showing that options for the purchase of other lands in that vicinity equally as good and upon equally as good terms could have been readily procured, had been transferred to the corporation by third parties dealing with it at arm's length, in sole consideration of the issuance and delivery to them of the capital stock of the corporation of the par value of $150,000, the transaction would have been presumed to be fraudulent, which presumption could be overcome only, if at all, by the strongest kind of showing of good faith upon the part of all of the parties engaged in the transaction. But where it also appears, as it does here, that the parties transferring these options to the corporation at such a gross overvaluation were the very parties who pretended to accept the transfer on behalf of the corporation and that they alone were in the control of the corporation and that the personal interest of each was subserved by the acceptance of the transfer in exchange for the stock, it conclusively establishes fraud. In the transaction involved here there was not such an exercise of judgment by the directors as to the value of the options as the statute intended should be exercised

[24] *Supra*, note 13.

[25] The defendant was one of the organizers of the corporation who had received $22,250 of stock for his *pro rata* interest in the options, he and his associates having contributed equally to an organization fund of $700. Of this fund $400 was spent in acquiring the options. The balance of $300 was returned to the promoters. The court did not allow the defendant a credit on his stock equal to his share of the $400. The apparent reason for this is that equally good land could have been bought at or below the option prices.

by a board of directors in the purchase of property or stock, and for that reason the pretended exercise of judgment by the directors is not conclusive upon any creditor of the corporation. And from this it follows that the defendant's indebtedness to the corporation upon his subscription, which exceeds the amount of plaintiff's judgment, is wholly unpaid and should be subjected to the payment of plaintiff's judgment so far as necessary to satisfy said judgment.

Likewise, in *Flint v. Sebastian* [26] the promoters bought oil leases in a "wild-cat" territory at a cost of approximately $10,000 and immediately assigned these leases in payment of subscriptions for $270,000 of stock in a corporation which they organized to exploit the leases. The defendants, who were incorporators and original subscribers for this stock, had subscribed for $225,000 of it in proportion to their respective contributions to the $10,000 promotion fund. Testimony below by credible witnesses showed that oil leases of the character here involved were selling in the vicinity at from $1 to $5 per acre and that many of the leases acquired by the defendants and assigned to the corporation were purchased at these prices. The plaintiff was a judgment creditor of the corporation in the amount of $8,441. Judgment below for the plaintiff was had for this sum, plus $1,662.67 and costs. The trial court found that the unpaid balance on the defendants' $225,000 of stock was $216,-562.50. This sum is almost exactly the difference between the par value of the stock and 225/270 of the cost of the leases to the promoters. In sustaining the judgment below the Missouri Supreme Court said in part:

The court's finding as to the respective amounts unpaid on the stock subscriptions of the defendants, and as to the respective amounts for which each is liable, are fully warranted by the official minutes of the special meetings of the stockholders of the company . . . in which they approved, ratified and confirmed the action of the company in issuing $270,000 of the capital stock to "its stockholders" in consideration for the transfer of certain oil leases, and by the testimony of the defendants Sebastian and Koerner to the effect that all of the stock subscribers, covering 270,000 shares, shared in the payment of $10,000 or $10,040 for said oil leases. . . . The holding of 225,000 shares of stock by these twelve defendants, and sharing proportionately in the total sum of $10,000 or $10,040 paid for 270,000 shares of stock, furnishes a sound and reasonable basis of calculation for the court's findings as to the respective amounts

[26] *Supra,* note 14.

paid by each of the defendants and the respective amounts remaining unpaid on the stock of each defendant.[27]

Here, it seems, the trial court used the cost to the promoters as the measure of the value of the property to the corporation and the appellate court found no error in that procedure. The correspondence between cost and value can hardly be considered an accident. The only other evidence in the case was testimony that equally good land could then have been bought in quantities at the same price as that which the promoters paid, and testimony that the leases were appraised at $200 two years after the corporation was organized.

Similarly, in *Babbitt v. Read* [28] where the cost of coal lands to the promoters was approximately one-sixth of the sum at which they capitalized it, the court said:

As to Read [one of the promoters and a defendant in the action], . . . the mere situation shows the character of the undertaking. The total money expended in purchasing coal properties was $1,150,000, or about one-sixth of the capitalization. It is, of course, conceivable that the promoters got such a fabulous bargain as this; but how likely is it? Moreover, if it were such a good bargain and the coal remained, as it did, it is scarcely possible that it should lose so much of its value as never to be able to pay a dividend, though subsequently organized on about its cost basis. The sale value of coal thereabouts was not more than $20 per acre, and the necessary value to justify the capitalization was over $140. . . .

Moreover, to suppose that these coal lands were so little subject to competition that one could buy them at one-seventh of their value is wholly unwarranted. The region was known, it was being freely exploited already, it was no secret El Dorado; if the lands had any such value in combination, it is not possible that the demand for them should not have created a higher price. Judge Mayer was therefore certainly right in finding that, whatever its value, the property as a whole was not worth more than $6,600,000. That was all he need find.[29]

[27] 317 Mo. 1344, 1364, 300 S. W. 798, 806 (1927).

[28] 236 Fed. 42, 46, 47 (C. C. A., 2d Cir., 1916), *aff'g*, 215 Fed. 395 (D. C., S. D. N. Y., 1914).

[29] The last sentence quoted deserves comment because it represents a fairly common situation in stock-watering cases. The capitalization was $6,-800,000. The legitimate claims of creditors against stockholders were less than $200,000. Hence, the ultimate fact necessary for the imposition of a liability upon the shareholders, so far as the question of valuation was concerned, was a finding that the property was worth not over $6,600,000. Even though the

And in *Rathbone v. Ayer*[30] the price paid by the promoters for an idle steel mill was $85,000, but they assigned it in payment of subscriptions for $500,000 of stock in a corporation which they organized. The trial justice considered that the cost price to the promoters was competent evidence both as to the good faith of the defendant directors and as a circumstance which might be taken into account in determining the value of the property, but that it alone was insufficient to cast upon the defendants the burden of proving that the property was not deliberately overvalued. For this reason judgment below was entered for the defendants. On appeal to the Appellate Division this judgment was reversed and a new trial ordered for the purpose of determining whether or not there was a deliberate overvaluation. In reversing the judgment below, the court said in part:

That the price paid for property is evidence of its value is too well settled to admit of discussion. . . .

The argument that the property when bought was the idle plant of a defunct corporation and when sold to the new corporation had become reanimated and thereby possessed of additional value is specious, and unsound. When bought it had the same elements and possibilities of value as when turned over to the corporation. That argument would apply to many purchases, particularly at auctions, where property is frequently and openly bought for speculative purposes. It has never been held, however, that the price paid was not evidence of value simply because the purchaser expected to make a profit. The answer to this and similar arguments is that the purchase price is sufficient evidence of value to put to his proof one who does not desire to be bound thereby. In the consideration of this question it should not be overlooked that this corporation did not create a demand or market for the plant. It was not the intention or expectation that the corporation should bring to the venture any additional capital, energy or ability beyond what these individuals possessed, and it

---

court may have believed that the property was not worth more than it cost the promoters, it was not necessary to find such a low value in order to hold the defendants liable. For this reason the case cannot be classed as one in which the test of value was the cost to the promoters, though the dicta of the court indicate that such would have been held if it had been necessary in order to give the plaintiffs complete satisfaction. But the relatively low cost to the promoters was accepted by the court as evidence of sufficient overvaluation to sustain a judgment for the plaintiffs.

[30] 121 App. Div. (N. Y.) 355, 105 N. Y. S. 1041 (1907), reversed on dissent of Kellogg, J., 196 N. Y. 503, 89 N. E. 1111 (1909).

is too plain for argument that under such circumstances the property was worth no more to them as a corporation than it would have been worth to them as individuals had they not covered themselves with the mantle of corporate protection. . . .

There was also such a remarkable disparity between the price paid by the defendant and his associates and the price at which they as individuals sold to themselves as directors the same property as to naturally suggest the necessity of an explanation not only as to this marvelously enhanced value but as to the rectitude of their motives and their good faith in selling the property to themselves as directors and in making such an extremely large profit out of the treasury of the corporation of which they were officers. . . .

It is apparent . . . from the opinion of the learned trial justice that he did not assume to determine any question of fact but erroneously held as a matter of law that the evidence of the prior purchase and sale of the property was insufficient to raise a question of fact for determination.[31]

Finally, in *Libby v. Tobey* [32] we find similar language to the effect that low acquisition cost to the promoters and immediate capitalization at a substantially higher figure constitute persuasive evidence of an excessive valuation. In this case twenty promoters acquired certain mineral rights at a cost of $7,500 and capitalized this property through the issuance of $225,000 in stock to themselves immediately thereafter. Of this stock they returned $60,000 to the treasury and most of the treasury stock was later sold for cash at 10 per cent of its par value (par $5 per share). The Maine statute concerning shareholders' liability to creditors was so worded as to charge shareholders with a liability on only such shares as the latter had *subscribed* for and held within certain time limits with respect to the date on which the creditor's claim was contracted. The court held the defendant liable on his *subscribed* shares in direct proportion

[31] 121 App. Div. (N. Y.) 355, 357, 358–59, 361, 362, 105 N. Y. S. 1041, 1043–44, 1045, 1046 (1907). On appeal the judgment of the Appellate Division was reversed and the judgment of the trial court was affirmed on the dissenting opinion of Kellogg, J. In the latter's view both the purchase price paid by the promoters and the price paid to them were evidence of the value of the property, but the two taken together did not establish a fraudulent overvaluation, since the discrepancy between the cost to the promoters and the cost to the corporation was the only evidence of an excessive overvaluation. The circumstances of the promoters' purchase were not in evidence and other evidence of the good faith of the promoters was strong enough to overshadow any presumption of bad faith which might arise from the discrepancy.

[32] *Supra*, c. III, note 42.

to the difference between the cost of the consideration to the promoters and the face value of the subscribed shares held by them after returning the $60,000 of stock to the treasury. The total number of shares so retained was 33,000 and the cost of the promoters' interest was $7,500. Hence the court held that only about twenty-three cents had been paid on each share and imposed a liability of $4.67 per share on the defendant. This was the exact difference between the cost of the property to the defendant and the par value of the shares subscribed and retained. The language of the court indicated its opinion that the low cost was evidence of an excessive overvaluation.

Other cases containing language to the same effect are cited in the footnote.[33] An examination of the language in these cases and those from which the above quotations are taken will reveal that these courts rely upon wide discrepancies between the cost of the promoters' interest and the capitalization thereof as evidence both of

[33] *In re* Phoenix Hardware Co., 249 Fed. 410, 413 (C. C. A., 9th Cir., 1918); *In re* Universal Rubber Products Co., 15 Fed. (2d) 62, 63–64 (D. C., W. D. Penna., 1926); Preston v. Cincinnati, C. & H. V. R. Co., 36 Fed. 54, 58 (C. C., S. D. Ohio, W. D., 1888), *aff'd,* 146 U. S. 630, 36 L. Ed. 1111, 13 Sup. Ct. 131 (1892); National Bank of America v. Pacific Ry. Co., 66 Ill. App. 320, 329 (1896), *mod.* and *aff'd,* 172 Ill. 149, 50 N. E. 19 (1898); Higgins v. Illinois Trust & Savings Bank, 193 Ill. 394, 400–01, 61 N. E. 1024, 1026 (1901), *aff'g* 96 Ill. App. 29 (1900); Cohen v. Toy Gun Manufacturing Co., 172 Ill. App. 331 (1912); Wallace v. Carpenter Electric Heating Manufacturing Co., 70 Minn. 321, 326, 328, 73 N. W. 189, 191–92 (1897); Shields v. Hobart, *supra,* c. III, note 36; Wetherbee v. Baker, *supra,* c. I, note 23; Hebberd v. Southwestern Land & Cattle Co., *supra,* note 14; Wolcott v. Waldstein, 86 N. J. Eq. 63, 64–65, 97 Atl. 951, 952 (1916); Huntington v. Attrill, 118 N. Y. 365, 375, 23 N. E. 544, 546 (1890); Bottlers Seal Co. v. Rainey, 243 N. Y. 333, 342–43, 153 N. E. 437, 440–41 (1926); Bailey v. Pittsburg & Connellsville Gas Coal & Coke Co., 69 Pa. St. 334, 339, 342 (1871); Union Pacific R. Co. v. Blair, 48 Utah 38, 47, 156 Pac. 948, 951 (1916); Manhattan Trust Co. v. Seattle Coal & Iron Co., 16 Wash. 499, 521, 48 Pac. 333, 340, 737 (1897), 19 Wash. 493, 515, 53 Pac. 951, 959 (1898) (dissenting opinion of Reavis, J.); National Bank of Merrill v. Illinois & Wisconsin Lumber Co., 101 Wisc. 247, 252–53, 77 N. W. 185, 187–88 (1898); Jackson v. Traer, 64 Iowa 469, 474, 20 N. W. 764, 766 (1884) (cancellation of debt for stock); Tooker v. National Sugar Refining Co., 80 N. J. Eq. 305, 314, 84 Atl. 10, 15 (1912). *Cf.* Voorhees v. Malott, 73 N. J. Eq. 673, 69 Atl. 643 (1908).

In the majority of these cases the language of the courts is directly in line with that quoted in the text above. In a few instances the language is less direct, but it seems to foot up to the same position as the language in the others.

overvaluation and of bad faith in making the overvaluation, though standing alone this evidence is never accepted as conclusive of either fact. Furthermore, there appears to be no basis in the courts' treatment of this item as evidence for a distinction between the meaning of "overvaluation" determined without regard to the directors' state of mind and that sort of overvaluation which must be found in jurisdictions which require the directors' opinion to be taken into account. A discrepancy between cost to the promoters and capitalization appears to be equally probative of the one as of the other. So far as the question of valuation is at issue, the ultimate question in either case appears to be "Was the directors' valuation unreasonable?" or, to put it positively, "Was the directors' valuation such as might have been made by reasonable men?"

In contrast to the above cases we find a number of cases in which the courts deny that a discrepancy between cost to the promoter and the par value of the stock issued is persuasive evidence of either an overvaluation or knowledge thereof. Considerations of space will not permit us to set forth these opinions in detail. The idea finds its clearest expression in the cases cited in the footnote below.[34] Reference to these opinions, and to those *contra* cited above, will indicate that the probative significance assigned to a discrepancy between cost to the promoters and capitalization is to a considerable degree dependent upon the peculiar circumstances of each case. No crystallized rule of probative significance has been developed in this connection, which is another way of saying that, standing alone, a discrepancy between promoters' cost and capitalization has no necessary bearing as evidence upon the question whether or not

[34] Clinton Mining & Mineral Co. v. Jamison, 256 Fed. 577, 581–82 (C. C. A., 3d Cir., 1919); Gamble v. Queens County Water Co., 123 N. Y. 91, 102 *et seq.*, 25 N. E. 201, 203 *et seq.* (1890); Rathbone v. Ayer, 196 N. Y. 503, 89 N. E. 1111 (1909), *rev'g* 121 App. Div. (N. Y.) 355, 105 N. Y. S. 1041 (1907), on dissent of Kellogg, J.; McMahon v. Pneumatic Transit Co., 85 N. J. Eq. 544, 547, 548, 96 Atl. 999–1000 (1916); Grant v. East & West R. Co. of Ala., 54 Fed. 569, 576 (C. C. A., 5th Cir., 1893); Union Pacific R. Co. v. Blair, 48 Utah 38, 54–56, 156 Pac. 948, 954 (1916) — opinion on application for a rehearing. See also: National Bank of America v. Pacific Ry. Co., *supra*, note 33; Finletter v. Acetylene Light, Heat & Power Co., *supra*, c. IV, note 7; Thomas v. Barthold, 171 S. W. 1071, 1073 (Tex. Civ. App., 1914), *rev'd*, 210 S. W. 506 (1919); Commonwealth v. Central Passenger Ry., 52 Pa. St. 506, 514–15 (1866); People *ex rel.* Westchester Street Railroad Co. v. Public Service Commission, 210 N. Y. 456, 104 N. E. 952 (1914), motion for rehearing denied, 211 N. Y. 533, 105 N. E. 1095 (1914).

a liability shall be imposed upon shareholders, or whether the stock is otherwise subject to legal disabilities because of the value of the consideration for which it was issued.

So much for the language used by the courts in this connection. Turning now to the decisions in cases in which the evidence disclosed the price which the promoter paid for the consideration given for his stock, we find a number in which the value found by the court exactly equalled the cost to the promoters.[35] Thus, from the standpoint of results, cost to the promoter appears to be very persuasive evidence of value. In the majority of these cases the purchase of the property by the promoter and its sale to the corporation for stock occurred almost simultaneously, thus eliminating the time element. Under such circumstances the price which the promoter paid is likely to be considered more persuasive evidence of value than it would be if a considerable time had intervened during which changes in value might occur. Although courts never say that promoters' cost is conclusive evidence of value, the large number of cases in which the value determined by the fact-finding body was identical with the promoter's cost indicates that fact-finding bodies tend to regard such evidence as substantially conclusive under many circumstances.

Where the net cost to the promoter is nil this result is easy to understand, since here the promoter contributes nothing to the enterprise except his conception of it, and promotional imagination is, by its nature, too intangible and too uncertain in value to receive very friendly treatment at the hands of courts charged with the duty of protecting creditors and innocent investors.

On the other hand, where the promoter has incurred an actual cash or other cost in assembling his enterprise, the refusal of many courts to sanction a higher capitalization is more difficult to under-

[35] Libby v. Tobey, *supra,* c. III, note 42; Flint v. Sebastian, *supra,* note 14; Higgins v. Illinois Trust & Savings Bank, *supra,* note 33; Foote v. Illinois Trust & Savings Bank, 194 Ill. 600, 62 N. E. 834 (1902); Garden City Sand Co. v. American Refuse Crematory Co., *supra,* c. III, note 33; *In re* Phoenix Hardware Co., *supra,* note 14; Shields v. Hobart, *supra,* c. III, note 36; Hebberd v. Southwestern Land & Cattle Co., *supra,* note 14; Jackson v. Traer, *supra,* note 33; Cohen v. Toy Gun Manufacturing Co., *supra,* note 33; Macbeth v. Banfield, *supra,* c. III, note 18; Wolcott v. Waldstein, *supra,* note 33; Bottlers Seal Co. v. Rainey, *supra,* c. III, note 17; Wetherbee v. Baker, *supra,* c. I, note 23; Bailey v. Pittsburg & Connellsville, etc., Co., *supra,* c. II, note 13; Tooker v. National Sugar Refining Co., *supra,* c. II, note 15; See v. Heppenheimer, *supra,* note 5. See also Atwell v. Schmitt, *supra,* note 13; Preston v. Cincinnati, etc., R. Co., *supra,* c. I, note 36.

stand except in terms of a recurrent inability of promoters to substantiate a higher valuation in terms which are comprehensible and legitimate from the standpoint of the average prudent men of which juries are supposedly composed. The practical effect of evidence as to promoters' costs seems to be that it throws upon the defendant shareholder the burden of justifying a higher valuation. In the case of a new enterprise this justification can generally take no other form than a showing of hopeful expectations, which are likely to be heavily discounted by juries in the face of the subsequent history of the enterprise belying these expectations. Certainly logic alone would not justify the erection of promoters' cost into an immutable standard of value. Nor has this been done, as the next group of cases to be mentioned will indicate.

In a number of cases where the evidence has disclosed the cost of property to the promoter, the courts have refused to base their findings of value upon that figure and have allowed shareholders a credit on their stock for a larger sum. For example, in *Enright v. Heckscher*[36] the cost to the promoter of certain mining locations was $880. In this case the enterprise was a going concern in need of funds for expansion. The mining locations were acquired by one of the directors at the cost indicated, and the company reimbursed him for his outlays. He surrendered these locations to the company for an issue of $1,000,000 of "fully-paid" stock and immediately donated the entire issue to the corporate treasury. A contract for the resale of this stock for $500,000 in cash had already been entered into, the defendant Heckscher taking half of it for a cash payment of $250,000 and the other half being taken by a banking firm for a like payment. Thus the corporation received for its $1,000,000 of stock $500,000 in cash and the surplus value of the mining locations over and above their cost of $880. In a suit by the trustee in bankruptcy against Heckscher to collect an unpaid balance of $250,000 on his stock for the payment of creditors, the trial court gave judgment for the plaintiff in the amount of $105,979.35. The difference between this sum and $250,000, the sum sued for, can only be accounted for in terms of a value assigned to the options in excess of its cost.

Similarly, in *De Shelter v. American Spring Water Supply Co.*[37] the cost to the promoters of a stock-in-trade, materials, etc., at a bankruptcy sale was $11,000. They capitalized this property at $49,-

[36] *Supra*, c. III, note 17. [37] *Supra*, c. III, note 30.

800 by an issue of stock. On a suit by a creditor against shareholders to collect an unpaid balance on the stock the court fixed the value of the property, as of the time when it was sold to the corporation, at $31,425. This was the exact price at which the corporation had sold its property two years after it had been organized and after many changes in the property had occurred. The fact that the promoters' cost was a price paid at a bankruptcy sale may explain the court's neglect of that item of evidence.

In *Rumsey Manufacturing Co. v. Kaime* [38] the promoters bought a stock-in-trade at a receiver's sale for $40,000. The appraised value of the property at the time ranged from $78,000 to $102,000, though the basis of the appraisal did not appear. On the advice of counsel that they could capitalize the property at its " full market value " the promoters exchanged the property for $75,000 of " full-paid " stock.[39] On a suit by a judgment creditor against shareholders to collect an unpaid balance on the stock, the trial court placed the value of the property at $57,000, thus holding the stock to be 24 per cent unpaid, and it ordered an assessment of 24 per cent against the defendant's stock. The judgment below was affirmed on appeal.

In *Finletter v. Acetylene Light, Heat & Power Co.*[40] the cost to the promoter of a license under a patent was $100,000 in cash and $500,000 of the stock issued to him for an assignment of his rights under the license. The corporation paid him $100,000 cash and $1,-400,000 in stock for his rights. The court held that the discrepancy between cost and capitalization did not raise any presumption of fraudulent overvaluation. The language of the court indicates that it regarded the rights as having been worth what the corporation paid for them.

In *Union Pacific R. Co. v. Blair* [41] sheep which cost the promoters about $2.75 a head were transferred about three months later to the corporation for stock at the rate of about $3.50 per head, the then

[38] *Supra,* c. III, note 36.

[39] The facts as reported are not clear. Either the promoters paid $60,000 for the property ($40,000 cash and assumption of $20,000 in liabilities), and capitalized it at $95,000, or they paid $40,000 cash for property which they capitalized at $75,000. In either case the net result was that property which they bought at $40,000, net, was capitalized at $75,000.

[40] *Supra,* c. IV, note 7. *Cf.* McMahon v. Pneumatic Transit Co., *supra,* note 34; Clinton Mining & Mineral Co. v. Jamison, *supra,* c. III, note 15.

[41] *Supra,* note 34.

prevailing market price. The stock so issued was held to be fully paid.

In *Gamble v. Queens County Water Co.*[42] a waterworks cost the vendor to the corporation about $69,000. The court held that this was not a measure of its value to the corporation and ordered a new trial with instructions to include in the value a fair profit to the vendor, as well as other items.

Other cases in which the court's conclusion concerning the value of property appears to bear no close relation to its cost to the vendor are cited in the footnote.[43] In most of these cases the value fixed by the court has been in excess of promoter's cost, though in a few of them the court regarded the value as being less than the cost to the promoter. In many of them the property was bought at a receiver's or bankruptcy sale, or it had an independent market value, or sufficient time had elapsed between purchase and sale to invalidate cost as an index of value.

To determine what quantitative relationships, if any, have existed between the ratio of the promoter's cost to the amount of the capitalization, on the one hand, and the decision reached by the court in stock-watering cases, on the other, the writer has made a study of the cases cited in footnotes 14–43, *supra,* inclusive. Wherever it was possible to do so, the ratio of the promoter's cost to the amount of the capitalization, and a similar ratio of the value determined by the court to the amount of the capitalization, have been computed. On the basis of this study the following conclusions have been reached. First, there is no necessary relationship between the decision which a court will reach and the ratio of the promoter's cost to the amount of the capitalization. The mere fact that property cost the promoter less than the amount of stock for which he exchanged it does not compel a decision that the property was overvalued in the exchange. Second, a wide discrepancy between the cost to the promoter and the amount of the capitalization generally shifts the burden of justifying a valuation in excess of the promoter's cost upon

[42] *Supra,* note 2.

[43] Rathbone v. Ayer, *supra,* note 34; Grant v. East & West R. Co., *supra,* note 34; Carp v. Chipley, *supra,* c. III, note 36; Raleigh Investment Co. v. Bunker, *supra,* c. III, note 60; Holcombe v. Trenton White City Co., *supra,* c. III, note 7; Commonwealth v. Central Passenger Ry., *supra,* note 34; People *ex rel.* Westchester Street Railroad Co. v. Public Service Commission, *supra,* note 34; Gilkie & Anson Co. v. Dawson Town & Gas Co., *supra,* c. III, note 17, *contra,* Penfield v. Dawson Town & Gas Co., *supra,* c. III, note 35.

the defendant shareholders. Third, the lower the ratio of promoter's cost to the amount of the capitalization the greater is the tendency of the courts to hold that there was an overvaluation. Fourth, in a considerable number of cases the courts have valued the property at the precise sum that the promoter paid for it. This tendency is particularly strong in cases where only a relatively brief period of time has elapsed between the date on which the promoter bought and the time at which the stock was issued.

CHAPTER VI

CAPITALIZED EARNING POWER AS EVIDENCE OF THE VALUE OF PROPERTY

It is often asserted by writers in business finance, especially by those writers who are less critical than others of current business practices, that the proper basis of capitalizing a corporation is the prospective earning power of the company. The theory underlying this point of view is that the real value of a business property depends entirely on its power to earn dividends and interest for its security holders. What the property may have cost in the first place, and even what it would now cost to reproduce its physically, is irrelevant except in so far as it may have an indirect bearing on the earnings that may fairly be expected from the corporation.[1]

Whatever may be the merits of this contention, we have here to consider the extent to which estimates of probable earning power have been relied upon by the courts in their decisions as to whether stock has been issued in excess of the value of property. In most cases in which the opinion of the court makes any mention of such estimates, it appears that they have been brought forth by the de-

[1] For a clear expression of this point of view see LOUGH, WILLIAM H., BUSINESS FINANCE (New York, 1917), c. VIII. Many writers who assume that capitalized earning power is the proper basis of capitalization for industrial companies would concede that it is not the proper basis for public utility companies where the amount of securities outstanding may have a close effect upon the rates which a company is permitted to charge. The assumption, however, that even for public utilities capitalized earning power constitutes the proper basis of capitalization underlies a defense of Mr. Harriman's much criticised recapitalization of the Chicago & Alton Railroad as brought forth by his official biographer, Mr. George Kennan, in THE CHICAGO AND ALTON CASE: A MISUNDERSTOOD TRANSACTION (New York, 1916). See also, from the pen of a railroad executive, FINK, HENRY, FEDERAL REGULATION OF RAILROAD SECURITIES AND VALUATION OF RAILROAD PROPERTIES (Roanoke, Va., 1910).

There can be little doubt that the average business man regards earning power as the proper basis of corporate capitalization, and for the most part he has adhered to this theory in practice. See U. S. BUREAU OF CORPORATIONS, REPORT ON THE STEEL INDUSTRY (Washington, 1911), Pt. I, pp. xx–xxii, 37–38, 239–51; U. S. INDUSTRIAL COMMISSION, REPORTS (1900–1902), Vol. XIX, pp. 616–18, 409–10.

fendant stockholders as a means of rebutting the contention of the creditors to the effect that the property was overvalued. The most typical case is one where the creditors point to a large discrepancy between the price for which the promoters have bought or agreed to buy the property and the amount of stock which has been issued against this property, as evidence of an overvaluation, and where the promoters in rebuttal have pointed to the estimates of prospective earning power which were made at the time of the incorporation by themselves or by the directors as justifying the excess in the valuation of the property over the price which the promoters agreed to pay for it. The question which we must now raise is whether the courts have accepted these estimates of earning power as in any way relevant to the problem of a reasonable valuation. We must also consider with what degree of skepticism the courts may have treated these estimates in view of the fact that the subsequent failure of the company has clearly shown that they were not justified by the actual turn of events.

We may turn first to a series of cases before the New Jersey courts where the validity of capitalized past and prospective earnings has been treated at some length.

The New Jersey Cases

See v. Heppenheimer [2] is, perhaps, the best known and most widely cited case in this group. Because it is one of the most notable cases in the whole field of stockholders' liability suits we shall outline it in detail. The case arose upon a bill by the receiver of the Columbia Straw-Paper Company against Heppenheimer and other stockholders of the company to recover from the defendants an alleged unpaid balance on shares of stock held by them.

Certain New York and Chicago lawyers, together with several other persons, procured through a man acting as a "conduit of title," options to purchase thirty-nine plants for the manufacture of wrapping paper from straw with a view to consolidating these plants under the single ownership and operation of a new corporation. The object of the promoters was to secure a monopoly of the manufacture of straw paper, eliminating the destructive competition

[2] 69 N. J. Eq. 36, 61 Atl. 843 (1905). See also Northern Trust Co. v. Columbia Straw-Paper Co., 75 Fed. 936 (C. C., N. D. Ill., 1896); Dickerman v. Northern Trust Co., 80 Fed. 450 (C. C. A., 7th Cir., 1897), *aff'd*, 176 U. S. 181, 44 L. Ed. 423, 20 Sup. Ct. 311 (1900).

which had theretofore prevailed in the industry, and reaping large profits through the ability of the new company to raise the prices of its products.

By the terms of the options approximately $2,250,000 was to be paid for the plants to their respective owners. Mr. Samuel Untermyer, the dominant figure in the promotion and one of the defendants in the action, stated that this figure represented the "appraised" value of the several plants. The basis of the appraisal is not revealed in the reported opinion, but it appears that the prices offered in the options for the various plants included an allowance for the good will of each plant. Payment was to be made in cash, preferred stock and common stock, approximately one-third of the purchase price to be satisfied in each medium of payment mentioned, except that the common stock was to be taken *at 50 per cent of par value*. Thus, at the very start, the scheme of organization contemplated the disposal of some of the common stock by the promoters to the vendors at an acknowledged discount of 50 per cent.

The corporation was formed through the conventional method of using law clerks as incorporators and original directors. These figureheads resolved as stockholders, and later as directors, that the corporation accept from the conduit of title, who represented the promoters, the thirty-nine plants, plus $200,000 cash for working capital, in exchange for $3,000,000 of "full-paid" common stock, $1,000,000 of "full-paid" preferred stock, and $1,000,000 of 6 per cent first-mortgage bonds secured by the plants to be acquired. Their resolution stated that in their judgment the plants were "fully worth" $5,000,000.

The securities mentioned were issued to the promoters for the agreed consideration and the following disposition was made of them: [3]

a) The common stock		$3,000,000
To the owners of the mills at the rate of $100 of stock for every $50 of the purchase price agreed to be paid in common stock, at a discount of 50%	$1,500,000	

[3] The statement which follows is a digest of the facts as reported in 69 N. J. Eq. 36 (1905). The other cases cited in note 2, *supra*, arose out of the same promotion and the facts as there reported suggest that a somewhat different disposition may have been made. All of the reports, however, indicate that approximately $1,000,000 of the stock went to the promoters.

As a 40% bonus with each bond sold for cash to the public or taken by the mill owners in lieu of cash payment	400,000	1,900,000
Retained by the promoters		$1,100,000
b) The preferred stock		1,000,000
To the mill owners at par	$ 750,000	
As an additional bonus of 20% given with each bond sold for cash or taken by the mill owners in lieu of cash	200,000	950,000
Retained by the promoters		$ 50,000
c) The bonds		$1,000,000

These were sold to the public for cash at par or were taken by the mill owners in lieu of cash which the options provided should be paid to them for their mills. With each bond sold, or otherwise disposed of, there was given a stock bonus of 60% of the par value of the bonds, of which 40% was common stock and 20% preferred stock. The bonds, or the proceeds of their sale, were distributed as follows: :

To the mill owners	$ 750,000
To the corporation for working capital	200,000
To Mr. Untermyer's firm for legal fees	50,000

The net effect of these transactions was a transfer of thirty-nine mills and $200,000 in cash to the corporation for $5,000,000 in securities, the deal being handled by the promoters in such a way as to leave in their hands, after the mill owners had been paid for their mills, something over $1,000,000 in stock which purported to be fully paid and non-assessable.

The incorporators and original directors who resolved to make this exchange of securities for property were utterly ignorant of the paper-milling business in general and of the value of these specific plants which they authorized their corporation to acquire. The only information before them was a list of the mills. They were not supplied with information as to the prices to be paid to the several mill owners, the value by appraisal or otherwise of each mill separately, the separate earning capacity of each of the mills, the contents and general tenor of the options, or with the probable value of each mill to the new corporation. The only basis for the valuation which they placed on the mills as a group was the hopeful and optimistic picture painted for the enterprise by the leading promoter, Mr. Untermyer. They knew that the latter was confident that the earning capacity of the plants would justify a capitalization of $5,000,000, and they understood their function to be a letter-perfect compliance with the instructions of this promoter.

The evidence disclosed that Mr. Untermyer's estimate of the value of the properties was based upon a capitalization of the prospective profits of the company which the latter could supposedly earn as a monopolistic manufacturer of wrapping paper. He estimated that net earnings would amount to $900,000. This figure was computed by multiplying the 90,000-ton capacity of the mills by an anticipated net profit of $10 per ton. Profits in the immediate past had been negligible because of intense competition. The cost of producing this grade of paper was about $20 per ton, and the prevailing selling price was little more than the cost of production. But Untermyer estimated that consolidation would reduce the costs and that the product could be turned out by the monopoly at a cost of $18 per ton. He further estimated that the selling price for the product could be raised to $28 per ton and maintained at that level because of monopoly control.

The reported facts do not disclose whether Untermyer's estimate of output was based upon the total productive capacity of the mills or upon the amount actually produced by these mills in the past and moved to markets at prevailing prices. The figures indicate that the ratio of estimated earnings to total capitalization was 18 per cent. If the interest on the bonds ($60,000) be deducted from the total estimated earnings and the balance available for the common and preferred stock related to the total stock capitalization, the resultant ratio is 21 per cent, a rate of capitalization which would seem to take into account the normal hazards of such an enterprise.

The company was organized in December, 1892. In May, 1895 it became insolvent and went into an equity receivership. The principal reasons assigned for its failure were: first, bad management of its affairs due to the difficulty of securing adequate management for a new combination of widely scattered plants in an industry which had just passed through a period of cut-throat competition; second, the starting up of old mills and the building of new mills as soon as the corporation raised the price of the product; third, the introduction of wood pulp as a substitute raw material for the manufacture of wrapping paper (a fundamental change in the industry which had already been introduced to some extent at the time the combination was organized); and fourth, the financial depression of 1893.

The plaintiffs charged that the portion of the stock retained by the defendants was issued without any valid consideration whatever; that the stock was issued for overvalued property, the valuation of which included items which were in no sense " property "; and that the valuation of the property which was transferred to the corporation in exchange for the bonds and stock was consciously and fraudulently excessive. They further charged that the formal proceedings by which the directors valued the property were a mere sham and in no sense a compliance with the statute. And, finally, they claimed that the defendants were the holders of unpaid stock and were therefore liable to creditors both at common law and under the statute.

The defendant stockholders did not seriously dispute the fact that the consideration for which they, as promoters, had bought the property was less than the par value of the securities issued for it by the corporation, but they contended on numerous grounds that no liability should be imposed upon them. Leaving aside their technical claim that the court did not properly have jurisdiction, they set up the following defenses against a liability to the plaintiffs: first, that their stock was issued for property as the statute permitted; second, that the difference between the capitalization and the price paid to the vendors of the property was made up by a capitalization of expected earnings; third, that this excess of valuation over the price paid to the vendors was *also* made up by the item of good will; fourth, that mere proof of overvaluation, assuming it to have been a fact, was not enough, since the valuation was made in good faith and without fraudulent intent, the good faith being manifested by the fact that defendants had invested over $500,000 in cash and services (for both of which they received bonds and bonus stock); fifth, that the practice of issuing stock of a par value in excess of the value of the tangible property received for it was a common corporate practice and was sanctioned by long usage; sixth, that the defendants had already lost between $300,000 and $400,000 cash in this venture and should not be required to bear any further loss; seventh, that there was no proof that any creditor had actually relied on the capitalization, without which proof no liability could be established; and, finally, that the defendants should be allowed to set off, against any liability which might be found, the amount of the bonds of the company which they held.

Replies of the plaintiffs to some of these contentions were: that the defense of good faith had no place in a transaction of this kind where the thing valued, being a mere capitalization of expected earnings, was not "property"; that the defense of "good faith" should not avail the defendants because the evidence showed that there was *no actual appraisal* of the property by a competent and disinterested board of directors; and that the claim for a value of good will did not support a valuation over and above the promoters' option prices since these prices already included a separate and specific allowance for the good will of each plant.

Despite these plausible arguments by defendants, the court, in a decision which caused something like consternation among many of New York's most respectable lawyers, held that the stock retained by the promoters (which exceeded $1,000,000 in par value) was wholly unpaid, as was likewise the stock given as a bonus with the bonds. The distinguished attorney-promoter, Mr. Untermyer, who was the only solvent promoter within the jurisdiction of the court, was held primarily liable to the receiver to the extent of the full par value of all his share of the stock retained by the promoters, as well as to the extent of the par value of the bonus stock which passed through his hands. His law partners and one other recipient of the promotion stock were held to be liable to a like extent on promotion stock taken by them. Those transferees of the bonus stock who had notice of the manner of its issuance were held secondarily liable. The exact amount which the creditors were able to collect on account of this holding did not appear in the published record of the case, though it was indicated that the creditors' claims exceeded $200,000 in amount.

Vice-Chancellor Pitney opened his discussion of the law and the facts of the case by phrasing the issue as follows:

> In short, they estimated the value of the property upon a capitalization of the profits expected to be made out of its use by control of the price of its product. So that, taking the aspect of the case most favorable to the defendants, the question which arises out of its ultimate analysis is, whether, under our statute above cited, it is competent and lawful to make up the valuation of the visible property to be purchased for stock issued, by adding to the actual market value, or cost of its reproduction, a sum of money ascertained by the capitalization of the annual profits expected to be realized

from a favorable marketing of the product of the company by a suppression of competition. Or, as I believe I asked counsel in argument, can prospective profits, however promising, be considered as *property*, as that word is used in the statute above quoted? [4]

He did not attempt to give a complete answer to this question at once, though he did say that the word "*property*," as used in the statute, construed by its context "refers to something visible and tangible" and that,

> If the question above put be the true one it seems to me that it answers itself, and adversely to the contention of counsel of defendants.[5]

and later, that,

> The present case is a painful illustration of the utter impossibility of giving the word "property" the construction claimed for it.[6]

and finally, he indicated his view that prospective profits were not "property" under the statute in the following statement:

> If, then, the promoters of this enterprise and the directors, who assisted them in adopting the valuation in question, consciously included in their valuation thereof "an estimate of matters which really are not property," which I have shown they did, then there was a conscious overvaluation of the property which amounts to a fraud on the act.[7]

The court then disposed of the claim that the alleged deficiency in value was made up in "good will." It accepted plaintiff's argument that an allowance for the individual good will of each of the separate enterprises was included in the option prices and that to include in the capitalization of the Columbia Straw-Paper Company a still further allowance for good will would be to count this item twice. It noted, further, that the new company had not in fact developed any good will of its own independent of the good will of the separate plants, and that the scheme of organization contemplated a complete destruction of the old good will of the individual establishments. In this connection and more or less as an aside (for the de-

[4] 69 N. J. Eq. 36, 42, 61 Atl. 843, 846 (1905).

[5] *Ibid.*, 43, 61 Atl. 846.

[6] *Ibid.*, 46, 61 Atl. 847.

[7] *Ibid.*, 58, 61 Atl. 852. The context indicates that the court's reference to "matters which really are not property" related to alleged goodwill and to prospective earnings.

fendants do not appear to have urged the point) the court noted that the consolidation of the ownership of the thirty-nine mills did not increase the total productive capacity, nor did it increase the range of the farming country in the neighborhood of each from which it derived its raw material. It said :

They were, in the main, widely separated from each other, so that the case is in marked contrast with those which occur where several properties lying contiguous to each other may be applied to a purpose for which they could not be used except under a combined ownership.[8]

The minor contentions of the defendants — that the practice of stock watering had become crystallized and sanctioned by usage; that the defendants had already lost a considerable amount of money in this venture and should not in " fairness " be compelled to lose more; that there was no proof that the plaintiffs had relied upon or been deceived by the capitalization; and, finally, that the defendants, as bondholders, should be allowed to set off against any liability imposed upon them as stockholders the amount of their bonds — were easily disposed of adversely to the defendants in ways which need not detain us here.

As to the major defenses set up by those whom the plaintiffs sought to hold liable, namely, that the stock issue was justified by a capitalization of expected earnings and that, even if overvaluation should be proven, no liability could be imposed on the defendants unless proof was given that the overvaluation was *fraudulent*, the court disposed of the latter claim by admitting that it was indeed the general rule, but that in the instant case the presumption of good faith was overcome by the showing of circumstances which indicated that *no actual appraisal* of the property had been made by a *competent* board of directors. The board, it appeared, had simply rubber-stamped the appraisals given them by their masters, the real promoters, and were not in any position to exercise the independence of judgment which alone would make their action final. Further, the court said the fact that the defendants had invested approximately $500,000 in cash and services in the enterprise and had accepted bonds in exchange therefor was no proof that they acted in good faith in valuing the property at $5,000,000. The $1,000,000 of bonds were secured by a mortgage upon the properties which the promoters had agreed to purchase at a price of $2,250,000 in cash and

[8] 69 N. J. Eq. 49, 61 Atl. 849.

stock and each taker of a $1,000 bond received a bonus of $600 in common and preferred stock. The court said:

> It is thus made clear that when the faith of these investors in the value of the property purchased was put to the actual test it went no further than to invest at par in first mortgage six per cent. bonds, secured by property estimated to be worth about twice the amount of the mortgage, to which bonds was added as a bonus, sixty per cent. of stock representing the value of the property above the mortgage.[9]

Turning now to the promoters' estimates of future earning power as the proper basis of capitalization, it will be recalled that the court stated the issue in this case in the form of a question as to whether a valuation of *physical* property may be made up by capitalizing prospective profits. It then resorted to an ill-chosen rephrasing of the question by asking whether prospective profits might be considered " property " as that word was used in the statute. Having placed itself in this unhappy situation it wriggled out of it by an unconvincing statement that by context the word, " property," referred to something visible and tangible. That this identification of " property " with something tangible was unfortunate is manifest by the court's later admission that good will is " property."[10]

At various places throughout the opinion the court indicated that the promoters had resorted to an overoptimistic, unfounded and unsubstantiated estimate of future earnings. On page 46 of the opinion the court said that future earnings could be taken into account only " to a limited extent " in estimating the value of property from which earnings are expected to accrue. On pages 46 and 47 it stressed the fact that the combination did not include all of the mills which it was intended to include. On page 49 it left-handedly criticised the action of the promoters in " counting their chickens before they were hatched," and stated that it could not see how the combination of the plants could be expected to enhance the value of the whole over the sum of the values of the separate parts. On page 50 it stressed the fact that the plants could readily and easily be duplicated. On pages 54 to 58, and on page 75, it referred to the fact that the directors' valuation was plainly not a disinterested one. On page 60 it referred to the demoralized condition of the wrapping-paper industry and the negligible profits which were being made in it. On pages 63 to 64 it emphasized the fact that the capitalization was based mainly upon

[9] *Ibid.*, 52, 61 Atl. 850.
[10] *Ibid.*, 44, 61 Atl. 846–47.

the optimistic hopes of Mr. Untermyer concerning the feasibility of reducing costs and raising prices to a monopoly level. On pages 68 and 69 the courts stressed the fact that the corporation was formed by " dummies " who had no real interest in the enterprise and that the same parties, acting as directors, authorized the issue of the $5,000,000 in securities without any knowledge whatever of the value of the consideration to be received for them. The valuation to which they certified was plainly made in the interest of the promoters and was computed without regard to the ordinary hazards which face every new enterprise as well as to the special hazards of this particular venture. On page 74 the court indicated that some of the directors must have known that their valuation was excessive since they knew that a 60 per cent stock bonus was to be given with each bond sold for cash or otherwise disposed of in financing the organization. This, the court said, was direct notice that the property was overvalued.

It can avail us little to detail further the many ways in which the court, convinced that the stock issue was based upon a capitalization of future earnings, indicated that the valuation was grossly excessive. The court nowhere denied that prospective profits might be capitalized, unless the *decision* of the case can be construed as such a denial. It indicated that future earnings could be taken into account to a limited extent, but denied that they were " property." Then, in phrasing what it considered to be a proper rule for corporate capitalization, quoted on page 72, *supra*, it used language which plainly indicated that future earnings must be considered.

Just what meaning should be assigned to the statements of the court that directors may issue an amount of stock for property equal to the amount of cash which they would pay for it, but that prospective profits are not " property " under the statute permitting the issuance of stock for property, is a matter of considerable doubt, for they seem to involve the contradictory assumptions: (*a*) that the proper basis of capitalization is the cash value of the property; and, (*b*) that prospective earnings may not be taken into account in *estimating* this value. Certainly it would seem that a board of directors, if it were deciding how much *cash* to pay for the property, must necessarily give attention primarily to the earnings which may be expected to result from the purchase of the property. And yet a New Jersey court, while in one sentence it assumes that the rule for stock issue is the same as the rule of a reasonable cash price, seems to say that prospective earning power is not to be regarded as "property" for the purpose of stock issue. To this statement one might reply that while prospective earning power is not in itself property, the rights to the particular assets, tangible and intangible, which are being turned over to the corporation are property, the *value* of which is almost entirely dependent on prospective earnings. The use by the court of language which characterizes property in terms of mere physical things, irrespective of the values which those things may have for purposes of profit, suggests a reversion to the older and cruder concepts of property, which, as writers in legal economics have shown, were entertained by most courts in earlier times.[11]

It is possible, however, to take a far more sympathetic view of the real attitude of the court if one overlooks the linguistic faults committed by it in explaining its position. Let us consider the facts of the case as they presented themselves. It was on record that the property against which $5,000,000 of securities were being issued consisted of plants for which, by the terms of the options, the owners were to receive only $3,000,000 in cash and in preferred and common stock. One half of this $3,000,000 was to be paid in common stock which by the very terms of the option contract was deemed to be worth only 50 per cent of par, thus cutting the actual consideration down to $2,250,000, a figure which Mr. Untermyer characterized as the "appraised value" of the properties including their good will. The entire difference between the full $5,000,000 of securities and the $2,250,000 consideration could be justified only on the ground that they represented an enhancement in value, due to the consolidation which it was hoped would bring about operating economies on the one hand and higher monopolistic prices on the other hand. It certainly would have taken a very innocent and simple-minded court to have assumed that this 100 per cent inflation was a *reasonable* estimate of the enhancement in value resulting from the consolidation. Not only did the facts as they subsequently developed clearly give the lie to any expectations such as were entertained by the promoters, but the prospects as they presented themselves at the time of the promotion were not such as would have caused reasonable and unbiased people to entertain any such expectation.

If more evidence were needed that the promoters knew full well, or at least should have known full well, that they were watering

[11] COMMONS, JOHN R., LEGAL FOUNDATIONS OF CAPITALISM (New York, 1924), *passim*, especially c. 2.

the stock, that evidence was supplied by the fact that they themselves contemplated the immediate issue of bonds to outsiders with a 60 per cent stock bonus. No single *one* of the facts brought out in the evidence was conclusive proof, perhaps, that the promoters had deliberately overvalued the property. Cumulatively, however, the facts gave such evidence beyond reasonable doubt, and the decision of the court holding the stockholders liable was the only one which could fairly have been reached.

Coming back again to the question as to the use of capitalized prospective profits, what the court seems really to have held was, not that these prospective profits must be left out of account, but simply that, as estimated by the promoters, they were altogether too optimistic to justify such a gross discrepancy between the $5,000,000 value placed by the promoters on the combined enterprise and the much smaller values placed by the owners on the separate plants. That this is the most plausible interpretation of the admittedly confusing opinion in the *See* case is born out by an analysis of the subsequent decisions of the New Jersey courts.

The following conclusions are offered as to the interpretation of the much-quoted *See* case. First, almost every statement by the court as to the proper basis of valuation is pure dictum, since the stock watering was so flagrant and so grossly excessive that it would have been established without regard to the controversial questions as to how the property should have been valued.

Second, certain sentences used by the court, taken alone, seem to state that capitalized prospective earnings do not constitute a proper basis of valuation, for the reason that estimated earning power does not constitute " property " and hence is not valid consideration for stock issue. Other sentences modify, and perhaps even completely destroy, the force of this position by stating that the earning power of the property must be given " consideration " in determining its value.

Third, while it is impossible to reconcile the precise language of the inconsistent statements noted above, a plausible interpretation of the court's real position can be given as follows: that while prospective earnings do not, in themselves, constitute " property," they nevertheless have a decided bearing on the value of those rights to tangible and intangible things which are rightly called, " property "; but that while estimates of future earnings must be given " due consideration," they must be supported by sufficient fact material to justify a holding that the valuation based on the estimate was a " reasonable " one.

Fourth, in a consolidation of hitherto independent business enterprises, a promoter who capitalizes the consolidation at a value far in excess of the prices which he pays for the properties and who justifies this excess capitalization solely on the assumption that greatly increased earnings will result from the combination, must face the burden of overcoming a natural suspicion that his assumptions were too optimistic to have reasonable justification. In the instant case, the promoter was unable to adduce evidence sufficient to overcome this suspicion.

Fifth, where the valuation of the property was made, on behalf of the corporation, by mere dummy directors who admittedly knew nothing about the situation that would permit of their making an intelligent appraisal, this fact alone will go far toward destroying the ordinary rule that the directors' valuations shall be accepted as final in the absence of " actual fraud " in the transaction.[12]

Another New Jersey case, *Holcombe v. Trenton White City Co.*,[13] brings out the point that if anticipated earnings are to be capitalized they must be discounted both for futurity and for risk. The case came before the Court of Chancery upon an application of the receiver of the Trenton White City Company for an assessment on capital stock for the benefit of creditors, the unliquidated claims of the latter amounting to approximately $40,000. The promoters of an amusement park to be located near Trenton, N. J., procured from a connecting street-railway company a ten-year leasehold on a tract of land, the lessor agreeing to furnish free current during a period of ten years for seventy arc lights on the premises. The lease also contained a clause permitting the lessee to purchase the land at any time within the life of the lease at a price of $35,000. This favorable lease was procured by the promoters at a cash cost of $4,000 (paid to a former lessee for discharge of a pre-existing lease which had four years to run), plus the payment to the street-railway company of the nominal sum of one dollar. The promoters also contracted: (*a*) for the construction of amusement buildings, the contractor

[12] Although this case was not appealed to the highest court of New Jersey it has long been recognized as a leading case and has frequently been cited with approval by the Court of Errors and Appeals of New Jersey and by the highest courts of other jurisdictions.

[13] 80 N. J. Eq. 122, 82 Atl. 618 (1912), *aff'd*, 82 N. J. Eq. 364, 91 Atl. 1069 (1913).

agreeing to take payment for his services in preferred stock of the company equal to 10 per cent of the cost of construction; (*b*) for the erection of certain carrousels at a cost of $5,000 below list prices (which latter the promoters admitted were excessively high); (*c*) for the laying of a cable by the Public Service Corporation from the city of Trenton to the park for the purpose of supplying lights; and (*d*) for the rental of roller skates on a percentage-of-net-receipts basis.

The promoters organized the Trenton White City Company with an authorized capital stock of $150,000 divided equally between preferred and common shares. In their capacity as incorporating stockholders they resolved that the board of directors be authorized to purchase from them the property rights and contract interests mentioned above for a consideration of $4,000 cash and $75,000 in "full-paid" common capital stock of the company. The preamble to the resolution stated that the property rights and contract interests would be of great value to the company, indispensable to its business, and that no other rights and interests of similar nature could be procured which would be of equal value to the company. At a subsequent meeting, the same persons, acting this time as the directors of the corporation, resolved to accept their own offer to sell and assign the property interests and contracts described in the resolution of the shareholders made at the incorporation meeting, and declared that they were "of the fair value of seventy-nine thousand dollars, and that the same are necessary and indispensable for the conduct of the business of this company."

In this way the entire common stock of the company was "paid up." All of it was then donated by the promoters to the company without the formality of issuing any certificates to them. Thereupon, a part of the common stock was distributed as a bonus to the subscribers to the preferred stock of the company, who agreed to pay par in cash for the latter. It was the holders of this bonus treasury stock who were sued for the benefit of creditors.

The plaintiff's (receiver's) bill set forth the manner in which the company was organized, alleged non-payment of stock subscriptions, and prayed for an assessment against subscribers for the full amount of common stock issued to them, or for such other sum as would be sufficient to meet claims of creditors and costs of liquidating the business. Upon filing of the petition an order was made requiring the persons shown to be stockholders to show cause why the prayer of the petition should not be granted, and afterwards a trial was held upon the question presented by the petition. It is not necessary for us to set forth the charges and defenses of the parties in detail. Enough has been indicated to show that the court was faced with a problem of valuation for stock-issue purposes, which is the only aspect of the case in which we are interested.

The facts before the court were insufficient to enable it to determine the exact amount of liability of the defendants, the value of certain parts of the consideration being in doubt. In substance, the holding of the court was that the defendants were liable to the plaintiff for so much of the full par value of their stock, minus the value of the lease, the lighting contract, and promoters' services, as should later appear to be necessary to liquidate the creditors' claims and the expenses of the receivership. The amount of the credits for the value of the lease, etc., was to be determined upon a further hearing in accordance with the principles of valuation laid down by the court in its discussion of the case.

After disposing of some preliminary matters, the court quoted the statute which permitted directors to purchase property for corporations by the issuance of stock " to the amount of the value thereof in payment therefor " and which provided that in the absence of "actual fraud in the transaction, the judgment of the directors as to the value of the property purchased shall be conclusive." [14]

The court's remarks upon the meaning of this statute were that " a solemnly expressed judgment of the board of directors of a corporation cannot impart value to property which has no value " and that the rule for valuation envisaged by it had been amply stated in the *See* case, *supra,* by the decision of which this court was bound. Although the court acquitted the directors of any charge of actual wrongdoing or fraud, it held the view that other conduct besides that of deliberate fraud on the part of directors would render stockholders liable on unpaid stock.[15]

[14] Sections 48 and 49 of the General Corporation Act (N. J. Pub. L., 1896, p. 293, 2 Comp. Stat. 1910, p. 1630). See v. Heppenheimer, *supra,* note 4, was tried under an earlier statute which did not contain the clause making the directors' judgment conclusive in the absence of actual fraud, but the court here, at page 141 of the opinion, 82 Atl. at pp. 626–27, stated that the clause added by the law of 1896 " introduced no novelty into the law, but is simply declaratory of the law " which had been developed by prior adjudications.

[15] In support of this view the court quoted the following language from Donald v. American Smelting & Refining Co., 62 N. J. Eq. 729, 732, 48 Atl. 771,

The court next disposed of the contention of the defendants that they were not original subscribers, but were assignees of the promoters to whom the stock was first issued. It stated that the defendants could not escape liability on this ground because, although the stock was first issued to promoters, the latter immediately donated all of it back to the company without any certificates having been issued to them. The defendants did not bargain with the promoters for a sale of the shares. On the contrary, the stock was issued direct to the defendants by the company without any representation as to how the stock was to be paid for. The implication is, apparently, that this fact should have put the defendants on notice that the shares were never paid for.

The court then characterized the case as being similar in most respects to *See v. Heppenheimer, supra.* It said that in both cases the proposition for the sale of what was called property and the acceptance of common stock in payment were embodied in previously prepared resolutions for the shareholders and directors; and (with less apparent justification), that the principal item in the valuation consisted in a then present capitalization of prospective or future profits of the company, an item which was not " property " under the statute; and, finally, that there was no actual appraisal of the property by the board of directors as contemplated by the statute.

But, said the court, the stockholders are entitled to have credited to the payment of their stock " the just and fair value " of the property conveyed to, and services rendered for, the company, and for which the stock was issued. Hence it is pertinent to inquire into the value of the property turned over to the company by the promoters. The court first considered the value of the lease and said:

> The true method of calculating the value of an unexpired lease is not by ascertaining the yearly rental value and then multiplying the figures by the number of years the lease has to run, but by calculating its value by the annuity tables — that is, by multiplying the annual value by the value of one dollar per year for the number of years in the unexpired term.[16]

---

772 (1901): "Their [directors'] honest judgment, if reached *without due examination into the elements of value, or if based in part upon an estimate of matters which really are not property* . . . may lead to a violation of the statutory rule *as surely as would corrupt motive.*"

[16] 80 N. J. Eq. 122, 153, 82 Atl. 618, 631 (1912). *Cf.* Babbitt v. Read, *infra*, note 45, wherein a similar view was taken by another court with respect to the value of unmined coal.

Although the promoters had acquired the lease at a cost of $4,000, plus a payment of one dollar made to the street-railway company for executing a new lease, the court said its value was not limited to the price which the promoters paid for it. The price paid to the street-railway company was a nominal one in view of the fact that this company expected the lease to result in a substantial growth in traffic. On the other hand, the court said it would not be proper to multiply the annual rental, saved by the Trenton White City Company because of this lease, by the number of years the lease had to run, because this method of computation would ignore the element of time discount which is applicable to all future payments. The report of the case does not reveal exactly what value the directors placed upon the lease, but it seems that they not only overestimated its rental value but also overvalued it by imputing to it a value equal to the difference between the price at which they could purchase the land under the terms of the lease and their estimate of the value of the fee-simple title to the land. This procedure the court also ruled was an improper one.

Further rulings of the court were: (*a*) that no credit should be made on the defendants' stock by virtue of the contract secured by the promoters for the construction of buildings at cost, plus a 10 per cent commission payable in preferred stock of the company; (*b*) that the defendants' were not entitled to a credit on their stock equal to the difference between the list prices for certain carrousels and the lower prices at which the promoters arranged for their purchase by the corporation, since the promoter who arranged for the discounts admitted that the list prices were in excess of what the carrousels were worth, but that a credit should be allowed for any value of the *services* of the promoters in negotiating these purchases at a discount; (*c*) that the stock of the defendants should not be credited with the cost of laying the feedwire from Trenton to the park, since this cost was paid by the public service company, but only with the amount of a fair compensation for the promoters' services in arranging for the work to be done; [17] and (*d*) that no credit of a sum equal to the value of the rented skates was due the defendants on their stock, since the skates did not become the property of the corporation. These several items were not "property" under the statute, and they could not be capitalized as such. All that

[17] The credits allowed here by the court were for services of the promoters rendered *prior to incorporation*.

the defendants were entitled to on account of them was a credit equal to the value of services rendered in making the arrangements.

Having thus indicated specifically the nature of the credits which should be made on the stock, the court laid down a rule of valuation by paraphrasing the language of Pitney, V. C., in the *See* case, *supra.*

After all the true test is this: If the White City Company had to its credit in the bank the sum of $75,000, would it have been willing to pay that price in cash for the property in question; would it be worth that sum in cash to the company? If confronted with that proposition the gentlemen who composed the board of directors of the White City Company, all of them business men, would have taken each item into deliberate and careful consideration. They would have been asked to say how much a ten years' lease of the property was worth, and they would have said that it was worth to them whatever was a fair rental value because it was turned over to them rent free, and they could have sublet or assigned the lease and thus made a rental to themselves. . . .

If, as in most cases, the promoters of the White City Company had not been themselves a majority of its directors it would have been necessary for them to have selected competent persons for the directorate — men who would act wholly in the interest of future stockholders, and who would not be biased or influenced by the persuasions of the proposed vendors or by friendship for either of them — and to have made to those directors a disclosure of all material facts. In this case, however, the promoters were themselves directors, and constituted a majority of the board; and this being so, it was their duty to have acted as an independent board of directors, with full knowledge, would have acted, namely, to have made a careful inventory and appraisement of all property to be purchased with stock or for cash, and to have either issued stock or paid cash, measure for measure — value for value.[18]

The parallel between this and the *See* case is apparent. The principal difference is that in the instant case the court acquitted the directors of any actual intent to defraud the public. However, the transaction viewed as a whole did not conform to the " reasonable (cash) valuation rule " and on this ground a liability was imposed. The court's position with respect to the valuation of the lease is illuminating on the question of what recognition may be given by directors to anticipated earnings in computing the value of property. The possibility of making a profit by exercising the option to purchase the leased property and selling the latter at a price in excess

[18] 80 N. J. Eq. 122, 159–60, 160–61, 82 Atl. 618, 634 (1912).

of the cost was too remote in this case to justify a capitalization of it. Perhaps the court felt that reasonable and intelligent directors would not sanction the listing of this possibility as an asset on the corporate balance sheet. Not only would such procedure be contrary to accepted accounting practice, but it is improbable that commercial bankers or other possible creditors would extend credit on the basis of it.[19] On the other hand, the saving of corporate expense through negotiation of a lease at a cost of $1 on land which would rent for $1000 per year was evidently regarded as a kind of future income which was sufficiently definite in amount and certain of realization to be capitalized under a rule which permits a corporation to issue stock for property and services in an amount equal to the cash price which directors would pay for them.[20]

The fact that the New Jersey courts, despite their affirmations in the *See* and *Holcombe* cases that prospective profits are not " property " under the statute, do not really mean to forbid a consideration of estimated prospective profits in the computation of a proper capitalization of newly incorporated enterprises, is borne out by the decision in *The Railway Review v. Groff Drill and Machine Tool Company.*[21]

The case arose upon a petition of the receiver of the company for an assessment against stockholders on behalf of creditors. A plant for the manufacture of a patented railway device, including machinery and the exclusive right to manufacture and sell the patented article in this country, was turned over to the Groff Drill and Machine Tool Company at a valuation based upon its earnings during the preceding year, capitalized at 6 per cent. Testimony showed that a detailed statement of earnings was exhibited to the directors and all of the evidence indicated that the capitalization was based

19 It is not intended to imply that the proper test of what items may be capitalized can be discovered by noting the items which accountants admit as assets on balance sheets. Good will, for example, is an item which under certain circumstances may properly be capitalized, even though conservative accountants might, under the same circumstances, exclude it from the balance sheet.

20 *Cf.* Rafferty v. Buffalo City Gas Co., *supra,* c. I, note 73. The latter was a suit by minority stockholders to enjoin the capitalization of an avoidance of future losses by acquiring a rival franchise through the issue of stock. See also Gamble v. Queens County Water Co., *infra,* note 52.

21 84 N. J. Eq. 321, 91 Atl. 1021 (1914), *aff'd,* 84 N. J. Eq. 508, 96 Atl. 1103 (1915).

upon these earnings, which had amounted to $12,000 during the previous year. Future prospects of the business " reasonably assured much greater profits " because the patented article had become standardized on certain railroads and it appeared at the time that the demand for it would " necessarily increase." In view of the record of earnings during the last year and in view of the favorable prospects for the enterprise, the directors capitalized the earnings of $12,000 at 6 per cent and issued stock to the owners of the enterprise in the amount of $200,000. The new company was a close corporation, the stock being retained by the parties who formerly owned and operated the plant. No distribution of securities to the public was made.

The contention of the plaintiff appears to have been that because the directors valued the property on the basis of its earning power it was *ipso facto* overvalued. The principal defense of the shareholders was that the record of the past earning power of the enterprise was the best possible index of its value for stock-issue purposes. The Court of Chancery advised an order denying the assessment and upon appeal the Court of Errors and Appeals unanimously affirmed the decision below.

The language of the lower court upholding the directors' valuation was, in part, as follows:

> I find nothing improper or unlawful in that valuation under the circumstances disclosed by the evidence. It may be assumed, as held in *See* v. *Heppenheimer, 69 N. J. Eq. 36,* that prospective profits, arising from the new conditions created by the transfer, are not elements that can be considered in ascertaining value for which stock can be issued. But it cannot be doubted that the established past and present earning capacity may be made a proper basis of valuation in appropriate circumstances. If a house should be purchased for purposes of rental the established past and present rental value clearly affords a stable basis of its valuation for the purpose named, and in like manner the established earning capacity of a business of the nature of the business here in question, must be regarded as a proper basis of its value, for such a business is necessarily purchased solely for and by reason of its peculiar earning capacity. Nor is it possible for any intelligent purchaser to wholly disregard future prospects. While our statute may not contemplate the capitalization of prospective future profits, it is clear that no present earning capacity can be made the intelligent basis of valuation without due consideration of future prospects; but where there are prospects of increased future earning capacity, the present earning capacity demonstrated by actual operation, clearly affords a proper

basis of valuation of a business of this peculiar nature if the future prospects are not also capitalized.[22]

At a later point in its discussion the court said:

. . . the new conditions which arose to render the patented article less valuable could not have been then anticipated.

The reasoning of the court in justifying its position that past and present earning capacity may be capitalized where future prospects are bright, but that *future earnings* may not be capitalized, although they *may be taken into consideration,* has its specious side. In the light of the language of the court quoted above it is conceivable that the decision might have gone the other way if the directors had estimated future earnings at $20,000 because of the favorable outlook for the enterprise and had capitalized this estimated figure at 10 per cent. The net result would have been a capitalization of $200,000, a figure which was regarded by this court as a conservative one. A 10 per cent rate might be regarded as reflecting more accurately the risks of small enterprises of the sort here in question than would a 6 per cent rate, though it is probable that a 20 per cent rate would have been nearer to the market rate for this type of venture in 1914. The point is that by sanctioning the use of a 6 per cent rate, as applied to existing earnings (obviously too low a rate except on the assumption that future earnings might reasonably be expected to increase materially), the court permitted the capitalization of future prospects just as effectively as though it had allowed the directors to estimate the earnings at $40,000 and to capitalize that figure at 20 per cent, which latter rate might well be regarded as appropriate for a small manufacturing enterprise with only a one-year record of earnings.

It will be noted from the quotation above that the court said in the same sentence that no present earning capacity could be made

[22] 84 N. J. Eq. 322–23, 91 Atl. 1021. *Cf.* Ewing v. Swenson, 167 Minn. 113, 208 N. W. 645 (1926), wherein the court said, " It must be true with corporations as with individuals that in business transactions the anticipated profits of an executory contract may be valued and accepted in payment." The case involved the question whether stock issued for a one-half interest in the anticipated profits from a construction contract which was made on a " cost-plus " basis, was " fully paid " in such a manner as to permit the issuing corporation to dispose of a portion of the stock, which had been donated to its treasury, without a liability of the purchaser to creditors.

the intelligent basis of valuation *without due consideration of future prospects,* and that where the future prospects are excellent the present earning capacity demonstrated by actual operation " clearly affords a proper basis of valuation of a business of this peculiar nature *if the future prospects are not also capitalized.*" This language of the court suggests that there is some esoteric distinction between *recognizing,* or *taking into consideration,* future prospects and *capitalizing* those prospects. We don't know what this distinction is, but it seems probable that when translated into economic terms the distinction will appear to have no foundation worth considering. As a stage in the process of imputing values to property for stock-issue purposes, *taking into consideration* the favorable nature of future prospects can be reflected in only two ways: first, in the determination of the *amount* of expected earnings to be capitalized; and second, in the *rate* of capitalization applicable to those earnings. Any consideration which will modify either of these factors will necessarily modify the resultant valuation. Since the court implied that the *amount* of the expected earnings to be used in the capitalization process was fixed absolutely by the past record of the enterprise, any *recognition* to be given to future earnings must necessarily be reflected in the rate at which they may be capitalized. The resulting effect upon the capitalization may be the same as though the court had permitted an addition to be made to the amount of past earnings because of favorable prospects. It is difficult to see, therefore, how the language of the court can be interpreted literally.

Although we cannot explain away the inconsistency in the court's language, there are a number of reasons why we should expect the court to approve the capitalization of earnings in this case despite its refusal to permit stock to be issued on that basis in the earlier cases discussed above. In the first place, the capitalization of the Groff Drill and Machine Tool Company was decided upon by the directors after considering a fully detailed statement of earnings for the previous year. They deliberated upon the question of value and reached a decision after weighing the pertinent facts. This is what the statute authorizing the issuance of stock for property contemplated. On the other hand, the directors in the *See* and *Holcombe* cases did not deliberate on the question of value. They exercised no judgment whatever in deciding to issue a given amount of stock for property but did exactly what they were ordered to do by the promoters, without regard to the factors which would influence rational men in deciding upon a valuation of the property for which they resolved to issue stock. In the second place, the Groff Drill and Machine Tool Company made no appeal to the public for the commitment of long-term funds. It was not a stock-jobbing scheme but a close corporation. Both the Columbia Straw-Paper Company and the Trenton White City Company appealed to the public for funds through the sale of bonds or stock. In the third place, the directors of the Groff Drill and Machine Tool Company had before them a record of *past* earnings, whereas the other two companies were organized without reference to any previous record of earnings and the directors' estimate of future earnings was based upon entirely new conditions to be created by the transfer of stock for property rather than upon existing conditions. And finally, it is not unlikely that the court was influenced by the fact that the directors used a *6 per cent rate* in capitalizing earnings. Express legal sanction of this rate in certain instances has doubtless caused jurists and laymen alike to impute to it a degree of validity in many circumstances to which it is wholly irrelevant.[23]

A recent pronouncement of the New Jersey Court of Chancery on the question of capitalizing prospective profits is found in the brief opinion in *Wolcott, Receiver v. Waldstein.*[24] So few facts are reported in the published opinion of the court that we are unable to say what the nature of the enterprise was. The case would hardly deserve mention, were it not for the significant dictum of the court concerning the capitalization of anticipated profits.

In this action by the receiver of a corporation to have its stock adjudged unpaid, and to procure an assessment on the shareholders for the payment of creditors' claims, it appeared that the cost to the promoters of certain undescribed property did not exceed $70,000. Acting as directors the promoters issued $250,000 of stock to themselves as the vendors of this property. There was thus a complete absence of independent judgment in the computation of the capitalization of the enterprise. The principal contention of the defendants appears to have been that the property was worth more than it cost them because there was reason to expect that under proper management the corporation would develop an earning capacity proportionate to its capitalization.

The court held that the defendant shareholders were liable to the

[23] *Cf.* Dee Co. v. Proviso Coal Co., *infra,* note 32.
[24] 86 N. J. Eq. 63, 97 Atl. 951 (1916).

receiver for the benefit of creditors for that percentage of the par value of each share held which was indicated by the ratio of what the promoters paid for the property to the par value of all the stock issued for it. Since $250,000 of stock was issued for property which cost the promoters only $70,000 the stock was 72 per cent unpaid.

In holding the defendant promoters and their transferees with notice (of the manner in which the stock was originally issued) liable to the receiver for the benefit of creditors, the court said in part as follows:

> The nearest approach to a justification of the valuation placed upon the property is to be found in the claim that the circumstances which existed at the time the valuation was determined upon may have justified a reasonable expectation that the corporation under proper management would develop an earning capacity proportionate to its capitalization. Future prospects or prospects of future profits can never be properly ignored in any intelligent valuation of property; but it is well settled that under our statute such prospective future profits cannot be made the basis of valuation for purposes of capitalization in a new enterprise with neither present nor demonstrated earning capacity.[25]

It said further, that any value for the property in excess of its cost to the promoters " which may have appealed to the board [of directors] must have been as anticipated future profits in an enterprise wholly untried and essentially experimental."

The court characterized this promotion as a case of obvious and gross overvaluation, and its holding that the property was worth no more than it cost the promoters was evidently based in large part on the fact that all of the evidence revealed this to have been a case of wilful and excessive overvaluation. The parties who valued the property at approximately 360 per cent of its recent cost to them were plainly actuated by self-interest in doing so. As the court put it;

> The personal interests and purposes of these three men were so far inconsistent with an impartial exercise of their statutory duty as to appropriately challenge the good faith of their valuation, especially in the light of all the circumstances disclosed by the evidence.[26]

This case was probably decided in large measure on the ground that the evidence impeached the directors' good faith and that in the absence of good faith on the part of the directors, property is not to be considered to be worth more for stock-issue purposes than it

[25] 86 N. J. Eq. 64, 97 Atl. 952 (1916). [26] *Ibid.*, 65, 97 Atl. 952.

cost the promoters, unless the latter can clearly demonstrate a greater value. Nevertheless, the dictum in the case concerning the capitalization of future profits is interesting and is consistent with the language and decisions of the New Jersey courts in the earlier cases which have been reviewed above.[27]

In 1913 a new clause was written into the corporation laws of New Jersey which appears to have originated in the language of the courts in the above cases. Chapter 15 of New Jersey Laws of 1913,[28] amending section 49 of the Corporation Act,[29] was a part of one of the famous " Seven Sisters Acts " which were passed in that year with the object of protecting the public from corporate abuses. The provisions of the act of 1913 which are material to the present discussion are:

> Provided, that when property is purchased the purchasing corporation must receive in property . . . what the same is *reasonably worth in money at a fair bona fide valuation;* and provided further, that no fictitious stock shall be issued; that *no stock shall be issued for profits not yet earned, but only anticipated.*[30]

The 1913 amendment also dropped from the previous statute the provision that, in the absence of actual fraud in the transaction, the

[27] Compare with the instant case Wallace v. Weinstein, 257 Fed. 625 (C. C. A., 3d Cir., 1919), in which the following statement appears: "They [agency contracts with automobile manufacturers] contained nothing more substantial than a promise of profits. Contemplated profits cannot be a basis of capitalization of a corporation under the Delaware law, for neither stockholders nor directors have any right to make a capitalization of prospective profits." The Circuit Court of Appeals cited See v. Heppenheimer, *supra,* note 4, Holcombe v. Trenton White City Co., *supra,* note 13, and Cooney C. v. Arlington Hotel Co., 11 Del. Ch. 286, 101 Atl. 879 (1917), *aff'd,* 11 Del. Ch. 430, 106 Atl. 39 (1918), in support of this statement. The last case was not in point, except in a constructive sense, for there the capitalization of prospective profits was not an issue, it having been decided in that case that services to be rendered in the future are not a valid consideration for stock issuance. But in the *Cooney* case the court frequently referred to the similarity between the New Jersey and Delaware statutes concerning corporations, and said " Interpretations of the New Jersey statute and practice under it are cogent to influence the Delaware courts in like cases." It seems probable that the courts of Delaware would hold, if the issue were raised, that no more significance is to be attached to anticipated earnings as a basis of stock issuance than has been allowed by the New Jersey courts.

[28] N. J. Pub. L. 1913, p. 28.

[29] P. L. 1896, p. 293, 2 Comp. Stat. 1910, p. 1630.

[30] The italics are mine. This section of the law was again amended by

judgment of the directors as to the value of property purchased with stock should be conclusive.

The most recent decision of the New Jersey courts concerning the capitalization of prospective profits was rendered in the light of the 1913 amendment quoted above, and both the language of the court and its decision are worthy of our careful attention. *Bryson v. Conlen* [31] was a final hearing on a bill of the receiver of an insolvent corporation, the Philadelphia Supply Company, to procure an assessment on capital stock. The defendant shareholders, Pierce and Fireng, desired to obtain from E. I. du Pont de Nemours & Company a lease of one of the buildings of the latter situated on its property at Carney's Point, New Jersey, and an exclusive right from that company to supply the inhabitants and persons at the three general camps of the du Pont Company at Carney's Point through a general merchandise store to be operated in the building in question. They employed the defendant, Conlen, a counselor-at-law, to negotiate for them to this end with the du Pont Company. Conlen evidently arrived at some agreement with the du Pont Company, for soon thereafter he, Pierce and one Baker (a figurehead for organization purposes) organized the Philadelphia Supply Company with an authorized capital stock of $50,000.

The first board of directors consisted of Conlen, Pierce and Baker. On November 15, 1915, at the first meeting of the board, the directors passed a resolution authorizing the company to purchase from Pierce with its entire capital stock,

> The exclusive privilege, right and authority from E. I. du Pont de Nemours & Company, of Wilmington, Delaware, together with a leasehold interest on a certain property at Carney's Point, New Jersey, to open a general merchandise store at said Carney's Point by which authority the company may supply exclusively the inhabitants and persons at the three general camps established by the E. I. du Pont de Nemours & Company, at Carney's Point, New Jersey.

This resolution was passed before any lease or contract had been effected, but about a month later the du Pont company executed a

---

Chapter 195 of the laws of 1917 (N. J. Laws, 1917, c. 195, p. 566), which contains the same language here quoted from the laws of 1913, except that the last clause beginning " that no stock shall be issued for profits not yet earned . . ." has been omitted.

[31] VII N. J. Adv. Rep. 273, 144 Atl. 723 (N. J. Ch., 1929).

lease to the Philadelphia Supply Company for the store contemplated by the resolution. The lease ran for one year at a monthly rental of $150, and was renewable for another year on the same terms. The lease mentioned nothing about an exclusive privilege nor did any other written instrument executed by the du Pont company. Whatever rights the promoters had in the lease were held in the name of Pierce for the equal benefit of himself and Fireng. They evidently thought that a store on the du Pont property would be a profitable enterprise and counted on an absence of competition. In fact, however, there was no contract preventing the du Pont company from opening a rival store, and other land near by which was suitable for similar stores was not under du Pont control. Furthermore, it was evident that the du Pont company could not compel the residents in the three camps to purchase exclusively from the store on their premises. This statement of the facts suggests the sequel. Rival stores were opened near by with the result that the Philadelphia Supply Company became insolvent. The receiver here sued for an order of assessment against Conlen, Pierce and Fireng, who were the original takers and holders of the entire capital stock of the company, for the purpose of providing funds for the payment of proven creditors' claims amounting to $7,632.90.

The contention that the du Pont Company was to grant to Pierce and Fireng an exclusive privilege was not supported other than by the statements of the defendant Conlen, for there was no written agreement to that effect and no representative of the du Pont company testified concerning the existence of any such privilege. That no such arrangement was contemplated by the lessor was indicated by the absence of any covenant in the lease to that effect.

The corporation was incorporated and its entire capital stock issued for the rights of the defendants in the lease in 1915. Hence the law applicable to the case was that embodied in the 1913 amendment quoted above.

The contention of the receiver evidently was that the capital stock of the corporation had been issued for no consideration, or for an inadequate consideration under the law, and that in consequence the defendants were liable to him for the benefit of creditors of the corporation to a maximum amount equal to the sum which the court might find remained unpaid on the stock. The answer of the defendants evidently was that the stock had been issued in good faith for a very valuable lease and for an exclusive privilege which the directors believed at the time to be worth at least the par value of the stock and that therefore no liability could be imposed upon the shareholders.

The court granted a decree for an assessment against the defendants for an amount sufficient to satisfy the claims of creditors and to cover expenses of the receivership.

Turning now to the opinion, the court began its discussion of the case by reviewing the legal background as set forth above. Noting the change in the law introduced by the amendment of 1913, it said:

> But even without attributing special significance to the circumstance that the 1913 act removes the earlier provision touching the conclusiveness of the action of the board in the absence of actual fraud, it appears to be now well established that in proceedings of this nature, in behalf of creditors, the rule touching evaluation is that defined in *See* v. *Heppenheimer, 69 N. J. Eq. 36,* and *Holcombe* v. *Trenton White City Co., 80 N. J. Eq. 122, affirmed 82 N. J. Eq. 364.* That rule may be said to be embodied in the plain and specific language of the act of 1913 above quoted.

Although admitting that the defendants had sought an exclusive privilege from the du Pont company and that they may have believed that they had acquired such, the court concluded from the evidence that no exclusive privilege had in fact been acquired by the company. All that the company acquired for its stock were such rights in the lease as the defendants had obtained. Concerning the value of the lease to the company the court said:

> That lease was a lease of a store on a tract of land of the du Pont de Nemours & Company for one year, with the privilege of an additional year, at a rental of $150 per month; the lease thus carried its own burden, and any value it had could only be the difference, if any, between the rental named and a fair rental value, and in addition a prospective ability of the insolvent to make large profits from its proposed business to be conducted in that store. In determining to purchase that lease, any purchaser would necessarily give consideration to the prospect of successful and profitable operation, but prospects of that nature in a new enterprise are not to be capitalized. *See* v. *Heppenheimer, supra.* In the absence of evidence disclosing that the property was leased at substantially less than a fair rental value the lease could not afford a basis for capitalization.

As a further basis for its decision that the defendants were liable to assessment the court laid particular emphasis upon the fact that the directors exercised no independent judgment in determining the amount of stock to be issued for the rights in the lease. It said:

> Nor is it to be overlooked that the board of directors of the insolvent who authorized the purchase were in truth the vendors. Conlen was the moving spirit in the whole enterprise. Pierce, the second member of the board, assumed to be the owner of the rights conveyed, but such rights as existed or were conveyed were in fact owned by defendant Fireng, equally with Pierce, and defendant Conlen cannot be said to have been without interest. Baker, the third member of the board was a mere dummy subject to the will of the others. For that board of directors to appraise the value of the rights to be sold was an empty form. In substance the three defendants named were selling to themselves. *Stewart* v. *Lehigh Valley Railroad Co.*, *38 N. J. Law 505, 522.* Clearly in its inherent force and effect the entire transaction can be considered as no more than an empty form to have the capital stock of the corporation issued as full paid stock and then divide the stock so issued among the vendors who authorized sale and purchase.

In conclusion the court stated that it was unable to find that anything of substantial value capable of capitalization passed to the insolvent corporation, and that an assessment must be made of the necessary amount to pay the corporate debts and expenses.

Both in the statute under which this case was tried and in the language of the court, we find the rationale of the earlier decisions by the New Jersey courts concerning the capitalization of prospective profits expressed with a fair degree of precision. Anticipated, unearned profits may not be the basis of corporate capitalization under the law of New Jersey, though prospects of future earning capacity cannot be ignored in the valuation of property which is acquired with the object of extracting income from its ownership and use. The New Jersey rule resolves itself into a question of the degree of prudence and business acumen which must be exercised in assessing the pecuniary value of potential income. By admitting that the defendants' interest in the lease might be capitalized to the extent of the difference between the capitalized value of a fair rental for the property and the capitalized value of the rental actually negotiated by the parties, the court granted that to some extent future profits, or more accurately, the saving of future expenses, may be capitalized. Its unexpressed justification for taking this position seems to have been that this difference was one which could be ascertained with substantial accuracy and represented an advantage for which intelligent, honest and disinterested directors would normally pay a cash price. But, to permit the entire capitalization to rest upon self-interested guesses of the promoters of the enterprise concerning the potentiality of this store to produce profits for its owners, based as it was upon an erroneous assumption that an exclusive privilege was involved, would clearly contravene the expressed legislative intention embodied in the 1913 amendment, and would unquestionably conflict with the position taken by the courts of the state in earlier cases which were tried under a law which was at least more tolerant in its literal phraseology toward the validity of directors' opinions concerning the value of non-cash considerations which they accept for stock.

In the light of the foregoing cases there seems to be little, if any, doubt that the New Jersey rule boils down to one which recognizes the futility of ruling out entirely all consideration of potential earning capacity when the issuance of corporate stock for property is in question, but which insists that the presumption that an earning capacity will be demonstrated in the future must be supported by such evidence as would persuade an unbiased and reasonably prudent director to authorize his corporation to pay cash for the right to receive the estimated income. And further, in such a case corporate stock with a par value is to be treated as though it were cash equal in amount to the par of the stock.

Capitalized Earning Power in Illinois

Courts other than those of New Jersey have rarely discussed prospective profits as a basis of corporate capitalization. There are, however, a few exceptions to which we should give some attention.

Dee Co. v. Proviso Coal Co.[32] was a suit by creditors charging the individual defendants with a liability on unpaid stock. The case came before the Supreme Court of Illinois on a writ of error.

The plaintiffs in error, Stephens and Westcott, started a coal-vending business in February, 1901, and conducted it as a partnership until February, 1903, when the enterprise was incorporated under the name of the Proviso Coal Company. Its entire capital stock of $25,000 par value was issued to them as full-paid stock in exchange for the assets and business of the partnership. Until November, 1902, about three months prior to its incorporation, the enterprise yielded only a small profit. During the next three months the partnership sold a large quantity of coal at a considerable profit, due

[32] 290 Ill. 252, 125 N. E. 24 (1919).

partly to the heavy demand for coal during these months, but more largely to a coal strike which prevented other dealers from getting coal. The partnership was receiving coal regularly under a favorable contract with the Lehigh Valley Coal Company by which the latter had agreed to supply the former with a certain quantity of coal at $6.50 per ton. This coal was sold at $12 per ton and, owing to the frantic public demand for coal, much of it did not have to be delivered but was taken from the cars by the consuming public without deduction for delivery costs. It was largely on the basis of the favorable record for these three months that the capitalization of the corporation was determined.

The business was continued until November, 1904, when, the sheds having burned, the enterprise was sold for $3,000 in cash and notes. The purchaser ran the business until 1911, at which time he made a voluntary assignment and creditors realized 19 per cent of their claims.

The contention of the defendants in error (the plaintiff creditors below) was that the property turned over by Stephens and Westcott in full payment of the entire capital stock was not worth $25,000 at the time of the transaction. The answer of Stephens and Westcott was that the property, business and good will of the partnership were worth in excess of $25,000 and that the capital stock was therefore fully paid. The master in chancery, to whom the case was referred below, reported that the business and property of the partnership were worth $25,000 and recommended that the bill be dismissed for want of equity. The chancellor in the Superior Court (trial court) sustained exceptions to the master's report and finally entered a decree finding the property to be worth not over $12,600 and holding Stephens and Westcott liable to creditors to the extent of $12,400, or $6,200 each. On appeal to the Appellate Court a rehearing was had and the Superior Court was reversed. The Appellate Court found the value of the tangible property and good will to have been $12,740 (the addition of $140 to the finding below being due to an admitted error in computing the amount of cash on hand) and $5,000, respectively, and the liability of Stephens and Westcott was reduced by the Appellate Court to $7,260, or $3,630 each.

On a writ of error the case was appealed to the Supreme Court, Stephens and Westcott assigning errors and the creditors assigning cross-errors. The assignment of errors questioned the conclusion of the Appellate Court that the property was worth only $17,740. It was insisted that expert testimony by public appraisers of similar property, opinions of local coal dealers, and evidence as to the prosperity of the business showed the property to have been worth at least $25,000. The parties examined as experts estimated that the property was worth at least $35,000. Their opinion was given on the hypothesis that the business had been carried on for about two years prior to incorporation; that the place where the business had been conducted was a rapidly growing village; that the annual volume of the business was 5,000 tons, sold at an average profit of eighty cents per ton; and that the physical property was worth $17,000. They capitalized estimated earnings of $4,000 at 10 per cent and concluded that the business was worth $40,000, or at least $35,000, and that since the physical property was worth $17,000, the good will was therefore worth $18,000.

The cross-errors questioned the allowance of $5,000 made by the Appellate Court for good will, the valuations of $3,500 for coal sheds, $3,000 for the land and switch track of which the corporation acquired a free use, the allowance of $2,300 for accounts receivable which in fact yielded only $760, and the allowance of $200 for the charter of the company.

The Supreme Court reversed the judgment of the Appellate Court and affirmed the decree of the Superior Court which had found the value of the property conveyed to the corporation to be not in excess of $12,600 and had held Stephens and Westcott liable to creditors to the extent of $12,400.

The language of the Supreme Court in justifying its decision was, in part, as follows:

These opinions [of the so-called experts] have a familiar sound as applied to taking in different plants in a merger into larger corporations and undoubtedly exemplify the theory and practice of those who have designs on the pocket-books of the public in forming such mergers. . . . Of course, everyone knows that $4,000 is ten per cent of $40,000, but there is no evidence that would justify a conclusion that under other conditions than those stated by the witness [an assumed volume of business at an assumed rate of profit] any retail coal business is sold on the basis stated by them. There is not the slightest reason to question the good faith or honesty of plaintiffs in error or any reason to suppose that they had any evil design against creditors or the public. Of course, they did not anticipate a business failure, but when it occurred the law cast upon them the burden of proving that the property had a cash value equal to the capital stock.[33]

[33] 290 Ill. 255–56, 125 N. E. 25 (1919).

The court continued its discussion by pointing out that there was no "substantial basis in the evidence" for the assumption that the annual volume of business would be as great as 5,000 tons or that the profits would amount to $4,000 annually; that the business had been run as a partnership for close to two years with little or no profit; and that the estimate of annual business was based on the unusual prosperity of the enterprise which had resulted from its fortuitously favorable situation during a coal strike in winter months when other dealers couldn't get coal at any price. As to the alleged good will, the court said that any prospective purchaser of this enterprise would have discovered upon investigation that it had not been yielding profits in normal times and would have concluded that it had no good will of any value.

For these reasons the court was unable to sustain the errors assigned. As to the cross-errors; it sustained the objection to the allowance of $5,000 for good will; refused to overrule the allowances of $3,500 for coal sheds and $3,000 for the free use of land and a switch track, on the ground that the valuation of these items was a matter of judgment which the court did not feel justified in disturbing; refused to reduce the allowance of $2,300 for accounts receivable to $760, the sum later realized on them, since there was insufficient evidence before it to determine their value; and finally, refused to allow the charter of the corporation to be counted as an asset in excess of its cash cost.

In conclusion, the court made the following statement concerning the manner in which stock may be issued for property and its bearing on this case:

> Property may be taken in payment for stock, but it must be done by a valid contract of bargain and sale. Payment with property for capital stock is no payment except to the extent of the true value of the property, and if property is taken at an overvaluation the stockholders are liable to make up the deficiency [citing Illinois cases]. The law required the plaintiffs in error, in paying for their stock, to give money or money's worth to the full amount of their subscriptions. The property was not worth the equivalent of $25,000 in cash, but the plaintiffs in error, as both sellers and buyers, took their partnership property at an over-valuation . . .[34]

The standard of valuation in Illinois appears to be much like the standard in New Jersey. There must be a disinterested and pru-

[34] *Ibid.*, 258, 125 N. E. 26.

dent estimate of the value of non-cash considerations which are given for stock, and if prospective profits are capitalized as a means of estimating that value, reasonable care must be used in estimating future earnings and in choosing the rate of capitalization applicable to them. Given the amount of the earnings and the appropriate rate, the computation of value is a simple matter of arithmetic. But the estimate of earnings must not be based upon the results of an unprecedented and plainly exceptional period of prosperity which could not reasonably be expected to continue, nor should the rate of capitalization be based upon an irrational hope for the continuance of such conditions.

Another Illinois case disallowing a 10 per cent rate of capitalization as applied to an unsubstantiated estimate of the amount of future earnings, is found in *Cohen v. Toy Gun Manufacturing Company.*[35] The case came before a branch of the Illinois Appellate Court on an appeal from a decree by the chancellor of the Circuit Court of Cook County. The case arose on a bill in equity by Cohen, an administrator of the estate of a creditor of the defendant corporation, against the company and certain stockholders (who were either original subscribers to the stock of the company or assignees thereof) to subject the unpaid portion of the stock to the payment of the complainant's claim which had been reduced to judgment. This judgment was based upon a tort liability of the company to the intestate. Another judgment creditor, whose claim was also based on tort, intervened and was made a party complainant. The total sum sued for was $6,300 and costs.

One Hazelhurst was the inventor of an improvement in toy guns and had applied for a patent. He sold to Cudahay a one-half interest in the patent for $5,000 cash and a further sum of $20,000 to be paid out of the profits of the manufacture and sale of the invention. In October, 1902, before letters-patent covering the invention had been issued, Hazelhurst and Cudahay formed the defendant corporation under the laws of Illinois and constituted themselves and three appointees the board of directors. As directors these five gentlemen authorized the issuance of the entire capital stock of $250,000 (2,500 shares of $100 par value) to the two promoters in payment for the assignment to the company of all right, title, and interest of Hazelhurst and Cudahay in and to the application and patent. Each of them acquired in this way, and by assignment from their nominees

[35] 172 Ill. App. 330 (1912).

who assisted in the organization of the company, one-half of the stock.

The patent was not granted until March 24, 1903, when it was issued to the company as assignee. Meanwhile, the company had not been successful, and in January, 1903, Cudahay, sold his interest in the enterprise for $15,000. This sum represented the amount of cash which he had invested in the venture, $5,000 of which he paid to Hazelhurst at the time of the transfer of the one-half interest in the patent to him, $5,000 as a loan to the company, and $5,000 in the payment of the company's bills as they fell due. In return for the payment of $15,000 he transferred to the purchaser his entire block of stock of $125,000 par value. Subsequently an explosion occurred at the company's plant which caused the death of the intestate and injury to others. Bankruptcy of the enterprise resulted, and at the bankruptcy sale in September, 1903, the patent was listed among the assets as having " uncertain value." The purchaser at that sale testified that although the patent was transferred to him he gave nothing for it and did not consider its value in making his bid. Total assets as listed and filed for the bankruptcy proceedings were valued at $17,639.12, exclusive of the patent. Liabilities were listed at about $14,000.00.

Testimony as to the value of the patent revealed the following: (*a*) a one-half interest in it was sold by Hazelhurst to Cudahay in September, 1902, for $5,000 cash and a charge of $20,000 on the earning capacity of a company to be formed to exploit the invention, a total present and future consideration of $25,000; (*b*) two patent experts placed the value at not to exceed $5,000 and $10,000, respectively; (*c*) the patent was not a basic one and the patent office rejected all claims regarding it except one; (*d*) the inventor, Hazelhurst, testified that he considered it to be worth $25,000 at the time the company was organized; (*e*) Cudahay and witnesses on his behalf testified that the usual way to value such a device was to take into consideration the profits that *might result* from the business, and Cudahay testified that, after making a careful investigation and giving due consideration to Hazelhurst's estimates of the demand for the patented device and the prospect of profits to be derived from its sale, he believed that an annual profit of from $25,000 to $50,000 could be made under proper management, and that although he had not placed any definite value upon the patent he thought it was capable of earning ample dividends on a capital of $250,000, and further, that he was not guilty of any fraudulent intent in valuing the patent at that figure.

The contention of the plaintiffs was that the patent was not worth more than twice the price at which Hazelhurst transferred a one-half iterest in it to Cudahay, that is **$50,000**, and that there remained an unpaid balance of **$200,000** on the stock issued to the promoters from which plaintiffs' claims should be satisfied by way of an assessment on the shares. No direct charge of fraud on the part of Hazelhurst and Cudahay was made.

The principal contentions of the defendants were that judgments based on tort damages are not " debts " for which the stockholders are liable to creditors; that the valuation was made in good faith; and that, therefore, the defendants were not liable to the plaintiffs, especially since no fraud was alleged in the bill.

The court below dismissed the bill for want of equity, in part because it found no actionable fraud in the transaction by which the stock was issued, and in part because it was unable to construe the various statutes of Illinois with respect to shareholders' liability to creditors in such a way as to impose a liability for tort damages. The Appellate Court reversed the lower court on each of these issues and remanded the cause with directions to enter a decree against Cudahay and one transferee of the stock in accordance with the prayers of the bill and the intervening petition.

As to defendants' plea of " good faith " the court said that unless there were entire good faith in such a transaction the stockholders are liable to creditors for the difference between the par value of the stock and " the actual value of the property taken " and that where it is plain that stock has been exchanged for property at a highly exaggerated value " a strong presumption of bad faith arises which will be conclusive unless rebutted." It expressed its notion of a proper rule of valuation in the following language:

> The law requires that the directors of a corporation obtain money or money's worth to the full amount of a stock subscription. If they see fit to accept property in lieu of cash, they can only take it at its fair cash market value, or, if it has no ascertainable market value, only at such a price as might be realized by selling the property to others for cash. They should ascertain the value of such property precisely in the same manner as they would do if they were about to invest their own money therein. The rule, that a mistake by directors in accepting property at too high a valuation in payment of a stock subscription cannot be regarded as a fraudulent over-

valuation, applies only where the transaction constitutes a valid contract of bargain and sale, made in good faith by the directors, and in the intelligent exercise of fair and honest judgment on their part, and does not apply to a sham transaction [citing several Illinois cases].[36]

In so far as the court was concerned with the capitalization of future profits in this case, its decision may be generalized as follows: that anticipated earnings of an essentially untried patent capitalized at from 10 to 20 per cent will not support an issue of full-paid stock as against creditors where other evidence makes it clear that the capitalization was excessive. The "other evidence" here was: (*a*) that there was no arm's-length bargain made between the corporation and the vendors of the patent, that is, no independent judgment was exercised in the determination of the value of the patent; (*b*) that shortly before the corporation was formed, a one-half interest in the patent was sold by the inventor to another promoter for $5,000 in cash and a charge of $20,000 on future earnings; (*c*) that two patent experts valued the patent at from $5,000 to $10,000; and (*d*) that the inventor himself testified that he regarded the patent to have been worth only $25,000 at the time of its sale to the corporation.

"The fair cash market value" of property which the court stated to be the proper basis of valuation is, in its essence, substantially like the New Jersey "reasonable cash value." Under both standards the directors must treat stock as the equivalent of cash and must estimate the value of the consideration intelligently and honestly. The plaintiff need not allege and prove an actual intent to deceive on the part of the directors under either rule, and under both rules the presumption of "good faith" which is ordinarily indulged on behalf of the directors is nullified by proof of circumstances showing that vendor and vendee were identical, or at any rate that no independent judgment was exercised in estimating the value of the consideration received for stock.

Capitalized Earning Power in Other Jurisdictions

The relationship of prospective earning capacity to a proper capitalization of corporations under California law is indicated in *Hasson v. Koeberle*.[37] This was an appeal by the plaintiff from a judgment of the Superior Court of Los Angeles County in favor of the

[36] 172 Ill. App. 347 (1912).

[37] 180 Cal. 359, 181 Pac. 387 (1919).

defendants. The plaintiff below, an unsatisfied judgment creditor of the corporation in the amount of $7,518.92, sued the defendant shareholders to collect the amount of his claim from an alleged unpaid balance on shares of stock issued for property.

The Ord Mountain Gold Company was incorporated under the laws of Arizona with an authorized capital stock of $1,000,000, divided into shares of $1 par value. On the date of organization certificates for 900,000 shares were issued to two promoters, Messrs. T. N. Hasson and G. L. Hasson, for certain mining properties. Thereupon the Hassons each donated back to the corporate treasury 250,000 shares of this stock. Soon afterwards the corporation reissued 5,000 shares of this treasury stock to Grossman, one of the defendants, for $250, and 4,000 shares to Koeberle, another defendant, for $200. Both of these sales were at the rate of five cents per share. About seven years later the plaintiff obtained a judgment against the company for $7,518.92, and, the corporation being insolvent, execution thereon failed and the judgment remained unsatisfied.

In bringing this action against the defendants as shareholders the plaintiff charged: (*a*) that the stock was issuel to the Hassons for grossly overvalued property; (*b*) that the Hassons were liable to creditors of the corporation for the unpaid balance on the stock; and (*c*) that by the rule laid down in an earlier case decided by the Supreme Court of California [38] the defendants, even if they were *bona fide* transferees for value, were liable to the plaintiff for the unpaid balance on the shares issued to them after being returned to the corporation by the Hassons. The defendants contended: (*a*) that the Hassons did not in fact return any stock to the corporate treasury and that therefore the issue to the defendants was an overissue of stock and, as such, was an *ultra vires* issue against which the rule of shareholders' liability for the difference between the value of the property and the par value of the stock should not apply; and (*b*) that, since it is common knowledge that there is no relation between the par value of mining stock and the assets of the corporation, creditors could not be supposed to rely upon any representation that the corporation had received assets equal to the par value of its stock, and hence the rule that shareholders are liable to creditors for an unpaid balance on stock should not apply to stock issues by corporations organized solely to develop and operate mining

[38] Perkins v. Cowles, 157 Cal. 625, 108 Pac. 711 (1910).

properties where all, or practically all, of the stock is issued in return for undeveloped claims of real but speculative value.

A mining expert for the plaintiff testified that if the indications were borne out by future development of the mine, the latter would attain an earning capacity which would enable the payment of "good dividends" on $1,000,000 of stock. This opinion was based upon an examination made after $150,000 had been expended in developing the mine. But the same expert testified that after the $150,000 had been so spent he was asked by one of the Hassons whether it would be wise to accept $250,000 for the property and his reply was that he thought that figure to represent "a very good value" for it. Another mining expert called for the plaintiff testified that at the time of the transfer of the property to the corporation he would have considered it worth between $25,000 and $35,000. This was the only testimony as to the value of the claims.

The court below tried the case on the theory that the opinion of the directors as to the value of the property was wholly immaterial, and confined the issue to the actual value of the property at the time of the transfer to the corporation. On this issue it found that the mining claims had a value not disproportionate to the amount of stock issued for them, that the consideration for the stock was "reasonable, just, and adequate," and that the property *would yield dividends* on $1,000,000. Therefore, it gave judgment for the defendants. Its finding was based upon prospective earning power as determined at a time subsequent to the transfer, after $150,000 had been spent in developing the mine. The Supreme Court reversed this judgment and remanded the case for a new trial for the reason that the capitalization, having been based upon prospective earning power, did not represent the "actual cash value" of the property.

Replying to the contention that the ordinary law of stockholders' liability does not apply to mining corporations, the court said that although *In re South Mountain Consolidated Mining Company*[39]

[39] 5 Fed. 403, 7 Sway. 30 (D. C., D. Cal., 1881), *aff'd,* 14 Fed. 347, 8 Sway. 366 (C. C., D. Cal., 1882). The question in this case was whether the acceptance of stock in a mining corporation creates any obligation to pay to the corporation or to its creditors the nominal value of the stock so accepted. The court answered this question in the negative and decided that a creditor of a mining corporation was left to the statutory liability of the stockholder for his *pro rata* share of the corporate debts, a statutory rule that is peculiar to California. The decision was based entirely upon an asserted difference between mining corporations, as organized in California, and other corporations. In discussing

constituted a precedent for this view, the rule announced in that case no longer properly expressed the law in force in California since the Supreme Court of that state had never given more than tentative recognition to the doctrine of the case and had certainly never approved it.[40] The alleged custom of issuing mining stock for property the value of which bore no relation to the par value of the stock was, according to the court, a clear infringement of California law. This law (by which the parties in the principal case were bound, since they had not pleaded the laws of Arizona, where the corporation was organized) had already been interpreted by the California courts as follows:

> ". . . the rule is that where the corporation and stockholder have agreed upon a given valuation for the property transferred, such valuation is binding and conclusive unless it is fraudulent in purpose or effect. But if the parties have put upon the property a valuation in excess of what they knew or believed to be its true value, this is a constructive fraud upon the creditors and the stock will be deemed paid only to the extent of the actual value of the property received in exchange for it."[41]
>
> . . .
>
> Consequently, unless the corporators knew or believed that the Ord Mountain mining claims were worth one million dollars, the stock is to be deemed paid only to the extent of the actual value of those claims at the time of the transfer to the corporation. We are also of the opinion upon a review of the cases that, however morally righteous was the belief of the corporators, if it was reached without intelligent examination into the elements of value, or by including items not really "property," or by the influence of self-interest, the issue would be as much a violation of the statutory and constitutional provisions as though it had been dictated by corrupt motives.[42]

---

the points at issue the court cited the custom of issuing mining stock with purely arbitrary par values which neither bore nor were intended, nor supposed by the public, to bear the slightest relation to the real value of the property, since the value was generally conjectural and very often imaginary. The appellate court said: "Mining corporations in California are, in these particulars, *sui generis*. They are organized and carried on upon principles, in these respects, wholly different from banking, railroad, insurance, and like commercial corporations having a *subscribed* capital stock. There is no agreement, express or implied, to pay up any particular amount of stock, and no one understands that there is. Certainly, none is intended by the parties." 14 Fed. 347, 349 (1882).

[40] See cases cited in 180 Cal., 359, 364, 181 Pac. 387, 389 (1919).

[41] Quoted by the court, 180 Cal. 359, 363, 181 Pac. 387, 388 (1919).

[42] *Ibid.*, 365, 181 Pac. 389.

At this point the court remarked that in determining whether or not the corporators did, in fact, honestly and intelligently believe the claims to be worth $1,000,000, considerable weight should be assigned to the fact that immediately after the stock was issued $500,000 of it was returned to the corporation and a short time thereafter $9,000 of it was sold to the defendants for $450 at the rate of five cents per share. It said:

These circumstances cast grave suspicion, to say the least, upon the existence of any honest and intelligent belief that the Ord Mountain claims were worth one million dollars.[43]

And finally, as to the bearing of prospective earning power on a proper valuation for the mining claims the court had the following to say:

The finding [of the lower court that there was no overvaluation] in effect rests upon the conclusion that the property was worth one million dollars, because it would pay dividends on one million dollars. It is not, however, found that the dividends referred to would be a reasonable or adequate return on an investment of one million dollars. Moreover, it is evident that future earning capacity rather than present cash value was adopted as a standard. We do not mean to say that prospective earning capacity, properly subordinated to other modes of ascertaining value, may not be considered in determining present cash value. We are compelled to conclude, however, that the court adopted a prospective earning power as the standard of value, and did not consider it as merely some evidence of present cash value which upon a review of the cases we take to be the standard approved by them. It was the duty of the court to determine this value by ascertaining as nearly as possible what a reasonably prudent investor who contemplated spending his own money would have been willing to pay for the Ord Mountain claims under the circumstances under which the corporators acted on the date of the transfer.[44]

Here again we have the idea expressed, even more clearly than in the language of the New Jersey courts, that prospective earning power may be used as a factor in computing the value of property to be exchanged for stock only in so far as this is one method of arriving at a prudent estimate of the cash price which intelligent and unbiased men would pay for the property. Recognition must also be given to the important question, whether the estimated amount of earnings will constitute a *proper return* for the type of enterprise

[43] *Ibid.*, 366, 181 Pac. 389.

[44] *Ibid.*, 366–67, 181 Pac. 389–90.

in question. Mining ventures, being risky affairs, should give promise of a larger return per dollar of stock issued than enterprises the probable earnings of which are more certain of realization and more stable in amount. Here, as in New Jersey and Illinois, the good faith of the directors or corporators may be impeached, not alone for an actual intent to deceive, but also by the showing of circumstances which lead by rational inference to the conclusion that no honest, disinterested, intelligent and prudent business man contemplating the purchase of the property with cash would have valued it at the figure placed upon it for stock-issue purposes by the directors. Nothing appears in the report of the case to indicate that the court had before it an exact estimate of the amount of expected earnings nor a rate at which the promoters and corporators capitalized the earnings. But the language of the court, just quoted, clearly means that if earnings are capitalized the parties using this method must prudently and intelligently reckon with the possibility and even probability that the earnings may not be realized.

Babbitt v. Read [45] is another case disapproving the reckless capitalization of anticipated earnings. This was an action by a trustee in bankruptcy of the Randolph-Macon Coal Company against certain promoter-shareholders and their transferees, to enforce a liability for unpaid stock subscriptions. The total of the claims proven in the bankruptcy proceedings was $2,376,041.43, of which $2,149,729.45 represented a deficiency judgment on a mortgage obligation which contained a " no-recourse clause," or waiver by the holders of bonds secured by the mortgage of all right to enforce any claim against stockholders for the payment of the mortgage debt.

Two of the defendants, Van Brunt and Kobusch, were the sole owners of surface and coal rights to some 23,000 acres of land in the state of Missouri. A coal mine located on this property was a going concern under their management. They conceived the idea of expanding operations by combining numerous potential coal properties which were then separately owned and by forming a corporation to take over the mining interests and to issue securities. To this end they acquired options and other interests in some 24,000 additional acres of supposed coal land. Altogether they owned or controlled by option or otherwise 47,000 acres of coal land and ten mines in operation.

[45] 215 Fed. 395 (D. C., S. D. N. Y., 1914), *aff'd,* 236 Fed. 42 (C. C. A., 2d Cir., 1916).

The defendant Read, a New York banker, and Gardiner, an eminent coal expert recommended by the banking firm of Spencer Trask & Company of New York, were associated with Van Brunt and Kobusch as promoters of the venture. Gardiner made a survey of the resources and commercial possibilities of the various properties as a combined unit and reported very favorably upon them. On the basis of current prices for mined coal and without regard to possible reductions in costs of production which might result from the combination, Gardiner estimated that the net earnings of the mines then in operation should be $375,000 in the first year and $600,000 in the second year. His estimates were based in part on the assumption that the mines could be more intensely operated if additional capital were raised, and in part on his opinion that the demand for coal would increase and that the market price of coal would either remain constant or increase. He also emphasized the favorable mining conditions in the region, the low cost of production as compared with the costs of competitors, the established reputation of the coal mined in this territory, the steadiness of coal prices, the absence of local competitive fields, the favorable situation of the property with respect to four great trunk-line railroads, the enormous coal resources thought to exist under the surface, and the fact that there were already ten operating mines on the premises.

In a second report to his associates he estimated that the property was then worth from $3,000,000 to $4,000,000 and that it would rapidly increase in value from the developments of the next two years. An important factor in his estimates was his assumption that the proposed enterprise would have adequate financial support.

On the same day on which Gardiner rendered his second report he, Read, Van Brunt and Kobusch entered into two agreements concerning the organization of the Randolph-Macon Coal Company and the distribution of its securities. The first agreement provided for the formation of the company with an authorized capital stock of $5,000,000 and an authorized first-mortgage bond issue of $3,000,000. This agreement further provided that in consideration of the transfer to the company by Kobusch and Van Brunt of all right, title, and interest in various plots of land aggregating about 47,000 acres which they controlled, the entire $5,000,000 of capital stock together with $1,800,000 of the first mortgage bonds should be issued to them. The balance of $1,200,000 authorized bonds was to be reserved for future financing. The second agreement made elaborate provision for the disposition of the bonds and stock thus to be issued to Van Brunt and Kobusch. The latter gentlemen agreed to transfer these $6,800,000 in securities to the banker, Read, to be held and disposed of by him substantially as follows:

1. Disposition of the $1,800,000 in bonds:
   - *a*) $600,000 to Van Brunt and Kobusch in payment for their actual cash outlays in acquiring the property and options for the company. These bonds were taken at a price of 90.
   - *b*) $1,200,000 to Read at a price of 90; proceeds to be used to purchase optioned property for the company, to improve and develop the property, and for working capital.

2. Disposition of the $5,000,000 in stock:
   - *a*) $2,000,000 to Kobusch and Van Brunt in full payment for their services in purchasing the properties for the company.
   - *b*) $1,850,000 to be retained by Read for services rendered and to be rendered in organizing and promoting the company in the capacity of banker and fiscal agent.
   - *c*) $150,000 to Van Brunt to be delivered to certain employees of the company. Any balance of this stock not so used was to be divided equally between Read, Van Brunt and Kobusch.
   - *d*) $500,000 to Gardiner, evidently in payment for his services in going to Missouri and making an engineering survey of the property and reporting his findings (Gardiner gave about two weeks of his time to this purpose) and for becoming president of the company.
   - *e*) $500,000 to be parceled out at the rate of $100,000 a year to Gardiner in full compensation for his services as president of the company. Gardiner was to receive all dividends on the entire $500,000 of stock from the start.

These agreements were carried out in detail. About ten days after Gardiner made his final report, the company was organized with the agreed capitalization by nominees of the promoters. These figureheads subscribed for the entire capital stock and appointed themselves the directors of the company. At the first meeting of the stockholders (consisting solely of the nominees of the promoters) one of their number offered to sell and convey, or cause to be conveyed, to the company in consideration of the payment and delivery of $5,000,000 par value of capital stock and $1,800,000 of first-mortgage bonds, the property and property rights aggregated by the promoters for the purpose. This offer was accepted, and in due course the securities were issued and transferred to the real parties at interest as indicated above.

The company was operated for about two years without profit, due to bad management of its affairs during an illness of Gardiner, to strikes, and to changed market conditions. At the end of two years the company was unable to pay interest on its mortgage debt, and foreclosure proceedings were soon instituted, as a result of which the property was sold for $100,000. Soon thereafter the company was adjudged a bankrupt and this action grew out of the company's bankruptcy.

The following facts are extracted from the evidence before the court:

1. The precise figures of $1,800,000 of bonds and $5,000,000 of stock at which the company was capitalized were not based upon an exact mathematical computation, but were regarded by the promoters as a minimum well within the value of the property as a consolidated and going concern with adequate capital. The basis of this opinion of the promoters, however, was the Gardiner reports to the effect that the property contained a large amount of coal which could be mined at a substantial profit over a long period of years.

2. The total cost of the property to the vendors (promoters) was $1,150,652.15.

3. The mining expert, Gardiner, had a wide reputation and was generally regarded as one of the most competent in the country.

4. Van Brunt and Kobusch evidently believed that the enterprise would be a success, for, prior to their connection with the Randolph-Macon Coal Company as promoters, they had acquired in their own right 23,000 acres, or substantially half of the property later turned over to the new corporation.

5. After the enterprise was launched, Read, Gardiner, and Van Brunt showed their faith in the success of the concern by lending money to it to help it meet its obligations.

6. This was not a stock-jobbing scheme. The stock was not dumped on the market or sold in any way to bring Read anything other than an underwriting profit. He sold the **$1,200,000** of bonds to The Metropolitan Life Insurance Company at 95 (thus making a gross profit on them of **$60,000**) and gave a 10 per cent stock bonus with the bonds. With minor exceptions this **$120,000** of stock given as a bonus was all of the stock which was distributed to the public.

7. Van Brunt and Kobusch sold a part or all of the **$600,000** in bonds to recoup their actual cash outlays.

8. The value of the property based upon the tonnage, times profit, minus amortization charges and royalties, ranged, according to estimates of witnesses for the defense, from **$12,000,000** to **$21,-000,000** depending upon the assumptions as to the amount of coal to be mined, the royalty and amortization rates, and the profit per ton.

Confining our attention to the question of overvaluation, we find that the plaintiff contended: (*a*) that the property was worth no more for stock-issue purposes than it cost the promoters; (*b*) that the law of Missouri, where the Randolph-Macon Coal Company was incorporated, should govern the case; (*c*) that the question of the good faith of the incorporators and directors was immaterial under Missouri law; (*d*) that even if the court should elect to decide the case without special reference to the law of Missouri the defendants should be held liable under the general law of the land because the issue of the capital stock in the manner indicated constituted an actual fraud, in that the stock was issued for property which was grossly and deliberately overvalued; (*e*) and that the method of basing the capitalization upon anticipated profits to be derived from the mining of coal years in the future was illusory, particularly where it was not certain that the company would have adequate working capital.

The defendants answered: (*a*) that the law of Missouri was not applicable to this case since the decisions of the Missouri courts, in respect of the subject-matter, were contrary to the well-established views of the federal courts; (*b*) that the transactions by which the stock was issued were undertaken in good faith; (*c*) that the defendants would be liable only in case actual fraud should be proven;

(*d*) that in fact the value of the property was greatly in excess of the par value of the securities issued for it; (*e*) that the proper and usual method of valuing mining properties, and the one which was used by the defendants, was the " tonnage basis " by which royalties and a proper charge for amortization of principal are deducted from the sum computed by multiplying the available tonnage of mineral by a minimum rate of profit; and (*f*) that the properties were worth much more under combined ownership than they were worth separately.

The United States District Court did not have occasion to fix a definite value for the property, but it did find on the record before it that the value was less than $6,800,000 by an amount sufficient to require defendants to pay all general creditors' claims with interest and costs.[46] The Circuit Court of Appeals, Second Circuit, affirmed the decree.

The District court gave elaborate consideration to the contentions of the parties concerning the question of what law should govern the case and concluded that the issues should be decided in the light of the law of the state in which the company was incorporated. As to the question of good faith the court acquitted the defendants of all suspicion of fraudulent purpose by saying:

> It is evident that these men thought that the property would earn its own way, and while, for various reasons, this result was not attained, I am satisfied that they honestly believed that the enterprise would stand the capitalization, and that they acted in that regard, in good faith. . . .
>
> . . .
>
> I am entirely satisfied (as I have heretofore indicated) that there was no fraudulent purpose or conduct in connection with the organization of this company. On the contrary, I am convinced that the promoters entered into the enterprise in good faith and with the greatest measure of confidence in its success. [Here follows a review of the evidence going to show that the

[46] The decree of the court went against the defendants, Read, the executors of Gardiner, and Van Brunt, requiring them jointly and severally to pay to the trustee in bankruptcy such amount as might be necessary to pay in full, with interest, the claims of those general creditors who should prove to be entitled to payment. Kobusch was not made a party to the suit. The decree went against the plaintiff so far as the claims of holders of the bonds with the " no-recourse clause " were concerned. The bill was dismissed as to those defendants who accepted bonus stock from Read at the time of purchase of bonds, as the court found them to have been *bona fide* purchasers without notice of any irregularity in the original issue of the stock.

promoters had great confidence in the ultimate success of the enterprise.] . . . Therefore this is not one of those cases where a number of men associate together for the purpose of putting on the market knowingly grossly overvalued stock, the proceeds of the sale of which they convert to their own uses. I think any one reading this record will be satisfied that all these men believed that they had a large proposition with splendid possibilities and that they believed so thoroughly in the future of the company that they were willing and were glad, in the main, to hold their stock until it reached a satisfactory market value.[47]

Turning next to the question of the value of the property, the court found that the views of the plaintiff and those of the defendants were radically different. The plaintiff contended that the value was not in excess of the cost of the property to the promoters, or about $1,150,000, whereas the defendants contended that the value, computed on the tonnage basis, ranged from $12,000,000 to $21,000,000, depending upon the rate of amortization, royalty rate, and the estimated amount of coal on the property. The court, noting that in its approach to the question of " actual value " it must discard all questions of good faith, pointed out that the defendants had made up their valuation by regarding the enterprise as a going concern with adequate capital resources, particular attention being paid to its anticipated earning capacity. It continued:

We are thus brought to a consideration of the theories of the defense, now presented as to value, but not developed prior to the incorporation of the company. Defendants contend that their experts have sustained calculations and not theories, but I cannot escape the conclusion that the testimony unfolds theoretical computations as distinguished from business market values . . . The tonnage basis of calculation is that which assumes the tonnage of coal in the ground irrespective, however, of the time that it would take to pay this coal on the surface ready for shipment and market requirements. There is much testimony on this subject, the net result of which is that the company owns coal in the ground of the aggregate value of many millions which, through a long period of years (indeed centuries) can or will be mined . . .

There is more than one difficulty with the theories of the defendants. Value, of course, means market value. It surely cannot be an abstraction. There is force in the argument of the plaintiff that actuarial figures dispose of the theories of the defendants. From the standpoint of practical business dealing, a ton of coal mined a century hence certainly cannot be worth a ton of coal extracted from the mine today . . . The real question is, How much,

[47] 215 Fed. 395, 403, 408–9.

under all the facts and circumstances, viewed from a practical business standpoint, were these properties worth? My own notion is that the real value was somewhere between the two extremes contended for by the parties hereto. It may very well be that there is substantial added value in collecting into a controllable whole a considerable number of units. Such control gives a better opportunity for influence upon the market and for economies in various directions of management and administration. But the difficulty is that there is no proof in this regard as to what, if any, increase in value, as such, there was between the units considered separately and these units when aggregated into a field of 47,000 acres; the plaintiff is right when he insists that the *evidence* fails to show a basis upon which added combination value may be figured.[48]

In affirming the decree of the District Court Judge Learned Hand of the Circuit Court of Appeals expressed himself as follows on the question of valuation:

As to Gardiner, the proof is beyond question; he puts the outside value on the whole property at $4,000,000, which, while we do not accept it, is too little to save him against the claims allowed by the District Court. As to Read, assuming Gardiner did not speak for him, the mere situation shows the character of the undertaking. The total money expended in purchasing coal properties was $1,150,000, or about one-sixth of the capitalization. It is, of course, conceivable that the promoters got such a fabulous bargain as this; but how likely is it? Moreover, if it were such a good bargain and the coal remained, as it did, it is scarcely possible that it should lose so much of its value as never to be able to pay a dividend, though subsequently organized on about its cost basis. [The court evidently refers here to the subsequent history of the property after its sale on foreclosure of the mortgage.] The sale value of coal thereabouts was not more than $20 per acre, and the necessary value to justify the capitalization was over $140. We may allow that consolidation into a single holding increased the value, but with what warrant may we say it increased the value sevenfold? Furthermore, we should be blind to the commonest facts of finance, if we allowed so transparent a disguise to pass muster. The constant effort to inflate capitalization so that the earnings shall not be too apparent could have no more characteristic an expression. That the incorporators honestly supposed that the property had a value beyond its bonded indebtedness we are quite willing to admit, but that they thought the stock at the time worth par passes belief. Their expectations did not constitute property until they could put them into the realm of such established certainty as would lead men generally to share them. The mere fact of the distribution of the sock as bonus demonstrates that they had not got so far as that.

[48] *Ibid.*, 415, 416.

The defendants' calculations of value were properly characterized by the District Judge as the merest speculation, and even then at the expense of the most commonplace actuarial theory. The peg to hang them on is the testimony that royalties are the "basis" of calculating value. Doubtless they are, but not upon the present full value of royalties payable a century hence. "Value" is what the thing will bring to-day in exploitation or exchange under some presently possible conditions. It has often been the custom in excessive capitalizations to try to justify watered stock issues by the statement that the value to the incorporators is such and such, greatly in excess of what they paid. That may or may not be true, according as the combination had enhanced the economic efficiency of the units, or as it results in the control of the market or the like. Some properties cannot be successfully sold; they are too big to have a genuine market. This perhaps was one, and perhaps its fairest measure of value lay in future exploitation; but just in so far as that exploitation involved the future it was subject to the discount of the future, even after the promoters' confidence became shared by the public. Moreover, to suppose that these coal lands were so little subject to competition that one could buy them at one-seventh of their value is wholly unwarranted. The region was known, it was being freely exploited already, it was no secret El Dorado; if the lands had any such value in combination, it is not possible that the demand for them should not have created a higher price. Judge Mayer was therefore certainly right in finding that, whatever its value, the property as a whole was not worth more than $6,600,000. That was all that he need find.[49]

This case is a fair example of the complexity of circumstance which determines the character of judicial decisions in suits to contest the validity of stock issued for property. The promoters capitalized their property at more than six times its cost to them and at more than one and one-half times the maximum valuation placed upon it by their mining expert. The bonds alone provided the means of acquiring the property from previous owners and nearly half of the stock, which exceeded the bonds in nominal value, was retained by two of the promoters for their "services" in promoting the enterprise. Over a third of the stock was given to Read for performing the simple task of arranging for the formal incorporation of the company and for future services as fiscal agent. Some of this stock was given away by Read as a bonus in order that he might sell the bonds at a profit. Gardiner, the other promoter, received $500,000 of the stock for devoting two weeks of his time in making a preliminary study of the project, and another $500,000 of it was reserved for the

[49] 236 Fed. 42, 46-47.

purpose of paying him a salary as president of the company. It was apparent that none of the promoters treated the stock as the equivalent of cash.

All of these circumstances taken together make it clear that no rational attempt was made to have the capitalization correspond to the value of the property. The promoters were characteristically optimistic about the latter and had their eyes on the rosy prospect of a prosperous future when they decided upon the capitalization. But it is impossible to say that any *one* item in the evidence was conclusive on the question of overvaluation. Did the court decide to hold the defendants liable because there was too great a discrepancy between what the promoters paid for the property and the amount of securities which they issued to themselves for it? We cannot say. Nor can we say that the court's decision was based upon its view that prospects are not property under the statute, or that future income must be discounted because of the fact that time must elapse before it is realized. Neither can we reconcile the statement of the court that the directors' opinion as to the value of the property was irrelevant under Missouri law, with its further statement that Gardiner's liability was unquestionably established *because* his own estimate of the value of the property ($4,000,000) was less than the capitalization.

Although we can give no *single* reason for the decision of the court, it is clear that a part of the justification for its decision lay in the fact that the promoters took entirely too prospective a view of the worth of the property when they reckoned up the future earnings without sufficient discount for time and risk. As the court put it, "Their expectations did not constitute property until they could put them into the realm of such established certainty as would lead men generally to share them." Future expectations must be supported by strong probabilities of realization. Mere guesses by self-interested parties will not be enough.

An opinion by a federal court interpreting the law of Alabama, *Grant v. East and West Railroad Co.,*[50] is worth mentioning because of the attention given by the court to capitalized earning power as evidence of the value of property in preference to the price paid for the property by the promoter at a forced sale.

The case arose upon a bill in equity for the foreclosure of a mortgage of the East and West Railroad Company of Alabama. An aux-

[50] 54 Fed. 569 (C. C. A., 5th Cir., 1893).

iliary and dependent bill was thereupon filed by James Grant, who held a certain portion of the mortgage bonds, against the respondents in the original bill, to declare void that portion of the bonds which were held by the respondents and to foreclose the mortgage for the benefit of the remaining bondholders. Grant's bill was based on the allegation that the respondents, Browning and others, had purchased the railroad property at a forced sale for $22,500, had spent $350,000 on improvements, and had then sold this property to the East and West Railroad Company, organized by them, in exchange for $375,000 of bonds and $375,000 of stock. Instead of contending that the bonds had been paid for but that the stock was a sheer bonus, Grant pleaded that the stock should be considered full-paid but that the bonds had been issued for no valid consideration and were therefore void. As " innocent holders for value " Grant and his associates claimed the benefit of the mortgage, but they also claimed that those bonds which were in the hands of Browning and of others with notice of the manner of their issuance should be cancelled.

The court below granted the foreclosure decree which was prayed for in the original bill but refused the relief demanded by Grant and others. The latter parties thereupon appealed and the action of the lower court was affirmed. The opinion under discussion was that of the appellate court, on a final hearing of the appeal.

Our concern with the opinion in this case relates only to that portion of it which deals with the contentions that the property was worth approximately what it cost the vendors, $375,000, rather than $750,000 at which it was capitalized. The constitution and code of Alabama provided for the issuance of stock for property at its " money value " and for the imposition of a liability upon subscribers to the extent of their failure to pay for their stock. Construing these provisions in the light of the facts of this case the court said:

The property of the Cherokee Railroad Company [a *pro tem* holder of the railroad property between its acquisition by the Cherokee Iron Company and its sale to the East and West Railroad Company] embraced a line of operative railroad 37½ miles in length, equipped for operation, well located for securing and doing business, then doing a thriving trade, out of which it was making, and for several successive years had been making, net earnings to the amount of near $40,000 a year. Its original promoters and managers had expended on it several hundred thousand dollars. It was acquired by the Cherokee Iron Company under such circumstances as enabled that company to get it at a bid which it can hardly be seriously contended measured its real worth or intrinsic value to a purchaser able and willing to complete it and operate it. *There could be no fraud or badge of fraud in such a purchaser claiming the benefit of his bargain, and valuing his property, when repaired and extended, according to its capacity to make net earnings,* and according to what it would cost to build and equip such a road, then and there, if it had never been built, and the right of way had yet to be acquired, and the road built from the stump. On this subject it can hardly be claimed that the testimony in conflicting. To an impartial mind accustomed to weighing evidence the overwhelming weight of the proof shows that the property was worth more than $375,000. And after a careful study of all the evidence offered we fully concur in the finding of the judge who heard the case at the circuit that "the weight of the testimony of experts and of others acquainted with the property is to the effect that the Cherokee Railroad was not overvalued." [51]

Here, as in the other cases reviewed above, there is no single piece of evidence to which we may ascribe the court's decision. Clearly, the court was of the opinion that property bought at a forced sale and improved by the purchaser is worth more than its cost. Under the particular circumstances of this case the court thought the property was worth what it would cost to reproduce it. There are two reasons why the court may have held this view. Either it felt that expert opinion that the property was not overvalued was conclusive, or it felt that the property was worth the face value of the bonds and stock because it had a demonstrated earning power of about $40,000 per year. This latter sum was less than six per cent on the capitalization, but the court very plainly said that promoters were justified in valuing a property of this sort on the basis of its earning power. It will be noted, however, that the court did not stop to discuss the point as to whether or not the ratio of earnings to capitalization was a proper one. Interest on the $375,000 of bonds would absorb $22,500 of the earnings, leaving only $17,500 for the stock, or less than 5 per cent. Perhaps this is the reason why the court mowed down the claims of the plaintiff with a double-edged sword, the other edge being cost of reproduction.

Finally, in *Gamble v. Queens County Water Company* [52] the court expressed the view that it was legitimate to take into account the prospective earning power of a completed waterworks in deciding

[51] 54 Fed. 576 (C. C. A., 5th Cir., 1893). The italics are mine.

[52] 123 N. Y. 91, 25 N. E. 201 (1890), *rev'g* 52 Hun 166, 5 N. Y. S. 124 (1889).

how much stock might properly be issued for the latter. The circumstances of the case have already been stated briefly above.[53]

In reversing the judgment below the court said:

The question which at once confronts the company is, would it be good policy to refuse to purchase at the price named ($110,000), with not only the possible, but the very probable contingency of seeing a portion of its own legitimate field of operations occupied by some rival, either to its entire exclusion, or else under circumstances where it would be obliged to compete for business? It might be that the company could well afford to pay such price, considering the prospective profits to be derived from supplying the village with water, and the driving out of any competition with it in such work. Any court considering all these facts, and taking all the circumstances into consideration, might reasonably come to the conclusion that the value of this property to the company defendant was the sum of $110,000.

The court below has not passed upon this question after taking all these matters into consideration, and if after doing so it should find the value of the property to the company was the last-named sum, then of course all basis for maintaining this action would be at an end.

But if after a critical examination of the facts the court should find the value of the property at the time of the proposed purchase to have been but $80,000 or $85,000, the vote to pay the sum above stated in stock and bonds, is not to be condemned as a fraud, unless the majority acted in bad faith. Possible or probable prospective value of property thus ordered to be purchased at a stockholders' meeting, may be taken into consideration upon this question of fraud, and actual good faith in the majority shareholders might be decided, among other things, by a consideration of the reasonableness, or the reverse, of such expectations of future value.[54]

[53] Pages 132–33.

[54] 123 N. Y. 91, 104–5, 25 N. E. 201, 204 (1890). *Cf.* Donald v. American Smelting & Refining Co., 62 N. J. Eq. 729, 48 Atl. 771, 1116 (1901), *rev'g* 61 N. J. Eq. 458, 48 Atl. 786 (1901). The facts of the two cases are very similar but the New Jersey court obviously followed a stricter rule. It is interesting to note, in contrast with the language of the New York court, that the dicta of the New Jersey court, 62 N. J. Eq. 729, at pp. 731–32, 48 Atl. 771, at 772, is the basis for the more fully developed "reasonable cash value rule" under which the capitalization of prospective profits has been subjected to particularly careful scrutiny by the courts of that state. By contrast, the New York court appears in a substantially similar case, to require that prospects of future profits be taken into account. However, the New Jersey cases condemning the capitalization of prospective profits have involved the rights of creditors.

It is also interesting to note that in the *Donald* case the court stated that a stricter rule applied to *contemplated* issues of stock than to issues already made, whereas the New York court states the reverse rule.

Although this was not a case calling for a determination of the exact value of property exchanged for stock, the dicta of the court make it very clear that the capitalization of anticipated profits is not regarded by the New York court with the apprehension characteristic of the courts of New Jersey. The New York court revealed its friendly attitude toward the capitalization of expected earnings in three ways: (*a*) by stressing the importance of the *value of the property to the corporation* for its own peculiar uses rather than the value to the vendor; (*b*) by insisting that " prospective profits " and " possible or probable prospective values " should have been taken into account by the trial court; and (*c*) by emphasizing as an element in value the prevention of competition or saving of business losses which could reasonably be anticipated through the elimination of a competitor.[55] The fact that creditors' rights were not involved may have accounted in part for the liberality of the court.

[55] The following cases are also worthy of consideration in their bearing upon the subject of this chapter: Barnard v. Sweet, 74 Colo. 302, 221 Pac. 1093 (1923); Buck v. Jones, 18 Colo. App. 250, 70 Pac. 951 (1902); Gillett v. Chicago Title & Trust Co., 230 Ill. 373, 82 N. E. 891 (1907); Garden City Sand Co. v. American Refuse Crematory Co., 205 Ill. 42, 68 N. E. 724 (1903), *rev'g* 105 Ill. App. 342 (1903); State Trust Co. v. Turner, 111 Iowa 664, 82 N. W. 1029 (1900); Libby v. Tobey, 82 Me. 397, 19 Atl. 904 (1890); Kingston v. Nichols, 221 Mich. 677, 192 N. W. 768 (1923); Durand v. Brown, 236 Fed. 609 (C. C. A., 6th Cir., 1916); Kelly v. Clark, 21 Mont. 291, 53 Pac. 959 (1898); Rathbone v. Ayer, 196 N. Y. 503, 89 N. E. 1111 (1909), *rev'g* 121 App. Div. (N. Y.) 355, 105 N. Y. S. 1041 (1907); People *ex rel.* Westchester Street RR. Co. v. Public Service Commission, 158 App. Div. (N. Y.) 251, 143 N. Y. S. 148 (1913), *mod.*, 210 N. Y. 456, 104 N. E. 952 (1914), rehearing denied, 211 N. Y. 533, 105 N. E. 1095 (1914); Williams v. McClave, 168 App. Div. (N. Y.) 192, 154 N. Y. S. 38 (1915), modifying and *aff'g* 85 Misc. (N. Y.) 184, 148 N. Y. S. 93 (1914); Rafferty v. Buffalo City Gas Co., 37 App. Div. (N. Y.) 618, 56 N. Y. S. 288 (1899); Finletter v. Acetylene Light, Heat & Power Co., 215 Pa. 86, 64 Atl. 429 (1906); Richardson v. Treasure Hill Mining Co., 23 Utah, 366, 65 Pac. 74 (1901); Manhattan Trust Co. v. Seattle Coal & Iron Co., 16 Wash. 499, 48 Pac. 333, 737 (1897); 19 Wash. 493, 53 Pac. 951 (1898).

For other cases see footnotes to the succeeding chapter.

CHAPTER VII

SPECIAL ASPECTS OF THE EARNING POWER BASIS OF CAPITALIZATION

The previous chapter has brought out the point that many courts, despite occasional statements which, taken alone, would seem to lead to a contrary conclusion, do in fact accept estimates of past and prospective earnings as evidence of the reasonable valuation at which property may be taken by a corporation in exchange for stock. Certain aspects of this general principle of valuation by reference to expected earning power remain to be discussed in the present chapter. They have been excluded from the preceding chapter mainly for the reason that the cases in which they appear do not raise the question of profits capitalization in its most direct form.

The explanation of the indirect way in which they raise the question is not far to seek. Promoters are professional optimists. They tend to a large extent to base the capitalization of their corporations upon expectations. These expectations are in last analysis reducible to a capitalized value of anticipated earnings. But as a general rule the promoters' hopes in this regard are not reducible to precise quantitative computations. They do not estimate future earnings at any exact amount and divide that sum by a rate which they have determined, after mature reflection, to be an appropriate one for the particular enterprise. Moreover, even if the promoters had made any such mathematical computation they would hesitate to disclose the fact in court. They know the danger of precise formulae and are loath to argue a case in terms of the propriety of any exact quantitative computation. The rate of capitalization may be criticized for failure to reflect the risks of the enterprise, or the manner of estimating future earnings may be attacked.[1] The situation is not unlike that discussed in an earlier chapter where it was pointed out that promoters prefer to get compensation for their services by issuing an excessive amount of stock for *physical* property rather than by a direct issue of stock for services. The latter is more vulnerable to direct attack.

[1] See, *e.g.*, Dee Co. v. Proviso Coal Co., *supra*, c. VI, note 32; See v. Heppenheimer, *supra*, c. VI, note 2; Babbitt v. Read, *supra*, c. VI, note 45.

Consequently, it is uncommon to find a case in which the promoters or shareholders have sought to justify the amount of stock issued by reference to a capitalization of prospective profits. More commonly the claim of overvaluation is met by a counter claim that the stock issue was based upon the value of the property "to the corporation," or upon the value which the property would attain as soon as the enterprise became established, or upon the increased value which would result from combining competing properties. To these special aspects of the capitalized earnings basis we now turn. They are: first, the use of prospective *versus* present value as a basis of capitalization; second, the question whether additional values resulting from a consolidation of properties may be included; third, the concept of "value to the corporation"; and fourth, the "reasonable cash value" rule as a standard of valuation. All four of these aspects of the problem are closely interrelated, and they are discussed separately only for the sake of convenient exposition.

Prospective Value versus Present Value as the Basis of Capitalization

The question that we raise here is whether property may be valued for stock-issue purposes, not at the relatively low value which a conservative appraiser would place upon a new and undeveloped property by virtue of the uncertainties of the promotion period, but rather at the much higher value which the promoters hope or expect to be justified when the business gets on its feet and becomes "seasoned." In short, may property be capitalized, not at its existing value, but rather at its prospective or potential value?

This question is not to be confused with the question whether prospective earning power may be capitalized. For all values, in the proper sense of the word, are simply a capitalization of prospective earnings. Our question is, rather, whether this capitalization must involve a full discount for the risk that the expectation may not be realized — a discount just as great as would be made on the market place, or as would be insisted upon by an intelligent investor who is considering whether or not to purchase an interest in the property before its earning power has been tested out.

On strictly logical grounds, this question would seem to leave no room for argument. If stock must be issued for full value, and if this value must be ascertained as of the time when the stock is issued, then it would follow as a matter of course that a present valuation, with full discounting for risk, rather than a prospective valuation, would be required. Yet courts are not always logical, and we must therefore not take any such conclusion for granted merely because it would seem to follow inevitably from the premise that value at the time of issue is the proper standard.

Let it first be noted that, whatever the courts may hold, American financial practice, particularly up to within the last few years, has sanctioned a capitalization based on values that are to be expected, rather than one limited to values that are already reflected in the market place, or even in the minds of the promoters themselves. A clear illustration of this practice is to be found in almost every railroad reorganization, where the reorganized company issues stocks and bonds in such large amounts that they are sure to sell at a heavy discount for years following the reorganization. As one railroad executive put it:

> And stocks so issued [in railway reorganization in excess of existing values] are in no sense fictitious. They represent actual values, and are drafts, for value received, on more prosperous times.[2]

The same idea was repeatedly expressed by promoters and business men before the United States Industrial Commission at the time when it made its exhaustive investigation of the "trusts." For example, when it was pointed out to Mr. H. O. Havemeyer that the sugar trust issued large quantities of trust certificates (later converted into stock of the American Sugar Refining Company) for plants which were losing money and which were worthless under conditions then existing, he replied that, although they were worthless under those conditions, they were "not worthless under the conditions that were about to prevail."[3] He referred to the expected enhancement in the value of the plants after monopoly should have been attained and prices for the product raised in consequence. The customary method of trust promotion which was in use at the time involved the issuance of quantities of stock against prospects, rather than against existing values.[4]

[2] Fink, Henry, *Over-Capitalization* (1908), 45 Ry. Age Gazette 487. Mr. Fink made the statement in commenting upon the increase in capitalization of the Norfolk & Western which resulted from the reorganization of that road in 1896.

[3] U. S. Industrial Commission, Reports (1900–1902), Vol. I, *Digest of Evidence*, p. 68, *Testimony*, p. 124.

[4] *Ibid.*, Vol. XIX, p. 617, Vols. I, XIII, Index, *s. v.*, "Capitalization," "Se-

Coming now to the opinion of the courts, we find them often stating, as a general principle, that it is the present value of the property rather than its future or expected value which must be considered. We also find them stating, in some of those cases where capitalized prospective earning power has been admitted as evidence of the value, that this earning power must be discounted for futurity.[5] A close study of the cases, however, clearly indicates that some courts have not followed out the full implications of this general principle and that they have allowed valuations to stand which can only be justified as being based upon potential, or expected future values. But there seems to be considerable divergence among various courts on this point.

Cases which deny that mere potential values may be capitalized. — Turning first to those cases which support the strict *present*-value rule, one may cite as perhaps the clearest expression of such a principle the California case, *Rhode v. Dock-Hop Co.*[6] This involved an action by creditors against stockholders of an insolvent gold mining company. The trial court had found the defendant stockholders liable for stock issued without full consideration. This holding was reversed by the Supreme Court of California for reasons that did not involve the basis of valuation of the property, but the latter court directed a new trial if the parties should choose to amend

---

curities." The usual practice was to issue preferred stock equal to the supposed value of the *tangible* property of the constituents (though in many instances the amount of preferred stock issued was more nearly an estimate of the supposed value of the enterprises as going concerns, including the value of good will, brands, etc.), and common stock in equal or greater amounts to represent intangibles such as promoters' services, earning power, good will and opportunity. The common-stock issues were in essence intended to represent enhanced values which the promoters hoped would result from the attainment of a monopoly position and from anticipated reductions in the cost of production. That these hopes were regarded as unsubstantial and visionary in the security markets is indicated by the fact that both the preferred and common stocks sold at substantial discounts. MEAD, *op. cit. supra* (c. I, note 8), pp. 336–55. See also, DEWING, ARTHUR S., FINANCIAL POLICY OF CORPORATIONS (Rev. ed., New York, 1926), Book IV, Appendix; U. S. BUREAU OF CORPORATIONS, REPORT ON THE STEEL INDUSTRY (Washington, 1911), Pt. I, pp. xx–xxii, 15–21, 166–80.

[5] Babbitt v. Read, *supra*, c. VI, note 45; Holcombe v. Trenton White City Co., *supra*, c. VI, note 13. See also Strickland v. National Salt Co., 77 N. J. Eq. 328, 336–39, 76 Atl. 1048, 1052 (1910), *aff'd* on other grounds, 79 N. J. Eq. 182, 223, 81 Atl. 828, 832 (1911).

[6] 184 Cal. 367, 194 Pac. 11 (1920).

their pleadings. The only point that is of interest here is the comment of the appellate court on the valuation of the property, a comment which may perhaps be regarded as dictum, except that it was probably designed to guide the lower court in the event of a new trial. The pertinent passage is as follows:

The stock had a par value of a dollar a share, and the shares which it was claimed the defendants owned, and which in fact they did own, were part of a lot of 599,995 shares issued as fully paid up, but in consideration for the transfer to the company of certain unpatented mining claims with the improvements upon them. These claims had been previously worked and abandoned by another company, and then relocated by one Knapp, who had been interested in the former company and was one of the promoters of the present debtor company. The history, character, and condition of these claims were such that it is well-nigh incredible that they had an actual immediate value of six hundred thousand, less five, dollars, or that the directors of the company believed that they had any such value. *The directors may have thought that there was a chance of the claims becoming of that value upon development and consequent demonstration of what they actually contained, but there is a very great difference between capitalizing a mining company upon the basis of what it is hoped its ground may be worth when developed, and capitalizing it on the basis of what its ground is actually worth undeveloped.*

When the capital of a corporation is paid in in something other than money, the thing accepted in lieu of money must be reasonably near its equivalent, and while the hopes or prospects for a property affect its immediate cash value, it is that cash value, and not the future value of the property if the hopes or prospects are realized, which must be taken as the basis of capitalization. . . . In this case, the court found that the directors of the company did not believe the claims to exceed in actual value two hundred and fifty thousand dollars, and if any criticism is to be made of the finding, it is that it is too favorable to the defendants, that the figure found is too great, rather than it is too small.[7]

Another California case of the same sort is *R. H. Herron Co. v. Shaw.*[8] This was an action against several stockholders of the Kern River Mining and Power Company to recover an unpaid balance on stock.

The authorized capital of the Company was $1,000,000, divided into shares of $1 each, of which the defendants held in the aggre-

[7] 184 Cal. 367, 369–70, 194 Pac. 12 (1920). Our italics.

[8] 165 Cal. 668, 133 Pac. 488 (1913).

gate 537,635 shares. The trial court found that certain persons owned water-rights, mining claims, and mining machinery and that in consideration of the transfer thereof to the company the latter issued 695,000 shares of its stock as fully paid and non-assessable. The court also found that nothing further had ever been paid for or on account of these shares, that the market value of the property did not then exceed $69,500, that the board of directors of the corporation did not believe that the then market value of the property was $695,000, but did believe that it exceeded $69,500, and believed that the property *could be developed to a value in excess of $695,000*, and that the directors " in issuing said stock for said property acted in good faith and in the honest belief that said property could and would be developed so that the said property would have a market value in excess of $695,000." The stock owned by the defendants was a part of the 695,000 shares referred to above. The report of the case does not reveal whether the defendants were the original takers of the stock or transferees.

It is evident, but not stated in the opinion, that the defendants sought to avoid liability by pleading the good faith of the directors in issuing stock equal in par value to the sum which they regarded to be the potential value of the property. A further defense was sought to be set up by pleading *In re South Mountain Consolidated Mining Co.*[9] as a precedent. The decision in the latter case was liberal to the holders of watered stock issued by mining companies, because the court felt that it was well known and universally understood by creditors and shareholders alike that mining companies issue stock for undeveloped properties whose value is wholly unknown and prospective. The theory of the decision in that case was based upon the grounds that the universality of the then current practice of mining companies of issuing stock in amounts fixed by mere guesses as to the probable value of mining claims when developed, rather than by known values, and the common knowledge that this was the general practice, justified the assumption that no creditor gives credit to mining corporations on the basis of the nominal amount of their outstanding capital stock.

Upon the findings stated above the trial court rendered judgment for the defendants, and the plaintiff appealed. The Supreme Court of California reversed the judgment below and denied the defendants a rehearing. Apropos of the value of the property the court said:

[9] *Supra,* c. VI, note 39.

The further fact found by the court that the directors acted in good faith and honestly believed that the property could and would be developed so that its market value would eventually exceed six hundred and ninety-five thousand dollars, does not relieve or excuse the stockholders from such liability [to creditors on stock issued for less than par]. As appellant's counsel well says, to hold that it would have that effect would be to sanction an arrangement to " throw the risk of the venture from the shoulders of the stockholders to those of the creditors." It is the value of the property in the condition it is in at the time of the exchange, the value as known to the parties and as they honestly believe it to be, that determines the liability, at least where there is no subsequent increase in value nor any intentional fraud. The parties may believe that the property will eventually rise to a value far above that at which it is exchanged, and they may willingly accept the hazard in view of the expected gain, but they have no right to demand that the creditor shall share the risk with them, in effect become their partner with no share in the profits, and lose his recourse on them if their speculation proves a bad one. The case cannot be distinguished in principle from *Vermont M. Co.* v. *Declez Granite Co.*, where stock of the par value of one hundred thousand dollars was sold for less than par in money. The parties may believe, and doubtless frequently do believe, that the money can be invested in property which can be developed so as to make it worth the par value of the stock. Whether the stock is invested in the property by direct exchange, or by first selling it for money and then buying the property from third persons therewith, the effect is the same and the same principle should control. The creditor is presumed to rely on the fact that the company has received, or will receive, full par value for the stock issued. He is not a partner with the stockholder, he cannot participate in the profits of their venture and he should not be required to assume their burden or hazard.[10]

The contention of the defendants that they should not be held liable to the plaintiff because of the decision in the *South Mountain Mining Company* case, *supra,* was overruled by the court on the ground that there was nothing in the record to indicate whether the company was organized to mine precious metals or to develop water power. The only indication that the company was to engage in mining was found in the use of the word " mining " in the corporate name. This the court considered to be insufficient to bring the case within the rule of the *South Mountain Mining Company* case, even if the court were to subscribe to the doctrine of the latter.

Judged by these two cases the attitude of the California courts

[10] 165 Cal. 668, 674–75, 133 Pac. 488, 490, 491 (1913). See also Hasson v. Koeberle, 180 Cal. 359, 366, 181 Pac. 387, 389 (1919).

concerning the capitalization of prospective profits appears to be identical with the New Jersey attitude. Prospective profits may be taken into account in computing the value of property to be exchanged for stock, but they must be discounted for futurity and risk. Likewise, potential values of speculative property may be considered in computing the present value of the latter, but their present significance must not be assessed by promoters and directors without regard to the probabilities of realization.[11]

Cases which recognize prospective values. — Perhaps the clearest instances of a readiness on the part of courts to accept a merely prospective value, rather than the then current value of the property, as a basis of capitalization are afforded by the usual run of mining cases. Owing to the impossibility of making an intelligent valuation of a mining prospect, most courts have been notably lenient toward promoters who have allowed their optimism full sway in the amount of stock which they have issued. Creditors, it has been held, should surely be on notice that they cannot rely on the par values of mining shares.

A few courts have gone so far as to hold that, where stock has been issued for undeveloped mining property, the rule of shareholders' liability for partly paid stock is really to be disregarded in the absence of special evidence of fraud.[12] Most courts, however, have not gone to this extreme. They have held, rather, that shareholders are liable on such stock if it has been issued in excess of a

[11] *Cf.* Kelly v. Clark, *supra,* c. VI, note 55, in which the facts, pleadings and results were much the same as in the two California cases reviewed in the text. The following cases indicate with greater or less force a judicial disinclination to sanction the capitalization of prospective values: Kaye v. Metz, *supra,* c. III, note 17; Berry v. Rood, *supra,* c. III, note 36; Gates v. Tippecanoe Stone Co., *supra,* c. III, note 15; *In re* Wyoming Valley Ice Co., *infra,* note 30. See also the cases cited *supra,* c. II, notes 10–12, denying that services to be rendered may be capitalized. And see Lea v. Iron Belt Mercantile Co., *supra,* c. III, note 17; State Trust Co. v. Turner, *supra,* c. III, note 18.

[12] This seems once to have been the rule in California (as interpreted by the federal courts). *In re* South Mountain Consolidated Mining Co., *supra,* c. VI, note 39. But the doctrine of this case has since been repudiated by the California courts. Hasson v. Koeberle, *supra,* note 10. But see Richardson v. Treasure Hill Mining Co., *supra,* c. VI, note 55, which substantially follows the South Mountain case, though the decision depended upon statutory construction which was not involved in the latter. See also Ross v. Kelly, 36 Minn. 38, 29 N. W. 591, 31 N. W. 219 (1887), wherein the decision rested upon a statute which was particularly liberal to mining corporations.

good faith valuation, but that in view of the impossibility of any accurate appraisal, the benefit of a very wide margin of doubt should be given to the shareholders. And they have also apparently accepted as a " good faith valuation " an estimate representing what the promoter hoped that the property would prove, later, to be worth, rather than an estimate as to what would be a fair price for the property at the time when the stock was issued.

One example of the readiness of the courts to accept prospective values in a mining case is *Young v. Erie Iron Company.*[13] This case arose upon a bill filed by a judgment creditor for the appointment of a receiver for the defendant corporation which was insolvent, and for an order directing the receiver to assess the shareholders of the company for the benefit of the plaintiff and other creditors of the corporation who should come in and prove their claims and share the expenses of the proceedings.

The manner in which the corporation was organized and its stock issued was as follows. E. H. and William A. Wright, father and son, leased some mining property under terms requiring the lessees to pay $6,000 annually, regardless of the amount of ore extracted, and 60 cents a ton if the amount of ore taken out in any one year exceeded 10,000 tons. Thereafter, they spent $3,000 on tools and labor in exploring and developing the land. They thought that the lease was very valuable, both because they had discovered what they thought was valuable iron ore on the land and because it was located near one of the profitable mines in upper Michigan. The ore discovered partook largely of the nature and character of the ore taken from this prosperous mine.

In order to finance the mine, the Wrights formed the defendant corporation, the capital stock of which was fixed at $500,000, divided into 20,000 shares of $25 par value. For the assignment of their lease and the improvements made on the property at a cost of $3,000, the Wrights received 17,000 shares of a nominal value of $425,000, of which $422,000 was for the lease. All of this stock was marked " fully paid and non-assessable." The remaining 3,000 shares of the authorized stock of the corporation were not issued at the formation of the company but were held by one of the Wrights as trustee for the corporation. The Wrights gave away, or sold at a nominal price, 600 shares of the stock issued to them to parties who had acted as additional incorporators. Work was commenced at the mine, ma-

[13] 65 Mich. 111, 31 N. W. 814 (1887).

chinery was purchased, and a branch line was built from the main line to the mine by a railroad corporation at its own expense. This spur was built upon advice of experts representing the railroad after they had examined the mine. Operations at the mine were apparently financed in part on credit extended by the Wrights and others, and in part by the sale of some of the Wrights' stock at prices ranging from 20 per cent to 50 per cent of par value, the proceeds of which were used for working capital.

In 1883 the corporation became insolvent, partly because of a depression in the iron market. In May of that year a mortgage bond issue of $60,000 was created to pay the corporate debts. The Wrights took $20,000 of these bonds at par in payment of that amount of corporate indebtedness to them. In September, 1883, the lease was forfeited for non-payment of royalty, at which time the company owed $70,000, exclusive of the royalty and inclusive of the debt to the plaintiff ($14,204.91) and to the Wrights.

The evidence clearly indicated that the Wrights thought that they were turning over a very valuable property to the corporation. Not only did they contribute their funds to it for the development of the mine before and after the company was organized, but their confidence in the enterprise was corroborated by the action of the railway company in laying a spur to the mine upon the advice of independent experts.

Yet the trial court, in holding the shareholders liable to the creditors, found that the value of the total property against which the stock was issued, including the value of the lease, did not exceed $100,000 and that at least $400,000 of the capital stock remained unpaid.

On appeal the supreme court reversed the decree of the court below and vacated it as against the defendants, dismissing the bill as against them. The record was remanded to the court below for such proceedings against the other defendants under the decree of the lower court as might be desired. The principal reasons, advanced by two out of four judges sitting, for the reversal were a finding that the Wrights had issued such a large amount of stock through a mistake in judgment as to the value of the mining lease and without any intent to deceive creditors, and a further finding that the defendants who appealed to this court were innocent purchasers of the stock. The other two judges concurred in the dismissal of the bill as to the defendants appealing, on the ground that there was no allegation in the bill that the creditor represented by the plaintiff did not know and fully understand that the capital stock was paid up by property purchased, and because it appeared from the evidence that the plaintiff's assignor knew how the stock had been issued. In view of the dismissal of the suit as to the appellants on the above grounds the court's discussion and conclusions concerning the value of the lease appear to be dicta, but it must be remembered that the decree below was vacated only as to the appellants. There were other defendants below and the terms of the interlocutory decree contemplated further proceedings with a view to discovering whether there were still other shareholders who might be brought under the terms of the decree. It would seem, that as to the defendants below who did not appeal and as to any other defendants discovered in pursuance to the order of reference, the language of the supreme court concerning the value of the lease would be determinative of the issue. This view is supported by the fact that there were other known holders of the stock within the jurisdiction who were responsible, and yet there is no record of an appeal by any of these from the decree of the lower court. Furthermore, one ground for the reversal of the decision below stated by the supreme court was its conclusion from the evidence that the lease was not overvalued deliberately but through a mistake in judgment.

Turning now to its discussion of the issues, we find that the court inclined to the view that the promoters were justified in thinking that their property was potentially very valuable and that their expectations in that direction would soon be realized. The acts of the promoters themselves and even the acts of independent parties were consistent with this view. The Wrights invested their money in the enterprise at the start. Later they sold some of their stock for cash and loaned money to the corporation to enable it to develop the mine. Experts representing a near-by railroad visited the mine and on the strength of its appearance and indications advised the railroad to construct a spur to the mine, which was done. The Wrights bought back at $10 a share some of the stock which they had previously sold at $5 and $8 a share in order to provide funds for the commencement of operations at the mine. All of these facts together with the fact that the Wrights made nothing out of the venture, but on the other hand lost their time and funds in their attempt to put the enterprise on a paying basis, were consistent with the conclusion that they had confidence in the enterprise. Throughout the court's discussion of this aspect of the case we find that it inclined to the view that it was legitimate for the Wrights to capitalize the lease on the basis of their hopes for the eventual success of the mine rather than upon any current price which could have been got for it. The following quotations from the opinion indicate this:

> I find no warrant in the testimony for the claim that the Wrights intended any fraud in the organization of this company. They honestly supposed that they had found value in this mine, and seemed to believe that it might become nearly, if not equally, as valuable as the Republic mine [a neighboring mine which was very successful], then worth from one to two millions of dollars. There is no doubt but at first the mine promised to be a very productive and valuable one . . .
>
> The evidence of the Wrights, and their action in the premises, confirm the claim of defendants' counsel that they honestly believed that, with a proper development of the mine, in a short time the stock of the company would be at par, if not above par. It is true, they gave away some of their stock, and sold more or less at $5, $8, and $12.50 per share, in order, as they claim, to get people interested in the company, and to procure funds to work the mine; but this action grew out of the necessity of the corporation . . . and is not at all inconsistent with the idea that the Wrights honestly thought that eventually the stock would be worth its face value. Money was needed and had to be obtained at a sacrifice . . . I am satisfied that at the outset, and up to near the time of the suspension of business by the defendant corporation, the Wrights thought they had a most valuable mine, and were going to make a fortune out of it, and that the stock would eventually be at par and above . . .
>
> The Wrights testify that they acted in good faith, and believed this leasehold interest to be of great value; and their actions, and the doings of others, seem to corroborate them. Whether they believed it to be worth the full sum of $422,000 is not clear, but it is evident that they thought it worth at least $200,000 or more, and honestly believed the stock, based upon the valuation in the articles of association, would ultimately in the near future be worth such valuation.[14]

Although the court's views concerning the value of the mining lease may be dicta, such dicta cannot be ignored in a study of this kind. They not only forecast the most probable reaction of the

[14] 65 Mich. 111, 120–21, 123, 31 N. W. 819, 820. The court evidently regarded the directors' belief that the stock would sometime sell at par as the equivalent of the belief that the mine would sometime be worth the par value of the stock which was issued for it.

courts, should they be faced with proper cases which directly raise the issue, but in many instances, as in this one, the cases go back to the trial court for further proceedings in accordance with the principles laid down by the appellate courts, and there can be little doubt that the future course of action of both the lower courts and the litigant parties is influenced by the views of appellate courts concerning the question of valuation whenever it arises.

In *Thurber v. Thompson*[15] we find the court suggesting that anticipated rather than present values are a proper basis for corporate capitalization. This was an appeal from a judgment in favor of the plaintiff, entered upon the verdict of a jury, and from an order by the trial court denying a motion for a new trial. The action was brought by a judgment creditor against six stockholders of the Lake Mahopac Improvement Company, a corporation organized for the purpose of laying out and subdividing land into building lots, and improving and selling the same. The defendants were sought to be charged, under section 10 of the act of 1853 concerning corporations, with the debts of the corporation because of the omission of the trustee to file a true certificate that the capital stock had been paid in.

The case was submitted to the jury by the court below upon the single question of fraudulent valuation of lands purchased by the company for business purposes and in payment for which a large proportion of the capital stock of the company was issued. Several witnesses who had long resided in the vicinity were called on behalf of the plaintiffs, and they gave their estimates of the value of the land. But it was clear that they based their estimates upon the value of the land for agricultural purposes. The defendants called as a witness a stockholder and trustee of the company who had acquired $10,000 of the stock of the company for cash and who was familiar with the locality and the value of the lands purchased. He testified that soon after the formation of the company he had offered to purchase several lots from it at considerable prices and that his offers had not been accepted. These offers indicated a total value for the land which approximated the capitalization of the company. The trial court granted a motion to strike out this testimony, to which ruling the defendants excepted.

On this appeal the court reversed the judgment in favor of the plaintiff and ordered a new trial.

[15] 21 Hun 472 (1880).

On the question of the value of the land given for stock of the company the court stressed the fact that the land had been acquired by the corporation, not for agricultural purposes, but for the purpose of bringing it into the market as village lots and villa sites, the value of which would be enhanced by extensive improvements. The following quotation from the opinion suggests that the court felt that future values to accrue from the establishment of the new conditions might be capitalized:

> In determining the question, as it was presented in this case, it was extremely important that the jury should have before them not merely the kind of evidence of valuation given by the witnesses produced by the plaintiff, but also evidence of the probable enhanced value growing out of the contemplated improvements made and to be made by the company, and of the public improvements which were expected to add largely to the value of the land for the new objects and purposes to which it was to be devoted. It would be extremely unjust to such a company as this to hold that farming lands upon which the site of a city or town is about to be established, and which are bought for that purpose, and mapped, plotted and subdivided into city or village lots, are to be viewed upon a question of over-valuation, merely as agricultural lands; and especially when the question to be tried is one of fraud, depending upon the good faith of the action of the trustees of a corporation which has purchased the property as the site of a city or town. In such a case as this it is and must be entirely competent to show at what prices portions of the lands have been sold for the latter purpose, and what offers have been made for parcels of the land with a view to their use as residences, or for the business purposes of a town or city. . . .

The court therefore ruled that it was error to exclude testimony as to the "village-lot value" of the land, since that testimony bore with considerable weight on the question of fraudulent overvaluation.

Although suggesting the view that prospective value rather than strictly present value may properly be capitalized, the *Thurber* case is by no means a clear-cut authority on this point. For the court may have been of opinion that, when the land was taken by the corporation under a plan to develop it for residence lots, *at that very time* it had a value dependent on its prospective use. The facts in the case are too meagerly reported in the opinion to warrant any confident conclusion on this point.

In *Buck v. Jones*[16] the appellant brought an action against two of

[16] 18 Colo. App. 250, 70 Pac. 951 (1902).

the stockholders of the Golden Horn Mining and Milling Company, a corporation organized under the laws of Colorado, to recover on a judgment previously rendered in his favor against the company.

The entire capital stock of $1,250,000 was issued in one certificate to Jones in consideration of the conveyance by him to the company of three mining claims. Jones immediately transferred $400,000 of the stock to the company for its use and benefit and transferred all of the remaining shares, except $112,750, to other incorporators and to unnamed parties. The mining locations were simple claims on which no work had been performed and in which no mineral had been discovered. The company lost all rights to the property through its failure to do any assessment work on it for three years and as a consequence became insolvent. The plaintiff, who held a judgment against the company in the amount of $300, sued the defendant to recover from the latter on allegedly unpaid stock.

The plaintiff alleged that the mining claims had no value except as prospects and that they were worth not over $1,000 at the time they were exchanged for the stock of the corporation. The lower court sustained the defendant's demurrer that the complaint did not show facts sufficient to constitute a cause of action.

On this appeal the judgment of the trial court was reversed on the ground that under the law of the state a mining claim must be made on a *mineral lode or vein,* the discovery of a vein or lode being an essential prerequisite to a valid location. Since the defendant had not discovered a lode or vein of ore he held no valid location, had no title to the property which he conveyed to the corporation for its stock, and hence any valuation placed upon his alleged claims was an overvaluation since the company received nothing for its stock.

Since this was the basis for the decision the court's statement of the rule for the valuation of mining property exchanged for stock was dictum, but we quote it below as an indication of the probable attitude of the Colorado courts on the question, should it arise in a proper suit. The court said:

In the case of corporations organized under the laws of this state for the development of mining property, the capitalization may be, and usually is, fixed with reference to prospective value, that is, to value which in the judgment of the parties the property actually has, but which development is necessary to disclose; and if such value is estimated in good faith, we think the stock issued in consideration of a transfer of the property should be regarded as full paid, notwithstanding the parties' judgment should afterward prove to be erroneous.

The language of the above quotation is interesting as bringing out two different concepts of property values. Ordinarily, the term, "value," is identified with valuation, with opinion, with estimate. If, for example, the owner of an undeveloped mine thinks that it will sooner or later prove to contain ore of a value of $1,000,000, we would say that he should value that mine today at some price less than $1,000,000, which discounts the risk that his expectation may be disappointed. In the quoted opinion, however, the court seems to assume that a promoter who confidently expects that later events will disclose a value of one million dollars is justified in capitalizing this prospect at the full million rather than at a heavily discounted figure such as five hundred thousand dollars. Even the admitted fact that intelligent investors would not buy the property except at some such discount for risk would not seem to belie the promoter's right to capitalize the property at its full "potential" value.[17]

Capitalization of a Supposed Enhancement in Value Due to Consolidation of Separate Properties

Among the cases that raise the question as to prospective or potential values are those in which the contention is made by defendant shareholders that the value of combined properties exceeds the sum

[17] See also the following cases in which the courts appear to have sanctioned a capitalization of prospective values: Gamble v. Queens County Water Co., *infra,* note 28; Rafferty v. Buffalo City Gas Co., *infra,* note 29; Rathbone v. Ayer, *supra,* c. VI, note 55; Kingston v. Nichols, *supra,* c. VI, note 55; Coffin v. Ransdell, Receiver, 110 Ind. 417, 11 N. E. 20 (1886); Penfield v. Dawson Town & Gas Co., *supra,* c. III, note 35; *In re* Pipe Line Oil Co., 289 Fed. 698 (C. C. A., 6th Cir., 1923); Finletter v. Acetylene Light, Heat & Power Co., *supra,* c. VI, note 55; Durand v. Brown, *supra,* c. VI, note 55.

A limit upon the capitalization of prospective values under the law of New York was suggested by the court in Huntington v. Attrill, 118 N. Y. 365, 382, 23 N. E. 544 (1890), as follows: "The fair value contemplated by the statute is that which the property had at the time of the sale and which constituted the consideration upon which the subscription to the capital stock of the company was satisfied. Then was the time the estimate of the value must, for that purpose, be deemed to have been made. *It could not be dependent upon subsequent success or failure of the investment further than such result may have been legitimately within evidential contemplation at the time of the sale in view of the uses, for which it may have had available advantages within itself.*" The italics are mine.

of the values of the separate parts. The assumption that a combination of competing enterprises would not only eliminate losses due to competition, but would also reduce the costs of operation, was the expressed economic basis for the formation of most of our business combinations, or " trusts " as they have generally been called.[18] The validity of this assumption as a general rule is not our present concern, though there is considerable evidence that it has often lacked sufficient foundation.[19] Our problem is to discover to what extent the courts will accept these apologetics of the promoter for a capitalization of a combined company that cannot possibly be justified on the basis of the values of the hitherto independent parts.

It was pointed out in the preceding chapter that some courts, notably those of New Jersey, have been very chary of valuations which can be justified, if at all, only on the assumption of a great future earning power that has not yet been realized. These courts have sometimes gone so far in their dicta as to say that earning power is not a proper basis of capitalization, although the decisions themselves do not indicate that any such extreme position has actually been taken. What these dicta do show, however, is a very proper judicial skepticism of speculative estimates of profits, made by interested parties. Similar skepticism might well be expected from judges with respect to the propriety of issuing stock against earning power which promoters anticipate to result from combinations.

Taking up, first, the New Jersey cases, we may note *Greer v. Almagamated Copper Company*,[20] which was not a shareholders'-liability case but an injunction suit by a minority stockholder to prevent the issuance of stock by the defendant corporation for shares of two other mining companies. Plaintiff contended that the purchase

[18] SEAGER, HENRY R., AND CHAS. A. GULICK, JR., TRUST AND CORPORATION PROBLEMS (New York, 1929), c. VI; JONES, ELIOT, THE TRUST PROBLEM IN THE UNITED STATES (New York, 1921), c. XI, XIX; U. S. INDUSTRIAL COMMISSION, REPORTS (1900–1902), Vols. I and II, *Review of Evidence*, Vol. XIX, pp. 604–5, 608–14, 620–22.

[19] JONES, *op. cit. supra*, c. XIX; MEAD, *op. cit. supra* (c. I, note 8), c. XVIII; DEWING, *op. cit. supra* (note 4), Book IV, c. 3 and Appendix. But see SEAGER AND GULICK, *op. cit. supra* (note 18) at pp. 659–61. A concise statement of the basis for the assumption that combination results in a value for the whole which exceeds the total value of the separate parts is made in Cleveland, C., C. & St. L. Ry. Co. v. Backus, 154 U. S. 439, 444, 38 L. Ed. 1041, 1045, 14 Sup. Ct. 1122, 1123–24 (1894).

[20] 61 N. J. Eq. 364, 49 Atl. 159 (N. J. Ch., 1901).

price of the shares was excessive and improvident from the standpoint of the minority shareholders of the defendant company. The principal contention of the complainant was that this purchase, by way of an exchange of stock or otherwise, would involve his company in numerous and expensive litigations then pending concerning the mining rights of the companies to be acquired.

It appeared from the evidence that the expensive litigation referred to by the complainant were all nuisance suits brought by a corporation of which the complainant was an employee, and that such of these suits as had been litigated had been decided adversely to the plaintiffs. The defendant company controlled, through stock ownership in other companies, substantially all of the mining rights in a particular section of Montana where the properties of the two companies to be acquired were located. These two companies owned or had mining rights in adjoining properties and were surrounded by mining claims of other companies controlled by the Amalgamated Copper Company. The mining laws of the Federal Government under which the properties were operated were such that contests between the various companies over the right to mine certain veins of ore in the region seemed inevitable, and it was for this reason that the Amalgamated Company was anxious to acquire a controlling interest in the two companies. The evidence also showed that the average market price for the stock of each of the companies during recent months was in excess of the price on the basis of which stock of the defendant was to be issued in exchange.

The court discharged the order to show cause why an injunction should not issue. Among the conclusions of the court supporting its decision was its finding that the allegation of an excessive price to be paid for the shares of the two companies was not a reasonable conclusion from the evidence. This finding was based upon four factors: (*a*) that the market price for the shares to be acquired was, and had been for a considerable time, in excess of the price to be paid for them; there was no evidence that the prices had been artificially "rigged," and these prices had been maintained in the face of general knowledge concerning the litigation on which the complainant relied to support his bill for an injunction; (*b*) the companies concerned had been able to pay considerable dividends from actual earnings; (*c*) counsel for the complainant had alleged in another action, contemporaneous with this proceeding, that the property of one of the companies to be acquired had a value substantially

tially in excess of the price which the Amalgamated Company proposed to pay for it; (*d*) the value of a controlling interest in the two companies to the defendant company might exceed the sum of the values of such interests if separately owned, because of the potential conflicts between separate owners concerning rights to mine the ore which underlay each. In this connection the court said:

The defendant has not presented any statement of the value of the properties of the Butte and Boston [one of the companies which it proposed to acquire], but relies upon the market value of its stock and the opinion of Mr. King, and upon its earnings for the last year or two. And it also relies upon the fact that the control of its stock would be of great value to the defendant for the purpose of preventing the clash of rights arising out of the Mining laws of the United States; and it is this which accounts for that portion of the affidavit of Mr. Rogers [a director and officer of the defendant company] in which he says that he would not advise the defendant company to purchase the majority of the stock of either company unless he could have that of both. And it may well be that the value of the stock of both companies to the defendant would be greater than is indicated by the value of either to be operated separately as independent properties. It may well be that the defendant corporation, controlling as it does, by the ownership of a majority of stock, substantially all the other mining claims at Butte, could afford to pay for the control of both the Butte and Boston and the Boston and Montana companies a sum which, in the aggregate, is greater than the value of either [21] of those properties if they are to be operated as independent concerns. And it must be observed that it is the value to the defendant corporation, the proposed vendee, which is to govern here, and not the value of their properties to the vendors.

It will be recalled that in *See v. Heppenheimer*,[22] which was discussed in the preceding chapter, the court refused to consider seriously the contention of the defendant stockholders that the consolidation in ownership of the thirty-nine paper mills enhanced their value. In this connection the court said:

It will be observed that the consolidation of the ownership of these thirty-nine mills did not increase in the least degree the producing capacity of each, nor did it increase the range of the farming country in the neighborhood of each from which they were to derive their raw material. They were, in the main, widely separated from each other, so that the case is in

[21] The court evidently meant " both " instead of " either."

[22] *Supra*, c. VI, note 2, *loc. cit.*, pp. 49–50, 61 Atl. 848–49.

marked contrast with those which occur where several properties lying contiguous to each other may be applied to a purpose for which they could not be used except under a combined ownership. Instances of this readily occur to the mind and are found in the books. Several small city lots, covered, if you will, with moderate dwellings, may be worth a great deal more for the purpose of erecting a large hotel or other building requiring considerable of ground space than the aggregate of the separate value of each for individual dwelling-house purposes. So several contiguous lots of unimproved land, under which a large vein of valuable minerals is known to exist, may be more valuable by reason of combined ownership, which enables the minerals to be sought for and brought to the surface much cheaper and to a better advantage than under separate ownership. So with regard to veins of ore cropping out to the surface under the peculiar mining laws in force in the Rocky mountain regions and so leading to insoluble problems of conflict of title as in *Greer* v. *Amalgamated Copper Co., 61 N. J. Eq.* (*16 Dick.*) 364. Something similar to that occurred in our own state in the case of *Meredith* v. *New Jersey Zinc and Iron Company, 55 N. J. Eq.* (*10 Dick.*) 211, see *pp. 214* and *215*. There the conflicting rights under the divers grants had rendered the solution of the questions arising thereout practically impossible, and a consolidation of ownership increased the value of both rights.

The above quotation is significant because it shows at one and the same time the willingness of the court to concede that enhancement in value, due to consolidation, may be validly claimed if supported by adequate evidence, and the reluctance of the court to accept such claims without forcible supporting evidence. The distinction between combinations of physically contiguous property, where the case for an enhanced value was thought to be a strong one, and combinations of physically distant properties, where the gains from combination would be of an intangible variety, suggests the possibility that the court was confusing the notion of value, which is necessarily a non-materialistic idea, with the notion of physical assets. Whether or not a combination will result in an increase in value depends, of course, simply on the question whether it will result in an enhancement of profits; and this result may be achieved by a consolidation of properties that are too widely separated to be operated as a unit. Yet it is probable that the court merely meant to distinguish between those cases where the economic advantages of combination were obvious and non-speculative, from those other cases where the advantages were doubtful. There is no reason to suppose that physical combination was thought of as a prerequisite to the claim of enhanced value, provided that adequate ground for expecting an enhancement should be established.[23]

The elimination of the damaging effects of competition has been the real or alleged basis for a large proportion of consolidations. In *Tooker v. National Sugar Refining Company* [24] this was the avowed object of the organizers of the defendant company. The enhanced value that was presumed to have been created by the combination was the only basis for the issuance of the common stock, since the owners of the constituent properties received only preferred stock for their plants and the common stock was retained by the organizers of the combination. The validity of the common stock was at issue in the case and the court held that it was issued contrary to law. Its owners were denied all rights as stockholders in the company except the power to vote to retire the common stock in the manner provided by law for the reduction of capital stock. Through a technicality they were not compelled by the decision to repay the dividends which they had received on this stock, but the court evidently regarded the stock as having been issued for no consideration whatever. It should be said, however, that the defendant shareholders did not stress the element of added value due to combination.

In *Donald v. American Smelting & Refining Company* [25] there is a dictum to the effect that the elimination of a competitor by consolidation may create a " legitimate item of value, according to the case," but the decision of the lower court, refusing to enjoin an issue of stock for the property of a competitor was reversed on appeal on other grounds, and the matter of enhanced value due to combination received no attention from the majority of the appellate court.[26]

In *Rural Homestead Co. v. Wildes* [27] minority shareholders sought

[23] From the standpoint of the decision in the See case it is perhaps significant that the promoters originally intended to combine *seventy* competing plants, and that in fact they succeeded in absorbing only thirty-nine. See Dickerman v. Northern Trust Co., *supra,* c. VI, note 2.

Although the question of valuation was not directly involved in the case, see Meredith v. New Jersey Zinc & Iron Co., 55 N. J. Eq. 211, 37 Atl. 539 (N. J. Ch. 1897), for a set of facts which would justify an assumption that consolidation would enhance the value of adjoining mining properties, according to a dictum in the See case, *supra,* note 22.

[24] 80 N. J. Eq. 305, 84 Atl. 10 (N. J. Ch. 1912).

[25] 61 N. J. Eq. 458, 466, 48 Atl. 786, 789 (N. J. Ch. 1901).

[26] 62 N. J. Eq. 729, 48 Atl. 771, 1116 (1901).

[27] 54 N. J. Eq. 668, 35 Atl. 896 (1896), *rev'g* 53 N. J. Eq. 425, 32 Atl. 676 (1895).

to annul an issue of 238 shares of stock of their company which were exchanged for a tract of land. The Court of Errors and Appeals reversed the decree below which set aside the transaction. Its grounds for reversal were that it was not improvident to issue the stock to acquire the land which was the only source of potential competition to the company's business, particularly since the stock was worth only 10 per cent of its par value in the market at the time. In so far as the latter reason was an operative factor in the decision, the holding may properly be criticised. None the less the opinion indicates a willingness on the part of the court to permit a corporate capitalization which can be justified only on the ground of values due to a reduction of competition.

In *Gamble v. Queens County Water Company* [28] an injunction was sought by a minority shareholder to restrain his corporation from issuing $50,000 in stock and $60,000 in bonds for the property of a potential competitor. The injunction was denied and a new trial ordered by the Court of Appeals in part because the court below failed to take into account several elements of value, among which was the value resulting from the elimination of a competitor through consolidation. This was not the sole ground for the decision but it was one element upon which the court relied to support its reversal of the judgment below. Likewise in *Rafferty v. Buffalo City Gas Company* [29] an injunction of like nature was refused on the ground that the plaintiff's bill ignored the element of value attributable to the elimination of a competitor.

The limits beyond which the court will not go in accepting a valuation based on the supposed benefits of combination were indicated in *In re Wyoming Valley Ice Company.*[30] A judgment creditor contested the validity of certain mortgage bonds which the Wyoming Valley Ice Company had issued, along with $200,000 of its stock, in exchange for the properties of several ice companies that were doing business in a certain area in Pennsylvania. In substance, the plaintiff's object was to set aside a foreclosure sale which had already taken place, in order that his claim might be adjudged su-

[28] 123 N. Y. 91, 25 N. E. 201 (1890), *rev'g* 52 Hun 166, 5 N. Y. S. 124 (1889). For a fuller discussion of the facts and other aspects of the case see pp. 115–16, 186–89, *supra*.

[29] 37 App. Div. (N. Y.) 618, 56 N. Y. S. 288 (1899).

[30] 153 Fed. 787 (D. C., M. D. Penna., 1907). See also Wiegand v. Albert Lewis Lumber & Manufacturing Co., 158 Fed. 608 (C. C. A., 3d Cir., 1908), which was decided on the law of the Wyoming Valley Ice Company case.

perior to that of the bondholders. At a sale by the trustee in bankruptcy the real estate of the company was purchased for $40,000 by a representative of the bondholders, who, after paying the costs in cash, was permitted to pay the balance in bonds secured by a first mortgage on the property. A return of sale to this effect was made by the trustee to the court, and exceptions were taken by judgment creditors. The plaintiff contended that the bonds and stock were issued for an inadequate consideration under the constitution and statutes of Pennsylvania and hence were void under the clause in the constitution which declared that " all fictitious increase of stock or indebtedness shall be void."

The United States District Court reversed the decision of the referee, sustained the exceptions to the return of sale, set aside the sale, and directed that the property be resold for cash unless the purchaser at the previous sale should within ten days pay in cash the sum remaining unpaid on his bid. In reaching its conclusion that the bonds were void under the Pennsylvania Constitution and statutes, the court said in part:

> The freedom from competition secured by the consolidation of these companies, and the economies made possible thereby, no doubt somewhat augmented these values, but certainly not to the extent which is claimed of which the subsequent bankruptcy of the company is proof, if there were nothing more.

The whole scheme of capitalization involved was predicated upon an assumption that consolidation would eliminate competition and enhance the value of the several properties in combination over their value as separate and competing enterprises. Hence the remarks of the court quoted above appear to have been in point. The facts showed plainly that $90,000 in bonds and $200,000 in stock had been issued for property the tangible value of which did not exceed $17,500. Competition soon sprang up and bankruptcy of the corporation was the result. Although the court was willing to admit that consolidation may enhance the value of the parts, its decision appears to have been entirely justified by the facts.[31]

[31] Compare *In re* Wyoming Valley Ice Co. with Manhattan Trust Co. v Seattle Coal & Iron Co., *supra*, c. VI, note 55. The facts and pleadings in the two cases were substantially similar, but the results were not identical. On the first trial of the Manhattan Trust Company case the reasoning and decision of the court were quite like the reactions of the court in the Wyoming Valley case. But on what was essentially a trial *de novo* the court turned a very

Finally, in *Babbitt v. Read* [32] we find a clear expression by the court concerning the matter under discussion in the form of a direct and an indirect statement of the conditions under which combination value may be capitalized. Certain coal properties had been consolidated and capitalized at a very large figure by a corporation which was formed to operate mines on the property. The enterprise became bankrupt and the trustee in bankruptcy sued to enforce a liability of shareholders on allegedly unpaid stock for the benefit of creditors. The capitalization of the company was nearly seven times the cost of its property to the promoters who sold it to the corporation for its entire capital stock and a large bond issue. In addition to other defenses the shareholders contended that the consolidation of the several adjoining mining properties under the single ownership by the corporation enhanced the value of the separate properties to an extent sufficient to cover the alleged unpaid balance on the stock. In considering this point the United States District Court admitted that combination of separate properties might enhance their value, but it was unwilling to indulge an assumption that such was the result in the case before it, because the *evidence* failed " to show a basis upon which added combination value may be figured." [33] Likewise, on appeal, the Circuit Court of Appeals admitted that combination *might* enhance the value of the constituent properties, but stated that this would depend on whether the combination enhanced the economic efficiency of the units or increased profits through a resultant control over the market. The court also pointed out that the mere *expectations* of the promoters that the value of the properties would be increased through consolidation were not within a workable definition of the term " property " for which the statute authorized stock to be issued, and that such expectations would not constitute " property " until they (the promoters) " could put them into the realm of such established certainty as would lead men generally to share them." [34]

---

friendly ear to the contention that a combination of contiguous coal properties enhanced their value, and its decision was predicated in part upon this assumption, though there was other evidence to justify the decision of the court.

[32] For a full statement of this case see *supra*, pp. 176–85.

[33] *Loc. cit supra*, c. VI, note 48.

[34] *Loc. cit. supra*, c. VI. note 49. *Cf.* Berry v. Rood, 168 Mo. 316, 324, 67 S. W. 644, 646 (1902). The referee, to whom the latter case was referred for findings of fact and for a statement of his conclusions, recommended that stock

Our conclusions on these combination cases may now be summarized briefly.

In the first place, it is clear that as a matter of law the courts have no definite rule that enhanced values resulting from combination of properties are not to be capitalized.

In the second place, however, it is equally clear that the courts have often shown a very sensible skepticism as to a capitalization which cannot possibly be defended except on the assumption of large and highly speculative benefits to be derived from consolidation of different properties.

In the third place, this judicial skepticism has had a far greater influence on the decisions relative to stockholders' liability to creditors than on the decisions relative to injunctions sought by minority stockholders. It will be noted that in the two cases where creditors were suing to hold shareholders liable for partly paid stock, the courts admitted the possibility that a combination might enhance the value of the property, but held that the facts did not warrant any such assumption in the case at hand. Mere self-interested guesses on the part of promoters that a great increase in profits would result from the elimination of competition were held in both these cases to be an insufficient ground for the valuation placed upon the combined properties by the directors.

On the other hand, in those cases where creditors' rights were not involved, the courts have hesitated to enjoin the issuance of stock for properties at a valuation based on the assumed benefits of combination. This more liberal attitude of the courts in injunction cases may be explained by their reluctance to interfere with *intra vires* matters of corporate management unless minority stockholders who object to the proposed issuance of stock can bring proof of improvident action bordering on fraud.

---

issued for supposed onyx deposits and a mill equipped with machinery for the reduction of ores be adjudged "fully paid." Aside from his conclusion that the promoters acted in good faith in valuing this property, the referee based his recommendation in part upon the assumption that a combination of onyx deposits and suitable machinery with which to work them enhanced the value of both. But the judgment below in favor of the defendant shareholders, which was rendered on the basis of the referee's report, was reversed on this appeal without regard to the supposition that combination of the parts of the inchoate enterprise enhanced the value of the whole. As so frequently occurs in cases of this kind, there were ample other reasons for the reversal.

"Value to the Corporation" as the Basis of Capitalization

In a preceding chapter it was pointed out that the peculiar nature of the property that is valued for stock-issue purposes has generally led the courts to discard "market value" as the proper basis of valuation. The reason for this is that the property in question has no outside market of buyers and sellers; or that, even if it has a market value for some uses, it may well have a much higher value for the particular purposes of the corporation. A promoter, for example, may receive stock in exchange for a vacant plot of land which he turns over to a new corporation organized to erect a hotel. The land may have no market value except for ordinary business-lot use. Yet the promoter may claim, with some show of reason, that the lot is particularly adapted for a hotel site and that it should therefore be valued at more than its "market value."

Faced with this contention, courts have frequently stressed the point that "value to the corporation" rather than market value, cost, or any other conventional basis, is here the correct test. This value to the corporation must be determined by reference to the earnings which the corporation may be expected to derive from the use of the property, and by reference to the further question of the price for which other, equally good, property could be purchased for the corporate purposes.

Huntington v. Attrill[35] was a case in which the New York Court of Appeals affirmed a judgment in favor of the plaintiff creditor against the original holders of stock issued for property at an alleged overvaluation.

A deed for about 120 acres of land bordering the ocean at Rockaway Beach, Long Island, was conveyed to the company, subject to a mortgage of $72,000. This land was part of 140 acres purchased by Attrill six months before the organization of the company for $80,000, of which he paid $8,000 in cash and gave the mortgage to secure the balance of $72,000. The object of the company was to purchase lands and to erect a hotel, bath houses, piers, a theatre and such other accessories as were usual or necessary for the completion and operation of a seaside hotel. The company was organized by Attrill and his associates, who proposed to finance the improvements on the land by the sale or other disposal of bonds of the company. Plans, which were later carried into effect, had been made for the construc-

[35] 118 N. Y. 365, 23 N. E. 544 (1890).

tion of a railroad from Rockaway Beach to New York City, as the success of the whole scheme rested upon easy communication between the beach and the city of New York. In order to carry forward the improvements on the property Attrill loaned a considerable sum of money to the company. The plaintiff loaned the company $100,000, taking as security $200,000 in bonds on which he later realized only $932. The enterprise subsequently failed and the land and improvements were sold at judicial sale for $175,000.

In affirming the judgment of the court below for the plaintiff, the Court of Appeals reviewed the evidence bearing upon the value of the property and upon the directors' belief concerning that value, and concluded that the circumstances were such as to justify the conclusion reached by the trial court that Attrill knew that the property was not worth the face value of the stock. The court said, further, that actual knowledge of overvaluation was not necessary to charge directors with responsibility. Knowledge of such circumstances bearing on the value of the property as would cause a man of ordinary discernment and sagacity to conclude that the property was worth less than the par value of the stock to be issued for it, was sufficient to charge a director having such knowledge with a liability under the statute.

The facts from which the court concluded that the defendants were chargeable with knowledge that they were overvaluing the property were as follows: (*a*) The amount of stock issued greatly exceeded the cost of the property to Attrill a short time before the transfer of the property to the company. This the court said was not conclusive on the question of deliberate overvaluation, but it had a bearing upon that question. (*b*) The defendants knew that the land had no market value, that its value was speculative and was preëminently dependent upon the success of the plans for the use of the land which the organizers contemplated.

But this discussion of the evidence going to show that the property had been deliberately overvalued was not essential to the decision, for the reason that an earlier decision by the Court of Appeals had settled the question involved.[36] It was held in that case that knowledge on the part of the directors that they were overvaluing property was not necessary to charge them with liability under the statute, but that the fact that they had signed an untrue report

[36] Torbett v. Eaton, 113 N. Y. 623, 20 N. E. 876 (1889), *aff'g* 49 Hun 209, 1 N. Y. S. 614 (1888).

which was false in any material representation was sufficient to support an action to recover a debt owed to the plaintiff by the company.[37]

The court then turned to the question of the value of the property and considered the claims of the defendants that error was committed by the trial court in the admission and exclusion of evidence. Some of the evidence was consistent with the view that the property had been overvalued by the directors through a mistake or error of judgment. The proposed railroad, later constructed, was expected to make the property very valuable as a seaside resort. Furthermore, Attrill manifested his confidence in the project by advancing considerable sums of money to the company for the construction of improvements. But the court said that what the property was expected to become worth in time was a matter entirely separate from what it was then worth and that the latter was the measure of the extent to which the stock was paid up.

The defendants had offered evidence as to the value of the property based upon comparisons with other seaside property at different places, but the evidence was rejected as non-admissible and the defendants excepted to its exclusion. Other evidence of the same character was sought to be introduced in the form of testimony of witnesses as to the value of the property, founded upon the knowledge of the witnesses concerning transactions in other property along the coast and not in the vicinity of the property in question. This evidence was also rejected by the trial court. It was contended by the defendants that since the property in question had no ascertainable market value, its value was dependent upon its advantages and ca-

[37] The case arose under Laws of 1875, c. 611, sect. 21. The law permitted the issue of stock for property, the latter to be taken at its "fair value," and required the filing of an annual statement concerning the capital stock of the company. This statement was to be signed by the officers of the company and submitted to a public authority. Section 21 provided: "If any certificate or report made, or public notice given, by the officers of any such corporation, shall be false in any material representation, all the officers who shall have signed the same, shall be jointly and severally liable for all the debts of the corporation, contracted while they are officers thereof."

The defendants and other officers of the company subscribed and swore to a certificate in which they stated that the amount of the capital of the company which was paid in full was $700.000. The plaintiff contended that this certificate was false because the property for which the stock was issued was not worth $700,000 and that the defendants knew that they had overvalued the property.

pacity for development and improvement as a seaside resort similar to Long Branch, Elberon, Coney Island and the like, to which reference would likely be had by the promoters of a new resort, and that the jury should be advised by evidence of the information which a purchaser would have on the subject, and of the facts which would or might influence him and his opinion of the value of the property for such purposes. The Court of Appeals concluded that there was no error in excluding this evidence from the consideration of the jury. Its inclusion would raise too many collateral questions of similarity and difference to justify reliance upon it. In this connection the court said:

The adoption of such a rule to the extent claimed, would open a wide field of speculative inquiry. If, however, it could successfully be affirmed that the influence, which would lead one man to an opinion, would be the common judgment of all prudent business men, there would be much force in the suggestion that the jury should by the evidence be furnished the opportunity to act upon such information, but since the reasons and influences which induce speculative enterprise, may be somewhat peculiar to those who engage in them, and the views of comparative advantages widely differ in respect to feasibility and results, it seems to be less conservative and reliable, as a rule of evidence, to attempt to base values merely upon comparison with those of other property at other places, resulting from its use . . . or upon opinions which witnesses may have formed solely on the relation in value arising from such use, and which they may assume it has to that which is the subject of controversy. The results, to follow, of development and use of the latter for similar purposes must be somewhat experimental and speculative.[38]

An attempt had also been made to introduce into the evidence the fact that the property with improvements made thereon was afterwards sold at a judicial sale for $175,000. The defendants excepted to the inclusion of this evidence but they were overruled. The Court of Appeals declared that there was no error in its admission on the question of value but it said that " it may have been entitled to but little force in that direction."

The concluding remarks of the court bear so directly upon the subject presently under discussion that they are quoted below in full to show that the standard of value to which the New York Court of Appeals subscribes is one which allows recognition to be given to the special utility to the company of the property the value of which is in question in stock-watering cases. The court said:

[38] 118 N. Y. 365, 379, 23 N. E. 544, 547–48 (1890).

The defendants' counsel requested the court to charge "that by the words 'at its fair value' in section 14 of the act, is meant the fair value of such property for the uses and purposes of the company in the conduct of its legitimate business and not the actual market value or the actual intrinsic value thereof at the time it is acquired by the company," and complain of the modification made by the trial justice in response to the request, that he knew of no value other than intrinsic or market value, and then proceeded to charge the jury to the effect that they had the right to consider, in determining the fair value of the property, its value for the use to which it was to be put, and the adaptability of it to any specific purpose, that they are constituent elements of intrinsic value, and although the value to be ascertained by the jury was that, at the time of the sale and conveyance to the company, any peculiar advantages, known or unknown, and even if known would make it advantageous to a few only, properly enter into consideration and go to make up the value as of that time. There was no error in the modification or in the refusal to charge as requested. The fair value contemplated by the statute is that which the property had at the time of the sale and which constituted the consideration upon which the subscription to the capital stock of the company was satisfied. Then was the time the estimate of the value must, for that purpose, be deemed to have been made. It could not be dependent upon subsequent success or failure of the investment further than such result may have been legitimately within evidential contemplation at the time of the sale in view of the uses, for which it may have had available advantages within itself. This was fairly submitted by the court to the consideration of the jury.[39]

Both the charge requested and that which was given directed the jury to take into account the value of the property to the corporation in view of the use to which it was to be put.

Although the view that the value of property for stock-issue purposes is its "value to the corporation for its purposes" has most frequently been expressed by the courts of New York, judicial affirmation of the notion is occasionally found elsewhere.[40] For example, *Clinton Mining & Mineral Company v. Jamison* [41] contains a clear statement by a federal court that the measure of the value of property for which stock has been issued is its "value to the corporation," as distinguished from its cost or other index of its worth. The case

[39] *Ibid.*, pp. 381–82, 23 N. E. 548.

[40] "Fair value to the corporation" is the standard adopted in the new General Corporation Act of Ohio. Ohio Laws, 1927, pp. 9–58, sects. 24 and 25 (Ohio Gen. Code, sect. 8623, subsects. 24 and 25).

[41] 256 Fed. 577 (C. C. A., 3d Cir., 1919). *Cf.* Greer v. Amalgamated Copper Co., 61 N. J. Eq. 364, 385, 49 Atl. 159, 167 (1901), quoted *supra*, p. 208.

reached the Circuit Court of Appeals on an appeal to reverse for error a judgment of non-suit granted by the trial court. The action was brought by a judgment creditor of the Imperial Gold Mining and Milling Company against an individual shareholder therein to recover the debt due on the judgment under authority of a South Dakota statute which subjected shareholders to an individual liability for the *debts* of their corporation to the extent of the amount unpaid on their stock. The statute provided, further, that any creditor of the corporation might institute action against any of its shareholders who had not fully paid for the capital stock held by him, in which case the court was required to ascertain the *amount* that was unpaid upon the stock held by each stockholder and render several judgment against each.[42]

The evidence showed that the Imperial Gold Mining and Milling Company was organized in 1899 under the laws of South Dakota. The incorporators had previously acquired several mining claims at prices which the court characterized as " nominal." The recited considerations in the deeds by which they acquired them footed up to about $50,000. These mining interests were transferred to the corporation for $50,000 in money and its entire capital stock of $1,000,000 (1,000,000 shares of $1 par value). Regarding this stock as fully paid, the vendors of the property returned to the corporation $750,000 of it as treasury stock for use in financing the undertaking. Thereupon the corporation executed a mortgage to secure $200,000 of bonds which it sold to the incorporators and others, giving one share of treasury stock as a bonus with each dollar of bonds subscribed. With the money thus raised, and with additional funds received from the sale of treasury stock at 25 to 45 cents a share, the corporation built reduction works and proceeded to operate the properties. The company operated for some eleven years but defaulted upon its bonds in 1910 and the mortgage was forclosed, resulting in the sale of the property in 1913. The reasons for the failure of the company were not stated, but the court surmised that there may have been a number of contributing causes, including exhaustion of the ore bodies and increased costs of extraction due to changes in the character of the ore.

The evidence also showed that the mining claims were not mere prospects at the time they were turned over to the corporation in

[42] South Dakota Civil Code of 1913, sect. 441 (S. D. Comp. Laws, 1913, vol. 2, p. 48).

payment for its stock. They were properties which had previously been developed by mining operations which had resulted in the extraction of a considerable amount of ore. An extensive footage of drifts, tunnels, cross-cuts and shoots had been run, exposing ore which varied from a low grade of $6 to a shipping grade of $20 a ton. Although no expert had measured up the ore, it was thought at the time that the exposed ore was worth at least $250,000 and that the whole mine was worth at least $1,000,000. This sum was based upon estimated quantities of high-grade and low-grade ores exposed and upon the probability of discovering additional ore on the claims because of their proximity to an adjoining mine which was working a very valuable vein of ore, the structure and character of which suggested that it extended beneath the surface acquired by the corporation. In making this estimate of a total value of not less than $1,000,000, consideration was given to the fact that a proposed cyanide works of the company was expected to reduce ores to metal at a cost of $3.50 per ton.

The trial court granted defendant's motion for a non-suit, not because of lack of proof of overvaluation of the property, but on the ground that the word " debts " as used in the South Dakota statute did not include an obligation of a judgment rendered in tort. The appellate court, however, side-stepped the meaning of the word, " debts," as used in the South Dakota statute on the ground that it was a matter which did not call for decision until overvaluation of the property had first been determined. Since the liability of the stockholder for the corporation's debts was predicated solely upon a deficiency in the payment of the stock, no recovery could be had against the defendant, whatever the meaning of the word " debts," unless overvaluation of the consideration were shown.

Before considering the proper basis of valuation the reviewing court discussed the distinction between the " good faith " and the " true value " rules, expressing preference for the former as representing the usual common-law doctrine. It held, however, that under either rule the plaintiff had failed to make good his charge that the stock had been issued for insufficient consideration, and it therefore affirmed the lower court in the judgment of non-suit. The fact that the promoters had themselves paid only a " nominal " consideration for their mining claims was no indication, it held, of the real value of the property. It said:

Nor is the cost of the claims to those who subsequently conveyed them to the corporation conclusive. The cost to the vendors is not a test of value [citing cases]. *We are concerned with their value to the corporation* and that value may exceed what it cost the vendors, who were doing little more than transferring the properties, whatever their value, from themselves as individuals to a corporation of which they were the owners and through which they expected to finance and operate the properties. Therefore, we do not regard the recited considerations in conveyances to the vendors or even in conveyances to the corporation evidence of the value of the properties in the hands of the vendee corporation *on which alone we could sustain a verdict that the properties were overvalued.*[43]

Turning again to the law, the court said that the evidence was insufficient to sustain a finding of overvaluation under either the "good faith" or "true value" rules. Under the latter all that the facts showed was a doubt "the benefit of which the courts give stockholders where there is ground for a difference of opinion as to the value of the property." And under the former there was no evidence indicating an absence of good faith or suggesting either fraud or fraudulent intent on which a verdict to the contrary could be sustained.

Furthermore, aside from the lack of evidence upon which a jury could base a finding of overvaluation, there was no evidence upon which a jury could fix *the amount* of overvaluation or the measure of the shareholder's liability under the South Dakota statute. The statute required that the court should determine the *amount* unpaid upon the stock of each shareholder. Hence, if this case had been submitted to a jury and it had found overvaluation it would have been without the means of rendering a verdict under the statute.

The only remaining testimony on the subject of overvaluation of the property was the fact of the foreclosure of the mortgage some ten years after the company began business. The court said that this did not show that the property was overvalued at the time the stock was issued. The question of value must be determined upon facts as they existed when the transaction was consummated, and the subsequent failure of the concern showing that the property had been overvalued in the beginning was not evidence upon which the court was willing to find that the property was not worth the face of the stock at the time it was taken over.[44]

[43] 256 Fed. 577, 582.

[44] See also the following cases with reference to the "value to the corporation" rule: Thurber v. Thompson, *supra*, note 15; Schenck v. Andrews, *supra*,

Capitalization of Property at Its "Reasonable Cash Value"

The final array of evidence supporting our hypothesis that the courts are not unfriendly to the capitalization of prospective profits is found in those cases in which the courts have stated that the proper basis of capitalization is the " cash price which an honest, unbiased, and intelligent board of directors would pay for the property if their corporation had the cash in its treasury "; or " the cash price which a prudent investor would pay for the property for the use contemplated by the corporation "; or " the fair cash market value " of the property; or " such a valuation as prudent and sensible business men would approve "; or a basis " which treats stock as cash "; or " the reasonable worth of the property in money "; or " money or money's worth." These dicta support the contention that the basis of capitalization which the courts are applying involves a capitalization of prospective earnings.

The New Jersey courts have said on two occasions [45] that the proper basis of corporate capitalization, where an issue of stock for property or services is involved, is the cash price which an honest, unbiased and intelligent board of directors would pay for the property or services if the corporation had cash available as a means of payment in an amount equal to the par value of the stock. The considerations for which stock was issued in these cases had no ascertainable market price. Their value was necessarily a matter of estimate or conjecture. The cash price which a prudent and disinterested

c. III, note 11; Lake Superior Iron Co. v. Drexel, *supra,* c. III, note 17; Rathbone v. Ayer, *supra,* c. VI, note 55; Gamble v. Queens County Water Co., *supra,* note 28; Greer v. Amalgamated Copper Co., *supra,* note 20; Boynton v. Andrews, *supra,* c. III, note 18; Macbeth v. Banfield, *supra,* c. III, note 18; Douglass v. Ireland, *supra,* c. III, note 17; McClure v. Paducah Iron Co., *supra,* c. III, note 17.

This concept or basis of valuation which is founded upon the peculiar utility of property to the corporation resembles the conventional justification by the accountant for his standards of balance-sheet valuation. Kester, Roy B., Accounting: Theory and Practice (2d ed., New York, 1925), Vol. II, c. 6; Hatfield, Henry R., Accounting: Its Principles and Problems (New York, 1927), c. II, especially pp. 74–75. It is a concept that is sometimes used in damage cases. Sutherland, J. G., A Treatise on the Law of Damages (4th ed., Chicago, 1916), Vol. 2, art. 448, p. 1455.

[45] *Loc. cit. supra,* c. III, note 25; *loc. cit. supra,* c. III, note 26. Content has been given to the rule by subsequent opinions and decisions. The Railway Review v. Groff Drill & Machine Tool Co., *supra,* c. VI, notes 21 and 22; Bryson v. Conlen, *supra,* c. VI, note 31.

board of directors would have paid in each case was not known. The property involved was business property the value of which was necessarily dependent upon its capacity to yield a revenue to its owner. We cannot conceive of an honest and unbiased board of directors, who are seeking to determine the cash value of such property, proceeding in any other way than by estimating the potential earnings to be derived from the property and, on the basis of their conclusions in that regard, setting a cash price which the corporation would be justified in paying. Of course, they would apply discounts to their estimates of potential earnings to cover the risks of ultimate realization as well as the factor of time discount; and the greater the uncertainty as to the estimate, the higher would be the discount.

Almost the same comments may be made concerning the rule announced by the California court,[46] the Illinois courts,[47] and the New Hampshire court.[48] In each case reference to the cash price which a prudent investor would pay for the property suggests, if it does not clearly indicate, a capitalization of anticipated earnings.[49]

[46] Hasson v. Koeberle, *loc. cit. supra,* c. VI, note 44.

[47] Gillett v. Chicago Title & Trust Co., *loc. cit. supra,* c. III, notes 30, 31; Cohen v. Toy Gun Manufacturing Co., *loc. cit. supra,* c. VI, note 36.

[48] Grafton County Electric Light & Power Co. v. State, *loc. cit. supra,* c. III, note 25.

[49] See also the following cases: Elyton Land Co. v. Birmingham Warehouse & Elevator Co., *loc. cit. supra,* c. III, note 15; Roman v. Dimmick, 115 Ala. 233, 238, 22 So. 109, 110 (1896); Grant v. East & West R. Co., *loc. cit. supra,* c. VI, note 51; Rhode v. Dock-Hop Co., *loc. cit supra,* note 7; Barnard v. Sweet, *supra,* c. VI, note 55; National Bank of America v. Pacific Ry. Co., 66 Ill. App. 320, 329–30 (1896), *mod.* and *aff'd,* 172 Ill. 149, 50 N. E. 19 (1898); De Shelter v. American Spring Water Supply Co., 182 Ill. App. 403, 411 (1913); Dee Co. v. Proviso Coal Co., *loc. cit. supra,* c. III, note 30; State Trust Co. v. Turner, *loc. cit. supra,* c. III, note 34; Hastings Malting Co. v. Iron Range Brewing Co., *loc. cit. supra,* c. III, note 34; Shickle v. Watts, *loc. cit. supra,* c. III, note 34; Farmers Bank of Frankfort v. Gallaher, *supra,* c. III, note 36; Garrett v. Kansas City Coal Mining Co., 113 Mo. 330, 337–38, 20 S. W. 965, 967 (1892); Van Cleve v. Berkey, 143 Mo. 109, 118, 136, 44 S. W. 743, 749, 750 (1898); Kelly v. Clark, *loc. cit, supra,* c. III, note 34; Hobgood v. Ehlen, 141 N. C. 344, 354–55, 53 S. E. 857, 861 (1906); Whitlock v. Alexander, *loc. cit. supra,* c. III, note 34; Caldwell v. Robinson, 179 N. C. 518, 524, 103 S. E. 75, 78 (1920); Gilkie & Anson Co. v. Dawson Town & Gas Co., 46 Neb. 333, 348, 64 N. W. 978, 982 (1895); Wetherbee v. Baker, 35 N. J. Eq. 501, 513 (1882); Macbeth v. Banfield, 45 Or. 553, 565, 78 Pac. 693, 696 (1904); Cole v. Adams, 19 Tex. Civ. App. 507, 512, 49 S. W. 1052, 1054 (1898); Lantz v. Moeller, 76 Wash. 429, 434–36, 136 Pac. 687, 688–89 (1913); Tuttle v. Rohrer, *loc. cit. supra,* c. III, note 34; National Tube Works v. Gilfillan, 124 N. Y. 302, 307, 26 N. E. 538, 539–40 (1891).

CHAPTER VIII

EVIDENCE OF OVERVALUATION BASED ON IMPLIED ADMISSIONS BY PROMOTERS AND OTHER INTERESTED PARTIES

In this chapter we consider several types of evidence adduced by plaintiffs to prove that stock has been watered, all of which take the form of proof that the promoters themselves, or their representatives, recognized the existence of an overvaluation. In view of the fact that deliberate or conscious overvaluation is the generally accepted test of a shareholder's liability, evidence of the type just mentioned may be expected to be particularly persuasive with the courts. Of course it is not to be expected that promoters will often go on record as stating in so many words that they are guilty of issuing stock at an overvaluation. Nevertheless, it has often been possible for plaintiffs to show that by their own action in trading in the stock or by the cash offers which they have made for the property, the promoters themselves recognized a high degree of inflation in the stock.

There are three types of action on the part of the promoters which have frequently been adduced by plaintiffs as express or tacit admissions of stock watering. They are: first, the simultaneous offer by a promoter to a corporation of property for a lower price in cash and a higher price in stock; second, the acceptance by a vendor in exchange for property of stock which has a definite market value lower than its par value; third, the acceptance by a promoter in exchange for property of stock, part of which he donates back to the company as treasury stock. In addition there are other somewhat similar types of evidence which occur so occasionally that they may most conveniently be brought into a fourth group of miscellaneous cases. Each of these four groups will now be discussed, the treasury stock cases being reserved until the last.

The Cash Price for Which Vendor Agrees to Sell the Property to the Corporation as Evidence of Its Reasonable Value

Suppose that a promoter secures options to purchase certain property and forms a corporation to take over and operate it. Suppose that he then sets up a board of directors and presents to them alternative offers to sell the property to the corporation for one million dollars in cash, or for two million dollars in stock. The directors, acting under the orders of the promoter, accept the latter alternative, which was probably the only one that was seriously contemplated. Subsequently the corporation fails and certain creditors sue the shareholders, alleging that the stock has not been fully paid and adducing the cash-offer price as evidence of a recognition by the directors themselves that the property was not worth more than one million dollars. What should be and what has been the reaction of the courts to this type of proof of overvaluation?

In cases of this kind the defendant shareholders have generally argued that the mere fact of a cash offer of one million dollars does not imply an admission, either by the directors or by the promoter-vendor, that the property was worth only this amount. They have contended that a vendor is often in urgent need of cash and that under pressure to secure a money payment he will not infrequently accept a smaller amount than the property is reasonably worth — a smaller amount perhaps than he could get for the property even in cash if he were able to go shopping for a better bid. To this defense, however, the plaintiff may reply that the accepted standard of value in stock-watering cases is the cash price which the directors of the corporation might reasonably pay for the property that is taken in exchange for the stock. It follows, they contend, that if a vendor has offered to sell the property for one million dollars in cash, no reasonable directors, dealing with the vendor at arm's length, would be justified in paying more than one million dollars for that property even though it might be argued that a higher payment could wisely have been made were it not for the willingness of the vendor to take a smaller sum.[1]

Turning to the cases bearing on this point, it will be recalled that

[1] There is ample evidence that the cash-or-stock alternative has been widely used by promoters. See U. S. BUREAU OF CORPORATIONS: REPORT ON THE STEEL INDUSTRY (Washington, 1911), Pt. I, p. 16; Robinson, Maurice H., *The Distribution of Securities in the Formation of the United States Steel Corporation* (1915), 30 POL. SCI. Q. 277, 279; U. S. INDUSTRIAL COMMISSION, REPORTS (1900–1902), Vol. I, *Digest of Evidence*, pp. 174–75, 190, *Testimony*, pp. 100–101, 851, 866, 883–84, 944; *Ibid.*, Vol. XIII, *Digest of Evidence*, pp. xli, lxv–vi, cix–cx, *Testimony*, pp. 37–38, 93–96, 249–52; MEAD, *op. cit. supra* (c. I, note 8) at pp. 102–3, 106–8; DEWING, ARTHUR S., CORPORATE PROMOTIONS AND REORGANIZATIONS (Cambridge, Mass., 1914), pp. 18, 54, 80, 206–7, 277.

in *See v. Heppenheimer*[2] the " appraised value " of the thirty-nine paper mills, according to Mr. Samuel Untermyer, the principal promoter of the Columbia Straw-Paper Company, was $2,250,000, and that these mills, plus $200,000 in cash raised by the sale of bonds, constituted the consideration for the issuance of $4,000,000 of stock and $1,000,000 in bonds. The price at which the promoters had the right, according to various options, to purchase the mills was about $2,250,000. Of this total $750,000 was to be paid in common stock of the corporation, taken at 50 per cent of par;[3] that is, for every dollar of this sum, two dollars in stock were to be given — a clear sign that the stock was not treated as the equivalent of cash. The remaining $1,500,000 of the purchase price was to be paid, half in cash and half in preferred stock at par, but as finally carried out the purchase involved a considerable substitution of bonds, preferred stock and common stock for the cash part of the agreed purchase price. To the extent that the vendors of the mills took securities in lieu of cash they received, for each $1,000 of appraised value payable in cash, $1,000 in mortgage bonds and a bonus consisting of $400 in common stock and $200 in preferred stock. Outsiders who purchased bonds at par for cash received a bonus of common and preferred on the same basis. Thus the whole scheme was revealed as one in which the promoters dealt with the stock at an acknowledged discount from its par value.[4] Furthermore, the difference between $2,250,000, the " appraised value " of the plants, and $5,000,000, the amount of securities issued for them, could not have been justified on the ground that the good will of the separate enterprises made up the difference, because the individual good will of each of the properties was by express terms included in the valuation thereof and was conveyed to the corporation as a part of the consideration for the purchase price mentioned in the options.[5] The entire arrangement here was so nearly like an offer by the promoters of a sum in cash or a much larger sum in securities that the court could hardly have reached any other conclusion than that the directors' valuation of the prop-

[2] *Supra*, c. VI, note 2.

[3] *Ibid.*, at p. 62, 61 Atl. at p. 854.

[4] As the court pointed out, the bonds were evidently well secured and should have sold readily without the inducement of a discount if the property values and estimated earnings claimed by the promoters were credible. Hence it could not be urged that the bonds were issued at a 60 per cent discount and the stock against full values.

[5] 69 N. J. Eq. 36, 43, 45, 61 Atl. 843, 846–47 (1905).

erty at $5,000,000 was a deliberate overvaluation designed simply to support a vast amount of watered stock.

In another New Jersey case, *Coler v. Tacoma Railway & Power Company,*[6] an offer by a corporation of $100 in its stock or $35 in cash for each share of a rival corporation was accepted by the court as evidence of a violation of the anti-stock-watering law. This was an application by a shareholder of a New Jersey corporation to enjoin a proposed merger. His application had been denied in the court below, but on this appeal the judgment below was reversed and a preliminary injunction was issued.

Two corporations, owning two separate electric street railways in the state of Washington, proposed to combine their properties and to capitalize the combined roads at an amount equal to the then present capitalization of the two corporations. An arrangement was made between the Tacoma Railway & Power Company, a New Jersey corporation, and the Seattle-Tacoma Interurban Railway, a Washington corporation, by which the former should transfer all of its property and franchises, except the right to be a corporation, to the latter company in exchange for 20,000 shares of full-paid stock of the par value of $100 per share. These shares corresponded exactly with the capitalization of the New Jersey company. The arrangement also provided that if any shareholder of the New Jersey company should refuse to exchange his shares of stock for an equal number of shares of stock in the Washington company, then the latter company was to pay to the New Jersey company $35 in cash for each share held by the dissenting shareholders, in lieu of the share-for-share exchange. The plan contemplated a dissolution of the New Jersey corporation and a distribution to its shareholders of the cash or stock to which they would severally become entitled under the terms of the plan.

The Court of Errors and Appeals reversed the judgment below on three grounds, one of which is germane to the present discussion and which was expressed by the court as follows:

> According to the decisions of the courts of Washington, it is unlawful to issue corporate stock as fully paid unless the corporation receives therefor money, or money's worth, to the face value of the stock, and, when such stock is issued for property, the judgment of the corporate directors respecting the value of the property is not conclusive as against innocent creditors, in whose favor shares so issued will be assessable until the face

[6] 65 N. J. Eq. 347, 54 Atl. 413 (1903), *rev'g* 64 N. J. Eq. 117, 53 Atl. 680 (1902).

value is paid in [citing cases]. Besides these decisions, the state constitution (article 12, paragraph 6) declares that "all fictitious increase of [corporate] stock or indebtedness shall be void." This phrase, "fictitious increase of stock," must, I think, include an issue of new stock when both the corporation and the recipient of the stock know that it is being issued for less than its face value.

Such knowledge is shown in the present case by the very terms of the proposal — for the Washington company offers a share of its stock, having a face value of $100, or in lieu thereof $35 in cash, as the unit of the price at which it will buy the property and franchises of the New Jersey company, thereby indicating, beyond dispute, that in this transaction the share and the cash are deemed of equal value. To the extent of sixty-five per cent. of the issue, the increase of capital stock will be therefore "fictitious," and, according to the constitution, "void." Such a scheme ought not to be forced upon an unwilling stockholder of the New Jersey company. He is entitled to require that his company shall not be stripped of its property and franchises for a counterfeit which is offered and about to be accepted as genuine.[7]

In *Barnard v. Sweet* [8] one important factor in the decision holding that stock was not fully paid as against creditors was the fact that the consideration for which $300,000 of stock was issued was simultaneously offered to the corporation by the promoter for that amount of stock, or for $200,000 in cash.

In *Shickle v. Watts* [9] a contractor agreed to take $20,000 in cash or a much larger sum in stock as partial payment for his services in constructing a gas works, and the court held him liable to creditors to the extent of the difference between the par value of the stock and the sum of cash in lieu of which the stock was taken. This was an action by judgment creditors against shareholders to collect an alleged unpaid balance on stock. Judgment below was for the plaintiffs and a single shareholder, Watts, appealed. The latter contracted to construct a gas works for the East St. Louis Gas, Light and Coke Company. For his work he was to receive $83,000. Of this sum $50,000 was to be paid in first-mortgage bonds secured by a first lien on the "works, property and franchises of the corporation," and the remainder, $33,000, was to be paid in cash. It was stipulated that $13,000 of the cash was to be paid by assessing the holders of the $50,000 of stock already outstanding, and the other $20,000 by the

[7] 65 N. J. Eq. 347, 350–51, 54 Atl. 413, 414 (1903).
[8] 74 Colo. 302, 221 Pac. 1093 (1923).
[9] 94 Mo. 410, 7 S. W. 274 (1887).

sale of new stock for cash. It was further stipulated that if the corporation failed to dispose of sufficient new stock to provide this $20,000 when due, then the defendant should receive in lieu thereof "cash stock of the corporation at the same rate as other shareholders in full compensation for his dues."

Watts built the works, receiving from the corporation $40,000 in bonds on which he realized by sale $38,504.16. No money was raised by assessing the old shareholders, nor did the company succeed in raising any funds by the sale of new stock. But the corporation did issue to Watts 1,500 shares of stock of the par value of $37,500. Of this stock he sold 300 shares of a par value of $7,500 and retained the balance of 1,200 shares. At the time this action was brought the account between Watts and the corporation remained unsettled.

The evidence showed: (*a*) that the stock had uniformly been issued to other shareholders at $12.50 per share (par $25); (*b*) that Watts had agreed to take stock on the same basis as the issue price to others; (*c*) that expert estimates of the cost of constructing similar works varied from $35,000 to $45,000. The court below found that the contract price for the gas works was 70 per cent beyond a fair and reasonable price and that the sum already paid on account of these works, in the form of bonds and stock, amounted to $57,254 ($38,504 from the sale of the bonds and $37,500 of stock rated at 50 per cent of its face value), or about $7,254 more than $50,000 which the court found to be the reasonable value of the works. The evidence was confusing as to whether the stock was issued as "fully paid" or was designated as "assessable" stock, but it seems reasonably clear that the nature of the agreement between the corporation and its various shareholders was that each was to receive his stock at 50 per cent of par without further liability to the corporation.

The decision of the court, affirming the judgment below against the defendant, appears to have been based entirely upon the fact that the defendant had agreed to take $20,000 in cash or $40,000 in stock at a discount of 50 per cent from its par value. It held that the defendant was liable for a maximum of $15,000 on the $30,000 of stock so issued to him which he had retained.[10]

Transactions of the sort disclosed in the four preceding cases bear upon the basis of valuation for stock-issue purposes in two ways.

[10] *Cf.* Coleman v. Howe, 154 Ill. 458, 39 N. E. 725 (1895); The Boulton Carbon Co. v. Mills, 78 Iowa 460, 43 N. W. 290 (1889).

First, they show that the directors did not think the consideration had a value equal to the par value of the stock. Hence, in so far as the directors' opinion is taken into account by the courts in deciding whether or not stock has been fully paid, the effect is to impeach the transaction and to throw upon the defendant shareholders the burden of explaining away the apparent inconsistency of his directors' actions. Second, they furnish the court with a starting point from which to proceed in determining the value of the consideration. A cash offer is ordinarily the result of careful weighing of the economic merits of a situation in which it is made, and measures with a fair degree of accuracy the quantum sought by the court, namely, the cash price which an honest, unbiased and intelligent business man would pay for the consideration accepted. It is not surprising therefore to find the courts fixing the value at a sum equal to the cash offer, and the maximum liability — if that question is involved — at the difference between the amount of the cash offer and the par value of the stock.

Market Value of the Stock of the Issuing Corporation as Evidence of Deliberate Overvaluation

Similar in effect to the stock-cash option cases reviewed above are those cases in which the market value of the outstanding stock of a going concern is less than its par value at the time that a new block of the stock is issued or proposed to be issued for a non-cash consideration. An offer of stock for property under these circumstances is substantially equivalent to a cash offer equal to the *market value* of the stock.[11] In all the cases of this character that have come to the writer's attention, the courts have either imposed a liability to creditors upon shareholders who held stock issued under such circumstances, or have enjoined the issuance of stock on the ground of obvious overvaluation of the consideration.

[11] The equivalence is not quite exact since an increase in the number of outstanding shares may be expected to have a depressing effect upon the market price, particularly if an attempt is made to convert the stock into cash within a relatively short time. This would be true even on such an active market as the New York Stock Exchange if the ratio of the new stock to the "floating supply" were large. On the other hand, if the element of "merger" is regarded favorably by the public or by insiders it is not improbable that the market value of the stock may rise and thus make it possible for the vendors to realize a larger amount of cash than the basis on which the purchase was effected.

In *Chouteau, Harrison & Valle v. Dean*[12] a creditor of a railway company sued a shareholder to collect the amount of his claim from an alleged unpaid balance on stock accepted by the latter in payment for services rendered to the corporation. Judgment below was for the plaintiff.

The defendant, a director of the corporation, was elected secretary and treasurer, an office which had always been a salaried one. It was verbally agreed between the defendant and the president of the corporation that the former should be paid for his services in connection with the office. After acting in that capacity for about nine months the defendant estimated the value of his services at about $2,500, and he and the other officers, as well as several other directors, agreed that he should be compensated in stock of the company. Since the stock was then worth in the market only 25 per cent of its face value, the defendant made out a bill for $10,000 and " paid-up " stock to that amount was directed to be issued and delivered to him. He later wrote a letter to the board of directors, asking that his account be reconsidered and stating that his $10,000 charge had been deliberately overstated because of the depreciated value of the medium in which payment was to be made. In this letter he requested that he be paid the " fair value " of his services in cash in lieu of stock and added that if this were not done any stock issued to him must be " fully paid, and free from any and all assessments, or for further or other payments thereon or therefor." The board refused to make a cash payment for the services and ordered the $10,000 of stock to be issued. The defendant received a certificate for the stock, but about a month later he wrote " cancelled " across the face of the certificate and returned it to the company. The president cancelled the stock on the company books and reported his action to the board of directors.

On appeal the court held that the stock was unpaid to the extent of the difference between the value of the services of the defendant and the par value of the stock, tacitly assuming that the value of the services did not exceed $2,500, and affirmed the judgment below in favor of the plaintiff. Holding that the cancellation of the certificate did not release the defendant from a liability to creditors, provided the stock was unpaid, the court said:

> The defendant in this case does not pretend that his services were worth more than $2,500, for which he was paid $10,000 in stock of the corporation.

[12] 7 Mo. App. 210 (1879).

The arrangement by which his account was made out for $10,000 was confessedly a mere disguise, intended to compensate the reduced market value of the stock. But such disguises can never avail to evade the law, which deals with the realities of a transaction, and not with its pretenses.[13]

Similarly, in *Enright v. Heckscher*[14] the fact that the stock of the defendant shareholder was sold to him by the corporation upon the payment of a cash price equal to the then market value of the outstanding shares (which was 50 per cent of the par value) was conclusive evidence that the directors did not regard the consideration, for which the stock had been issued shortly theretofore, as having a value equal to the par value of the stock. This evidence was likewise accepted by the court as a partial proof that the value of the consideration was less than the face value of the stock.

In *Strickland v. National Salt Company*[15] a holder of dividend scrip of the defendant company appealed from a ruling of the receiver of the latter disallowing his claim on the ground that the scrip originated as a part of an illegal transaction which had involved an excessive issue of stock for property contrary to the law. The court sustained the action of the receiver.

The plaintiff was a transferee of certain written promises of the defendant company which grew out of an exchange of stock of the United Salt Company for stock of the National Salt Company. The National company absorbed the United company by giving to the shareholders of the latter, stock of the par value of $250, plus a promise to pay $106.25 in semi-annual installments over a period of five years, for each share of the United stock. The $250 of National stock consisted of one and one-quarter shares each of preferred and common stock, and the semi-annual installments were exactly equal in amount to the dividend on the preferred stock and a 10 per cent dividend on the common stock. During the five-year life of the dividend scrip the stock of both companies was pledged with a trustee as security for the performance of obligations undertaken by the parties, and the trustee was instructed to apply the dividends received on the National stock to the payment of the installments.

The dividend scrip was non-negotiable in form. The evidence revealed the following: (*a*) that in arranging for the exchange of stock

[13] *Ibid.*, p. 215.

[14] 240 Fed. 863 (C. C. A., 2d Cir. 1917).

[15] 77 N. J. Eq. 328, 76 Atl. 1048 (1910).

the parties sought merely to make a fair bargain on a *relative* basis without regard to the par value of the stock; (*b*) that the directors of the National company did not appraise the value of each share of the United company at $356.25; (*c*) that the president of the United company offered to sell his stock at $65 a share; (*d*) that the market value of two and one-half shares of National stock was $143.75.

In sustaining the action of the receiver disallowing the claim of the plaintiff which was based upon the dividend scrip mentioned above, the court laid considerable stress upon the wide discrepancy between the market value of the National stock and its par value. Certainly, said the court, no business man would ignore this discrepancy and it is not reasonable to suppose that the directors did so. There was no evidence of the value of the United stock other than the fact that the president of that company had offered a large block of it for sale at from $60 to $65 per share. But the market value of two and one-half shares of the National stock given in exchange for each share of United stock was $143.75. No seller of the United stock could have accepted the National stock on the assumption that the latter was worth its par value of $250 in the face of the market verdict of $143.75. Furthermore, the National stock so accepted was subject to a five-year suspension of dividends and the court said that the application of a proper discount for this fact would bring the market value down to about $100 instead of $143.75. The addition to this of the discounted value of the dividend scrip of the nominal value of $106.25 would give an approximate total market value of less than $200. A value of this amount was insufficient to support the issuance of $250 in stock and $106.25 in dividend obligations. Hence the court concluded that the dividend scrip was issued in fraud of the law, and since the scrip was non-negotiable the defense of illegality was valid as against the plaintiff.

Although there was other evidence to support the decision, it seems probable that the principal ground on which the court concluded that the defendant company's stock had been issued for a deliberately overvalued consideration was the wide and evident discrepancy between the market value of the stock and its par value. On appeal the decision was affirmed on other grounds.[16]

Finally, in *Donald v. American Smelting & Refining Company* [17]

[16] 79 N. J. Eq. 182, 223, 81 Atl. 828, 832 (1911).

[17] 62 N. J. Eq. 729, 48 Atl. 771, 1116 (1901), *rev'g* 61 N. J. Eq. 458, 48 Atl. 786 (1901).

one of several reasons mentioned by the court for enjoining an issue of stock for property was the relatively low price, as compared with its par value, at which the stock was selling in the market at the time.

The case came before the Court of Chancery of New Jersey on an application by minority stockholders for a preliminary injunction to restrain the defendant corporation from increasing its authorized capital stock from $65,000,000 to $100,000,000, and from issuing $45,200,000 of stock in exchange for: (*a*) the plants and business of M. Guggenheim's Sons; and (*b*) $12,000,000 in cash which was also to be supplied by the Guggenheims. The injunction was requested on two grounds, the first of which was not considered by the court because it was admittedly not established by the plaintiff. The second contention of the plaintiffs was that the smelting and refining plants of the Guggenheims, including their mining leases and contracts, were not worth more than $10,000,000, their alleged cost of reproduction, and that this property plus the $12,000,000 in cash was not a full equivalent for the $45,200,000 of stock to be issued.

The motives which led to the attempt of the American Smelting and Refining Company (hereinafter called the Refining company) to absorb the Guggenheim interests do not appear in the reports of this case, but it is apparent from other sources [18] that, when the Refining company was organized, less than two years before this action was begun, the promoters desired to include the plants and other assets of M. Guggenheim's Sons in the enterprise, but the latter were unwilling to come in on the terms offered. It is apparent that the directors of the Refining company were anxious to secure the Guggenheim business, not merely for their properties, but for the business capacity and experience of the Messrs. Guggenheim and the removal of the principal competitor of the Refining company.

The $45,200,000 of stock to be issued to the Guggenheims was to consist of an equal number of preferred and common shares. The amount was determined, through negotiation by the directors of the Refining company with the Guggenheims, on a *comparative basis*. That is, in negotiating the terms of the merger the parties did not concern themselves with the question whether the Guggenheim prop-

[18] See Report to the Stockholders of the American Smelting & Refining Company, (May 10, 1922); Moody, John, The Truth about the Trusts (New York, 1904), pp. 45–53; U. S. Industrial Commission, Reports (1900–1902), Vol. XIII, *Digest of Evidence*, pp. cix–cxi, *Testimony*, pp. 93–96.

erties were worth the par value of the stock to be issued to them. As testified by Mr. Daniel Guggenheim:

> From the outset the purpose of both parties was to reach a just conclusion as to *comparative values,* and to determine on that basis what amount of the securities we would justly receive for our business and properties as against those of the American company, represented by its outstanding $54,800,000 of stock.[19]

In December, 1900, prior to the announcement of the plan to consolidate the two concerns, the common stock of the Refining company sold in the open market at $41 a share and the preferred stock at $91 a share. Shortly thereafter, when the plan for consolidation had been announced, the common stock rose sharply to $63 per share and the preferred to $99.50 per share.

The complainants' bill alleged that the Refining company's stock already outstanding had been issued as fully paid for property, but that the capital of the company had since become impaired, and that the company had no working capital. It also contended that the low market price of the outstanding stock, prior to the announcement of the merger plans, proved this contention and showed that the property of the company was not then worth the par value of its stock. According to the complainants, the comparative method used in determining the amount of stock to be issued to the Guggenheims would be valid only in case the assets of the Refining company were fully worth the par value of its outstanding stock, and their contentions were directed to show that the latter assumption was not justified by the facts. Putting their case differently, they stated that the cost of reproducing the physical property of the Guggenheims was not in excess of $10,000,000 and that this sum, added to the $12,000,000 of cash working capital to be contributed, gave a total of $22,000,000 or $23,000,000 less than the face value of the stock to be issued.

In their answer the defendants denied that the capital of the Refining company was impaired, and alleged that the company had an adequate working capital and was earning at the rate of about 8 per cent upon its capitalization. They also contended that the market value of the outstanding shares of the Refining company was not a fair measure of the value of its property, and that the alleged deficiency of $23,000,000 in the value of the tangible property of the Guggenheim business was more than made up by intangibles such

[19] 62 N. J. Eq. 729, 734, 48 Atl. 771, 773 (1901).

as the goodwill, business capacity of its managers, and high earning power.

The lower court denied the injunction. Holding that the alleged capital impairment of the Refining company was not supported by evidence and that the company had ample working capital and was making excellent profits, the court said that on this showing it could not conclude that the company's stock did not "fairly represent the value of its property." The bearing of the low market price of the stock upon the question at issue was thus disposed of by the court:

> But it is said that Mr. Guggenheim's affidavit shows that prior to December last the preferred stock was selling for ninety-one cents on the dollar and the common for forty-one, and that this is proof of what the property is really worth. Undoubtedly the market price of stock is some evidence of value, and often satisfactory evidence; but Mr. Untermyer argued, and not without force, that investors are apt to look with some degree of doubt or suspicion upon a new industrial undertaking, and to manifest an unwillingness to take the stock at its real value until time has demonstrated the company's stability and earning power, and he argued further that the stock of this very company which, in December, sold for ninety for the preferred and forty for the common, in the month following sold for ninety-nine and one-half and sixty-three, thus showing how uncertain an indication of the value of this particular property the market price of this stock is. Taking all the foregoing facts together, I cannot say that it is proved to my satisfaction that the property of the smelting company is not worth $54,800,000, and that consequently, on the basis of relative values, the Guggenheim property is not worth $45,200,000.[20]

Returning to the statute law of New Jersey, the court said that in order to justify the injunctive relief prayed for it was necessary for the court to find not only that the Refining company's property, and consequently the Guggenheim property, was not worth the par of the stock, but also "that the directors, in the *bona fide* exercise of their discretion, could not think so; that having consciously overvalued these properties, they resorted to the device of relative valuation to cover up what they knew." This was a finding which the court said was impossible on the proofs as they then stood.

The contention that there was a deficiency of $23,000,000 in the value of the Guggenheim property was brushed aside by the court on the ground that this figure was based upon an appraisal of the physical property alone and that it ignored the value of the good will and

[20] 61 N. J. Eq. 458, 465–66, 48 Atl. 786, 789 (1901).

earning capacity of the Guggenheim business, and the advantage of eliminating competition.

On appeal the ruling of the lower court was reversed and a preliminary injunction was granted. The appellate court stressed the point that the exchange of stock for property was to be made on the basis of the *relative* values of the two hitherto independent businesses. The mere fact that the issuance of $45,200,000 of stock of the Refining company might be a fair *quid pro quo* for the assets and business of the Guggenheims would not make the transaction legal unless it could be assumed that the Guggenheim business was worth the full par value of the stock which was to be issued in exchange for it. The fact that the market value of the stock of the Refining company was well below par created a strong presumption that the Guggenheim property was also worth less than the equivalent of par, since it was not lightly to be assumed that the Guggenheims would accept less, in market value of the stock, than their property was reasonably worth.

As to defendant's contention that the Refining company's stock had a " real " value, as distinct from a market value, equal to par and therefore that the Guggenheims might not regard this stock as a depreciated form of currency, the court held that no adequate proof of this contention had been adduced. The mere fact that the Refining company had earned 8 per cent on its stock during the preceding year was held not to be conclusive, since " the earnings of a single year hardly afford satisfactory evidence of the value of the company's property . . ." [21]

In conclusion the court said:

> In view of the undefined nature of the property for which $23,000,000 of stock is to be issued, of the illegitimate basis on which the price to be paid for that property appears to have been fixed, and of the probability that the stock has been rated by the parties at its market value rather than at par, we think proper ground is shown for restraining the completion of the contract until further investigation can be made.[22]

Although the decision of the Court of Errors and Appeals granting the preliminary injunction hardly appears to need a justification outside of the facts set forth in the opinion, an examination of some

[21] *Cf.* The Railway Review v. Groff Drill & Machine Tool Co., *supra*, c. VI, notes 21, 22; Dee Co. v. Proviso Coal Co., *supra*, c. VI, note 32.

[22] 62 N. J. Eq. 729, 735, 48 Atl. 771, 774 (1901).

of the facts bearing upon the antecedent history of the American Smelting & Refining Company may be worth while and may serve to throw added light on the decision.[23] The company was originally organized in April, 1899, by consolidating under one corporate ownership a number of smelters, refineries, and mines or mining rights. The promoters obtained options to purchase the various properties for a total of $27,400,000 in cash, but the vendors were given an opportunity to accept preferred stock of the company in amounts equal to the several option prices and a bonus of common stock equal to 70 per cent of the option prices. An underwriting syndicate was organized and to the extent that the vendors failed to take stock in lieu of cash the necessary funds were supplied by the syndicate. The syndicate and promoters received 30 per cent of the common stock as compensation for their services. In this manner $54,800,000 of "full-paid" stock was originally issued, consisting of equal amounts of common and preferred stock. The preferred was issued against tangible assets and the common stood for good will, patents and processes. No attempt was made to place an accurate valuation upon these latter items. It was the current promotion practice at the time to issue preferred stock in an amount equal to the appraised value of the tangible property and an equal amount of common stock to represent intangible values inherent in the separate business enterprises as well as those economic advantages which were expected to result from combination of competitors and the attainment of monopoly. This common stock was, in part, given as a bonus to the vendors in order to persuade them to accept preferred stock in lieu of cash for their plants and, in part, it was used to defray promotion expenses; the promoters, accountants, lawyers, and investment bankers sharing it roughly in proportion to the value of the services rendered by each.[24]

[23] The statement in the text concerning the manner of organizing the American Smelting & Refining Company has been taken from the following sources: REPORT TO THE STOCKHOLDERS, ETC., *supra,* note 18; HANDBOOK FOR STOCKHOLDERS OF THE AMERICAN SMELTING & REFINING COMPANY (compiled for use of stockholders prior to the annual meeting, April 6, 1921); MOODY, *op. cit. supra,* note 18; U. S. INDUSTRIAL COMMISSION, REPORTS (1900–1902), *loc. cit. supra,* note 18.

[24] The common stock was a cheap gamble on the future of the enterprise. Its modern equivalent is the cheap or costless option or option warrant so widely used in current corporate finance, particularly in the field of investment trusts and financial holding companies.

As stated above, the Guggenheims refused to come into this combination on the basis of the offer originally made to them. It is not known what the original offer to the Guggenheims was, but the book value of their plants was $3,647,000 two years later, and there is reason to believe that the original offer was approximately $11,000,000 in stock of the American Smelting & Refining Company.[25] The negotiations in 1900, and the resulting offer which led to the suit discussed above, were conducted with a view to according to the Guggenheims the same treatment as that received by the owners of the original properties. Half of the stock to be issued was to represent tangible property and the other half was to represent good will, processes, business connections, and managerial ability. The directors of the Refining company were particularly anxious to absorb the Guggenheims, because the latter were the principal competitors in the industry and were noted for their business capacity and experience in this line. The foreign business of the Refining company and the sale of certain of its products were handled by the United Metals Selling Company with which two of the directors of the Refining company, Messrs. H. H. Rogers and Leonard Lewishon, were identified. Foreseeing that the consolidation of the Refining company and the Guggenheim firm would result in a loss of this business to the United Metals Selling Company because the Guggenheims were equipped to handle it, these two directors caused the suit for an injunction to be brought.

It may be significant that at about this time the United States Industrial Commission was engaged in a comprehensive exposé of the manner in which combinations of this character (including the American Smelting & Refining Company) had been promoted in recent years, and of the excessive amount of watered stock which had resulted from the current type of promotion. Numerous combinations had been promoted and incorporated, particularly under the laws of New Jersey, and the capitalization of these new "trusts" was known to bear little if any relationship to the value of the underlying tangible properties. Capitalization of hope was currently in vogue and it is probable that the courts, no less than the public, were impressed with the alarming extent to which this practice had gone.

[25] See Report to Stockholders, *supra*, note 18, p. 6; Handbook, *supra*, note 23.

This, then, was the background out of which the *Donald* case came before the courts. To what extent the court was aware of it is not known. It made no reference to it in the opinion. But it is not difficult to understand the attitude of the appellate court if it were aware that all of the common stock of the Refining company had been issued two years previously for nothing other than the hope that the company would succeed as an industrial combination. In the light of such knowledge the low market value of the stock would assume considerable significance and the reason for the unwillingness of the court to sanction the *comparative* method of valuation would be apparent.

It seems clear that the lower court knew quite well that the value of the Guggenheim property was probably less than the par value of the Refining company stock to be issued for it. But it is probable that this court didn't consider such a discrepancy to be a vitally important matter (especially in litigation on the part of minority shareholders), and that it considered relative values to be the really important question. Hence, while it didn't dare to defy the New Jersey statute to the extent of saying, " Absolute values are not important in cases of this kind," it did the next thing to it by putting all of the burden of proof on the plaintiffs and by resorting to a sophistical argument to the effect that the low market value of the shares was irrelevant in a suit by minority shareholders to restrain an issue of stock for property.[26]

[26] The subsequent history of the manner in which this conflict between the directors of the American Smelting & Refining Company was compromised out of court furnishes an illustration of the way in which the shareholders' injunctive relief fails to prevent stock watering and even encourages policies which are detrimental to the interests of shareholders and creditors. Upon the granting of an interim injunction by the Court of Errors and Appeals of New Jersey the majority directors negotiated with Messrs. Rogers and Lewishon, the dissenting minority, and secured a dismissal of the suit, thus enabling the merger to be carried out on the original terms. It is reported that Rogers and Lewishon were bought off with a commercial bribe in the form of a contract granting to the United Metals Selling Company an exclusive agency for five years for the sale of silver and copper products (with some exceptions) of the smelting and refining company, on terms which were regarded as burdensome to the latter. It is difficult to see how such a contract would be other than detrimental to the interests of creditors of the company and to the innocent shareholders who did not receive a collateral benefit under it. See REPORT TO STOCKHOLDERS, *supra*, note 18, pp. 5–6; Moody, *op. cit. supra* (note 18) at p. 51.

Other Types of Evidence Tending to Show Knowledge of Overvaluation

Closely resembling in effect the suits discussed in the two preceding sections is a group of cases wherein some agreement or act of the defendant shareholders or of the directors of their corporation, collateral or incident to the organization and initial financing of the enterprise, has demonstrated, either that the directors did not regard the consideration for which they authorized stock to be issued as being worth the par of the stock, or that reasonable and unbiased business men would not have so regarded it. Space will not permit a detailed consideration of the opinions and decisions in all such cases, but we shall review several of them for purposes of illustration.

Douglass v. Ireland [27] was an action by a creditor against a shareholder to collect on unpaid stock. One Horton had an option to purchase a furnace and mining premises, together with standing timber near the furnace, for $40,000, of which $30,000 was the price of the furnace. He and four others, including the defendant, incorporated the "Black River Iron & Mining Company of New York" and as directors authorized the issuance of its entire capital stock of $300,000 to Horton for his option. Horton divided $200,000 of the stock with his associates for no apparent consideration. He donated the remaining $100,000 of stock to the corporation to be sold by it to raise working capital and to pay the contract price for the furnace, timber, etc. This latter stock was reissued at prices ranging from forty to sixty cents on the dollar. The defendant bought $25,000 of the stock for $10,000, in addition to receiving $5,000 of stock from Horton as stated above. At the trial the jury placed the value of the property at $65,000 and the trial court gave judgment for the plaintiff.

On appeal the judgment was affirmed. The court said:

> It is a very significant fact, as alleged, giving character to the transaction, that the seller of the property was willing to and did divide with his co-trustees, the bargainers, two-thirds of the nominal consideration he received for it. This is entirely inconsistent with the idea that the sale was a *bona fide* sale for the supposed actual value of the property, and without explanation would be conclusive evidence that the purchase by the trustees was not, in the exercise of an honest judgment and the discretion vested in them, at the real or supposed value of the thing purchased; but that under

[27] 73 N. Y. 100 (1878).

color of a compliance with the provisions of the act of 1853 [which amended the act of 1848 to permit the issuance of stock for property], the purchase of the property and the issue of the stock was a palpable evasion of, and fraud upon, the law. . . .

The property was held by Horton, under executory contracts of purchase, upon which nothing had been paid; the purchase-money being wholly unpaid. The contract-price for the furnace property was $30,000, and the contract was made but about a year before the sale to the company. The contract for the woodland had been entered into but about five months before the sale to the company, and was for $10,000, to be paid for as the wood should be cut. One-third of the stock issued was immediately retransferred to the company, to be sold by it to raise a "working capital," and enable the company to prosecute its business, and this stock was sold at prices ranging from forty to sixty cents on the dollar of its par value, the defendant buying his at the lowest price named. In this sale of stock by the corporation to the defendant we have the estimate of both buyer and seller — that is, of all the trustees of the company of the value of the property acquired and owned by the company, and represented by the nominal capital of $300,000. By that sale and purchase they fix the value of the property at only $120,000, which is nearly double the value proved upon the trial and found by the jury. The defendant cannot complain if the property is valued at his own price.

The surrender and re-transfer of $100,000 of the stock to the company, without consideration, is some evidence that the $300,000 was not regarded as the value of the property, but that it was so treated with a view to absorb the entire capital stock, and the sale of the stock received by the company at prices stated was very persuasive evidence of the opinion entertained by the trustees of the value of the property as represented by the stock.[28]

A similar situation resulting in a similar decision is found in *Blake v. Griswold.*[29]

In *National Tube Works Company v. Gilfillan*[30] the manner in which the promoters dealt with their stock after it had been issued to them for a non-cash consideration appears to have been the basis for the decision that the defendant shareholder was liable to a creditor of the corporation. The plaintiff, an unsatisfied judgment creditor of the Brooklyn Marine Power Company, brought this action against one who was a shareholder, trustee, and president of the power company.

The corporation was organized with a capital stock of $300,000,

[28] *Ibid.*, pp. 105–6.

[29] 103 N. Y. 429, 9 N. E. 434 (1886).

[30] 124 N. Y. 302, 26 N. E. 538 (1891), *aff'g* 46 Hun 248 (1887).

all of which was issued to the defendant as full-paid stock for the assignment to the company of certain unpatented inventions in marine machinery. The defendant held the rights to these inventions as trustee for the inventor, Bliven. In accordance with prior agreements the stock was disposed of as follows: $100,000 to defendant as trustee for the corporation; $50,000 to defendant in payment of a debt of $15,000 owed him by Bliven; $5,000 to Dexter in payment of a debt of $2,500 owed him by Bliven; $13,500 to various persons in order to qualify them as directors and to induce them to act as such; $131,500 to Bliven for his inventions.

The case was tried before a jury which found that the property purchased at $300,000 was really worth only $75,000 and gave a general verdict for the plaintiff.

On appeal to the supreme court the judgment was affirmed. It said in part:

> The issuing and division of these certificates in this manner was evidence of an understanding that the inventions for which the capital stock was in form wholly issued, were not worth the amount agreed to be paid for them. If they had been, no satisfactory reason appears why the inventor, Bliven, should have immediately returned 200 shares to the company, and delivered 100 shares to the defendant in payment of an indebtedness of $15,000. These 100 shares nominally amounted to $50,000 which would not have been given to pay the indebtedness which has been mentioned, if the property obtained by the company had been of equal value to this stock. At least these were facts which the jury could well consider, and from which they could determine that the inventions were not only worth less than the prices agreed to be paid for them, but that it was so understood by the defendant and the other parties to these transactions. And that it was intended before the shares were issued that they should be divided and disposed of in this manner, appears by an agreement made between the defendant and A. Perry Bliven. . . . By this agreement, precisely this division of the shares of the company was provided for, which it is reasonable to assume would not have been done, if the inventions taken by the company had been considered by the defendant of the value, or fair value, of this stock. At least one-third of the stock without any apparent consideration was returned to the company, and 100 shares received by the defendant in payment of the proportionately small indebtedness of $15,000.[31]

Other evidence mentioned by the court which may have contributed to its decision was the fact that the inventions were never

[31] 46 Hun 248, 251 (1887).

patented and the fact that the two other companies, which had been organized to exploit these inventions, had failed.

The case was appealed to the New York Court of Appeals which refused to reverse. It said:

> According to the evidence, the jury made a liberal estimate of the real value of the inventions when they found that they were worth $75,000. The good faith of the trustees, including the defendant, as one of the most active in the transaction of this business, may be inferred from the foregoing facts. If they honestly considered the inventions worth $300,000, why was one-third of the avails, $100,000 in stock, donated to the company by Bliven? Why did the defendant accept $50,000 in stock in payment of a debt of $15,000? Why was $5,000 given to Dexter to pay $2,500? Why was $13,500 in stock given to persons to induce them to become trustees? Would $300,000 in money have been disposed of in this way? The arrangement to thus dispose of the stock was made before the purchase and became a part of it. The facts were all known to the trustees, including the defendant.[32]

Similarly, in *McClure v. Paducah Iron Company*,[33] a creditor's suit, the fact that several of the directors of a corporation accepted $100,000 of stock, the issue of which they had authorized, in satisfaction of a debt to them of $50,000 was regarded by the court as persuasive evidence that they did not believe that the consideration for which the stock was issued was worth the face value of the stock.

On the other hand, in *Finletter v. Acetylene Light, Heat and Power Company* [34] the rule appears to be *contra* to that found in the foregoing cases. The court did not regard the promoter's liberal distribution of his shares, after having received them from the corporation in payment for the assignment of certain patent rights, as indicating that the stock had been issued for deliberately overvalued property. This was an action by a receiver for the benefit of creditors against shareholders to collect an alleged unpaid balance on stock issued for the patent rights. The decree below dismissed the bill as to the defendants and an appeal was taken on grounds of error.

Suckert and Dickerson held a patent for producing liquefied acetylene gas and supplying it cheaply to consumers. Vincent secured from them an option to purchase a license under the patent for the territory in and around Philadelphia. He paid $10,000 for this option, which gave him the right to buy the license for $90,000

[32] 124 N. Y. 302, 306, 26 N. E. 538, 539 (1891).

[33] 90 Mo. App. 567, 583–86 (1901).

[34] 215 Pa. 86, 64 Atl. 429 (1906).

in cash, plus a certain percentage of the capital stock of a corporation to be organized to produce the gas under the license. Vincent induced Adams and Napheys, two of the defendants, to form the company. The original subscribers were friendly capitalists who paid $100,000 in cash to the company for a like amount of stock. This cash, together with $1,400,000 of stock, was given to Vincent in exchange for an assignment of the license. Vincent then gave to the patentees, Suckert and Dickerson, $500,000 of this stock and $90,000 in cash under the terms of his agreement with them. He also divided $500,000 of his stock with Napheys, Adams, and Dickerson, the last having advanced the $10,000 with which Vincent had obtained the option. Vincent turned over $400,000 of stock to the cash subscribers who had paid in the original $100,000 of cash. This was a 400 per cent stock bonus which had evidently been agreed upon in advance.

The company failed, due to the action of insurance companies in refusing to insure buildings using the liquefied gas.[35] This action was taken by the insurance companies after an explosion had occurred in an industrial plant using the gas.

The principal contention of the plaintiff was that the $900,000 of stock, which was not turned over to the patentees by Vincent but was distributed by him among his associates, was not full-paid and was, therefore, liable to assessment.

In affirming the dismissal of the suit the court said that the manner in which Vincent had disposed of his stock was not proof of deliberate overvaluation. According to the court, this was the natural way to induce coöperation of capitalists and technicians in management for the advancement of the new enterprise and was perfectly consistent with an honest belief on the part of the directors that the rights under the patent were fully worth the par value of the stock.[36]

While there is some force to the court's position, it seems clear that the decision can be justified only on the assumption that stock may be issued for property at a valuation which is merely prospective rather than at a cash price which reasonable investors would then have paid in view of the extreme risks involved.

The several cases which follow bring out another type of evidence

[35] *Cf.* O'Bear-Nester Glass Co. v. Antiexplo Co., 101 Tex. 431, 108 S. W. 967, 109 S. W. 931 (1908).

[36] *Cf.* American Tube & Iron Co. v. Hays, 165 Pa. 489, 30 Atl. 936 (1895).

which has been relied upon by the courts to support decisions of overvaluation. In these cases a sale to a corporation of property for a large block of stock has been preceded by cash dealings or agreements among the promoters with respect to the property on the basis of a much lower price.

Carp v. Chipley [37] was a case holding a shareholder liable to creditors on watered stock. Mabee owned a trade-marked process for the manufacture of a medical compound known as "Targarette," and had applied for a patent on the process. He sold a one-half interest in the process, trade-mark, and patent application to Davis for $5,000 cash. For a short time the product was marketed with slight success. The business did not yield satisfactory returns and Davis decided to sell his interest in it. He offered to reconvey his one-half interest to Mabee for $4,450 and the sale at this price was ultimately effected, Davis taking Mabee's note for $4,450 secured by the pledge of $25,000 of stock in a corporation formed to exploit the process. Mabee and Chipley, a capitalist whom Mabee had induced to take a financial interest in the enterprise, formed a corporation and arranged the issuance of $99,600 of stock to Mabee for his right, title and interest in the compound, registered trade-mark, and application for a patent. Mabee returned $49,600 of this stock to the company's treasury to be used in raising working capital. The balance of $50,000 was divided between Mabee and Chipley. The latter loaned his $25,000 of stock to Mabee who pledged it with Davis to secure Mabee's note for $4,450.

The referee to whom the case was referred found that the value of the compound "Targarette" and all of the property transferred therewith to the company, was not over $25,000, and that at least four of the five directors knew this to be a fact. On the basis of this finding the trial court held the defendants liable.

The case was appealed and the judgment below was affirmed as to one plaintiff but reversed as to the other for reasons that need not concern us here. The following language from the opinion of the Appellate Court indicates, in part, the reason for the decision:

> The referee found that the value of the Targarette preparation, the business, etc., transferred by Mabee to the corporation, did not exceed $25,000 in value. In view of the fact that Mabee had a short time prior to selling to the corporation sold to Davis one-half interest in this preparation for $5,000, and repurchased it on the eve of the formation of the company for

[37] 73 Mo. App. 22 (1898).

$4,450, and in view of the manipulations made by Mabee and L. M. Chipley with a large portion of Mabee's nine hundred and ninety-six shares of stock, it can not be doubted for a moment that the referee was extremely liberal in the limit he fixed, beyond which the value of this property could not be placed.[38]

Similarly, in *Hastings v. Scott*[39] the fact that the promoters had valued a mining property at $12,000 for the purposes of a partnership agreement and had shortly thereafter valued it at $30,000 for stock-issue purposes formed the basis for a decision holding shareholders liable to a trustee in bankruptcy on an unpaid balance due on the stock. As the court put it:

> The fact that the owners of the property in forming a partnership in relation thereto less than four months before the formation of the corporation had placed a value of only $12,000 upon it is of itself an important fact to be considered in determining the value of the property when the corporation was formed.

Again, in *Macbeth v. Banfield*[40] we find the same type of evidence tending to defeat the contention of defendant shareholders in a suit by a trustee in bankruptcy for the benefit of creditors, but there was further evidence that the promoters had agreed among themselves that the stock should be issued as fully paid for a payment of 50 per cent of par.[41]

Two men by the name of Kaupisch sold a one-half interest in their creamery business to the defendant, Banfield, and to one Rand, for $5,000 cash. Of this money $1,000 was immediately used to pay accounts payable of the creamery concern. On the next day the property and business of the creamery, together with the remaining $4,000 cash, were turned over to a corporation organized by these parties and $20,000 of its capital stock was issued to them in ex-

[38] 73 Mo. App. 22 (1898), pp. 34–35.

[39] 248 S. W. 973 (Mo. App., 1923). *Cf.* Berry v. Rood, 168 Mo. 316, 67 S. W. 644 (1902) — concerning the value of onyx works put in for $90,000 of stock despite an agreement to reimburse the vendor for all excess in value over $15,000.

[40] 45 Or. 553, 78 Pac. 693 (1904).

[41] *Cf.* Coleman v. Howe, *supra,* note 10; Jackson v. Traer, 64 Iowa 469, 20 N. W. 764 (1884); Boulton Carbon Co. v. Mills, *supra,* note 10; Moore v. United States One-Stave Barrel Co., 238 Ill. 544, 87 N. E. 536 (1909); Shickle v. Watts, *supra,* note 9; The First National Bank of Chanute v. Northup, 82 Kan. 638, 109 Pac. 672 (1910); Chittenden v. Thannhauser, 47 Fed. 410 (C. C., S. D. N. Y., 1891).

change. Thus the parties valued the property for purposes of the transaction *inter se* at approximately $10,000 and immediately thereafter valued it at $20,000 for stock-issue purposes.

Furthermore, all four of the promoters agreed in a written instrument executed on the day they subscribed for stock of the new corporation, that neither should sell his stock to outsiders, and that in case any desired to sell his stock the remaining original parties should have an option to buy it at 50 per cent of its par value. The agreement stipulated 50 per cent of the par value of the stock as liquidated damages in case of any breach of this contract. One of the Kaupischs testified that the plan contemplated by all of the parties was that each should receive his stock for a payment of 50 per cent of par value.

On appeal the judgment of the lower court, holding the defendants liable to the plaintiff up to a maximum of 50 per cent of par value, was affirmed. The prior deal on this basis among the promoters, and their agreement to a like effect after the company was formed, were apparently the principal reasons for the decision.

In *Cohen v. Toy Gun Manufacturing Company* [42] a sale of a one-half interest in certain patent rights by one promoter to another at a price of $25,000, and a later transfer of the patent rights to a corporation organized by them for an issue of $250,000 of stock was the basis of the decision holding the shareholders liable to creditors on a finding that the patent rights were not worth over $50,000.

A further type of evidence indicating knowledge of overvaluation is the fact that the promoters, shortly after receiving stock in exchange for property, sell it for a price materially less than par. This circumstance is particularly strong evidence if the sale at a discount has been made under an agreement entered into before the stock was issued.

Libby v. Tobey [43] was a case in point, although there was other fatally damaging evidence of gross and deliberate overvaluation. The action was brought by a creditor of a mining company to recover from the holder of allegedly unpaid stock. In giving judgment for the plaintiff, the court pointed out the following circumstances: first, the property for which the stock was issued had cost the promoters less than 3 per cent of the par value of the stock; second, the promoters, after receipt of the stock, immediately returned 25 per cent of it to the company as " treasury stock "; third, most of this treasury

[42] 172 Ill. App. 330 (1912).

[43] 82 Me. 397, 19 Atl. 904 (1890).

stock was at once resold by the corporation at 10 per cent of its par value; fourth, the promoters themselves soon sold at similar discounts some of the stock which they retained. The court commented as follows on these circumstances:

> The total actual cost to these associates, including $2,500, expended in improving and developing the property, was not over $375 each, or a fraction less than twenty-three cents a share for 1650 shares each.
>
> That the property was not actually worth the sum of $240,000, at the time it was purchased is too evident to require discussion. The price paid, as well as the acts of the purchasers immediately after the organization in voting to sell the capital stock of the company to the amount of $45,000, at fifty cents a share, or at one tenth of its par value, — the sale of a considerable portion of the treasury stock within sixty days of the organization at that figure, — the fact that the whole $60,000 of treasury stock was sold at prices ranging from fifty cents to one dollar and fifty cents a share, — and the very low figure at which many of the stockholders sold their stock, — is evidence from which we may well infer that the value of $240,000, placed upon this property by the corporation, was not a "*bona fide* and fair valuation thereof." [44]

Kaye v. Metz [45] was a suit by a trustee in bankruptcy to recover an alleged unpaid balance on stock. The court below rendered judgment for the plaintiff in the amount of $45,432.20.

The corporation was organized with a capital stock of $500,000, divided into 500,000 shares. Of this stock $400,000 was issued to promoters for leaseholds on the basis of their potential value as oil lands. The defendants contended that this constituted full payment for the stock and resisted the suit on that ground. The court below found that the value of the leaseholds was $100,000 and that the directors knew that the value did not exceed this sum and had no reasonable grounds for thinking otherwise. The defendants claimed that this finding was not supported by the evidence. The evidence on the question of value was not extensive. One promoter, who was also an incorporator and a director of the company, testified that he believed the property was worth $400,000 in the sense that he believed that oil of this value would ultimately be taken out. But other witnesses who were familiar with the locality testified that in their opinion the leaseholds were worth not over $100,000, and were probably worth less.

[44] 82 Me. 397, pp. 403–4, 19 Atl. 905 (1890).
[45] 186 Cal. 42, 198 Pac. 1047 (1921).

In sustaining the judgment below the court stressed the fact that immediately after the resolution to purchase the leaseholds for stock as indicated above was passed, the directors resolved to place the remaining 100,000 shares of stock on the market at the price of twenty-five cents per share. The court said in part:

It was also shown that all of the directors, including Smith and Metz, the holders of said lease, were present at the meeting of the directors at which the transaction was closed, and that immediately after the passage of the resolution authorizing the purchase of said lease by the corporation for said amount of stock the same directors passed another resolution that the remaining one hundred thousand shares of stock of the company should be placed on the market at twenty-five cents a share. This was done accordingly and a large part of the one hundred thousand shares was sold at that price. The greater part of the stock in question here was the stock originally transferred to Smith and Metz in exchange for said lease. It had been acquired afterward by the appellants with knowledge of all the circumstances. The conduct of these parties in immediately putting the remaining stock on the market at twenty-five cents a share was a clear indication that they then believed that the stock already disposed of to Smith and Metz had no real value above that amount. It is true that Jameson testified that it was necessary to sell at that price in order to raise the money with which to develop the property and that this proceeding was not an unusual one in the oil business. It still remains true, however, that the court may well have inferred from this circumstance that the directors, all of whom consented to this sale at the reduced price, did not believe that the stock had a greater value. We are, therefore, of the opinion that the finding is sustained by the evidence and that under the doctrine above stated it must be deemed paid up only to the extent of one hundred thousand dollars, or one-fourth of the par value.[46]

Similarly, in *Kelly v. Clark* [47] the decision, granting to a creditor of a mining corporation recovery from shareholders on unpaid stock,

[46] *Ibid.*, pp. 51–52, 198 Pac. 1050–51. But see Harrison v. Armour, 169 Cal. 787, 792, 147 Pac. 1166, 1168 (1915), where the court said: — "The fact that cash sales were made at twenty-five cents per share [par value $1] is no proof that an issue of stock in exchange for patent rights was intended to be or was at the same rate. The two transactions are essentially different, and the nature of each must be determined from its own facts." See also, Young v. Erie Iron Co., 65 Mich. 111, 121, 31 N. W. 814, 819–20 (1887), where the court said that gifts of stock by promoters to influential parties in order to obtain their interest, and sales of stock by the promoters at $5, $8, and $12.50 per share, which they had issued to themselves at its par value of $25 in exchange for property, were not inconsistent with a belief on the part of the promoters that the stock would eventually become worth its face value.

[47] 21 Mont. 291, 53 Pac. 959 (1898). *Cf.* Enright v. Heckscher, *supra*, note 14;

appears to have been based upon the price at which the promoter sold some of the stock which was issued to him for property.

Donation of Stock to the Treasury of the Corporation as Evidence of Deliberate Overvaluation

Of all types of evidence indicating an implied admission that watered stock has been issued, the fact that promoters have resorted to the device of donated treasury stock has been most frequently adduced.

Treasury stock may be defined as stock which has once been issued by a corporation as full-paid stock but which has been received back by the company either through gift or purchase.[48] As a promotion device it is a means by which promoters may raise cash capital for their company through the sale of nominally full-paid stock at a discount. The following illustration is typical of the practice in its simplest form.

A promoter of a mining venture secures options on mining property and forms a corporation to take over and develop the mine. In exchange for the property, which his options permit him to buy for $100,000, the directors of the corporation (all of them being his appointees) vote to issue $1,000,000 of " full-paid and non-assessable " stock. They solemnly go on record as holding the opinion that the property is " fully worth " the par value of the stock that is to be issued against it. After receiving the stock, the promoter at once turns back half of it to the corporation, and the corporation thereupon reissues it for cash at 20 per cent of par. The proceeds are used for working capital or for any other corporate purpose.

The object of resorting to this circuitous method of financing is to make the treasury stock " full-paid " before it is issued to investors for cash at a discount. Were it not for this assurance that the stock carries no further liability for payment, cash purchasers could not be found unless the stock could be issued at par, and this latter

---

Raleigh Investment Co. v. Bunker, 285 Mo. 440, 450, 452, 227 S. W. 121, 124 (1920).

[48] An investigation of the contents of a corporate treasury might reveal a variety of stock certificates, including the following: authorized but unissued stock; pledged stock; purchased stock; forfeited stock; donated stock. The present discussion is limited to the last type, namely, stock which has been issued for a consideration and donated to the corporation, or to an agent or a trustee for its benefit.

possibility is out of the question since the promoter proposes to retain so much stock that no sensible investor would buy an interest in the company on the basis of the par value of the stock.[49]

There are various ways, more complicated than the one stated in the above illustration, for accomplishing the same result. One of them is to have the promoter turn over the redundant stock which he receives in exchange for his property, not to the corporation itself, but to a trustee. This trustee then sells the stock for cash at a discount and turns over the proceeds (sometimes minus a selling commission) to the corporation. Or the trustee may be an agent for the sale of bonds of the company and may give a bonus of treasury stock with each bond sold. Counsel for the promoters evidently hope that this more circuitous method will stand legal scrutiny more effectively in a subsequent shareholders'-liability suit than will the simpler device of a donation of stock directly to the corporation. However, the cases that have been studied for the purpose of this chapter

[49] The doctrine of Handley v. Stutz, 139 U. S. 417, 35 L. Ed. 227, 11 Sup. Ct. 530 (1891), permitting the sale of par-value stock at a discount without liability of the purchaser for a further payment to creditors, is restricted to a going concern which has become financially embarrassed so that it cannot sell its stock at par, and to sales of stock by such concerns in order to raise funds with which to continue the enterprise as a solvent concern, rather than to sales of stock for expansion purposes. See BONBRIGHT, *op. cit. supra* (c. I, note 1) at pp. 429–31. Even then the rule is not universal. *Ibid.*, p. 431.

More frequently the same difficulty of selling new stock at par is faced by the corporation at its inception. In either event, the stock purchaser tends to refuse to risk the possibility that Handley v. Stutz will not be applied and demands further assurance that the stock will not be subject to calls by creditors. Even then, if the purchaser of treasury stock pays a price below par, or if he accepts it as a bonus, the court may hold that he is on *constructive notice* that the stock was not fully paid when it was originally issued and may impose a liability upon him on that ground. Holcombe v. Trenton White City Co., *supra*, c. VI, note 13; Stoecker v. Goodman, 183 Ky. 330, 209 S. W. 374 (1919); Cooney Co. v. Arlington Hotel Co., *supra*, c. VI, note 27; Smith v. Schmitt, 112 Or. 687, 231 Pac. 176 (1924); Scully v. Automobile Finance Co., *supra*, c. II, note 11; See v. Heppenheimer, *supra*, c. VI, note 2; Alling v. Wenzel, 133 Ill. 264, 24 N. E. 551 (1890); Campbell v. McPhee, 36 Wash. 593, 79 Pac. 206 (1905); Blake v. Griswold, *supra*, note 29; Gillett v. Chicago Title & Trust Co., *supra*, c. VI, note 55; Scott v. Barton, 285 Mo. 427, 226 S. W. 958 (1920); Gordon v. Cummings, 78 Wash. 515, 139 Pac. 489 (1914). But see: Davies v. Ball, 64 Wash. 292, 116 Pac. 833 (1911); Berry v. Rood, *supra*, note 39; Kingston v. Nichols, 221 Mich. 677, 192 N. W. 768 (1923); California National Supply Co. v. Dinsmore, 52 Cal. App. 513, 199 Pac. 552 (1921); California National Supply Co. v. O'Brien, 51 Cal. App. 606, 197 Pac. 414 (1921).

do not reveal that the courts make any distinction between these two methods of doing the same thing.

To a layman it would seem almost self-evident that a promoter who receives $1,000,000 in stock for property and who at once turns back $500,000 of that stock to the corporation, by this very act betrays his own opinion that the property is not worth the full million dollars at which he is capitalizing it. This assumption would seem to be doubly justified where the treasury stock is subsequently sold by the corporation, in accordance with a prearranged plan, at much less than par. Yet the courts have not always held that the mere proof of such a financial practice is enough to establish deliberate overvaluation. On the contrary, they have listened with more or less sympathy to defendants' argument that the property was reasonably valued at the full amount of stock which the promoter received rather than at the lower amount of stock which the promoter retained.

The argument for the defense is that the promoter may own property which, as part of a going concern, equipped with working capital, is worth at least one million dollars but which could not be sold in the market for any such figure because no one but the promoter recognizes, or is willing to exploit, its commercial possibilities. Only by securing the support of other investors who will contribute cash capital can the promoter develop the full value of the property.[50] These investors, however, cannot be attracted to a new and untried enterprise unless they are given an opportunity to buy stock at a real bargain — at less than the stock is "really worth." Consequently the promoter is forced to turn over some of his stock to the corporation for resale at a discount to other investors, retaining an amount of stock the par value of which is less than the property was worth.

This contention on the part of defendant shareholders has a certain color of plausibility. Yet it smacks suspiciously like the argument that the *potential* value of a property, rather than its existing

[50] See, *e.g., In re* Pipe Line Oil Co., *loc. cit. infra,* note 52; Lake Superior Iron Co. v. Drexel, *loc. cit. infra,* note 56; Insurance Press v. Montauk Wire Co., *loc. cit. infra,* note 57; Manhattan Trust Co. v. Seattle Coal & Iron Co., 19 Wash. 493, 501–2, 53 Pac. 951, 955 (1898); Davies v. Ball, 64 Wash. 292, 298, 116 Pac. 833, 835 (1911); American Tube & Iron Co. v. Hays, 165 Pa. 489, 495 *et seq.*, 30 Atl. 936, 938 *et seq.* (1895). *Cf.* Willock v. Dilworth, 204 Pa. 492, 495–96, 54 Atl. 278, 280 (1903); Kingston v. Nichols, 221 Mich. 677, 686–87, 192 N. W. 768, 772 (1923). See also 1 Cook, *op. cit. supra* (c. I, note 37), sect. 47.

and acknowledged value, is the proper basis of capitalization — a defense which, as was noted in a previous chapter, has been verbally rejected by most courts.

Judging from the recorded cases in which judges have expressed their opinion on the subject, the courts are divided as to whether the donation of stock to the corporation by the promoter is persuasive evidence of overvaluation. No court, to be sure, has gone so far as to hold that it is conclusive evidence, but there is much difference of opinion as to the weight to be given it.

Taking up the cases which have belittled the importance of the use of treasury stock as proof of overvaluation, we may note, first, a decision by a United States Circuit Court of Appeals, interpreting the law of Delaware, *In re Pipe Line Oil Company.*[51] This was an action by the trustee in bankruptcy of a Delaware corporation to levy an assessment equal to 100 per cent of the par value of shares held by the defendants who took their stock as a bonus along with notes of the corporation for a cash payment equal to the face value of the notes. The referee had held that the stock of the defendants was assessable for the benefit of the plaintiff up to 100 per cent of par, and had entered an order to that effect. The facts concerning the original issue of the stock were as follows: Smith and Hall held leases on 170 acres of oil land and a contract to supply oil to an oil company. Their nominees incorporated the Pipe Line Oil Company and resolved to accept the leases and the contract in payment for an issue of $150,000 of stock. Smith, Hall, and one other promoter, acting as the sole directors of the company, voted to accept this mode of payment and to sell $75,000 of notes to raise working capital. They donated $75,000 of the stock issued to them to the corporate treasury for its use as a bonus to facilitate the sale of the notes. Of the latter, $62,000 were sold at par and an equal amount of " treasury stock " was given to the purchasers. The proceeds, less a 25 per cent selling commission, were paid into the treasury of the corporation. No proof whatever was taken below as to the actual or reasonably estimated value of the property at the time the stock was issued for it.

From the mere fact of the immediate return of 50 per cent of the stock to the corporate treasury and the simultaneous adoption of a plan to use it as a bonus to promote the sale of notes, the referee drew the inference, practically as one of law, that the property was

[51] 289 Fed. 698 (C. C. A., 6th Cir., 1923).

not worth more than $75,000 and that so much of the valuation placed on the property as had been applied to pay up the stock returned to the treasury was a fraudulent overvaluation, and that such stock was wholly unpaid. The District Court vacated the order of the referee levying the assessment and this appeal was on a petition of the trustee in bankruptcy to review the order of the District Court.

The Circuit Court of Appeals affirmed the vacation of the order of assessment and gave directions to hear further evidence to determine whether there was a *prima facie* case of "actual fraud in the transaction," such being necessary to any assessment under the Delaware law. On the question of overvaluation the court said:

What were here involved were oil leases and (it is said) a contract for the purchase and transportation of the output of a prospective large producer. Such property is notoriously of speculative value. It may have no fixed, or market, value, and yet be truly valuable. Indeed, we do not understand it to be urged that, if the directors had fixed the value at $150,000 and issued all the stock therefor as fully paid, and done nothing else, there would be any presumption of fraud to be drawn merely from the fact that the enterprise failed.

The proof of fraud is said to be found in the practically simultaneous turning back of one-half of the stock for the avowed purpose of being used to promote the sale of notes for working capital. This develops a peculiar characteristic of a mining prospect, strikingly true of an undeveloped oil lease, and perfectly familiar to all. Its value depends upon the existence of available capital for development. No one would doubt that it would often be reasonable for the owner of such a prospect to give one-half of it as a bonus to anyone who would lend the perhaps large amount of capital necessary for exploitation. It might well be, it being a question of fact, that $75,000 would be a high price for oil leases helpless for lack of capital, and $150,000 would be a reasonable price for the same leases if and when the necessary capital could be borrowed. To carry out this theory in connection with a corporate enterprise, perhaps the only form in which capital could be secured — a typical method which would directly embody the complete theory — would be for the entire capital stock to be issued to the lease owner as fully paid by the transfer of his leases, and for him then to give one-half of his stock to the individual whom he might persuade to lend the corporation the necessary capital, or to divide it pro rata among investors he might procure. He might do this himself, or he might put it in the hands of a trustee for that purpose.

We see nothing in such a course of business which would raise a presumption that there had been "actual fraud in the transaction" by which the value of the property was agreed upon. There is no substantial difference in principle between such a transaction and one where he returns some of the full-paid stock to the treasury of the corporation, to be disposed of by it on any terms satisfactory to him, in aid of raising working capital. Young v. Erie Co., 65 Mich. 111, 31 N. W. 814. The sole question, then, as before, must be: "Was there actual fraud in the transaction by which the valuation of the property was fixed?" We do not say that such simultaneous surrender of part of the stock received might not tend to show fraud in the valuation; whether it would and how persuasive it would be, would depend on the facts of the case, and upon facts not to be found in this record.[52]

Somewhat similarly in *Sherman v. S. K. D. Oil Co.*[53] the court said:

If the land conveyed to the corporation was reasonably believed by the directors to be worth five hundred thousand dollars the stock would have been thereby paid up and it would make no difference whether the corporation subsequently sold the stock returned to it for more or less than par. As between the creditor of the corporation and the stockholders the validity of the transaction does not depend upon the fact that the corporation subsequently received back a large proportion of the stock originally issued in payment for the lease. The rights of the parties must be determined with reference to the original transaction, from which it appears that the directors issued five hundred thousand dollars of stock for ninety thousand dollars worth of property.

And in *Clinton Mining & Mineral Co. v. Jamison*,[54] wherein 75 per cent of the stock issued to promoters for mining claims was returned to the corporate treasury and a part of it sold at prices ranging from 25 per cent to 45 per cent of par and a part of it given away as a 100 per cent bonus with bonds, the court said:

No exception can be taken to a transaction of this kind when the stock is full paid.[55]

In *Lake Superior Iron Co. v. Drexel*[56] it was said:

In this case the evidence was very persuasive, that the trustees, in exchanging the stock of the company for the property taken, were endeavoring to evade and circumvent the law, but it was not conclusive. Another

[52] 289 Fed. 698 (C. C. A., 6th Cir., 1923), at pp. 701–2. *Cf.* Ewing v. Swenson, 167 Minn. 113, 208 N. W. 645 (1926).

[53] 185 Cal. 534, 546, 197 Pac. 799, 804–5 (1921).

[54] 256 Fed. 577 (C. C. A., 3d Cir., 1919).

[55] *Ibid.*, p. 581. *Cf.* Davis Bros. v. Montgomery Furnace & Chemical Co., 101 Ala. 127, 130, 8 So. 496, 497 (1892); Kingston v. Nichols, *loc. cit. supra*, note 50.

[56] 90 N. Y. 87, 94–95 (1882).

view of the evidence was possible, and that is, that the parties believed the property to be worth $2,500,000, for the uses and purposes of the corporation, and that the trustees actually gave the entire stock for it. The title to the stock passed out of the company, and Blair, Foster & Struthers [the vendors of the property and the promoters] could then do with the stock what they pleased, sell it, give it away, or re-transfer a portion of it to the company, in order that the business of the company might be successfully prosecuted, and thus the sixteen thousand shares of stock still held by them rendered more valuable.

When they transferred the nine thousand shares they made a transfer of actual stock which had been paid for, which belonged to them, and which, but for their agreement with the company, they could hold against it. The fact that they were under obligation to devote a portion of the stock received by them to the purpose of creating, through a trustee, a working capital for the company, by which they were to be benefited more than all others, no more altered the real nature of the transaction than if they had agreed to contribute a large sum of money toward the working capital instead of stock. . . . Whether the form the transaction took was a mere sham, intended as an evasion of the statute, was a question of fact for the determination of the jury.

Likewise in *Insurance Press v. Montauk Wire Co.*[57] the court said:

The individual defendants then transferred back to the company a certain amount of stock [25 per cent of the issue] which was to become the property of the company and to be disposed of by it for its own benefit. Such a condition is not unusual in companies of this character. In order to make its stock of any value, it was essential that the company should have a working capital in addition to the patents, and the persons who had exchanged their patents for the stock of the company were willing to give to the company a portion of the stock so that the working capital could be secured and thus give value to the remainder of the stock.[58]

On the other hand, expressions *contra* to the foregoing are even more numerous in the cases examined by the writer. A number are quoted below for illustration.[59]

[57] 103 App. Div. (N. Y.) 472, 476, 93 N. Y. S. 134, 136–38 (1905).

[58] The essentials of the doctrine expressed in the foregoing quotations are also found in the following: Manhattan Trust Co. v. Seattle Coal & Iron Co., *loc. cit. supra,* note 50; Davies v. Ball, *loc. cit. supra,* note 50; Willock v. Dilworth, *loc. cit. supra,* note 50; American Tube & Iron Co., *loc. cit. supra,* note 50; Finletter v. Acetylene Light, Heat & Power Co., 215 Pa. 86, 90, 64 Atl. 429, 430 (1906); Arnold v. Searing, 73 N. J. Eq. 262, 267–68, 67 Atl. 831, 833–34 (1907).

[59] In addition to the language which follows in the text see Libby v. Tobey, *loc. cit. supra,* note 44; Douglass v. Ireland, 73 N. Y. 100, 105–7 (1878); Na-

. . . and this was manifestly a scheme devised to have this stock issued and divided among these stockholders, because Mr. Haughey, the leading defendant, the only one who has answered here, and on whose behalf it has been strongly argued that it was worth a great sum of money, and that $1,000,000 was not an excessive valuation, turned over to the company nearly one-half of the capital stock issued to him, which he would not have done if the patent had belonged to him and was of the value which he said it was. It is in evidence that the stock was turned back to the treasury according to some understanding or agreement. . . . If a proceeding of this kind can be sanctioned by the court, it would be a very simple matter for all stockholders to avoid payment for capital stock issued to them. . . .[60]

• • •

The verdict of the jury establishes the fact that the stock was issued in excess of the value of the licenses, and it also establishes the actual fraud. There was evidence to justify the verdict. In fact, we do not see how the jury could have reached a different conclusion. It is incredible that the licenses were worth $1,000,000, for it is incredible that Mumford would have given this stock back to the company, and so lost the licenses and the stock in addition, if the licenses had been worth $1,000,000. He would have been giving the company $1,500,000, for he knew that Ceballos & Co. had offered in writing to buy the stock from the Syndicate [the corporation] for $500,000 and that the offer had been accepted . . . The whole purpose of the transaction with Mumford clearly was to make the stock "full-paid and nonassessable." . . . It is impossible to believe that the directors were acting in good faith when they sold to Mumford stock which they had already sold and fully expected to deliver to Ceballos & Co., and which they subsequently did deliver. . . .[61]

• • •

---

tional Tube Works Co. v. Gilfillan, *loc. cit. supra,* note 31, *loc. cit. supra,* note 32; Carp v. Chipley, *loc. cit. supra,* note 38; Wallace v. Carpenter Electric Heating Manufacturing Co., 70 Minn. 321, 334, 73 N. W. 189, 193 (1897); Easton National Bank v. American Brick & Tile Co., 69 N. J. Eq. 326, 329, 60 Atl. 54, 55–56 (1905), *aff'd,* 70 N. J. Eq. 722, 64 Atl. 1095 (1906), *rev'd* in part on other grounds, 70 N. J. Eq. 722, 64 Atl. 917 (1906); Lea v. Iron Belt Mercantile Co., 147 Ala. 421, 424, 42 So. 415, 416 (1906); Blake v. Griswold, 103 N. Y. 429, 435–36, 9 N. E. 434, 436–37 (1886); Bottlers Seal Co. v. Rainey, 243 N. Y. 333, 342–43, 153 N. E. 437, 440–41 (1926); Thurston v. Duffy, 38 Hun 327, 329–30 (1885); Gardner Valve Manufacturing Co. v. Halyburton, 87 N. J. Eq. 689, 693–94, 102 Atl. 893, 895 (1917). See also Babbitt v. Read, 236 Fed. 42, 46 (C. C. A., 2d Cir., 1916); See v. Heppenheimer, 69 N. J. Eq. 36, 74, 87, 61 Atl. 843, 858, 863 (1905); Scott v. Barton, 285 Mo. 427, 438–39, 226 S. W. 958, 960 (1920); Colonial Trust Co. v. McMillan, 188 Mo. 547, 568–69, 87 S. W. 933, 940 (1905).

[60] Honeyman v. Haughey, 66 Atl. 582, 583 (N. J. Ch., 1906).

[61] Enright v. Heckscher, 240 Fed. 863, 869–70 (C. C. A., 2d Cir., 1917).

It may be remarked at this point that in determining whether or not the corporators did in fact honestly and intelligently believe the Ord Mountain claims to be worth one million dollars the circumstances attending and following the transfer should be taken into consideration. Immediately following the transfer, shares of the par value of one dollar each and of the total par value of five hundred thousand dollars were returned to the corporation. A short time thereafter several thousand of these shares were sold to the respondents at five cents a share. These circumstances cast grave suspicion, to say the least, upon the existence of any honest and intelligent belief that the Ord Mountain claims were worth one million dollars.[62]

From the foregoing quotations it is apparent that, in their verbally expressed opinions at least, judges differ greatly as to the weight which should be given to the use of treasury stock as evidence of stock watering. The question is still open, however, as to whether this cleavage of opinion is really embodied in the decisions. Do some courts actually decide for the plaintiff largely on the basis of evidence that a promoter has given back a part of his stock to the corporation, whereas other courts pay little or no attention to this circumstance? It goes without saying that any such analysis of the motives underlying actual decisions as distinct from mere opinions is extremely difficult.[63] An effort in this direction, however, has been made by the writer through an intensive study of the cases cited in footnotes 49 to 62, *supra*. In each case the proportion of the promoter's stock which was donated back to the corporate treasury and the percentage of par value at which it was resold by the corporation have been computed, and the resulting ratios have been compared with the decision reached by the court.

The conclusions reached from this analysis are largely negative. There is no evident correlation between the percentage of treasury stock turned back to the corporation and the decision by the court that the original consideration was or was not overvalued, or that a liability should or should not be imposed upon shareholders. The mere fact that a large proportion of the stock was returned to the treasury has not necessarily resulted in a liability being imposed, nor has the converse been true. But the outcome in a considerable majority of cases suggests that the presence of treasury stock tends to

[62] Hasson v. Koeberle, 180 Cal. 359, 365–66, 181 Pac. 387, 389 (1919).

[63] Not the least of the difficulties in the way of this type of analysis is the fact that evidence of overvaluation almost never appears singly. There are usually several types of evidence, *pro* and *con,* and correlation of the decisions with any one of them is therefore practically impossible.

be accepted as probative, in some degree, of an overvaluation. However, this tendency appears to be correlated in no way with the *proportion* of stock returned to the treasury.

Likewise, in most cases in which the evidence disclosed that the treasury stock was sold or otherwise disposed of at less than par value the courts have imposed a liability upon shareholders, but no correlation between the decision and the price is discoverable. The only positive conclusion which has been reached in this connection is that the courts have more frequently imposed a liability in treasury-stock or bonus-stock cases than they have refused to do so. The probability of a liability being imposed upon shareholders in a treasury-stock case appears, from the cases studied, to be a little better than two to one, but the sample is too small to justify any quantitative inferences. Because the number of treasury-stock cases found in any one jurisdiction is so small it is not even possible to erect any jurisdictional divergences.

Conclusions on treasury stock.—What, then, is the evidentiary significance of the return by promoters of a part of their stock to the corporate treasury, or its return and resale at a price below par? For the purpose of stating an answer to this question we may classify evidence into several degrees of probative significance. They are: (1) *Evidence which is so irrelevant or so confusing to a fact-finding body as to be inadmissible;* (2) *Evidence of some probative value*—that is, evidence tending to lead to a conclusion on the question at issue, but the force of which and the inferences to be drawn from which are matters about which reasonable men might differ materially; (3) *Prima facie evidence*—that is, evidence tending strongly to establish a conclusion concerning the question at issue, but which is not conclusive and must therefore be submitted to the fact-finding body for evaluation; and (4) *Preponderant or conclusive evidence*—that is, evidence of sufficient strength to justify a directed verdict or the setting aside of a contrary verdict as against the weight of the evidence.

Taking these four possibilities, we find: first, that no courts have held the treasury-stock evidence to be inadmissible; second, that no courts have held this evidence to be conclusive; third, that there is a divergence between courts as to the weight to be attached to the evidence, some courts tending to attach very little weight to it, and other courts making it, in effect, *prima facie* evidence of a deliberate overvaluation. The weight of authority, however, is that a treasury-stock transaction, especially if followed by a reissue of this stock at a large cash discount, is very strong evidence that the directors, in valuing the property at the par value of the stock, were guilty of a deliberate and therefore " fraudulent " overvaluation.[64]

[64] At present any supposed necessity for the use of treasury stock in either the initial or subsequent financing of corporations has been obviated by the use of non-par shares. In practice these can be sold for their market price without regard to any purely nominal figure, except in a few jurisdictions where a minimum price must be received for non-par shares. Where a speculative call upon the future of an enterprise is regarded as essential to the successful sale of senior securities, non-par stock, or more commonly, option warrants for the purchase of common stock, may be given to the investor for a nominal consideration without fear of damaging legal consequences. See, however, Stone v. Young, 210 App. Div. (N. Y.) 303, 206 N. Y. S. 95 (1924).

CHAPTER IX

CONCLUSIONS

The primary object of this study has been to answer the question as to what the courts mean by " value " when they interpret the laws which require that stock must be issued for property or services at a fair valuation. Do they use " value " as the economist uses the term, to mean market price? Do they mean value to the owner as contrasted with market value? Do they identify or confuse value with cost? Finally, are the courts subject to the same criticism which has been made against them in other types of valuation (especially in public utility valuation cases), that they lack any definite standard or concept of the illusive word, " value " ?

In this concluding chapter it is proposed: first, to summarize briefly the conclusions of the preceding chapters; second, to state our conclusions as to the standard of valuation developed by the courts in stock-watering cases; third, to consider the effectiveness of the American anti-stock-watering laws as a means of protecting creditors and other investors; fourth, to review briefly the similar laws in England and Germany; fifth, to suggest the direction which the corporation laws should take in the effort to give greater protection to investors against the evils that have been associated with stock watering.

Summary of Preceding Chapters

Chapter I explains how and why the promoter exploits the nominal value of shares and discusses the evils which may result from his activity. It also shows how common-law and statutory rules have been developed for the protection of innocent shareholders and creditors against damage resulting from an original underpayment for shares, by requiring full payment and by imposing upon shareholders a liability to creditors for any unpaid balance on stock. The system of control thus established raises, quite obviously, a problem of valuation. For if payment may be made in services or in property other than cash, it must be established that *the value* of the property or services was less than the par value of the shares issued for them, before a liability of the taker may be imposed.

Chapter II discusses the types of consideration that are not valid for stock-issue purposes. Many courts hold that certain items, though they may conceivably have some economic value, do not constitute valid consideration. The explanation of the decisions in these cases was found to lie, in part, in the specific wording of the statutes. Many items excluded, such as agreements to render future services to the corporation, promissory notes, the use of a man's name, prestige and influence, have been held to be neither " money paid," " labor done," nor " property actually received." Others, such as services of the promoters rendered prior to incorporation, have apparently been ruled out on grounds of policy. The issue of stock for such items has been regarded as dangerous from the standpoint of those whose interests were sought to be protected by the anti-stock-watering laws, not only because a reliable valuation of these items is extremely difficult even under the most favorable circumstances, but also because of the danger that the promoter's self-interest will persuade him to exploit this difficulty.

Chapter III discusses the sharp distinction which appears in many judicial *opinions* between the " good faith " rule on the one hand and the " true value " rule on the other. The latter rule purports to require the court to ignore the opinion of the directors as to the value of the consideration accepted for stock, whereas the former grants a *prima facie* validity to the directors' judgment. On investigation, however, the distinction between the two rules is found to be largely a verbal one. Although there are some procedural consequences resulting from the adoption of one rule as opposed to the other, the actual decisions in the cases do not indicate that the holdings of the courts with respect to the question of overvaluation are influenced by their acceptance of one rule or the other. For in all jurisdictions, even in those which adhere to a " true value " doctrine, the crucial question is whether a valuation was *reasonable* in the light of the apparent facts rather than the question whether it was objectively correct or " true." Indeed, there appear to be fewer differences in results between the operation of the " true value " rule and the ordinary " deliberate overvaluation " variety of the " good faith " rule, than there are between the results under the New Jersey and Illinois type of " good faith " rule on the one hand and the ordinary " good faith " rule on the other. The insistence in New Jersey, Illinois, and a few other jurisdictions upon the exercise of prudent and unbiased judgment in the determination of the value of property has had more far-reaching results than has the Missouri dictum that the " true value " of the property is the quantum sought and that in determining this value the opinion of the directors is of no consequence.

Chapter IV discusses the language used by courts in defining " value " and points out that this language is too vague and contentless to indicate what basis of valuation is to be applied. For the most part the courts have merely repeated the meaningless phrases found in the statutes, such as " fair value," " full value," " actual value," " real value," and " reasonable value," without making any real distinction between these various terms.

Some light, however, has been thrown upon the nature of the standard of valuation by judicial statements that " value," as distinct from cost to the promoter or vendor of the property, is the proper test of whether or not there was an overcapitalization; that this " value " is to be taken at the time when the stock was issued rather than at some prior or subsequent time; and that " value " should be taken to mean " value to the corporation " or value for corporate purposes rather than value in an independent market. Moreover, although most courts have gone no farther in defining the standard than to say simply that it is the value to the corporation at the time the stock is issued, a few of them, notably New Jersey, have attempted to be more explicit by stating that the par value of the stock should not exceed the amount of *cash* that might reasonably have been paid by the corporation if payment had been made in cash.

Chapters V to VIII, inclusive, present a detailed study of the cases with the object of discovering a more specific content for the vague standard of valuation suggested in the statutory and judicial definitions. Our working hypothesis in the study of these cases has been that the standard of valuation could be discovered directly or indirectly by reference to the significance attached by the courts to various types of evidence which have been admitted or excluded in stock-watering cases.

Chapter V begins the case analysis with a study of the various types of *cost* as evidence of the value of property. Neither the original cost of the property, nor its cost of reproduction as of the date of valuation, has been adduced very frequently as evidence. Slight significance has been attached to the original cost except in those very rare cases where the original cost was incurred shortly before the property was transferred to the corporation. This is a logical consequence of the rule generally followed by the courts that " value " for capitalization purposes pertains to the time at which the stock is issued.

Cost of reproduction, on the other hand, has played a more significant role as evidence of the value of property at the time when it was capitalized. Logically, this type of evidence has a more direct bearing upon the value of property on the date when the latter is surrendered to the corporation than has original cost. Nevertheless, it has appeared infrequently as evidence in stock-watering cases owing largely to the non-reproducible character of the property which is commonly exchanged for stock, or to the difficulty of estimating the reproduction cost. Under certain circumstances it may be admitted as evidence of considerable weight, but we have found no case in which it was held to be conclusive evidence. In a few cases it appears to have been the principal item of evidence on which the decisions have been based, but in each instance there have also been other types of evidence tending to support the decision.

On the other hand, the cost of the property to the promoter, or other vendor who sold it to the corporation, has frequently been adduced as evidence and has played a more significant role than any other type of cost as evidence of overvaluation in stock-watering cases. Although courts generally admit that the cost of property to the vendor is not *conclusive* evidence of the value of the property for stock-issue purposes, they do admit it as evidence which must be taken into account. Indeed, where the vendor has secured the property shortly before turning it over to the corporation the price at which he bought it is generally regarded as evidence so persuasive that it casts upon the defendants the burden of justifying a higher valuation by depriving them of the benefit of the normal assumption that they acted prudently or in " good faith." Moreover, a distinct tendency has been found on the part of juries, and of other fact-finding bodies, to hold that there has been an overvaluation wherever the cost to the vendor was relatively low as compared with the face value of the stock issued. In many cases the value found by the court or jury has exactly coincided with the cost to the vendor. In most cases, however, there has been other substantiating evidence bearing out the conclusion reached, and there have been a number of cases in which a very great discrepancy between the par value of the stock and the cost to the vendor did not result in a finding of overvaluation.

Chapter VI discusses prospective earning power as a basis of valuation and concludes that, despite some *dicta* to the contrary, it is generally accepted as valid evidence. But capitalizations based upon mere unsupported guesses as to the amount of future earnings are generally rejected, especially where the rights of creditors are involved; and in a few jurisdictions, notably in New Jersey, California, and Illinois, ample discounts for futurity and risk must be applied. In New Jersey, in particular, great emphasis is placed upon the necessity of unbiased, honest, and prudent judgment on the part of directors when they value property by reference to its estimated future earning power.

Chapter VII considers certain matters closely related to the capitalization of prospective profits. Although many courts refuse to permit the capitalization of mere potential values, as opposed to present, discounted values, there is a substantial body of opinion and decision *contra,* particularly in cases involving the issue of stock for mining rights and patents. These latter cases are not easy to reconcile with the more general run of cases except in terms of the difficulty of assessing the value of mines and patents and on the assumption of the courts that no one really supposes that the nominal capitalization of such enterprises is significant.

The same chapter points out that, although the courts do not appear to have any definite rule that enhanced values resulting from combination of properties are not to be capitalized, they have often shown a sensible skepticism concerning capitalizations which cannot possibly be defended except on the assumption of large and highly speculative benefits from consolidation. This skepticism has been particularly effective in suits relative to stockholders' liability to creditors, as opposed to suits by minority shareholders seeking to enjoin a proposed issue of stock. The more liberal attitude of the courts in injunction cases may be explained by their reluctance to interfere with *intra vires* matters of corporate management unless proof is offered of improvident action bordering on fraud.

The discussion of the combination cases is followed by a brief review of those cases which emphasize the concept of "value to the corporation" as distinct from mere sale value or market value. The friendly ear which courts have given to the argument of a peculiar "value to the enterprise" implies a capitalization of prospective earnings.

Finally, this chapter emphasizes the fact that the capitalization of earnings as a basis of valuation is implied by the insistence of many courts that property must be valued at the cash price which an intelligent and prudent investor would pay for it. This standard of valuation subsumes many of the rules of the courts with reference to the weight which may be assigned to particular types of evidence. It also implies the necessity of discounting estimated potential values for futurity and risk.

Chapter VIII concludes the discussion of *evidence* by assessing the importance assigned to certain implied admissions by promoters and other interested parties that the property was overvalued. Where a promoter offered to sell his property to the corporation either at a cash price, or at a higher price in stock, the low cash offer has been held to be persuasive evidence of deliberate overvaluation. Some cases, indeed, hold it to be conclusive evidence. Moreover, if the stock taken by the promoter in exchange for property has a definite market value at the time when the exchange was made, this market value has been accepted as *prima facie* evidence that the property surrendered was not worth more than the *market value* of the stock accepted in payment for it. Other types of evidence, similar in import and effect, have also been reviewed in this chapter.

As a part of the subject of " admissions against interest," Chapter VIII discusses those cases in which it appeared that the promoter donated all or a part of his stock back to the corporation as " treasury stock " in order that it might be reissued for cash at less than par. On its face such a donation, particularly if coupled with immediate resale of the stock at a large discount, would seem to be a confession of an overvaluation of the consideration for which the stock was originally issued. But the courts have been divided with regard to the significance which they have attached to it. They have ruled that treasury-stock transactions are admissible evidence on the question whether the overvaluation alleged was deliberate, and they have also admitted them as evidence to be taken into account in determining *the amount* of overvaluation, but no courts have held this evidence to be conclusive of either question. Some courts attach very little weight to it and others have, in effect, made it *prima facie* evidence of a deliberate overvaluation. The weight of authority is that a treasury-stock transaction, particularly if followed by a reissue of the stock at a substantial discount, is very persuasive evidence that the directors deliberately overvalued the consideration for which the stock was originally issued.

CONCLUSIONS CONCERNING THE BASIS OF VALUATION

It will be observed from the foregoing summary that our detailed examination of the cases has yielded little except negative results. The courts do not appear to have worked out any specific philosophy of corporate capitalization, certainly none which is capable of being summed up in a shorthand expression. Considered in the large, the nearest approach which they have made to the development of any general standard of valuation is the common requirement that the directors must determine their valuations with the prudence and intelligence of the ordinary business man.

This is hardly an objective standard, and no crystallized rules of law can be deduced from it. Only a predisposition to find a "rule," whether one exists or not, would enable us to be more specific in our statement of the courts' position. Clearly, this "rule of reason" implies a capitalization of prospective profits, for that is the basis on which the average business man determines the price which he will pay for producer's goods. But the limits within which profits may be capitalized are not indicated in any definite way in the cases. In only a small minority of the opinions and decisions does the problem directly appear as one of estimating the *amount* of anticipated earnings and discounted this sum at a *rate* which measures both futurity and risk.

However, in the application of this vague, general standard a few semidefinitive rules have been developed. They may be enumerated as follows:

1. "Value" of property or services for stock-issue purposes refers to the value at the time the stock is issued. In the determination of this value, the circumstances as they appear at that time are to be taken into account. The subsequent success or failure of the enterprise is presumed to be ignored. There are a few exceptions to this rule against "hindsight." [1]

2. "Value" means "value to the corporation for its purposes" rather than value to anyone else, or market value in the strict sense of the price for which the property could then have been sold. This highly individualized concept of value is sometimes frankly admitted. It is more frequently implied. The rule is not absolute. If

[1] *Cf.* footnote 7, c. IV, *supra*.

there is a reliable objective test of the value to others at the time, this may be taken into account. How persuasive the latter would be as evidence depends upon how reasonable it would be for the directors to ignore it.

3. Original cost (when incurred shortly prior to the promotion), and cost of reproduction are admissible evidence of the value. Normally they are not persuasive evidence.

4. The cost of the property to the promoter is evidence bearing upon the reasonableness of the valuation which he placed upon it for stock-issue purposes. If that cost was materially below the amount of stock issued, the discrepancy is sufficiently persuasive as evidence to place on shareholders the burden of justifying a higher valuation. This is particularly true if the cost was incurred at, or shortly before, the time when the stock was issued.

5. With the exception of some mining and patent cases, the usual rule is that adequate discounts for time and risk must be applied where the amount of stock issued has been based upon estimates of future earnings or potential values. But the cases do not indicate any precise procedure to be followed here. The acturial aspects of this problem are neither discussed in the opinions nor revealed in the decisions. The implication in some opinions is that the discounts must be " reasonable," but what is " reasonable " is made to depend upon the circumstances of each case.

6. Certain acts of promoters are commonly regarded as tacit admissions of deliberate or unreasonable overvaluation, and as very persuasive evidence of the *fact* of overvaluation. The more important of these are: (*a*) offers to sell property to a corporation for an amount of cash or for a much larger amount of stock; (*b*) issues of stock for property when, at the same time, the market value of identical stock is less than its par value; (*c*) sales of property by promoters *inter se* at a relatively low cash price, followed by a resale of the property to the corporation for an amount of stock which is greatly in excess of the cash price; and (*d*) large donations of " treasury stock," especially when they are followed by an immediate resale of the donated stock at a discount.

7. In a few jurisdictions great emphasis is placed upon the principle that the directors should deal with the unissued stock as though

it were cash equal in amount to the par value of the stock. The courts in these same jurisdictions look with disfavor upon valuations made by self-interested parties.

8. The benefit of any doubt concerning the value of property for stock-issue purposes will normally be given to the defendant stockholder unless there is persuasive evidence tending to impeach the directors' valuation.

The Ineffectiveness of Our Anti-stock-watering Laws

American legislators have sought to lessen the evils of watered stock by the enactment of statutes requiring an initial equivalence between the par value of shares issued and the " value " of the consideration for which they are issued. For the protection of creditors, reliance has been placed in the common-law and statutory rules which impose upon shareholders a liability to creditors for any unpaid balance on shares that results from a deficiency in the value of the consideration given for the stock.

Aside from the many technical grounds upon which the shareholders may escape from liability to creditors,[2] the major difficulty with this system of social control of stock watering lies in the practice of issuing shares for property or services and in the absence of any satisfactory measure of the " value " of property or services for capitalization purposes. The foregoing discussion of the law and cases pertaining to stock watering has disclosed a complete absence of any definite rules for the determination of appropriate valuations.

The failure of the courts to develop any definitive measure of value for the purposes of corporate capitalization is important, because the effective operation of the legislative scheme focalizes upon a problem of pecuniary valuation which is generally dissociated from market phenomena or other conventional tests of value. The whole device for control breaks down at the point where it becomes necessary for a court to decide whether or not the consideration against which the stock was issued was overvalued. Except in extreme cases where there could be no reasonable doubt that the stock was watered, the law fails to accomplish its purpose because, in order to obtain redress, the creditor must successfully traverse a treacherous realm of opinion and belief concerning the value of the consideration which was given for the stock, and must at the same time overcome a strong

[2] Bonbright, *op. cit. supra*, c. I, note 1.

judicial disposition to give the benefit of all reasonable doubt concerning the value, to the shareholder. Each of these difficulties would be partially overcome were it possible to apply some objective measure of value to the facts of each case.

But no such measure has been developed by the courts. At the outset, the adoption of a definite standard of measurement was discouraged by the fact that at common law, shareholders' liability to creditors was grounded in the law of fraud. The applicability of fraud doctrines to this particular type of legal situation was tenuously developed and embodied in the so-called " trust fund " and " holding out " theories of shareholders' liability.[3] An essential corollary of each of these theories is that, in order to charge shareholders with a liability to creditors, there must be proven not only the fact that the consideration given for the stock was overvalued but also a state of mind on the part of the directors which would charge them with a constructive fraud. Hence, aside from the difficulty of valuing producers' goods for any purpose there was introduced the necessity of taking into account the special frame of mind of the valuer. It is not surprising, therefore, that no definite basis of valuation was evolved from the common-law background.

In time the common law pertaining to watered stock was supplanted by the enactment of constitutional and statutory provisions designed to charge shareholders with a pecuniary responsibility for an unpaid balance on stock. With few exceptions,[4] however, these enactments had no effect upon the law of shareholders' liability nor upon the principles and practice of the courts in determining whether in any given case such a liability existed. No new basis of valuation was introduced by the legislative enactments. In many instances the courts simply held that the statutes were a mere legislative expression of the existing common-law rule that, in the absence of fraud in the transaction, the directors' valuation could not be impeached. In others the statutes themselves were so worded as to indicate that this was the intention of the legislators.

The upshot has been that the creditor, or other person who has sought to impeach the directors' valuation, has been compelled to bear the burden of fathoming the human mind on the delicate question of value. In consequence, the directors and incorporators have

[3] See references cited *supra*, c. I, note 52. See also Hale, *op. cit. supra*, c. I, note 22; Wallstein, *op. cit. supra*, c. III, note 7.

[4] See Bonbright, *op. cit. supra*.

been allowed to guess at the value of the consideration for which they have issued stock and the accuracy of their conjectures has been granted *prima facie* validity by the courts. Moreover, the experience of courts with stock-watering cases has not resulted in the development of any crystallized rule whereby this assumed validity of the directors' judgment may be tested. As we have already noted, the greatest length to which the courts have gone in the direction of defining a standard of valuation applicable to stock issuance has been to hold the shareholders responsible for the failure of their directors to exercise unbiased, prudent and intelligent judgment in making their valuations, and to submit the question of fact to the jury or other fact-finding body as to whether the directors' valuation reflected the proper frame of mind.

The reasons for the failure of the courts to develop a more definite test of overvaluation are many. A number of the more important ones are as follows: (1) The common-law heritage that " fraud " is an essential element in any legal overvaluation of property for stock-issue purposes. (2) Statutory expression of this common-law rule. (3) The fact that stock alleged to have been " watered " has usually been issued for producers' goods of more or less unique character, or for services, each of which has lacked independent realizability in a going market and both of which are difficult to evaluate at best. (4) The absence of any statutory definition of the term " value " and a prevalent uncertainty as to the meaning of the term. (5) The tendency of the courts, which is due to a considerable extent to the absence of objective data concerning the value of the consideration involved in many cases, to concede that " value " means " value to the corporation," coupled with a tendency to indulge a presumption that the directors are best qualified to adjudge the value so defined; (6) The retrospective character of the valuation. The valuation of the court is made as of the date upon which the stock was issued. The time elapsed between the date of the stock issue and the date of the trial varies from a few months to fifteen or twenty years. This introduces many difficulties of proof and encourages the court to grant the benefit of doubt to the directors who were responsible for the original valuation. (7) The fact that in many cases the facts and pleadings do not require the court to determine an exact valuation for the non-cash consideration which was given for the stock. For example, if the complaining creditors' claims amount to $3,000, all that the court need find to support a judgment for the plaintiffs is that there was an overvaluation of *at least* $3,000. The stock in question may have amounted to several millions of dollars and a reasonable valuation of the property exchanged for it may have been several hundred thousand dollars less than the par of the stock, but if this were in fact the situation, all that the fact-finding body need determine in order that the plaintiffs might recover is an overvaluation of at least $3,000.[5] Finally, (8) The fact that a number of courts seem to doubt whether creditors are in fact deceived by overcapitalization and for that reason tend to give the benefit of the doubt concerning the valuation to the directors. All of these factors encourage the use of a hazy and more or less flexible standard of valuation in stock-watering cases and contribute to the ineffectiveness of any system of control of excessive stock issues.

We do not believe that the courts may fairly be censured for their failure to develop a definite standard of valuation for stock-issue purposes. The reasons enumerated above for the coarseness of the standard which they have developed constitute a sufficient answer to most of the criticisms which might be advanced. To these may be added the fact that our statutory and judge-made law with respect to stock watering has been developed in a young and growing country. The economic background from which this law has been evolved was one in which many factors conspired to encourage rapid industrial development. This, coupled with the difficulty of setting any exact value on the types of property which are commonly exchanged for stock, may account in large measure for the freedom allowed to the promoter as well as for the tendency of the courts to accept his judgment as final unless there is clear evidence to the contrary.

Moreover, there does not appear to be any alternative basis of valuation which the courts might adopt as a uniform standard that would be practicable in the sense of affording both the proper protection to creditors and investors and the desirable degree of freedom to the promoter.[6] Space will not permit a complete discussion of all of

[5] For example, Babbitt v. Read, 236 Fed. 42 (C. C. A., 2d Cir., 1916).

[6] For discussions of various bases of corporate capitalization, see the following: BONBRIGHT, JAMES C., RAILROAD CAPITALIZATION (New York, 1920), c. III; Bonbright, *Earning Power as the Basis of Corporate Capitalization* (1921), 35 POL. SCI. Q. 482; DEWING, ARTHUR S., FINANCIAL POLICY OF CORPORATIONS (Rev. ed., New York, 1926), Book II, c. 2–7, inclusive; GERSTENBERG, CHARLES W., FINANCIAL ORGANIZATION AND MANAGEMENT (New York, 1928), c. XVIII, XXIX; LOCKLIN, DAVID P., REGULATION OF SECURITY ISSUES BY THE INTERSTATE COMMERCE COMMISSION (Urbana, Ill., 1927), c. VI; LOUGH, WM. H.,

the various objections to the several alternative bases of valuation, but we shall mention a few of them very briefly. In this discussion of alternatives we have assumed that it is desirable to establish an equivalence, at the time stock is issued, between the par value of the stock and *the value* of the consideration given for it. Although we doubt the desirability of establishing any such equivalence, this is the underlying theory of our present laws with respect to corporate capitalization, and our discussion is offered in the light of the law as it now stands.

Original cost of property is not a satisfactory measure of its value for stock-issue purposes. In many, perhaps in most, instances this figure cannot be ascertained; but even if it is known it bears no necessary or definite relationship to the value of the property.

A second alternative, the *cost to the corporation,* is out of the question as a basis of capitalization for the obvious reason that in all cases where the problem of valuation is involved, the cost to the corporation consists of the very stock whose full payment is in question.

The *cost to the promoter* who sells the property to the corporation may involve the same circuity. Frequently the cost to the promoter consists of a part of the stock which he obtains in exchange for his property. The face value of the purchase stock is obviously no measure of the value of the property so purchased. If, on the other hand, the cost to the promoter was recently incurred and was met with a cash payment, this cash cost may be a serviceable index of the value of the property. There are many circumstances, however, where this would not be the case. For example, the promoter may have bought at a genuine bargain price. If the amount of stock which he can have issued to himself for the property is limited to his cash outlay, he can obtain a profit only by selling his shares at a premium.

On the other hand, if the promoter purchased the property with cash and a considerable time has elapsed between the date of his purchase and the sale to the corporation, this remote cash cost to him will hardly be a satisfactory index for the measurement of the value of the property to the corporation. It is interesting historical data, but it is out of date.

The *cost of reproducing property* at the time stock is issued for it is another basis which might be used under certain circumstances.

BUSINESS FINANCE (New York, 1922), c. VIII; MEAD, EDWARD S., CORPORATION FINANCE (6th ed., New York, 1928), Vol. I, c. XIX, XX; U. S. INDUSTRIAL COMMISSION, REPORTS (1900–1902), Vol. XIX, pp. 408–12.

Supporters of this view would argue that if stock is issued for property the amount of the stock should exactly equal what it would cost the corporation to acquire equally efficient property. But there are numerous practical and theoretical difficulties in the way of a universal application of this measure of value in stock-watering cases.

In the first place, the difficulty of ascertaining is insuperable in the cases of inventions, good will, unexplored mineral deposits, uniquely situated land, etc. In the case of less unique items, the problem of accurate depreciation and obsolescence measurement renders ascertainment difficult. In the second place, this basis of valuation ignores the importance of the time element in values. Property may be worth a great deal more now than the cost of its physical reproduction, solely because of its time utility. Finally, the cost-of-reproduction basis is defective because it fails to allow for the intangible values of the going concern.

The *market value* of property might be regarded as the proper measure of the amount of stock that may be issued for it. In view of our assumption that corporate capitalization should represent *values*, the market-value basis would have much to support it were it not for the fact that the type of property for which promotion stock is usually issued has no ascertainable market value. This is due either to the unique character of the property or to the fact that there are no offers of, or bids for, identical property.

Moreover, even if the property has an ascertainable market value, it does not follow that in all cases this value is the best measure of the amount of stock which should be issued for it. The market can't always be supposed to appreciate the real merits of new ventures because it can't be expected to be " in the know " in all cases. Valuable coal land may be used as a pasture for sheep. Its market value may be based upon its use for that purpose. If a company should be organized to exploit the coal, would it be proper to restrict the amount of stock to the pasture-land value of the property?

Closely resembling the market-value basis of corporate capitalization is the *earning-power* basis which is commonly justified by writers on corporation finance, business men, and promoters. Here again, and still bearing in mind our assumption that it is desirable to have par values represent *the value* of the consideration received, the principal difficulty with this measure of capitalization is the problem of ascertainment. In most promotions the earning power of the enterprise must be estimated without the benefit of any past record. Not only must the *amount* of the potential earnings be estimated but the appropriate *rate* at which the earnings should be capitalized must be determined in order to arrive at a valuation based upon earning power. The majority of promotion valuations arrived at in this way will be mere conjectures which are based to only a negligible degree upon historical fact. The results are mere guesses.

The fatal objections that have just been noted to *any* single standard or measure of value explain why the courts have held that values must be estimated in the light of the particular circumstances surrounding each issue of stock, and that in estimating the value in any particular case, account may be taken of any one, several, or all, of the foregoing bases of valuation.[6]

A rule of this kind has both the advantages and the defects of its eclecticisms. The advantages lie in its broad scope and universal applicability, and in the fact that it seeks to protect the interests of both the promoters and the public. The defects lie in the uncertainty and lack of precision with which the standard must be applied.

Legal Devices for the Control of Stock Watering in England and in Germany

Before suggesting possible legislative reforms for our domestic evil of watered stock it seems desirable to review the manner in which England and Germany have sought to protect the public from the dangers of excessive corporate capitalization. Our reason for inserting here a brief review of the laws of these two countries with respect to corporations is our conclusion that those laws contain some valuable precedents which deserve the careful consideration of anyone who proposes reforms in our domestic legislation with respect to watered stock.[7]

[7] In the discussion which follows we have confined our attention to share-issuing companies of the ordinary form (the "company limited by shares" in England, and the "Aktiengesellschaft" in Germany) which most closely resemble our own corporations in having a share-capital divided into freely transferable shares. In both countries the law provides for other forms of corporate organization and exempts them from many of the requirements to be mentioned below.

In England the law provides for "private companies" the principal characteristics of which are: (*a*) restricted transferability of shares; (*b*) number of shareholders (excluding employees) limited to fifty; (*c*) prohibition of invitations to the public to subscribe for any shares, or debentures, or debenture stock of the company. These companies are sometimes called "limited partnerships" because they partake of the characteristics of both of the forms of

The Control of Stock Watering in England

In strong contrast to our American system of prohibition and penalty, the effective operation of which depends upon judicial valuation, is the legislative scheme which has long prevailed in England.[8] The fundamental feature of those sections of the British Companies Act which deal with corporate capitalization is *publicity* with regard to the payment made for shares, rather than any prohibition of stock watering. Indeed, it is fair to say that the law is designed to disclose the amount of " water " in stock rather than to prevent stock watering. The sections of the law which prescribe the terms on which a public offering of shares may be made insist upon the availability to the public of all pertinent information essential to the formation of an independent judgment as to the value of the property or other consideration represented by the shares. Detailed information concerning the manner in which stock is issued must be disclosed, and severe personal liability for the correctness of this information is imposed upon those responsible for the promotion and conduct of the affairs of the corporation. It is not our purpose at this point to

---

organization which the name implies. They enjoy considerably greater freedom than does the ordinary corporation, both with respect to the ease of organization and in the greater absence of governmental regulation thereafter. For descriptions of this type of company see the British Companies (Consolidation) Act, 1929 (19 & 20 Geo. 5, c. 23), sects. 26–29 and PALMER'S COMPANY LAW (13th ed., London, 1929), c. 37.

In Germany the analogous form of organization ("Gesellschaft mit beschrankter Haftung" — partnership with limited liability) has been provided for by statute since the act of April 20, 1892. The outstanding characteristics of this form of organization resemble those of the British "private company," but the shares are less readily transferable than are those of the "private company." See KUHN, ARTHUR K., A COMPARATIVE STUDY OF THE LAW OF CORPORATIONS (New York, 1912), pp. 67–68; REPORT OF THE COMPANIES ACTS (AMENDMENT) COMMITTEE, June 27, 1895 (the so-called Davey Committee Report, Cmd. 7779), Appendix, pp. 25–26.

Special legislation with respect to close or private corporations, of which the "private company" and the "Gesellschaft mit beschrankter Haftung" are examples, would certainly seem to be a desirable, if not a necessary counterpart of strict regulatory legislation concerning corporations such as is found in Germany and in England. Indeed, it would seem to be desirable in any case. Weiner, Joseph L., *Legislative Recognition of the Close Corporation* (1929), 27 MICH. L. REV. 273.

[8] For a brief history of the development of the British Companies Act from 1862 to 1929 see PALMER'S COMPANY LAW (12th ed., London, 1924), c. I; *ibid.*, (13th ed., London, 1929), c. I.

enter into a detailed description and discussion of the legislative provisions whereby these results are obtained by the British statute.[9] But the bare outlines of the legislative scheme may be indicated.

A cardinal principle of the first comprehensive consolidation of British company law [10] was that, in the case of a company limited by shares (limited liability company), the nominal or face value of the shares was payable in full, either in cash or its equivalent.[11] This payment was regarded as a price paid for the privilege of limited liability,[12] and the capital fund resulting from a full payment of the shares was, from the standpoint of creditors, considered to be a proper substitute for the unlimited liability of private traders.[13]

But there are three primary ways whereby the integrity of this capital fund may be impaired. The first is through the issue of shares for cash at a discount. The second is through the issue of shares for property or services taken at a price in excess of their value. The third is through the payment of dividends out of the capital fund, a device which is beyond the scope of this inquiry, but one in which the problem of valuation is closely analogous to that which we have studied. We shall consider each of these devices briefly.

The issue of shares for cash at a discount. — Prior to the Com-

[9] For detailed description and discussion of the latest revision of the Companies Act (19 & 20 Geo. 5, c. 23, May 10, 1929) see: PALMER'S COMPANY LAW (13th ed., London, 1929); Hunt, Bishop C., *Recent English Company Law Reform* (Jan., 1930), 8 HARV. BUSINESS REV. 170. See also, Ten Eyck, Andrew, *Some Precedents in British Law and Practice for Safeguarding Securities* (July, 1924), 2 HARV. BUSINESS REV. 385; Barlow, Montague, *The New Companies Act, 1900* (1901), 11 ECON. JOUR. 180.

[10] Companies Act, 1862 (25 & 26 Vict. c. 89).

[11] *Ibid.*, sects. 6, 8, 11, 38; reenacted in Companies Act, 1908 (8 Edw. 7, c. 69), sects. 2, 3, 14, 123. *Cf.* Companies Act, 1929 (19 & 20 Geo. 5, c. 23), sects. 1, 2, 20, 157. See also Ooregum Gold Mining Co. of India v. Roper (1892), A. C. 125; Baglan Hall Colliery Co., (1870), L. R. 5 Ch. App. 346.

[12] Ooregum Gold Mining Co. of India v. Roper, *supra*.

[13] Schuster, Ernest, *The Promotion of Companies and the Valuation of Assets According to German Law* (March, 1900), 10 ECON. JOUR. 1. The Companies Act of 1862 made no express provision in regard to the payment of dividends. It was assumed from the first, however, that dividends could be paid only from *profits*, and not out of capital. But by judicial interpretation the term " profits " came to be exceedingly equivocal and in time the way for considerable impairment of the original capital fund was opened through the assignment of various meanings to the term. See footnote 44, *infra*, for references.

panies Act of 1928, it was *ultra vires* of a corporation to issue its shares for cash at a discount,[14] and the same was true, *a fortiori*, of an issue of bonus shares.[15] However, by legalizing the payment of a commission for subscribing to shares, the Companies Act of 1900[16] permitted the frank and open practice of what had previously been achieved through an inflation of the price which the vendor of property received in cash or shares. The essential safeguard to the public was presumably provided by requiring the amount or rate of commission to be stated in the prospectus, or statement in lieu of a prospectus, issued in connection with the offer of the shares to the public, or in any circular or notice inviting subscription for shares. As a further protection, section 7 of the Companies Act of 1907[17] required that the total amount of commission so paid or allowed, or so much of it as had not been written off, should be stated in every balance sheet of the company until the whole of it had been written off. Thus, although it was possible, prior to the Act of 1928, to issue shares at a discount by abusing the privilege of paying or allowing a commission to subscribers, the public was protected to a considerable extent by various provisions of the law which required the substance of such transactions to be revealed to all who might be interested. This disclosure was regarded as ample justification for permitting the payment of unlimited commissions so long as the latter were authorized in the company's articles.

The Wrenbury Committee of 1918 noted the existing state of facts and recommended that permission be granted to issue shares at a discount, frankly and directly, inasmuch as the law as it then stood permitted the same end to be achieved through the payment or allowance of a commission.[18] To prevent abuse of the privilege the

[14] See Ooregum Gold Mining Co. of India v. Roper, *supra*, note 11; *Re* Almada & Tirito Co. (1888), 38 Ch. D. 415, 423; *Re* Addlestone Linoleum Co. (1887), 37 Ch. D. 191; Welton v. Saffery (1897), A. C. 299; Mosely v. Koffyfontein Mines, Ltd., (1904) 2 Ch. 108; *In re* James Pitkin & Co., W. N. (1916) 112.

[15] *Re* Eddystone Marine Ins. Co., Ltd., (1892) 2 Ch. 423; *Re* Alkaline Reduction Syndicate, (1896) 45 W. R. 10.

[16] 63 & 64 Vict. c. 48, sect. 8. Similar provision is found in 8 Edw. 7, c. 69, sect. 8, and in 19 & 20 Geo. 5, c. 23, sect. 43.

[17] 7 Edw. 7, c. 50. See also, sect. 90 of the Companies Act, 1908 (8 Edw. 7, c. 69), and sect. 44 of the Companies Act, 1929 (19 & 20 Geo. 5, c. 23).

[18] Wrenbury Report (July 15, 1918, Cmd. 9138), sect. 45, which reads as follows: "The evidence before us is that commercially the issue of shares at a discount is desirable. There is, we agree, no principle in this. It is a concession to commercial experience. Principle, however, has as instanced above al-

Committee recommended that no issue of shares at a discount should be permitted until five years after the commencement of business by the corporation and that the price at which shares are to be sold should not be less than 5 per cent below the market value of the outstanding shares of the same class, or 5 per cent below the value of the shares for transfer-tax purposes in the absence of a market price. Moreover, the Committee recommended that the discount should never exceed 50 per cent of the nominal value.[19] No action was taken on these suggestions of the Committee until the enactment of the Companies Act of 1928.[20] The committee of the Board of Trade, appointed in January, 1925, to consider and report upon the advisability of amending the Companies Acts, divided on the question of the wisdom of permitting the sale of stock at a discount, but referred to Parliament the recommendations of the Wrenbury Committee.[21]

---

ready been abandoned, and issue of shares at a discount is but accepting in practice that which has already been conceded in fact by allowing payment of commission in consideration of a person subscribing for shares."

[19] *Ibid.*, sect. 46.

[20] 18 & 19 Geo. 5, c. 45. With the exception of section 92 pertaining to house-to-house offers of shares, this Act did not come into force until it had been replaced by the Companies Act of 1929, which consolidates the Companies (Consolidation) Act of 1908 and subsequent amendments.

[21] See Report of the Company Law Amendment Committee (May 8, 1926, Cmd. 2657). Section 19 of this Report reads as follows: "This matter was fully dealt with in the Report of the Wrenbury Committee, paragraphs 45 and 46. There is a substantial but by no means overwhelming body of commercial opinion in favor of giving companies power to issue shares at a discount and there is no doubt that in many cases such a power could be extremely useful. The Committee as a whole is not prepared to dissent from the findings of the Wrenbury Committee. Some of us think that the change might be attended by risks which it is not easy to guard against and in particular the consequential inflation of the nominal issued capital of a company might lead to unsound finance. Other members of the Committee take the view that the suggestion that shares cannot be issued at a discount under the existing law is misleading, seeing that shares can be issued as fully paid up for goodwill, patents and other items of that character, the value of which is uncertain and fluctuating, and that if the issue of shares at a discount were frankly authorized and the public notified that shares could be issued at a discount it might induce the public to realize that the nominal value of a share is no guide whatever as to its intrinsic worth, and that a share is nothing more than a token representing a certain proportion of the profits and assets of the company. For the same reason some members of the committee are inclined to favor the issue of shares of no par value, for if a share has no nominal value on the face of it a person taking such share cannot be misled as to the value of the share by the amount printed on

On the strength of those recommendations the present law [22] provides that a company may issue at a discount shares of a class already issued, provided that: (1) a resolution authorizing such issue has been passed by a general meeting of the shareholders of the company; (2) the issue has been sanctioned by the court; (3) the resolution specifies the maximum rate of discount at which the shares are to be issued; (4) not less than one year has elapsed between the date of issue and the date on which the company became entitled to commence business; (5) the shares to be issued at a discount are issued within one month after the date on which the court has approved the issue, or within a greater time if an extension of time is granted by the court.

In granting authority to issue shares below par, the court is required to take into account all of the circumstances of the case. Moreover, every prospectus relating to the issue of the shares, and every subsequent balance sheet issued by the company, must contain particulars of the discount allowed or of so much of the discount as has not been written off at the date of the issue of the document in question. Default in complying with these latter provisions concerning balance sheet and prospectus imposes liability for a fine upon the company, and upon every officer of the company who is in default. Similar publicity is required with respect to any commissions allowed to persons for subscribing or obtaining subscriptions to shares, and the amount of such commission is limited to 10 per cent of the price at which the shares are issued.[23] It is unlawful to issue any form of application for shares in a company unless the form is issued with a prospectus, which must set forth in complete detail the facts essential to an independent judgment concerning the merits of the security.[24]

---

the face of the certificate as the nominal value thereof. If the recommendation of the Wrenbury Committee is adopted we think that the limit of five per cent below market value should be increased to ten per cent."

[22] Section 47 of the Companies (Consolidation) Act of 1929 (19 & 20 Geo. 5, c. 23, sect. 47).

[23] *Ibid.*, sects. 43, 44.

[24] *Ibid.*, sect. 35, subsection (3). Offers of participations in underwritings and offers not made to the public are excepted. In these latter cases the public is protected by the provisions of section 40 pertaining to allotments and the statement in lieu of a prospectus which must be filed with the Registrar of Joint Stock Companies. The public is also protected by the provisions of section 38, which is intended to prevent a company from evading the prospectus

These provisions, coupled with the requirement that every prospectus or statement in lieu of prospectus must be filed with the registrar of companies where they are open to public inspection, and the necessity of filing annual returns with the registrar setting forth particulars concerning discounts allowed on the issue of shares,[26] assure to interested members of the public the opportunity of discovering the terms on which a company has disposed of its capital stock.

Thus, although we find that it is now permissible to issue shares for cash at a discount, the public is afforded protection in those sections of the law which require complete disclosure of what is to be done or has been done in this regard. In amending the law to permit a direct issue of shares at a discount, the English legislature has given open recognition to the business fact that shares are in practice

---

provisions of the law by allotting the whole of a proposed issue to some other company or banking group which would then offer the shares to the public. Section 35 and its companion, the Fourth Schedule to the Act, relate to matters which must be set forth in every prospectus "*issued by or on behalf of a company.*" The italicized phrase is a loophole through which the law was evaded prior to the enactment of the Companies Act of 1928, sect. 32 (now sect. 38 of the Companies Act of 1929). See PALMER'S COMPANY LAW (13th ed., London, 1929), p. 374. Section 38 of the 1929 act provides that a document containing an offer of shares for sale shall be deemed to be a prospectus issued by the company if the company has allotted or agreed to allot any shares with a view to any or all of them being offered to the public. An intention to make a public offer is presumed if any of the shares are offered to the public within six months after the allotment or agreement to allot was made or if at the time the offer to the public is made the company has not received the whole consideration therefor. Such an offer of shares is subject to the provisions of the law relating to the prospectus; the persons making the offer have the same responsibilities as though they were named as directors in a prospectus; and the offer must state the place and time at which the allotment contract may be inspected and must also state the amount of consideration received or to be received by the company for the shares to which the offer relates.

It should also be noted that section 380 of the Companies Act of 1929 states that unless the context otherwise requires "'Prospectus' means any prospectus, notice, circular, advertisement, or other invitation, offering to the public for subscription or purchase any shares or debentures of a company."

[26] With regard to the filing of the prospectus or statement in lieu of prospectus, see sections 34, 38 and 40 of the Act of 1929. With regard to publicity of accounts revealing discounts allowed on the issuance of shares, see sects. 108, 110, 113, 130. See also section 98 which applies to annual returns as well as to the register of shareholders and provides cheap and ready access to the annual accounts of the company.

issued for less than a full consideration, and has, through the requirements concerning publicity, made available to those members of the public who need protection the means of their salvation within the limits of their rationality and business prudence.

Permission to issue shares at a discount is particularly desirable in England in view of the consistent refusal of Parliament to sanction the use of non-par shares.[26] The new law should assist companies whose shares are selling below par to avoid excessive debt by making it possible for them to sell shares at the price obtainable for them in the market. A leading authority on British company law doubts whether corporations will make much, if any, use of this liberty.[27] As he points out, the necessity of obtaining the approval of a court before issuing shares at a discount may go a long way toward discouraging applications, particularly in view of the availability of alternative devices for obtaining indirectly the same or similar results. This has been done by issuing shares of a low nominal value carrying the same rights as shares of a higher nominal value, or by issuing shares for a consideration other than cash. The latter suggestion leads us to our second method of setting up a fictitious capitalization.

The issue of shares for overvalued property. — We have already noted the early doctrine of British company law that the nominal value of shares must represent full actual payment in " money or in money's worth," and we have pointed out how the doctrine has been violated, first by the payment of commissions to subscribers, and now by the amended law permitting the issuance of shares at a discount for cash. The justification for Schuster's statement that the doctrine was also violated " by the absence of any provisions insuring that the property in which the capital is invested in the first instance is taken at a price representing its true value," [28] remains to be discussed.

Section 25 of the Companies Act of 1867 [29] restricted the power to pay for stock otherwise than in cash by providing as follows:

[26] See Hunt, *op. cit. supra* (note 9), pp. 175–76. See also, Report of the Company Law Amendment Committee, *supra*, note 21.

[27] Palmer's Company Law (13th ed., London, 1929), p. 114.

[28] *Op. cit. supra*, note 13. Compare his further statement that " The amount of the nominal capital with which a company is started in England is purely arbitrary, and need not stand in any relation to the value of the assets by which it is represented." *Ibid.*

[29] 30 & 31 Vict. c. 131.

Every share in any company shall be deemed and taken to have been issued and to be held subject to the payment of the whole amount thereof in cash, unless the same shall have been otherwise determined by a contract duly made in writing and filed with the Registrar of Joint Stock Companies at or before the issue of such shares.

The evident object of this section was to compel disclosure of the nature of the *quid pro quo* for which shares were to be issued and to thrust upon shareholders the responsibility for a full payment in cash until such disclosure had been made. As one writer puts it:

A company might accept payment in peppercorns, if the directors honestly believed them to be worth the par value of the shares; but if so, the fact of such payment must be disclosed to the public. If the contract was not recorded, the shareholder was bound to pay the value of the shares in cash, even though he might have given full value in property or services.[30]

This provision of the law was found to operate unjustly at times, however. In practice, promoters who issued "watered" shares to themselves in exchange for overvalued property were careful to see that the contract was recorded in order to escape further responsibility, whereas persons who had actually given a full consideration in property or services for their shares were later held liable for a full payment in cash because of a failure to record the contract.[31]

For this reason the cash payment provision of section 25 of the Companies Act of 1867 was repealed in 1900 [32] and subsequent enactments leave the repeal untouched. The policy of the law, however, has not been changed by the repeal. That policy is that persons dealing with the company are entitled to a full disclosure of the character of the consideration for which shares have been issued as "fully paid" by the directors. Hence we find that the law which repealed the section, as well as subsequent amendments to British company law, contained substitute publicity provisions which require a disclosure of the nature and extent of the consideration other than cash which is given for shares.[33] Furthermore, severe penalties are imposed upon the directors and other officers for failure to com-

[30] MACHEN, ARTHUR W., MODERN LAW OF CORPORATIONS (Boston, 1908), Vol. I, p. 638.

[31] *Op. cit. supra* (note 27) at p. 115; MACHEN, *op. cit.*, sect. 795.

[32] By sect. 33 of the Companies Act of 1900 (63 & 64 Vict. c. 48).

[33] 63 & 64 Vict. c. 48, sect. 7; 8 Edw. 7, c. 69, sect. 88; 19 & 20 Geo. 5, c. 23, sect. 42.

ply with the requirements concerning publicity. In other words, the statutes permit freedom of contract to subscribers who pay for shares in property or services and impose upon them no other burden than that which they agree to assume (except in the case of fraud or collusive overvaluation), but impose a heavy financial penalty upon the officers and directors of the company for failure to record and thus make available to the public the nature and extent of the payment given.

Moreover, for the following two years after an issue of shares for a consideration other than cash, complete particulars concerning the nature of the consideration must be set out in every prospectus, or in every statement in lieu of prospectus, which is issued.[34]

Finally, the Annual Return of the company must state the number of shares issued as wholly or partly paid up for a consideration other than cash and the extent to which it has been agreed that they shall be deemed paid up.[35] This Annual Return must be kept open to members for inspection free of charge and to all others upon payment of a nominal fee.[36] Members may obtain transcripts of the Return at a negligible cost, and a copy of the Return must be filed with the Registrar of Joint Stock Companies where it is open to public inspection. Moreover, the Annual Return must include a certified copy of the last audited balance sheet of the company, with all documents attached which are required by law, as well as a copy of the last report of the auditors of the company. The balance sheet must state the manner in which the fixed assets were valued, and the value of such intangibles as good will, patents, and trade-marks must be stated separately on the balance sheet until written off.[37] Failure to comply with the requirements enumerated above involves a pecuniary liability of directors and officers of the company and sometimes of the company itself.

Despite the many provisions for the disclosure of essential information, the terms of the British company law leave no doubt that (subject to the qualifications mentioned above concerning the sale of shares for cash at a discount and the payment of selling commis-

[34] 63 & 64 Vict. c. 48, sect. 10; 7 Edw. 7, c. 50, sect. 2; 8 Edw. 7, c. 69, sects. 81, 82, and Second Schedule to the act; 19 & 20 Geo. 5, c. 23, sects. 34–42, and the Third, Fourth, and Fifth Schedules to the act.

[35] 19 & 20 Geo. 5, c. 23, sect. 108 and Sixth Schedule. And see sect. 113 concerning the contents of the Statutory Report.

[36] *Ibid.*, sects. 98, 110.

[37] *Ibid.*, sects. 110, 124. See also sect. 113.

sions) shareholders are obligated to pay the company the full face value of their shares.[38] A liability for the unpaid balance on shares is imposed upon shareholders and the responsibility for full payment continues so long as the shares are not fully paid up.[39] The courts have held, however, that payment may be made in either " money or money's worth " and that in the absence of fraud the value of the consideration given will not be inquired into if a valid contract for the payment of the shares in specified property or services has been made and the details duly recorded as required by law.[40] In other words, the court will not revise the discretion of the directors unless the arrangement is plainly fraudulent or collusive, and the mere fact of a discrepancy between the nominal value of the shares and the value of the consideration given in payment is not, in itself, evidence of fraud.

Where, however, the arrangement for payment in property or services is fraudulent or shows on its face that the consideration given to the company is illusory, or is clearly less than the nominal value of the shares, the latter are not fully paid[41] and the shareholder may be held liable to pay for the shares in full.[42]

Our conclusion from the foregoing is that under British company law little attempt is made to protect the public through enforcement of the principle that shares must be fully paid. Rather, the protection takes the form of enforced publicity concerning the character of the payment which has been made or is to be made. A distinct relaxation of the original principle is manifested not only in the permission granted to issue shares at a discount and to credit subscribers with commissions on the shares which they take, but also in the *prima facie* validity granted to any contract made by the directors for the

[38] 8 Edw. 7, c. 69, sects. 2, 3, 14(2), 123(1)-(iv); 19 & 20 Geo. 5, c. 23, sects. 1, 2, 20, 157.

[39] 8 Edw. 7, c. 69, sect. 123; 19 & 20 Geo. 5, c. 23, sect. 157; Ooregum Gold Mining Co. of India v. Roper, *supra*, note 11; *In re* Wragg, Ltd., (1897) 1 Ch. 796, 808.

[40] Pell's Case, *In re* Heyford Co., (1869) L. R. 5 Ch. App. 11; Baglan Hall Colliery Co., *supra*, note 11; *In re* Wragg, Ltd., *supra*, note 39, and cases reviewed therein at p. 827 *et seq*. See also: *In re* Theatrical Trust, (1895) 1 Ch. 771; *In re* Innes & Co., (1903) 2 Ch. 254; Ooregum Gold Mining Co. of India v. Roper, *supra*, note 11; *In re* Richmond Hill Hotel Co., (1867) L. R. 2 Ch. App. 527; Gardner v. Iredale, (1912) 1 Ch. 700.

[41] *In re* Wragg, Ltd., *supra*, note 39, p. 836; Hong Kong & China Gas Co. v. Glen, (1914) 1 Ch. 527.

[42] *In re* James Pitkin & Co., *supra*, note 14.

acceptance of property or services at an agreed price, provided the agreement is recorded. The justification for the whole device lies in the presumptive protection given to the public by compliance with the publicity provisions of the law and the severe personal penalties imposed upon corporate officials for defaults in this connection.[43]

The payment of dividends out of capital.—The impairment of the value of the capital fund—which is supposed to be contributed by the shareholders—through the payment of "unearned" dividends has already been mentioned as a subject of too great intricacy to be included within the scope of this inquiry, although the problems of valuation for the protection of the public are closely related to those which we have studied in this monograph. The best reason for excluding it here, aside from the limitations of space, is the fact that it has been ably studied and the results lucidly stated by another investigator of the problems of judicial valuation.[44]

In brief, the law of England appears to permit the payment of a dividend out of the "profits" of a particular year despite past losses. Each year is treated as a unit and previous deficits need not be made up before a dividend can be paid. Moreover, in computing the "prof-

[43] Civil liability is provided in the several publicity sections of the Companies Acts already cited. There is also a criminal liability. See sect. 84 of the Larceny Act, 1861 (24 & 25 Vict. c. 96). Deliberate disobedience of the law is an essential element for the imposition of a criminal liability.

Apparently, it is still an open question whether a mere omission to comply with the statutes will result in a criminal liability. PALMER'S COMPANY PRECEDENTS (12th ed., London, 1922), Pt. I, p. 224. The right to sue for compensation in damages sustained through reliance upon misstatements in the prospectus is given in sect. 84 of the 1908 act (8 Edw. 7, c. 69), and in sect 37 of the 1929 act (19 & 20 Geo. 5, c. 23). See also sects. 82 and 281 of the 1908 act and sects. 40 and 362 of the 1929 act.

[44] Weiner, Joseph L., *Theory of Anglo-American Dividend Law: the English Cases* (1928), 28 COL. L. REV. 1046. See also: Weiner, Joseph L., *Theory of Anglo-American Dividend Law: American Statutes and Cases* (1929), 29 COL. L. REV. 461; Weiner, Joseph L., and James C. Bonbright, *Theory of Anglo-American Dividend Law: Surplus and Profits* (1930), 30 COL. L. REV. 330; REITER, PROSPER, PROFITS, DIVIDENDS AND THE LAW (New York, 1926).

The English cases and principles emerging from them are fully discussed in PALMER'S COMPANY PRECEDENTS (11th ed., London, 1912), Pt. I, c. IX, pp. 857–908. The discussion and cases are brought up to date in PALMER'S COMPANY PRECEDENTS (12th ed., London, 1922), Pt. I, pp. 838–52, and in PALMER'S COMPANY LAW (13th ed., London, 1929), pp. 222–33. See also the critical comments of Schuster, *op. cit. supra*, note 13.

its " of any particular year depreciation in the value of the " fixed capital " need not be taken into account. The result of these rules appears to be that a dividend may be paid when the balance sheet for the fiscal period shows a deficit. The consequence is that the ideal of a permanent fund on which creditors of a limited liability company can rely has been abandoned in practice in England. Considerable impairment of the original capital fund contributed by the shareholders has been permitted through the equivocal definition of the term " profits " which has been erected by judicial interpretation.[45]

The Control of Stock Watering in Germany

The legal devices for the prevention of stock watering in Germany closely resemble those established in England by the Companies Acts of 1862 to 1929.[46] In contrast to the English legislative scheme, however, the German law is designed to give assurance that the value of the consideration given in payment for capital stock shall correspond with the nominal paid-in capital of the company and that corporate possessions of the same value shall continue to repre-

[45] Some offset to this situation is provided by the various sections of the law which require the annual balance sheets to state the manner in which the assets have been valued and to separate the fixed from the " floating " assets. The law also provides for the availability of annual balance sheets to the public. See Companies (Consolidation) Act, 1929 (19 & 20 Geo. 5, c. 23), sects. 98, 108, 110, 122–30, 135–38. See also the Sixth Schedule to the act.

[46] The best general discussions in English of the German law pertaining to Corporations are the following: KUHN, ARTHUR K., A COMPARATIVE STUDY OF THE LAW OF CORPORATIONS (New York, 1912), pp. 65–85, 122–34, 157–60; SCHUSTER, *op. cit. supra*, note 13; Weiner, Joseph L., *Balance Sheet Valuation in German Law* (1929), 48 J. OF ACCOUNTANCY 195; REPORT, of the Departmental Committee Appointed by the Board of Trade to Inquire What Amendments Are Necessary in the Acts Relating to Joint Stock Companies Incorporated with Limited Liability under the Companies Acts, 1862 to 1890 (the so-called Davey Committee Report, Cmd. 7779, June 27, 1895), Appendix, pp. 11–40, consisting of a *Memorandum, Oral Testimony,* and *Extracts* from letters submitted by Dr. Ernest J. Schuster to the Committee. The writer has also had the privilege of examining an unpublished article by Mr. Joseph L. Weiner, *Prevention of Stock Watering with Especial Reference to German Law,* written by the author after he had spent several months in Germany investigating the operation of German company law.

See also THE GERMAN COMMERCIAL CODE (London, 1911), translated and briefly annotated by A. F. Schuster. A brief bibliography of the German works on the subject is contained in A GUIDE TO THE LAW AND LEGAL LITERATURE OF GERMANY (U. S. Library of Congress, 1912).

sent the capital stock unless the latter is reduced in a manner provided by law.

Added to the provisions tending to this result are a number of requirements which compel disclosure of: the nature and value of non-cash considerations to be given in payment for stock; the circumstances from which it appears that the property to be accepted in lieu of cash is worth the amount for which it is to be taken; the transactions whereby the company came to acquire the property, together with all prices paid within the preceding two years for the purchase or construction of it; the results of operation during the previous two years, if a going business is taken over and paid for in stock; annual balance sheets and profit and loss statements; promotion expenses; promotion agreements; and the articles of incorporation. Severe civil, and even criminal, liability is provided by the law for a failure of the following persons to live up to the requirements of the statutes: promoters (including by definition all persons who sign the articles or who take shares in payment for property or services); members of the managing directorate and board of supervision; the bankers or other persons who offer the shares for sale to the public; persons receiving any part of the promotion expenses not included in the return of promotion expenses; and persons guilty of wilful concealment, or of wilful or reckless infliction of loss on the company.

It is not our purpose to set forth in detail the provisions of the German law which have been designed for the protection of shareholders and creditors against the evils of watered stock.[47] We may, however, mention several of the outstanding features of the German system which differentiate it from that of England. As in England, the capstone of the legislative structure is publicity of those facts pertaining to the organization and administration of the corporation which are, or should be, of interest to creditors and investors in forming an intelligent opinion of their own concerning the merits of the enterprise as a credit or investment risk. Under both systems of regulation information is made available to the public concerning the nature and value of the consideration which is given for stock, as well as the subsequent record of the enterprise as a going concern.

The distinguishing features of German corporate law and financial practice which are worthy of mention here are: (*a*) the elaborate safeguards (particularly the independent audit) which are designed

[47] This has been done by Kuhn, *op. cit. supra*, note 46.

to prevent the overvaluation of property which is exchanged for shares; (*b*) comprehensive and consistent rules for the valuation of assets on the balance sheet; and (*c*) the participation of responsible bankers as promoters of new corporations, coupled with the practice of selling the new shares to the public at a premium.

Safeguards against overvaluation. — The articles of association of a German corporation must be signed by at least five intending shareholders and must be entered in the local mercantile register which is open to the public. They must state particulars as to: (1) any special advantages which are to be conferred on any individual shareholders; (2) the nature of any consideration other than cash against which any shares are to be issued; (3) contracts for the purchase of property or the construction of works for cash, including the name of the vendor or contractor and the price to be paid; (4) the total amount to be paid by the company for services rendered in connection with the promotion of the company. These matters are hereafter referred to as the " promotion agreements." All agreements for the acceptance of property in payment for stock which are not specifically set forth in the articles are invalid as against the corporation.

In all cases in which shares are to be issued for a consideration other than cash, or in which contracts for the construction or purchase of works are entered into, the promoters must prepare and sign a declaration stating the circumstances from which it appears that the property to be acquired is worth the price to be paid for it. This declaration must disclose all transactions leading up to the ultimate sale of the property in question, including all prices paid within the two preceding years for the purchase or construction of any part of the property. If the company is to acquire the business of a going concern, the results of operating the business during the previous two years must be disclosed in the declaration. The term " promoter " includes all those who have signed the articles of incorporation as well as those to whom shares are to be issued for any consideration other than cash.

The first duty of the managing board (executive) and of the board of supervision (directorate) is to examine the promoters' declaration and to test the accuracy of the statements contained in it. They must make an independent inquiry concerning all of the incidents of the formation of the company, including the allotment and payment for shares. Their examination must relate particularly to the accuracy and completeness of the statements made in the promoters' declaration with reference to the payment for stock in property. The results of these inquiries must be embodied in written reports.

If any member of either board signed the articles as one of the organizers, or is to be the recipient of any particular advantage or compensation by reason of the formation of the company, or if the company is to issue shares for property or agrees to purchase any property for cash, *independent auditors* must be appointed by the local chamber of commerce or other similar body in the place at which the company is to be registered. If there is no such local body, then the auditors must be appointed by the two boards. These auditors must examine the circumstances surrounding the promotion of the company, with particular reference to the accuracy and completeness of the promoters' declaration concerning the value of property to be turned over for stock. The auditors may demand further information concerning the subject of their inquiry than is contained in the promoters' declaration and reports of the two boards. If differences arise between the auditors and the promoters concerning the scope of the examination, the authority which appointed the auditors is empowered to give a binding decision as to whether the demand for further information is justified. As long as the information sought is not forthcoming, the auditors may refuse to report and in this manner prevent the incorporation of the company.

The foregoing provisions are reinforced by publicity requirements. Registers for mercantile purposes are kept by the local courts, and the entries made in them as well as the documents filed in connection therewith are open for public inspection. The articles of incorporation must be entered in the register and the following documents (among others) must be filed: (*a*) the promotion agreements referred to above; (*b*) the promoters' declaration; (c) a detailed statement as to the promotion expenses; (*d*) the reports of the two boards concerning the organization of the company, referred to above, and all exhibits to which they refer; (*e*) the report of the auditors. The local court must publish an extract of the articles, containing, among other things, particulars concerning the promotion agreements.

Numerous civil and criminal penalties are imposed upon promoters and upon the members of both boards for losses arising from inaccuracy or incompleteness of any of the documents required for registration. No criminal liability is imposed, however, in the absence of proof of deliberate misstatement of fact. The promoters are directly responsible to the company for loss occasioned by reckless overvaluation of any property acquired by the company. Persons receiving any part of the promotion expenses not included in the return of promotion expenses are jointly and severally liable with the promoters for the return thereof to the company. Finally, anyone who issues a prospectus before the registration of the company, or who within two years after incorporation publicly advertises the shares for sale is answerable to the corporation for any inaccuracy or omissions from the promoters' report pertaining to the organization of the company and the payment of its capital stock. Such a one is responsible for any damage caused by reckless overvaluation of payments in kind unless he neither knew, nor by the exercise of the diligence of a prudent trader would have known, of the overvaluation.

The special feature with regard to the civil liability of the foregoing parties is that the liability is joint and several and runs to the corporation rather than directly to the injured shareholder. But the corporation can be compelled to sue if 20 per cent of the stock is voted in favor of such action. Waivers and compromises of the liability of these various parties are barred by statute for several years following the organization of the company and are invalid at any time unless approved at a general meeting by the holders of more than 80 per cent of the stock.

The most striking feature of the whole legislative scheme for the protection of investors and creditors against the acceptance of overvalued property in payment for stock is undoubtedly the *independent audit*. Experience teaches that it is unwise to leave the delicate matter of valuing non-cash payments to the judgment of self-interested parties. The promoters and vendors have every reason to overvalue the consideration and the directors may be their nominees with no will of their own. At any rate, the organizers and first officers of a new company are not likely to exercise impartial judgment in the matter, because they generally have a direct or an indirect interest in accomplishing what the promoters wish to be done.

There is good reason to believe that the independent audit in Germany has not fully accomplished the purposes for which it was intended. Certain defects in administration have developed which have destroyed most of its supposed value.[48] Incompetent auditors

[48] See Davey Committee Report, *supra*, note 46.

have frequently been appointed. This has been due in part to defects in the machinery for their appointment and in part to the inadequacy of the compensation provided. There can be little doubt, however, that the independent audit has had some beneficial effects in the way of discouraging acts on the part of promoters which might later lead to suspicion.

Valuation of assets in balance sheets. — The second distinguishing feature of German company law is the comprehensive way in which the preparation of balance sheets is prescribed by law.[49] The rules for balance-sheet valuation of assets appear to be direct corollaries from the basic principle of German law stated as follows by Schuster:

> . . . There is one principle which should never be disregarded, whenever the principle of limited liability is conferred by law; the liability of a fund having a fixed and ascertainable value should be substituted for the unlimited liability of individuals. The value of this fund should on the formation of the company correspond with the amount of its nominal capital, and precautions should be taken to prevent, as much as possible, the diminution of this fund during the subsequent stages of the company's existence. Company law should, therefore, find means to assure (*a*) that the value of the property which represents the capital of a company on its formation shall correspond with the amount of the nominal paid-up capital of the company; (*b*) that property of the same value should continue to represent the paid-up capital of the company as long as it is not increased, and that on any increase of the paid-up capital the property representing the increase should be of a value at least equal to the nominal amount of the increase.[50]

According to German law an annual balance sheet and profit-and-loss statement must be prepared by the managing directors. These documents, supported by a report of the supervisory board upon the financial condition and affairs of the company, must be presented to the shareholders at the annual meeting. A majority at the general meeting may appoint independent auditors for the purpose of testing the accuracy of the balance sheet or of investigating other matters relating to the organization and management of the company. If holders of 10 per cent of the stock demand it, the auditors must be appointed by the court if there is reasonable ground for supposing that the report is inaccurate or violative of the law or

[49] WEINER, *op. cit. supra*, note 46; SCHUSTER, *op. cit. supra*, note 13.
[50] SCHUSTER, *op. cit. supra*, note 13.

articles of incorporation. Such a report by the auditors must be filed at the mercantile registry.

If the balance sheet and profit-and-loss statements are approved at the general meeting they must be published immediately in the papers in which the company's announcements are published and must be filed in the local registry.

Aside from these provisions for publicity, the balance sheet must be drawn up in a certain way. Current assets having a market value must be valued at the lower of cost or market. Other assets are to be valued at not in excess of cost. Buildings, plant, and other fixed assets which are not intended for resale may be valued at cost, regardless of a lower market value, provided an adequate deduction for physical depreciation is made or an equivalent sum is set up in a depreciation fund.[51] Organization expenses may not be included among the assets. The par value of the capital stock and all reserve and depreciation funds must be included among the liabilities. The difference between assets and liabilities which results when the assets have been valued in this manner is the amount of the profit or loss and must be separately stated at the foot of the balance sheet.

These accounting rules have a definite bearing upon the maintenance of the original capital fund for the benefit of shareholders and creditors. They prevent the payment of dividends out of unrealized appreciation in the value of assets, or despite the depreciation or depletion of the fixed assets. Wasting-asset companies must set up a renewal fund which is accumulated out of earnings at the rate at which depletion progresses.

As a safeguard of financial solidity the law provides for a compulsory reserve-fund consisting of accumulated earnings (at the rate of 5 per cent of net profits per annum) equal to at least 10 per cent of the capital stock of the company, plus the amount of any premiums paid on the issue of shares. This statutory reserve fund is not available for the payment of dividends but may be used to cover losses. To the extent that this cannot be done the losses must be debited against profit-and-loss account, and no dividend can be paid until any deficit in the profit-and-loss account has been covered

[51] If stock is issued for property it may apparently be taken onto the balance sheet at a figure equal to the valuation placed upon it by the independent auditors. From the standpoint of investors and creditors this possibility appears to be shorn of its possible harmful effect by the publicity provisions of the law.

by earnings. Additional reserves for dividend equalization may be set up, however.

The sale of shares at a premium. — The final characteristic which space will permit us to mention is not a matter of law but of promotion practice. In America as well as in England it has been customary for the promoter to make a profit through an overvaluation of the consideration given for his stock and through a sale of this stock at or below par. In America little attempt is made to compel disclosure of the manner in which the promoter has paid for his shares. That is left to the ingenuity of shareholders and creditors who later claim that the stock was watered. In England, on the other hand, the promoter is required to disclose the nature of the payment which he made for his stock.

There was a time when the system in Germany resembled the American. The promoter made his profit through the sale at or below par of stock which had been issued to him for overvalued property. That system is no longer in vogue in Germany. For the last forty years or more the promoter has made his profit through a sale of his stock *at a premium.* Instead of the promoter's profit being added to the nominal capitalization of the company, it is added to the price which the public must pay for its shares.

A part of the explanation of this practice lies in the strict requirements enumerated above concerning the valuation of non-cash considerations given for stock. These requirements were introduced by the company law of 1884 and by the revised Commercial Code of 1897. Too many checks upon the promoter's valuation were introduced by these laws to make it easy for him to inflate the nominal value of his shares. Moreover, his personal responsibility for losses caused by overvaluations is too great in case of detection, and detection was greatly facilitated by the requirements concerning publicity of the promotion arrangements.

Perhaps the explanation of the modern practice lies to some extent also in the development within the last fifty years of a new relationship of the large German banks to industry. Much of the promotion of corporations is done by banks, which combine underwriting and share-issuing activities with ordinary commercial banking. The common method of organizing a company is for the promoters to subscribe for all of the shares and hold them until they can be sold to the public at a premium. Without the assistance of bankers it is improbable that promoters could finance such transactions. Moreover, since the law imposes upon all persons who publicly offer shares for sale within two years after the registration of a new company, a joint and several liability with the organizers for the accuracy and completeness of the various reports mentioned above, there is every incentive for the banker who is both a promoter and a share-merchant to insist upon a conservative initial valuation and to sell the shares on the basis of earning power. The system is not free from evils, of course, since manipulated accounts may be made to present a favorable earning statement at the time the shares are offered, and purchases may be made on this false basis.

Finally, the practice of selling shares at a premium may be due in part to the discovery that the public could be induced just as easily to pay an excessive price based upon demonstrated or estimated earning power as upon an excessive par value. The sale of shares at a premium is no guarantee that the purchaser will not pay too much for them. But it has the advantage of giving the first purchaser from the promoters direct information that the premium represents a promoter's profit. Moreover, the creditor is benefited by the practice because there is less likelihood that the nominal value of the shares will be misleading.

Reform of Domestic Law

The futility of attempts to make par values serve a useful purpose. — Any suggestions for the reform of our anti-stock-watering laws must be made in the light of our conclusion that all attempts to make the par value of shares correspond to the net value of corporate possessions are bound to prove abortive. This conclusion follows from the fact that, even if an initial equivalence could be set up, its significance would soon be lost through shifts in the value of the corporate assets. Moreover, even if an equivalence could later be maintained, we doubt whether any feasible scheme for the control of stock watering can be erected around the necessity on the part of complaining parties of proving a discrepancy between the par value of stock and the *value* of the consideration for which it was issued. The value of the types of property commonly exchanged for stock is so much a matter of opinion that it cannot be made a satisfactory measure of shareholders' liability.

These points will be clearer if we recall for the moment the purpose of a stated or par value for corporate shares. We have already pointed out in an earlier chapter that the sole significance of par value lies in its use as a publicity device. It is intended to serve a useful function by revealing the amount of the shareholders' contribution to the corporate venture. A hypothetical example will afford us an illustration of this point and will also enable us to indicate wherein par values fail to live up to this mission under present conditions.

Let us suppose that a promoter has purchased the plant and equipment of a textile manufacturer. Suppose, further, that the cash price which the promoter paid for the property was $500,000 and that he plans to turn over the plant and equipment to a corporation which he will form and which will issue to him its entire capital stock in payment for the property. How much stock (measured in par value) should the promoter issue to himself in exchange for this property?

The question which we are raising is, How does it concern the public whether the promoter issues $500,000 of $5,000,000 of stock against his purchase? Since the enterprise is not a public utility, it seems improbable that the possible influence of overcapitalization on the price charged for the product will be raised in a court. The only apparent harm which the law may be interested in preventing is not a direct [52] injury to the consumer of textile products, but rather an injury to investors who may be induced to take a financial interest in the company and who may be misled by an excessive issue of stock. This leads us to the conclusion that the par value of a share of stock lies solely in its use as an accounting or publicity device for the disclosure to investors and creditors of information useful to them.

If, in our illustration, the law restricted to $500,000 (the cash cost to him) the amount of stock which this promoter could issue for his property, then the par value of the stock would carry a significant burden of information for the investor and creditor. It would show that the shareholders have made an initial investment of $500,000 in the enterprise. This is an historical fact of some significance. It indicates the sum of money which the shareholders have risked in

[52] As has been noted in Chapter I, the laws against stock watering by industrial concerns, as opposed to public utilities, can hardly be construed as attempts directly to protect the consumer. But they may very well be construed as attempts to give the consumer indirect protection. Any injury done to corporate creditors or stockholders through the sale of fraudulent stocks or bonds is also an injury to the consuming public, in that it results in a waste of the capital resources of the country. The consumer will suffer from the repercussions of this kind of waste.

the venture and which must stand the brunt of any losses resulting from subsequent transactions. At the start it would be a fair indication of the value of the shareholders' equity and as such could be relied upon for purposes of credit extension. This would follow from the fact that the promoter's self-interest would have dictated as low a price (and hence capitalization) as possible, and from the fact that any gain or loss resulting from the bargain would fall first of all on the promoter and only secondarily upon the creditor.

Under our present law, however, the amount of the stock need not be restricted to the promoter's cost. The promoter may offer the property to the corporation for $1,000,000 of stock, and his nominees, acting as directors of the newly formed corporation, may solemnly resolve to issue that amount of " fully-paid " stock to him in payment for the property. Their resolution will state that in their judgment the property is fully worth the face value of the stock. Unless their valuation is obviously excessive it will have *prima facie* validity in any later suit in which it is urged that the property did not constitute a full consideration for the stock. If the company should fail and creditors seek to collect an alleged unpaid balance on the stock, the shareholders would probably be successful in maintaining that the cost to the promoter is no proper criterion of the value of the property to the corporation and that, in view of the prospects for future earnings and in view of the other surrounding circumstances at the time the company was formed, the property was reasonably worth $1,000,000 to the corporation.

As contrasted with a capitalization based upon the cost of the property to the promoter, of what possible use can this figure of $1,000,000 be to creditors and investors? It stands for no historical fact. It is not a measure of the extent to which the stockholders have shared in the risks of the venture. It represents simply a self-interested guess. Here we see a serious flaw in our existing law with respect to corporate capitalization. To the extent that the law declines to accept some objective test as the measure of proper capitalization, such as the price paid by the promoter, and to the extent that it accepts in lieu of an objective test the estimates by interested parties of the future earning power of the company, to this extent does it almost completely defeat the object of anti-stock-watering laws. These laws should be designed to aid the investor to form some intelligent judgment of his own as to the merits of the enterprise. The laws are useful only so far as they make the par value of the shares mean something significant to a person who is trying to decide whether to lend or not to lend, or whether to buy a share of stock or to leave it alone. It is perfectly absurd to assume that a statement by corporate directors (representing the promoters) as to what they think the property is worth can be of any material aid to investors in deciding what they, the investors, think the property is worth.

What is needed, if par-value stock is to be used at all, is not a par value representing an estimate by promoters of the earning power of the enterprise, but rather a par value which represents some objective fact on which prospective investors can be guided in their own evaluation of the risks which will be incurred by a financial commitment in the enterprise. The fact that seems to have the most significance for this purpose is the cash price which the promoters, themselves, have paid for the property which they are turning over to the corporation. Even this cash price, to be sure, represents a valuation of the property by the promoters, since only by an estimate of the future profitableness of the company can promoters determine what price they are justified in bidding for the property. Nevertheless, this estimate is one of far greater significance than an unsupported statement by directors as to their *opinion*, since it is an estimate on which the promoters themselves are acting. Under the present law, which allows directors to place an unsupported valuation on the property, self-interest tempts the directors to make the figure as *high* as possible, whereas under a law requiring the capitalization to be based upon the promoters' cost, self-interest will tend to keep the figure as *low* as possible.[53]

But one may inquire how the promoter may obtain payment for his services if the suggestion that the promoter's cost be made the basis of capitalization is embodied into law? The promoter is entitled to a fair profit on the transaction, and the proposed basis of capitalization will prevent him from making any profit at all unless he can sell his stock at a premium. One must admit the cogency of this argument as applied to present American conditions. The very reason why most promoters resort to watered stock is that the shares can be sold to the public at a price less than par and still yield a generous

[53] The promoter may deliberately misstate the cost price and state that his cost was $700,000, instead of $500,000. This type of fraud, however, is much more easy to establish and, therefore, is more dangerous to attempt than is the more subtle type of fraud involved in an overstatement of one's opinion concerning the value of property.

profit to the promoter. If now the law should be changed in such a way as to require the promoter to take his profit entirely through the sale of his stock at a premium, it might make promotion on a profitable basis extremely difficult. For several reasons, however, we doubt whether this argument has sufficient force to carry the case.

In the first place, the difficulty of selling new stock issues at a premium, or even at par, is due very largely to the prevalence of stock watering in American promotions. Investors expect as a matter of course that the amount of stock issued in any given instance is far in excess of the cost of the property to the promoters, and they are naturally unwilling to pay face value for an issue which experience tells them is almost sure to be worth far less than par. If, however, the law were so changed and so well enforced that waterless promotions became the general rule, investors could be educated to the purchase of promotion shares at prices above par value, just as they have been educated to the purchase of shares in newly formed banks at a premium. An illustration of what might be expected is afforded by financial practice in Germany where, as we have already noted, the general rule is for new shares to be offered to the public at a premium.[54]

In the second place, it may be argued with much force that a law preventing the capitalization of promoters' profits, even if it did result in making promotions much more difficult, would be all the more desirable for that very reason. There is much to be said for the opinion that no one who is not thoroughly familiar with the mechanism of finance should experiment in the purchase of promotion stocks. Since only those persons who are unfamiliar with financial methods are likely to be influenced materially by par values, the only effect which a stricter anti-stock-watering law would have would be to discourage the purchase of promotion stock by the uninitiated investor. This result alone might justify the law.

In the third place, there is at present the alternative of issuing shares without par value. In view of the presence of this alternative, there is much more reason for making our laws governing par-value shares far more strict than ever before. Possibly a still better policy would be to amend the corporation laws so as to forbid absolutely

[54] It is unsafe, however, to draw too many inferences from the German practice, particularly in view of the sponsorship of most promotions in Germany by large and powerful banks. In many instances these banks are the real promoters in every sense of the word. See references cited *supra*, note 46.

the issue of shares with a par value. Unless, however, the legislators are willing to take this drastic step, there is good reason to support a far more rigid policy with respect to the old type of shares.

The principal difficulty with our proposal to base corporate capitalization upon the cost of property to the promoters is the fact that there are many cases of promotion where this rule could not be observed, because no cash price to the promoters is agreed upon. To revert to our illustration above, it was assumed that the promoter bought the plant and equipment for a cash consideration of $500,000. Suppose, however, that the former owner of the mill had agreed to take stock in the new company in full or in part payment for his property, and suppose that he had not given a cash option, which might prove inconvenient in case creditors should discover this option price and should use it as evidence of the admitted value of the property. In such a case, one cannot fix upon $500,000 or any other figure as the cash price which the promoter agreed to pay or which the vendor agreed to accept. It is certain that the importance of this change in the law would be greatly reduced because of the fact that it would have limited application.

In view of this fact it would seem to be desirable, in all cases where the promoter has not paid a cash price for his property, to follow the German precedent and require an independent audit of the value of the consideration to be accepted for stock. This requirement need not be so broad as to include private or close corporations where no appeal for funds is made to the public. In order to insure that competent auditors will be appointed, the law should require that they be certified public accountants selected by an unbiased authority such as a blue-sky commission. This audit should be made before the right to offer shares to the public has been granted and the law should provide for full and compulsory publicity of the auditors' report and the basis of valuation used. In general, the law should provide for the following: (*a*) an independent determination of the value of the consideration to be accepted in payment for stock; (*b*) full publicity of the basis of valuation used and of the promotion arrangements whereby the promoters are to obtain any benefits; (*c*) responsibility of promoters, directors, and those who offer the shares to the public (within a limited time after the incorporation of the company) for the completeness and accuracy of the information made available to the public.

Alterations in the law along the lines suggested would materially strengthen the position of shareholders and creditors as opposed to the promoters. But the improvement in their position would not be the result of establishing an equivalence between par value and the *value* of the consideration received in payment for shares. It would result rather from the establishment of rules of conservatism in corporate capitalization and more particularly from the availability of precise information concerning the basis on which shares have been issued. In view of these facts we see no good reason why par values should be retained. As we view the matter, any attempt so to amend the corporation laws as to make par values serve a useful purpose is foredoomed to failure.

The very fact that stock is so frequently issued not for cash but for other property, and the further fact that there is no objective basis on which this property may be valued and by which any alleged overvaluation on the part of the directors can be tested, is final in favor of abandoning the use of par values altogether. Perhaps exceptions should be made in the case of financial institutions where payment for the capital stock must be made in cash and where the assets remain for the most part in liquid form, but for industrial companies as well as for public utility companies par value is a nuisance and not a help. The present laws permitting its issue should be repealed, or, if this step seems too drastic, the responsibilities of promoters and directors with respect to par-value stock should deliberately be made so strict that the issue of such stock will be discouraged.

Non-par stock as a remedy. — Although the logic of the situation is clearly in favor of abandoning or discouraging par values, it does not follow that the removal of par values will of itself solve our problem, which is to provide the investor and creditor with the means whereby they can form an intelligent opinion of their own concerning the value of the enterprise. This is true because non-par-value shares reveal no figure to which creditors or investors may refer as a measure of the contribution of shareholders to the enterprise. They must consult the balance sheet of the corporation for this information and if the balance sheet may be falsified as readily as par values, the widespread, and perhaps universal, adoption of non-par shares will bring us little nearer to the solution of our problem than that provided by the present laws with respect to shareholders' liability.[55]

[55] Bonbright, James C., *The Dangers of Shares Without Par Value* (1924), 24 Col. L. Rev. 449, 465 *et seq.*

It is true that the removal of par values will eliminate such deception as has resulted from the engraving of a nominal value upon share-certificates. But this is not enough. The means must be provided whereby there is made available to investors and creditors the information necessary for the formation of their own opinions concerning the contributions made by shareholders to the corporate treasury. Unless it proves feasible to adopt a non-par balance sheet, as well as a non-par stock certificate, that is, unless a form of financial statement can be devised which does away with pecuniary valuations of the fixed assets by interested parties, we are still faced with the same problem, though in a somewhat different form, that presents itself in the case of an overissue of par-value shares. This problem is the difficult but insistent one of requiring the company's promoters, who alone are intimately familiar with the nature of their property and who are directly interested in exaggerating its good points, to give information on the balance sheet which is sufficiently significant as an indicator of the price which the promoters paid for the privilege of sharing in the enterprise, sufficiently simple and direct in form that persons do not need to be expert accountants in order to understand its meaning, and sufficiently objective and verifiable that fraudulent misstatements can be exposed and punished.

But if we must abandon as hopeless all effort to make the par value of stock into a useful measure of the value of the real assets of the company, what reason is there to hope that we can make the balance sheet any more truthful and objective? How does the one bring us any nearer to a solution of our difficulty than the other?

Although there is doubtless a foundation for skepticism concerning the proposal to shift the burden of disclosure to the balance sheet, there are several reasons why a truthful and significant balance sheet as a more practicable goal than a truthful and significant par value. In the first place, there is the important fact that it is not so difficult to enforce rules of conservatism in balance-sheet valuation as it is to enforce rules of conservatism in par values. A promoter, for example, may think himself seriously handicapped if he is unable to include a promoter's profit in the par value of the stock which his company is to issue to him for his property. Even though it is doubtful whether this difficulty is as serious as promoters often think it to be, there is little question that it reflects a prevalent attitude in the financial world. We do not believe that this same difficulty would prevail against a rule requiring the capital assets of a new company to appear on the books at their cost price to the promoter — assuming that the promoter has purchased the assets for a cash consideration. The reason for this difference lies in the fact that the sale of non-par stock at a price in excess of its book value is probably not as difficult as the sale of par-value stock at a price in excess of its par value.

A further and more important reason why it is probably more feasible to use the balance sheet rather than the nominal capitalization of a company as a guide to investors is the fact that the balance sheet does not merely provide a single item which is supposed to represent the sum of the values of all of the assets contributed by the shareholders. It does the far more important thing of dividing these assets into different types. Aside from a record of earnings which is not ordinarily available in the early stages of a new enterprise, it is only through reference to detailed and specific information concerning the separate assets and the price paid to the promoter for his services that an intelligent opinion may be formed concerning the net position of the company at any given time. It is such information that is demanded by the banker before he advances funds to a corporation, and similar information should be available to the public.

The object of a standardized balance sheet which would separate the tangibles from the intangibles, disclose the manner of valuing each, and reveal both the amount and medium of payment of the promoter's compensation or profit, is to give to creditors and investors a basis by which they can check the asserted values of the assets as stated by the promoters. If, for example, a comparatively new enterprise is represented by a balance sheet with tangible values stated at $100,000 and with good will stated at $900,000, investors are put on their guard by the appearance of such a tremendous item of good will.

The problem of standardizing the balance sheet is certainly a difficult one and can be solved only by the work of expert accountants. It may be that the additional requirement of an appraisal by reputable auditors, who are to be selected not by the promoters but by some independent authority such as a blue-sky commission, may be necessary. In any case the appraisers should not be selected by either the promoters, the original directors, or the original shareholders, since their interests are largely identical. Furthermore, care should be taken to assure the selection of appraisers who are competent.

Difficult as is the problem of affording adequate protection to investors and creditors against the evils of watered stock without unduly hampering promotion and corporate management, we suggest that certain minimum requirements may be covered by statute. In the first place, we feel that the issue of par-value shares should be discouraged except, perhaps, by financial institutions. This could be accomplished by prohibiting the issue of stock for property in excess of the cash cost of that property to the promoter or other vendor to the corporation. Disclosure of this cash cost should be made not only on the balance sheet but on a public record in the form of a sworn statement by the vendor. Severe penalties for deliberate misstatement should be imposed.

This statement should be filed with the secretary of state and with the recorder of deeds in the county in which the company has its principal office. The statement should be open to public inspection and transcripts should be made available to the public at nominal cost. There should also be filed with the same officials a sworn statement by the promoters (which term should, by definition, include all signers of the articles of incorporation and all vendors who are to accept shares of stock in payment for property), setting forth all dealings in the property during two years prior to the sale to the company which have been made among the promoters or their nominees in contemplation of the promotion. The object of this latter requirement would be to disclose any successive sales or options among the promoters or their friends which have resulted in an inflation of the cost price to the ultimate vendor to the company.

In all cases in which the vendor to the company has not obtained his property by a cash outlay, or in which services are to be the consideration for a stock issue, there should be an independent appraisal of the value of the consideration by competent and disinterested persons, and the amount of stock issuable should be limited to the appraised value. In this case the appraisers should be required to sign a report setting forth the basis of the appraisal and the circumstances from which it appeared that the value agreed upon was appropriate. This report should also be available to the public and the balance sheet should state the method of appraisal and refer to the appraisers' report. Here, too, previous dealings with respect to the consideration during the preceding two years should be disclosed. Severe civil and even criminal liability should be imposed upon the promoters (as above defined) for any deliberate misstatement or deliberate withholding of essential information in any report signed by them for the purpose of any public record.

These requirements would provide the public with more significant and more reliable information than is now available and would practically force the promoter to sell his par-value stock at a premium if he is to make a profit. It is probable that as a matter of practice such stock could be sold at a premium only on the basis of demonstrated earning power. This would, in effect, compel the promoters to carry the risks of their ventures until success becomes measurably apparent.

Summarizing our major proposal concerning non-par stock, we suggest that the following minimum requirements might well be embodied in statute:

A. Reports to be filed upon the issue of stock for a consideration other than cash:

1. Wherever shares are to be issued for a consideration other than cash there must be filed with a public authority, and be open to inspection, a sworn statement (signed, in the case of a new company, by the incorporators, original directors, promoters, and vendors, and, in the case of a going concern, by the directors and vendors), indicating the agreed valuation of the consideration and the circumstances from which the valuation appears to be justified. Any basis of valuation used must be set out in the statement, including any past record of earnings for the previous two years. The statement must be filed within thirty days after the stock is issued and the offer of the stock for sale to the public, prior to the filing of this statement and the auditors' report mentioned below, should be prohibited. The agreed valuation must be credited to the capital stock account in the absence of expressed intention to the contrary.[56]

2. This statement should disclose all transactions effected during the preceding two years with respect to the consideration given for the stock, which were made in contemplation of the promotion among the parties who sign the statement or between them and parties whom they represent. These disclosures

[56] *Cf.* Berle, A. A., Jr., *Problems of Non-Par Stock* (1925), 25 Col. L. Rev. 43, 48, reprinted in Studies in the Law of Corporation Finance (Chicago, 1928), c. IV, by the same author; Bonbright, *op. cit. supra,* note 55.

should relate particularly to the prices at which the property has changed hands during this period.

3. There should also be filed a detailed statement of the promotion expenses and the manner in which they have been or are to be paid.

4. A further statement should be filed revealing the nature of any options given or to be given to the promoters or vendors entitling them to obtain management shares or other stock, and the terms of the arrangement.

5. The auditors' report mentioned below.

B. Independent audit and publication of results:

1. In every case where shares are to be issued for a consideration other than cash, qualified and independent auditors must be appointed by an unbiased authority. These auditors must examine all of the reports to be filed by the promoters, vendors, etc., mentioned above, and submit a concurring or dissenting report and the reasons therefor. The auditors should have full powers to investigate the matters to which the promotion reports pertain and their report should relate particularly to the valuation of the consideration accepted for stock. The valuation of the promoters, vendors, etc., should be conclusive in the absence of deliberately false statements, but the dissenting opinion of the auditors should be made a matter of public record and should be noted on the initial balance sheet of the company. In the case of deliberate misstatement by the promoters, vendors, incorporators, or original directors in any of the promotion reports, they should be jointly and severally liable to the corporation for any loss or damage resulting therefrom. The qualification, appointment, and remuneration of the auditors should be carefully prescribed by statute in order to provide for the services of competent and disinterested men.

C. The issue price of stock of a going concern:

1. Where stock is to be issued for cash, the price at which it is to be offered should be determined by the directors, subject to ratification by the holders of a majority of the outstanding

shares of the class to be issued, and like ratification by the holders of a majority of shares of each class junior thereto.

2. Where stock is to be issued for a consideration other than cash the number of shares to be issued should not exceed the number determined by dividing the agreed purchase price by a figure representing the book value per share of the stock of that class already outstanding. If no stock of that class is already outstanding, the number of shares to be issued for any given consideration should be subject to the approval of the holders of a majority of the shares which will be junior to the new stock.

D. Balance-sheet valuation and disclosures:

1. The assets must be classified as between tangibles and intangibles.

2. The method of valuing each asset must be stated in a footnote to the balance sheet. If an asset is taken onto the balance sheet on the basis of its previous earning power, that fact must be stated and the record of earnings disclosed in a footnote or schedule attached to the balance sheet. If the value cannot be accurately ascertained, the fact should be noted.

3. In each case in which an asset was acquired by an issue of stock, a footnote should indicate the fact and state the number of shares issued for it.

4. Promotion expenses, underwriting fees, and commissions allowed for the sale of stock must be stated separately on the assets side of the balance sheet to the extent that they have been capitalized, and must be carried there until written off.

5. No unrealized increases in the value of the assets should be carried to the profit-and-loss account or be the basis of a cash dividend. Stock dividends or increases in capital surplus account against unrealized appreciation in the value of assets may be allowed, provided these increases are separately stated as such among the assets.

6. Exceptional losses should be noted on the balance sheet with a notation of any adjustments of surplus account which have

been made on account of them. A statement should also be made concerning the extent to which current income has been charged with such losses and the period over which they are to be amortized.

7. The surplus account of every company should be itemized with respect to the source, and the availability of each item for the payment of dividends should be clearly indicated. For this purpose the surplus account should be subdivided into four parts: (1) earned surplus resulting from ordinary operations; (2) surplus resulting from realized profit on the sale of fixed assets; (3) surplus resulting from unrealized appreciation or revaluation of assets; (4) paid-in surplus.

E. Annual balance sheets and profit-and-loss statements:

1. Annual balance sheets prepared in accordance with the above principles must be submitted annually to stockholders and be filed with the same public authority who is the custodian of the promoters' and auditors' reports.

2. A like requirement should be made with respect to annual profit-and-loss statements. These statements should be more than mere totals. They should be in sufficient detail to permit of analysis.

F. Prospectus:

1. Every public offer of shares for sale by the company or by any security dealer or salesman should be accompanied by a prospectus containing a copy of the latest balance sheet and profit-and-loss account, if any. The prospectus should either refer to the auditors' and promoters' reports which have been filed, or else set them out in full.

G. Escrow of speculative stock:

1. It may be desirable in all cases where shares are issued for intangibles such as patents, copyrights, trademarks, secret processes, formulas, good will, or promotion fees, to require, as a condition precedent to the sale for cash of other stock of the company, that the stock issued for intangibles of this

> variety shall be held in escrow until the cash subscribers have received certain minimum cash dividends which are shown to the satisfaction of the blue-sky commission to have been actually earned, and on dissolution or insolvency to subordinate the rights of the owners of the stock in escrow to the rights of cash subscribers. Exceptions to this rule could be made in cases where the intangibles taken over have a demonstrated earning power, or where the stock is issued by a going concern having an established earning power. This would further strengthen the position of innocent shareholders, and creditors would be in a position to inform themselves by reference to the reports suggested above.[57]

One further question of law is raised by our discussion of remedies and the proposals sketched above. If we assume that the solution of our problem is first to remove par values, and second to require greater publicity of promotion arrangements and greater accuracy and uniformity in the balance sheet and operating statements, how are we to enforce these requirements against persons who disregard them? There seems to be no good reason why a severe civil and perhaps even a criminal liability should not be imposed upon the promoters, incorporators, vendors and original directors for deliberately misstating the facts required to be recorded in the promotion reports which we have suggested should be filed. Clearly, also, a severe civil liability ought to be imposed upon the directors of going concerns for deliberate misstatements in the annual balance sheets and operating statements of the company. The history of promotion in this country makes it clear that any law which would impose a liability upon the initial directors for a false statement in the first balance sheet of a company would be defective in that the directors are often persons of no financial responsibility who have been chosen to do the bidding of the promoters. It would do little good to obtain judgment against these directors.

What is needed is an effective means of reaching the promoters themselves, even though these promoters attempt to hide behind dummy directors. A statute is needed which will name not only the

[57] A provision of this kind is proposed in section 14 of the THIRD TENTATIVE DRAFT OF UNIFORM SALE OF SECURITIES ACT, which was submitted to the thirty-seventh annual meeting of the National Conference of Commissioners on Uniform State Laws, Buffalo, N. Y., August 23–29, 1927.

directors, but also the incorporators, promoters, and vendors of property as responsible for the accuracy of the disclosures concerning the consideration accepted for stock. Moreover, both the promoters and the initial directors should be held responsible for the accuracy of the balance sheet of a new company.

If the above suggestions are embodied into law there will be no need to impose upon shareholders a liability to creditors. The shareholder's liability to pay for his stock should be made to depend upon his contract. His responsibility to the company should be the obligation to pay to the company what he agrees to pay, or to deliver to the company the specific property or other consideration which he agrees to deliver. The creditor will be protected by the publicity provided in the various reports and annual accounts. Subsequent purchasers of shares will also have the means available for their own protection.

Many of the proposals enumerated above have been inspired by precedents established by the British and German law concerning promotion and company management. They are supported to some extent by the recently enacted General Corporation Act of Ohio.[58] Many of the provisions of the Uniform Business Corporation Act (which was ably drafted in its final form by Professor Robert S. Stevens and was approved by the National Conference of Commissioners on Uniform Laws in July, 1928, and by it recommended for enactment) indicate what practical lawyers believe should and can be accomplished along the lines suggested above.[59] The Uniform Act was in a tentative stage when the Ohio act was framed and enacted, with the result that many of the provisions of later drafts of the Uniform Act were incorporated into the Ohio act and much that was put into the Ohio act was taken over into the Uniform Act.[60] The Uniform Act has since been substantially adopted by Louisiana and Idaho and rejected by the draftsmen of the 1929 Tennessee act as not being adaptable to their local conditions. The committee which

[58] Ohio Gen. Code, sect. 8623, subsections 1–136 (Ohio Laws, 1927, pp. 9–58, as amended by Ohio Laws, 1929, pp. 413–62). For a fully annotated draft of the act and a discussion of its provisions see Report of Committee Respecting Revision of Ohio Corporation Law, *supra*, c. I, note 16.

[59] See Handbook of the National Conference of Commissioners on Uniform State Laws (1928), pp. 334–418. The explanatory notes to this final draft of the act contain many valuable comments upon modern corporation law.

[60] Letter from Professor Robert S. Stevens to the writer. This is also evident from a comparison of the two statutes. See also, Report of Committee Respecting Revision of Ohio Corporation Law, *supra* (note 58) at p. 15.

drafted the recent revision of the corporation law of Indiana made substantial use of the Uniform Act.[61]

The justification and explanation of the stock-issue provisions of the Uniform Act have been clearly stated by its draftsman.[62] It represents a distinct advance over existing law in many particulars. From the point of view of this study its particular merits lie in the fact that an affidavit must be filed containing " an accurate, detailed and itemized description of the consideration received or to be received in payment for shares allotted, or allotted since the last report," and " a statement of the valuation put by the incorporators, shareholders or board of directors, as the case may be, upon the consideration other than cash received or to be received in payment for shares allotted, or allotted since the date of the last report, and, in case of shares allotted as a stock dividend, the amount of surplus transferred to capital in respect of such dividend, whether all or any part of such surplus was created by a revaluation of assets, and, if so, the value of the assets on the books of the corporation before and after such revaluation, the amount of the surplus or deficit before such revaluation, and the amount of the surplus after such revaluation." [63] We believe, however, that this provision would be materially strengthened from the standpoint of those whose interests it is designed to safeguard, if the basis of valuation used, or the circumstances from which it appeared that the valuation was proper, had been required to be stated in the affidavit. A check upon the promoters' and directors' valuations by independent authority would also seem to be distinctly desirable.

Another significant provision of the Uniform Act, which was modeled after section 38 of the new Ohio act, is section 24 dealing with the method of valuing assets for the purpose of estimating the fund available for the payment of dividends. This section requires that amounts of surplus arising from unrealized appreciation or revaluation of fixed assets shall be shown on the books of a corporation as a separate item apart from surplus profits or paid-in surplus. It requires that proper allowances for depreciation, depletion and losses shall be made. It prohibits the payment of cash dividends from

[61] Indiana Acts, 1929, c. 215, p. 725.

[62] Stevens, Robert S., *Stock Issues under the Uniform Business Corporation Act* (1928), 13 Cornell L. Q. 399. See also the explanatory notes to the Ninth and Tenth Tentative Drafts of the act as well as those appended to the Final Draft.

[63] Sect. 18, par. I, subsections (*b*) and (*c*) of the act.

unrealized appreciation in value or revaluation of fixed assets; from unrealized profit on treasury stock; from unrealized profits due to increases in the value of inventories; and other unrealized items of a similar kind. Companies with wasting assets are not required to amortize depletion prior to dividends.

These requirements are desirable, but the law could safely go much further in prescribing the form and content of the balance sheet.

Finally, the Uniform Act, as approved by the Conference of Commissioners on Uniform Laws and by the American Bar Association in 1928, is deficient in that it does not contain section 21 recommended by the committee which prepared the Tenth Tentative Draft of the Act. This section imposed penalties of heavy fines and/or imprisonment upon incorporators, subscribers, shareholders, and directors for deliberate and intentional overvaluation of the consideration with which subscriptions for shares were made payable, and upon any incorporator, officer, or director who deliberately and intentionally made, or consented to the making of, any false statement in any paper filed in any public office as required by the provisions of the act. Not only might section 21 of the Tenth Draft have been retained, but it might have been strengthened by imposing similar penalties for the omission from the public statements of any information required to be stated.

Despite these deficiencies in the Uniform Act it is, from the standpoint of modern conditions of corporate finance, by far the most intelligently drafted piece of legislation concerning corporations that has been proposed, with the possible exception of the new Ohio law. It is to be hoped that it will be universally adopted. It deals intelligently and constructively with the concept of capital stock when non-par shares are issued and its requirements with regard to the handling of surplus and to the payment of dividends are consistent with the interests of sound finance under a regime of non-par shares.

TABLE OF CASES

INDEX

COLUMBIA UNIVERSITY PRESS
Columbia University
New York

FOREIGN AGENT
OXFORD UNIVERSITY PRESS
Humphrey Milford
Amen House, London, E. C.

Bei Fragen zur Produktsicherheit wenden Sie sich bitte an:
If you have any questions regarding product safety,
please contact:

Walter de Gruyter GmbH
Genthiner Straße 13
10785 Berlin
productsafety@degruyterbrill.com